Why Docudrama?

Why Docudrama?

Fact-Fiction on Film and TV

Edited by
Alan Rosenthal

Southern Illinois University Press
Carbondale and Edwardsville

Printed in the United States of America
02 01 00 99 4 3 2 1

Library of Congress Cataloging-in-Publication Data
Why docudrama? : fact-fiction on film and TV / edited by Alan Rosenthal.
p. cm.
Includes bibliographical references.
1. Historical films—History and criticism. 2. Historical drama—History and criticism.
PN1995.9.H5W58 1999
791.43′658—dc21
ISBN 0-8093-2186-6 (cloth : alk. paper) 97-52387
ISBN 0-8093-2187-4 (pbk. : alk. paper) CIP

The paper used in this publication meets the minimum requirements of American National Standard for Information Sciences—Permanence of Paper for Printed Library Materials, ANSI Z39.48-1984. ♾

For
Phylis and Alfred
for all the many years of love and support

Contents

Acknowledgments

First, my thanks to all the authors who appear in this book and who allowed me to use their articles. In this category, special thanks are due to Jerry Kuehl, who went out of his way to amend his article at my request, and to Douglas Gomery, who voluntarily updated his classic piece on *Brian's Song* so as to make it even more relevant for this book.

A special debt is also owed to John Corner, George F. Custen, David Edgar, George MacDonald Fraser, Todd Gitlin, and Derek Paget. In these cases, the authors and/or their publishers allowed me to make selections from certain articles and book sections whose length prevented their publication in full. This excerpting of articles is not a practice I like but was forced on me by limitations of space. I appreciate having been allowed to make such selections and to have been trusted to exercise my judgment in these matters.

Occasionally I have taken the liberty of changing the name of an article or book extract in the interests of variety and clarity. Without this device I would have had twenty-five similarly titled articles, all sounding something like "Docudrama: Fact or Fiction?" or "Docudrama: True or False?" I hope the authors and the readers will forgive me.

I discussed the concept of this collection with many friends over about three years, but five people above all others guided my steps and gave wonderful advice. My good friend Henry Breitrose was, as usual, in at the beginning and with humor and patience filled in many gaps for me. Michael Eaton also entered the project early, treated me to innumerable Soho dinners and enlightened me as to how writers really work. Derek Paget, for his part, proved to be a gold mine by informing me about British films, writers, and sources I'd never heard of, having been out of England for so long. Meanwhile, an ever patient Ian McBride sent me cassettes and scripts, even though I sometimes assigned him to another Scottish family and misnamed his correct Granada title.

The fifth man on the roll of honor is Leslie Woodhead. Leslie introduced me to the idea of docudrama more than ten years ago and inspired me with enthusiasm for the genre. Since then he has gone out of his way to provide me with material and introductions and to bless me with his wisdom and anecdotes. This book would not have been possible without his friendship.

As usual, my overall guiding light was Jim Simmons. This is the third book on which he has given me his editorial help, and his quiet humor, patience, judgment, and terrific enthusiasm were invaluable all along the way. To all the above five, and to Jim, my thanks and gratitude.

Finally, my thanks to Kathryn Koldehoff, who did a superb job of copyediting on a very difficult manuscript.

Introduction

In April 1990, an English docudrama called *Who Bombed Birmingham?* cast serious doubt on the conviction of six men for the bombing of two British pubs in 1974. Prime Minister Margaret Thatcher said at the time that "a television program alters nothing." She was wrong. The film engendered a new inquiry, and the men were eventually released. Such a reexamination of legal guilt had also been the object of Abby Mann's 1985 film *The Atlanta Child Murders,* but in the Atlanta case the accused stayed in jail.

In February 1993, almost three years after the airing of *Who Bombed Birmingham?,* one item above all others dominated the American news media. This was the story of David Koresh and his Branch Davidian cult followers, who were besieged at Waco, Texas, by the FBI. What intrigued me, as I followed the events, was that Koresh was said to have mused with one reporter about who would play him in the film. Maybe Tommy Lee Jones or Bruce Willis.

The end was no joke. Koresh died in a blazing inferno along with eighty others. Yet he was right. They did film his life as *Ambush in Waco,* though he didn't stay around long enough to say whether they did a good job.

It was an amazing story. It had sex, charismatic personalities, weirdos, religious battles, the lot. No writer could have invented a juicier story. It was made for the screen. Once more, fact was better than fiction.

Taken from the headlines, *Who Bombed Birmingham?, The Atlanta Child Murders,* and *Ambush in Waco* made news in their own right and illustrate something of extreme interest. Whether you call them docudramas, drama-docs, fact-fiction dramas, or something even more exotic, one thing is clear: reality-based stories, taken from topical journalism, are the most popular drama genre on U.S. and British television today. In fact, it would be a most unusual week in which Americans did not see featured on TV at least two or three stories based on real incidents. And it has been that way for a long time.

Many of the docudramas have been highly praised. Many have been called rubbish and condemned with an invective unusual even for jaded TV critics. Thus Richard Corliss of *Newsweek* simply dismissed the three network dramas on Amy Fisher, the "Long Island Lolita," as "Trashomon." Though quality can be debated, what is very true is critic Howard Rosenberg's remark that "where docudrama goes, controversy is sure to follow."

Films based on fact are obviously not just confined to the small screen, but in terms of numbers, stories based on real happenings make up only a small percentage of the output of the feature industry. However, in recent years these films have managed to generate discussion way out of proportion to their numbers. This can be seen, for example, in the case of Warren Beatty's *Reds,* and it is particularly true in regard to Oliver Stone's *JFK* and *Nixon.*

What we seem to be witnessing is the growth of a very specific group of films and TV programs of increasing popularity, a group that seems to merit its own genre category. Now obviously, most dramadocs can already comfortably be fitted into the standard genre compartments of Western, gangster, detective film, and so on. *The Longest Day* slips easily into the war division. The TV miniseries *Sinatra* and *The Jacksons: An American Dream* are backstage musicals. And *Hoffa* and *Bugsy* are gangster pictures. Nevertheless, films based on fact raise so many questions regarding truth, morality, exploitation, effect, audience expectation, and other issues that, for purposes of study, it is profitable to regard them as belonging to a different species called *docudrama.*

Yet what are we talking about? What is this hybrid form that floats uneasily between documentary and fiction? What *is* docudrama? There is, before all else, the difficulty of the name and the bewildering labeling. *Docudrama. Dramatic reconstruction. Faction. Reality-based film. Murdofact. Fact-based drama. Biopic.* Maybe we should announce a competition for something definitive, but that might bring worse horrors like "factovies" or "factoramas." For the sake of simplicity, and as there is no single accepted name for the genre, I mostly use the term *docudrama* throughout this book.

Of course the problem is not really in the name but in defining the parameters of docudrama. A fairly prosaic but workmanlike definition of TV docudrama is that given by Tom Hoffer and Richard Alan Nelson. They call it

> A unique blend of fact and fiction which dramatizes events and historic personages from our recent memory. . . . It is a TV recreation based on fact though it relies on actors, dialogue, sets and costumes to recreate an earlier event. The accuracy and comprehensiveness of such a recreation . . . can vary widely and is conditioned not only by intent but also by factors such as budget and production time.[1]

Leslie Woodhead, a very distinguished English producer-director and former head of Granada TV's docudrama section, presents the problem a little differently:

> [Instead of hunting for definitions] I think it much more useful to think of the form as a spectrum that runs from journalistic reconstruction to relevant drama with infinite graduations along the way. In its various mutations it's employed by investigative journalists, documentary feature makers, and imaginative dramatists. So we shouldn't be surprised when programs as various as *Culloden* and *Oppenheimer* or *Suez,* or Cabinet reconstructions refuse tidy and comprehensive definition.[2]

Woodhead's presentation is excellent, though many would dispute the word *relevant.* Are all the dramas about the British royal family relevant? Not really. And can this word be applied to the hullabaloo around the Menendez brothers or O. J. Simpson? Probably not. Furthermore, Woodhead's definition tends to be limited to TV and to exclude feature films.

Clearly, the real operative word for Woodhead is *spectrum,* and if you wanted you could claim that fact-fiction goes back beyond Shakespeare. In other words, docudrama covers an amazing variety of dramatic forms, bound together by two things. They are all *based on* or *inspired by* reality, by the lives of real people, or by events that have happened in the recent or not too distant past. Furthermore, they would seem to have a higher responsibility to accuracy and to truth than does fiction. In short, fact-fiction film can be considered a special genus, worthy of study in its own right.

The aim of *Why Docudrama?* is to look at the dominant questions and controversies confronting docudrama today by assembling a diverse and provocative collection of writings on the subject. The hope is that, taken together, the essays will give a broad overview of the key problems in the field and also reveal the prevailing attitudes of network television and the film industry to the genre.

One major concern of this book is whether docudrama has a serious function to perform in society or whether it is just another branch of irrelevant popular entertainment. The emphasis is on major docudrama issues and questions. What kind of a genre is it? What are its problems and possibilities? What subjects should it be covering? How does it relate on the one hand to straight documentary and on the other hand to classic drama? Who should be the senior partner, the "docu" element or the "drama?" Is there room for experimentation within the form? If it has a serious function, what is it, and how should it best be carried out? And why is the genre so heavily criticized? The book attempts to stimulate discussion and thinking by raising questions and focusing the debate. The challenge is deciding where we go from here; my hope is that this book will provide a few hints and suggestions.

Why Docudrama? arises out of my work as a documentary filmmaker and out of two early books I did on nonfiction filmmaking called *The Documentary Conscience* and *New Challenges for Documentary.* In preparing materials for both books, I kept banging up against the subject of docudrama and getting more and more frustrated that I could find so little on the subject. As Steve Lipkin states in his chapter, "Fiction film studies have neglected to find a niche for dramatic re-creations of actual events, and documentary studies bypass docudrama as belonging to fiction."

Later I started exploring the subject in depth as a result of growing friendships with Leslie Woodhead, director of *Invasion* and *Why Lockerbie?,* and Antony Thomas, producer of that wonderful and notorious film *Death of a Princess.* Both men opened my eyes to the possibilities of docudrama and to the possibility of making strong social and political statements about current affairs that could be made in no other way. Practically and intellectually, this was highly attractive to me.

As I began to get the broad picture, however, I realized there were a number of intriguing theoretical and practical issues about the form that warranted serious discussion. Had people written on these topics? Well, here and there, yes; but the articles were scattered and hard to find. Though major journals, such as *Cineaste, Film Quarterly, Jump Cut,* and others devoted to serious discussion of documentary, were emerging in the seventies, the topic of docudrama was rarely discussed, except when films like *Malcolm X* and *JFK* emerged to their five minutes of fame and controversy.

The situation was no better in regard to serious books on the subject, though two pioneering works deserve to be cited as being both highly readable and excellent academic forays into the neglected byways of docudrama. The first, Derek Paget's *True Stories,* is a political and sociological exploration of docudrama's modes of representation on radio, stage, and screen in England.[3] The second, George F. Custen's *Bio/Pics,* is a fascinating study of how the Hollywood biographical film created public history.[4] A much less scholastic book, but interesting for some of its insights and always entertaining, is George MacDonald Fraser's *Hollywood History of the World.*[5]

The subject of docudrama has also come up tangentially in the recent surge of books on film and history, the most interesting writing being done by Robert A. Rosenstone and John E. O'Connor.[6]

Given the dearth of articles and the existence of only two or three key works on docudrama itself, I thought there might be room for an anthology that would bring together the significant thinking on the subject, an idea strengthened by my basic attitude toward the subject. Docudrama is an important issue. It has an effect on society far greater than has the average documentary, and its academic neglect is a disgrace. Nothing illustrates this more clearly than the question of docudrama and its influence on change, one of the many questions raised in this book. For example, *Roots, Gandhi, Malcolm X,* and *In the Name of the Father* were all germinal films in the formation of public opinion and attitudes toward civil disobedience, black pride, and the war in Northern Ireland. All were flawed, with fiction being sold as truth. This too strengthened my impulse to provide a forum for the discussion of docudrama. So, gradually, this book was born.

Why Docudrama? is divided into three parts. Part one covers the main theoretical, political, and sociological problems of docudrama. The authors define docudrama and examine its rationale. They look at issues of form and discuss docudrama's connection with and separation from documentary and mainstream fiction filmmaking. In particular, they discuss the history and development of docudrama on TV and film. Finally, they open up a discussion of the place of truth in docudrama, the main critiques of the form, and audiences' susceptibilities and expectations.

After theory, history, and problems, the main concern of part two is filmmaking practice. Thus, one of the purposes of part two is to examine how docudrama as a "commodity" is created in the United States and England. The authors discuss how Hollywood, commercial television networks, producers, and writers work and think and look at the objectives, difficulties, and accommodations of those producers and writers in a commercial world. The authors also confront some of the political obstacles of the form. Some of part two is essay, some is case study, and some is interview.

The aim of the last section of the book, part three, is twofold: first, to present an in-depth critique of a number of controversial docudramas; second, to offer a detailed examination of some of the controversies discussed earlier in the book. Most of the essays have been selected because the films the authors discuss—ranging from *Battleship Potemkin* and *Roots* to *Schindler's List*—have helped form and shape public opinion on a few key historical and political issues. The authors of a number of the essays also look in a fairly provocative way at the overall presentation of history by the genre.

Though the book is divided into discrete subjects, discussions naturally and inevitably overlap. Thus, Leslie Fishbein's critique of *Roots* is also extremely relevant to part two, with its focus on network television practice. Similarly, Todd Gitlin's discussion of *Bitter Harvest,* although centered on the compromises of TV, would have been equally at home in part three. Irene Shubik's chapter on her work in British TV and Robert Rosenstone's on *JFK* and history could likewise have been placed elsewhere. This is all to the good, as my intention is that the essays will bounce off, provoke, contest with, and also reinforce each other, rather than remain isolated, closed statements of opinion.

Although all books demand that choices be made, the anthologist's task is especially difficult. With luck there are more good articles than can fit, but this ideal situation can be both a blessing and a curse: a blessing because there is supposedly so much good material to choose from, a curse because so much of value has to be dropped for want of space. I read a great number of articles in making the current selection, so a brief word on choice is needed.

First, I have limited myself to British and American films. This is partially through budgetary necessity and also because of my own inadequacies in dealing with a wider field.

Second, besides looking for the best and most interesting articles of the past few years, I also decided to try to avoid as far as possible anthologizing well-known and overexposed essays that could easily be found elsewhere. This led to the almost total exclusion of essays on *Malcolm X* and *JFK*.[7] I also decided to avoid simplistic critiques, of which there are hundreds.

That having been said, I should mention that there are four articles I really regret having to leave out because of space considerations: essays by Harry Watt, Brian Winston, Richard Grenier, and John Caughie. Watt's wry observations are contained in his autobiography, *Don't Look at the Camera,* and give chapter and verse for the development of docudrama under John Grierson.[8] Brian Winston's essays "Non Narrative" and "Sincere and Justifiable Reconstruction" take up the story from Watt and show how vital were the elements of story, reconstruction, and narrative development to early British documentary.[9] Richard Grenier's essay on Gandhi sets out to illustrate how easily docudrama distorts history and becomes simple hagiography; it should be read alongside discussions of *Malcolm X*.[10] Finally, John Caughie's "Progressive Television and Documentary Drama" was omitted even though it presents an excellent discussion of Ken Loach's *Days of Hope*.[11] Unfortunately, too much of the article overlapped the essays of Paget and Corner.

Once I had narrowed the field, I also set up guidelines for readability and intellectual rigor. The readability element is, for me, a sine qua non, especially in regard to film theory, which runs the danger of a certain self-inflicted marginalization—that is, elitism so extreme that the message becomes inaccessible to the ordinary film viewer. At the same time, intellectual rigor is necessary to provide the basis for, stimulate, and provoke argument and discussion. On this score, purists may object to my using a number of newspaper and popular magazine articles, labeling them beneath academic concern, but I have no apology. The articles and chapters chosen represent for me the clearest and most accessible views I could find on the subject.

Theory obviously has a tremendous part to play in any book even remotely touching on modern television and film studies. One must clearly be aware of how literary studies have redirected critical analysis and the work of Richard Williams, Stuart Hall, and others in the investigation of ideology and culture. Nor can one advance very far without paying attention to the Frankfurt school of sociological analysis and to studies based on feminist theories, structuralism, deconstruction, postmodernism, and other approaches. In fact, beware the scholar who fails to cite Christian Metz, Michel Foucault, György Lukács, Louis Althusser, Fernand Braudel, Fredric Jameson, and Hayden White in their discussions of film and the nature of reality and historical representation.

I admit all this but believe these applications of theory to docudrama are best left to later scholars. My objective at this stage is merely to clear a path in the desert and point the way forward. This is done with the knowledge that others will undoubtedly come later and construct wonderful buildings and landscapes, all in accord with the visions of their chosen masters, gurus, and disciplines.

I have tried to be complete, but it is clear there are still a number of essential docudrama topics that merit further exploration. The most serious of these omissions, which various authors touch on, is the almost complete absence of any *meaningful* discussion of the docudrama audience.

The most commonly repeated criticism of docudrama, floating through both popular and scholarly articles, is that the audience will be misguided by docudrama. It will fail to understand the difference between fact and fiction. It will be misled regarding history. Its opinions will be shaped by fictitious wishful thinking. In its political understanding it will be led astray. In all of this, I must admit, I am as guilty as the next person in making assumptions about the nature of the audience and its understanding and assimilation of the docudrama form. But do we really have *facts* on which to base our assumptions?

Clearly, two subjects cry out for more research and examination: the first is audience perception; the second, effect and action. Each is related to reception theory, a conceptual attempt to understand the position of the audience. Examination of how the audience understands the film would add a new dimension to the debate about whether the work is seen as truth or fiction or a peculiar mixture of both. Work on effect would clarify what docudrama does in terms of propaganda and attitude change. Now, media effects and attitude change are not exactly new subjects. The two-step theory of change and the uses and gratifications theory have been around for years and are in every beginning text on social psychology. Maybe the time has come to start applying these theories to docudrama, but I am not sure. I suspect that we would end up with more mystification than ever.

Another topic absent from most discussion is the issue of *new* docudrama forms. British documentary experimented with docudrama in the forties and made various breakthroughs. In the sixties, Peter Watkins's *Culloden* showed what could be done if you grafted the immediacy of current-affairs news techniques onto a historical drama to give a vital sense of place and reality. A few years later, *The War Game* showed what could be done when documentary style was wedded to fictional story and interviews. Since then, experiment in form has been minimal, reflecting the general state of television drama.

In England, Dennis Potter's breakthrough series *Pennies from Heaven* and *The Singing Detective* showed how music, fantasy, reality, and flashback could illuminate and invigorate TV drama. Unfortunately, the influence of Potter has not yet crossed the Atlantic. In the United States, as in England, docudrama stays rooted in conservative realist forms, except for such tentative experiments as *Citizen Cohn* and *The Positively True Adventures of the Alleged Texas Cheerleader-Murdering Mom.* In the former, the author plays around with dream appearances of people from Roy Cohn's past. *Texas Mom,* for its part, frames a chronological murder comedy within the framework of a documentary discussion with the principals and brings the whole thing off superbly.[12]

It is clear, then, that there is little mainstream experiment, but why is discussion needed? Primarily to prod and invigorate the form. Without experiment, without searching, there is a danger the form will die from familiarization, overuse, contempt, and lack of vigor.

One can talk about docudrama from a hundred viewpoints. In the end, one has to ask, Does it really matter, or are we dealing with interesting but abstract academic questions? Personally, I think docudrama, or the branch of it that deals with the basic questions of politics, history, and the social good, is one of the best things to have emerged from modern media. A corollary to this statement is that only when the issues of the form are clarified will it become evident how docudrama can best work, both as entertainment and for the general good of society.

The real challenge, then, may be the challenge of function—to determine what docudrama should be doing and how it can bring about positive social change. I am realistic enough to know that its main commercial object will be to entertain and to provide tantalizing and sensational stories for a mass public based on the day's headlines. But ideally I would like it to do more, to go on telling the stories that, as Woodhead puts it, cannot be told by conventional methods and that focus on the major questions that concern all of us.

In 1980, Antony Thomas made *Death of a Princess* and exposed the poverty and dilemmas facing the average woman in Saudi Arabia. It was a film full of devastating criticism, which could have been expressed no other way. In 1989, Granada made *Who Bombed Birmingham?* and helped free five men held in jail under a wrongful conviction. Like Thomas's film, *Who Bombed Birmingham?* was a film many argued should not have been made. In the end, both films showed the power and the possibility of docudrama in an era when the mass media are becoming increasingly impoverished, both artistically and culturally. If the best of the docudrama output, like *Princess* and *Birmingham,* can go on asking the hard questions and reexamining the most pertinent issues of our time, then there is still hope.

Notes

1. Tom W. Hoffer and Richard Alan Nelson, "Docudrama on American TV," *Journal of the University Film Association,* 30, no. 2 (spring 1978): 21.
2. Leslie Woodhead, "The Guardian Lecture: Dramatised Documentary," BFI, 19 May 1981.
3. Derek Paget, *True Stories: Documentary Drama on Radio, Screen and Stage* (Manchester: University Press, 1990).
4. George F. Custen, *Bio/Pics* (New Brunswick, New Jersey: Rutgers University Press, 1992).
5. George MacDonald Fraser, *The Hollywood History of the World* (New York: Fawcett Columbine, 1989).
6. See *Revisioning History,* ed. Robert A. Rosenstone (Princeton, New Jersey: Princeton University Press, 1995); *Image as Artifact: The Historical Analysis of Film and Television,* ed. John E. O'Connor (Malabar: R. E. Krieger, 1990); and the series of essays on film and history in the *American Historical Review* 93 (December 1988).
7. See *Cineaste,* vol. 19, no. 1 (1991): 8–44, for eleven articles on JFK; and see *The JFK Reader* (New York: Applause Books, 1992).
8. Harry Watt, *Don't Look at the Camera* (New York: St. Martin's Press, 1974).
9. Brian Winston, *Claiming the Real: The Documentary Film Revisited* (London: BFI, 1994).
10. Richard Grenier, "The Gandhi Nobody Knows," *Commentary,* March 1983, 59–72.
11. John Caughie, "Progressive Television and Documentary Drama," *Screen* 21, no. 3 (1980).
12. For a postmodernist view of what can be done experimentally with film and history, see Sumiko Higashi's chapter on *Walker* in part three of this book.

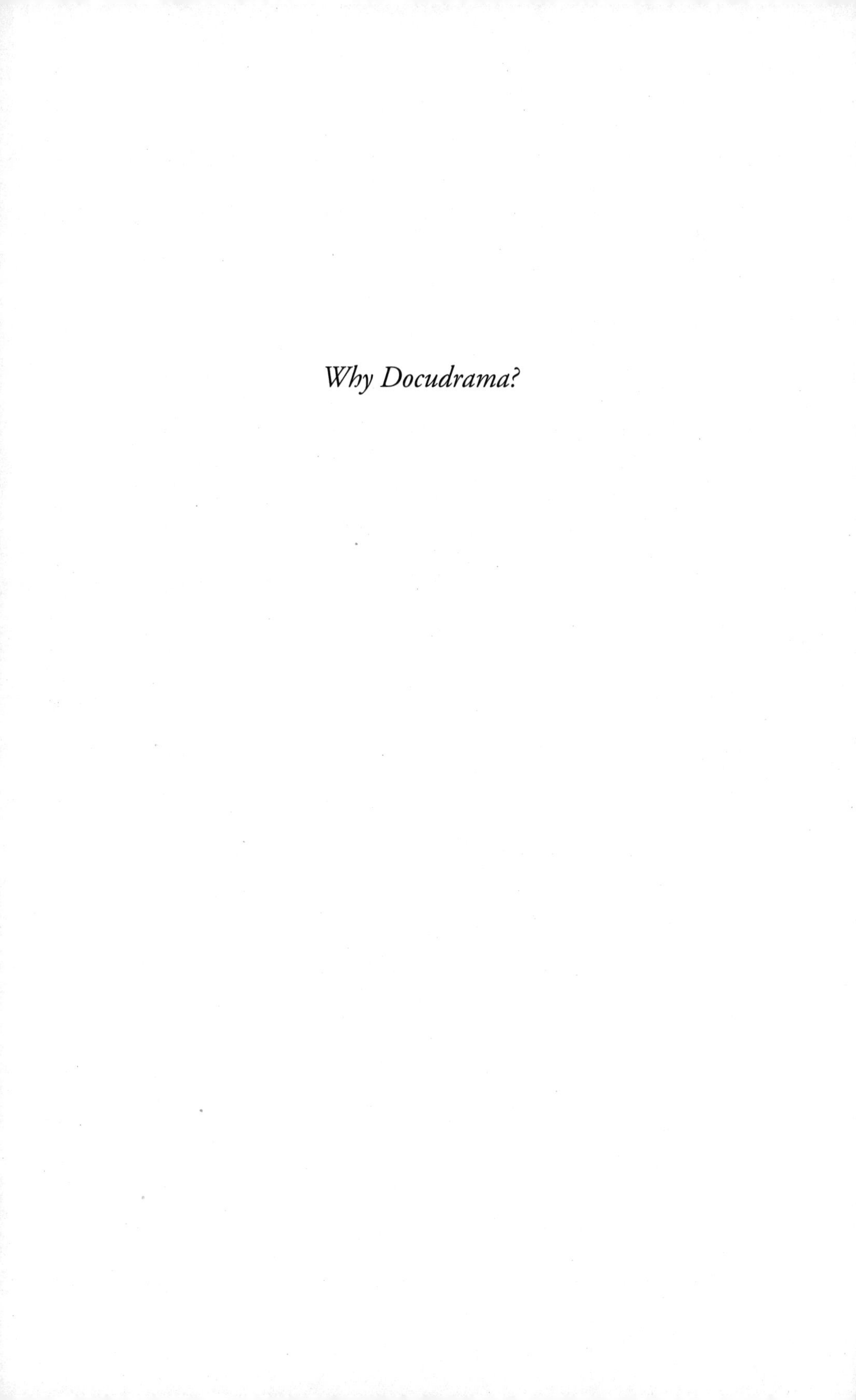

Why Docudrama?

Part One

Taking the Stage: Developments and Challenges

The pieces assembled in this part provide a general overview of docudrama, seen from the perspective of the eighties and nineties. Their general purpose is to clear the decks, so to speak, and focus on the main issues that have come to the fore in the last decade. I have tried to keep a logical thrust to the ordering of the essays, but it has not been easy: each writer touches on four or five recurring topics.

In the end, my choice has been to go from development to the rationale and appeal of the form and to conclude with criticisms of the genre. Where possible, I have separated discussion of British docudrama from discussion of U.S. docudrama, as they may be two different creatures. This settled, part one begins with a number of essays in which the authors discuss the history of the form and then opens out to debate the very nature of docudrama, its problems, and possibilities.

The idea of presenting reconstructions of real events on film is almost as old as the cinema. Ray Fielding, for example, in his account of the newsreel, relates how incidents from the Spanish-American War and First World War were restaged for a gullible American public and passed off as authentic.[1] For his part, D. W. Griffith restaged pageants from the Civil War in *Birth of a Nation,* but unlike that of the newsreels, his artifice was apparent to the audience.

Though D. W. Griffith, Cecil B. DeMille, and other Hollywood directors of the twenties attempted to restage historical or biblical incidents, the first really serious use of the form can be attributed to the Russians. The films of Sergei Eisenstein and Vsevolod Illarionovich Pudovkin, such as *October* and *The Fall of St. Petersburg,* are too well known to need much discussion here.

Quite clearly, their films imbued the form with a strong political bent. They also raised, in a very provocative way, some of the basic questions of truth and influence that surround us to this day. What is curious and troubling, though, is how much of Eisenstein's and Pudovkin's work is still exhibited today as if it were genuine archive material of the Russian Revolution.[2]

The real expansion and development of docudrama dates from the thirties and can conveniently be divided into four areas of study: (*a*) the Hollywood studio fact-fiction epic, or docudrama; (*b*) experiments with the form by British documentary filmmakers in the late thirties and forties; (*c*) British television docudrama since the early sixties; and (*d*) docudrama on American television since the early seventies. Obviously, a fifth category might have been created from the work of modern directors, such as Oliver Stone and Sir Richard Attenborough, but I am not sure there is enough volume there to merit a separate classification.

In "Hollywood and World History," the opening essay of this book, George MacDonald Fraser argues that the classic Hollywood studios took history seriously and should be praised for giving such a vivid and remarkable picture of the past to a mass audience. Known for his comic but very accurate historical novels, Fraser claims that the visual feel and the overall sense of the age might be as important as getting the facts right.[3] In his view, Hollywood is not a university. Its objective is not to teach history but to fashion drama. This is fine, as Fraser puts it in chapter 1, "provided a writer does not break faith with the spirit of history by willful misrepresentation . . . he or she may take liberties with the letter—but as few as possible." As will be seen, this is not a view that many critics like.

George F. Custen, author of the second chapter, "Clio in Hollywood," takes a more jaundiced view of Hollywood's version of public history in presenting an introduction to the story of the studio biopic, or biographical picture, which provided about 4 percent of Hollywood's annual output from 1927 to 1960. What Custen does is show how, for thirty years, Hollywood created and sustained a monochromatic view of history. In the pretelevision era, Hollywood assumed a key role in setting out the public agenda for what topics were deemed to be of importance, and it also guided the public's perception of these issues. In short, classic Hollywood was for decades a major force in the teaching of history, a force probably more important than the home or the school. And yet for years, the nature of the message was never questioned or discussed.

The chapters by John Corner, "British TV Dramadocumentary: Origins and Developments," and Derek Paget, "Tales of Cultural Tourism," take the story one step further. Both deal with the work of the early British documentarians in fact-fiction and go on to describe how docudrama then became one of the jewels in the crown of British TV. Corner and Paget also open up questions of form. Any student of documentary history knows that the practitioners have always strained at the form, and most scholars now accept that documentary was never pure, always pushed toward fiction. Thus in *Claiming the Real,* Brian Winston writes cogently of the thrust, from Robert Flaherty through John Grierson onward, to incorporate into documentary the strategies of drama and conventional narrative.[4] Again, in his autobiography, *Don't Look at the Camera,* Harry Watt provides details about how the modes and possibilities of docudrama pervaded his work from *North Sea* to *Target for Tonight.*[5] Watt's book also shows how and why docudrama also appealed to so many of the other Griersonian recruits, like Humphrey Jennings and Arthur Elton.

As Corner correctly points out, the use of docudrama became particularly prevalent in the Second World War. Here the "idea was to take a documentary theme (the submarine service, for example, . . .) and treat this by 'particularizing' it around a story line with characters, which could be given an intimate rendering using the depictive methods of feature fiction." These films, of course, show the difficulties of defining docudrama. Here, very often, real people were placed in real settings and told to repeat their customary work against a fictitious story line.

The problems of defining docudrama become more acute as one observes British television in the sixties. The two key films of this era discussed by Corner, Paget, myself, and others in this book are *The War Game* (1965) and *Cathy Come Home* (1966). Both were pioneering and groundbreaking teleplays and became the focus of national attention. But are they docudramas? *The War Game,* by Peter Watkins, grafted a documentary style, which included interviews, onto a drama with voice-over narration, which follows the prelude and aftermath of the use of atomic bombs on England. Jeremy Sandford's *Cathy Come Home,* made for the BBC, used the research culled from hundreds of interviews to create a fictitious picture of a homeless family moving from one desperate situation to another. Both films were hailed as docudramas but would probably be regarded by purists as being outside the form.

Tom W. Hoffer and Richard Alan Nelson, in "Docudrama on American Television," describe in detail the evolution of the form in the United States in the same period. The original article from which this chapter is drawn was written in 1978 and has since become the classic text on the history of early TV docudrama.

Douglas Gomery, in "*Brian's Song:* Television, Hollywood, and the Evolution of the Movie Made for TV," then presents a case study that complements Hoffer and Nelson's article and fleshes out the relationship between Hollywood and the television industry between 1950 and 1970. Gomery also adds a short afterword, which brings the situation up to date. (Although they deal with practice, the contributions of Todd Gitlin in part two and Leslie Fishbein in part three are also helpful in broadening the discussion.)

After absorbing the picture painted by Hoffer, Nelson, and Gomery on the one hand and by Paget and Corner on the other, one thing becomes very apparent. Though using the same term—*docudrama*—each group is talking about an almost entirely different animal. The British version has to do with reconstructive political and social investigation. The American version thrives 90 percent of the time on entertainment biographies and sensational scandals. A further difference is that, whereas British TV docudrama tends to be tied to the news bureaus, U.S. docudrama is usually the province of the drama and entertainment divisions of the networks.

The two men most connected with the development of docudrama in England in the seventies and early eighties are Leslie Woodhead and Peter Goodchild. Woodhead, a noted documentarist, was the key figure in the creation of the Specialist Docudrama Department at Granada TV. His films include *Strike,* about the Lenin shipyards in Poland, and *Invasion,* about the 1968 Soviet invasion of Czechoslovakia. Goodchild, for his part, chose to use the BBC Science Features Department for such miniseries as *Marie Curie* and *Oppenheimer.* Other docudrama makers of note who also made major contributions during this time include Chris Rallings and Michael Latham, the producer of *The Explorers.*

What currently characterizes British television docudrama is the seriousness of its form, which is much closer to journalism and news than to conventional drama. Though it uses dramatic forms, characters, and dialogue, its motivating force is that of the restless inquirer and investigative reporter. Overall, it is motivated by the idea of bringing about change and working in the public interest, and many of its practitioners continually talk of an underlying contract of trust with the audience in regard to truth. It wants to uncover and reveal for the public good and not just in the name of higher ratings.

This last comment, however, may not be quite as accurate now as it was in the eighties. In recent years, both Granada and the BBC have often joined forces with HBO to produce docudramas. As the budgets have increased under coproduction deals, so has the use of name stars, highly paid writers and directors, and the importance of high audience figures.[6]

By contrast, the U.S. member of the family has always pursued the audience, emphasized entertainment value, and had a rather loose regard for truth.

Hard news dramas tend to be pushed aside in the race for the O. J. Simpson sensations and the Menendez brothers' story and in the pursuit of titillating sleaze and the beautiful murderer of the week. Serious docudramas occasionally surface—like *Friendly Fire, Citizen Cohn, And the Band Played On,* and *The Missiles of October*—but they are few and far between.

As docudramas have multiplied on television, so have the questions proliferated about its form. This is particularly true of the last ten years, when more and more attention has been paid to a number of complex issues, including questions of definition and the boundaries of the form, its separation from documentary, its appeal, and its purpose. Many of these questions overlap, and it is not surprising that a number of the essays selected for this first part deal with two or three of the issues in one go.

In the introduction, I quoted the docudrama definitions of Hoffer and Nelson and of Woodhead, and both of their chapters explore the subject in some depth. The same question is, of course, also touched upon by Corner in his survey of docudrama history. (The question of definition is also discussed by Steve Lipkin in "Defining Docudrama" in part three of this book. The important thing for Lipkin, however, is the examination of the differences between docudrama and documentary, including their ethical problems, which he does by using examples from *JFK, Schindler's List,* and *In the Name of the Father.* One of Lipkin's main observations is that the coding of each form is completely different. Docudrama has replaced the indexical unstaged image of documentary with quasi-indexical narrative. He also argues that, like melodrama, docudrama suggests a lost moral structure that can be recovered and restored.)

The problem of defining the form, or discussing its separation from documentary, is made increasingly difficult when it keeps reappearing in new guises every day. This was particularly true of the late eighties, when dramatized "recreations" of real-life events kept surfacing everywhere. As Richard Zoglin wrote, "Tabloid shows like Fox's *America's Most Wanted* and NBC's *Unsolved Mysteries* use 'recreations' to reenact just about everything from grisly murders to purported UFO sightings."[7]

This blurring of boundaries between documentary, docudrama, and news is one of the most interesting and possibly frightening phenomenon to appear on television. It also led me at one time to consider including Bill Nichols's essay "At the Limits of Reality" in this book. I dropped the idea because his discussion is more relevant to documentary issues. Nevertheless, Bill Nichols's work is well worth surveying for a deeper investigation of the boundaries of

TV forms and the problems that will sooner or later have an impact on the future of docudrama.[8]

The appeal of docudrama is another of those subjects that has come to the fore in recent years and can be approached from three directions. The easiest question to ask is, What is the appeal of the form for the commercial entertainment–oriented producer? The answer is clear. Docudramas that are based on sensational headlines, such as *The Raid on Entebbe* and *Diana: Her True Story,* deliver huge audiences. The stories, having been presold by massive coverage in other media, translate easily and comfortably into high ratings, which bring high financial returns.

But why *are* the ratings of U.S. TV docudramas so high? What *is* the attraction for the audience? Many people have tried to provide answers. Documentary producer Peter Davis talks about the audience's *hunger* for factually oriented fiction and general voyeuristic passions.[9] But not everyone is willing to see appeal simply in terms of satisfying the raw desire to spy. Writing in an edition of the *Journal of the Directors Guild,* discussing trends on television, producer Tony Eltz put the matter this way: "There's value for the viewer in seeing that a very scary thing has an explanation. For example, we recently produced *Deadly Medicine,* which helped viewers understand why a nurse might be driven to murder 32 babies."[10]

John Matoian, CBS's vice president for movies and miniseries, has his own comments on the appeal of the murder docudramas. "People are looking for windows in behavior. Hopefully they'll gain insight from these kind of movies."[11] The question of audience appeal is also tackled by many of the authors in this book, with varying responses. Hoffer and Nelson, for example, state that "the revival of the docudrama on American commercial television was directly conditioned by public interest in newsmakers and the Watergate scandals, network experimentation to build mid-1970 audience ratings . . . and the appeals inherent in the American Bicentennial."[12]

Finally, one is curious about the hold docudrama has on the serious filmmaker. For Hoffer and Nelson, part of the answer is that writers can espouse controversial ideas in relatively safe historical formats. David Edgar, a teacher of drama and a noted dramatist in his own right, argues that, on certain subjects, we (the audience) no longer have any shared experience (see part two). The power of docudrama is to give credibility to the playwright's analysis of the unbelievable happenings of our time. Docudrama's duty is to expose an audience to a subject it is interested in but knows nothing about. For myself, the most satisfying statement of docudrama's appeal to the concerned writer-producer, and also a definition of its raison d'être, is given by Leslie Woodhead in "The Guardian Lecture: Dramatized Documentary." In one of the most important chapters in the book, he describes docudrama as "a form of last resort, a way of doing things when conventional documentary can't cope." What story cannot be told using conventional documentary methods? For Woodhead, it has ranged from the Soviet invasion of Czechoslovakia in *Invasion,* to the blowing up of Pan Am flight 103 in *Why Lockerbie?,* and to the story of the *Exxon Valdez* in *Dead Ahead: The* Exxon Valdez *Disaster.* While Woodhead's dramatic aim has been to re-create history as accurately as possible, his broader aim, echoed by David Edgar and the Granada group, has been to screen dramas of crucial *public concern* and interest.

In his chapter, "Where Are We Going and How and Why?" Ian McBride basically reinforces Woodhead's argument and approach. This is not surprising, as McBride assumed Woodhead's mantle as head of factual drama at Granada TV when Woodhead left to go independent. However, McBride also points out how, in the last ten years, Granada's docudramas have left foreign soil and have become increasingly controversial as the programs have explored cover-ups by the British police and the secrets of British politics.

Derek Paget exhibits in his chapter, mentioned earlier, a certain amount of skepticism toward the morally elevating purposes claimed by Granada TV and many British producers. He sees docudrama as an easy, undemanding trip across the borders of experience. In brief, every issue eventually becomes mediated through a docudrama, which is a salve to the conscience but merely keeps the problem in its place. It is an interesting attitude but not one I agree with. I admit it is often difficult to gauge the effects of docudrama, but they can be traced. A simple example is the reexamination by the British courts of the guilt of six men accused of bombing a British pub, after Granada TV's *Who Bombed Birmingham?* named four others as the alleged real killers.

While docudrama is tremendously popular, it has also drawn the wrath of a great number of critics. Thus Jerry Kuehl, one of the most serious opponents of the form, wrote for the British magazine *Vision,*

> Many docudramas are produced with little regard for historical truth, or psychological plausibility, but with every regard for pecuniary advantage. To see the names of real people with public reputations attached to characters drawn from the stockpile of drama stereotypes . . . is enough to alert the viewer to the fact that he or she is in the presence of a program which intends to exploit, but not satisfy an audience's curiosity.[13]

Another vitriolic critic of the genre is Walter Goodman of the *New York Times,* who has stated in no uncertain terms that "The only good docudrama is an unproduced docudrama." Continuing in the same vein, this is what he had to say about *The Final Days,* the TV miniseries about the conclusion of Richard Nixon's presidency: "What's wrong? Several things. Real people are treated sometimes flatteringly, sometimes cruelly, as though they were made for TV. They exist for our amusement. Real events, which deserve analysis, and perhaps action, are presented in a hyped-up watered-down way that short cuts thought." [14]

Many of the problems just raised are discussed and enlarged upon by Jerry Kuehl in "Lies about Real People," the last chapter in this part. Kuehl continues the discussion from his *Vision* article and argues that docudrama should always be avoided where documentary is possible.

Docudrama raises certain theoretical problems that can be put fairly simply: Where is the center of truth in this form, and how believable or how suspect is it? Now, one of the underlying assumptions of documentary is that it is supposed to be more honest and accurate than fiction. As Brian Winston puts it, "On the basis of Grierson's notion of the separation of form, we have established a hierarchy of truth in film whereby documentary stands higher than fiction." [15] Though docudrama aspires to join documentary on this upper level, the difficulty is that whole areas seem to be opening up where fiction is presented as fact, as reality. I would argue that in most cases this doesn't cause too many problems. The audience perceives, for the most part, what is fact and what is fiction and where license with fact has been taken. But there are obviously situations where the mixing of fact with fiction and dramatizations masquerading as documentary can be dangerous and misleading.

Broadly speaking, I think that two or three elements need to combine to create such a problematic situation. First, the audience must completely or almost completely misread the fiction as fact. Second, the misleading fictional elements must be of real consequence to the story and to the sense of the characters and the basic situation under discussion. Third, the subject being presented must be one that can, or is meant to, affect our ongoing social or political actions and attitudes in a fairly important way.

Given these three elements, I find few problems with *North Sea, Yankee Doodle Dandy, Barbarians at the Gate,* or *The Amy Fisher Story.* However, Richard Attenborough's *Gandhi* and Spike Lee's *Malcolm X* disturb me profoundly with their simplistic pictures of martyrs and superficial recounting of history, much in the same way that *October* disturbed some of the better critics seventy years ago.

The confused boundary lines between fiction and fact can be seen in two highly publicized television presentations, *Washington: Behind Closed Doors* and *The Atlanta Child Murders. Washington* was fiction but clearly based on

Nixon's Watergate years. It was this assumed claim to authenticity that made it special. However, within the program, *unproved* rumor about John F. Kennedy's involvement with CIA assassination schemes was casually paired with Nixon's *proved* inclination to indulge in illegal activities. In CBS's *Atlanta Child Murders,* aired in February 1985, doubt was cast on the just conviction of a man for two of the twenty-eight slayings that shocked Atlanta between 1979 and 1981. CBS called the film a "fact-based drama," but many residents of Atlanta claimed that the film distorted the truth. CBS finally agreed to label the film as "containing some fiction." An editorial on the film in the *New York Times* stated:

> "Fact-based drama" not only defrauds the news but assaults it, hit and run. The dramatists never stay around for rebuttal or new facts. . . . But dissension gets no place in docudrama. And if new evidence were to turn up next week, only CBS news would be left to clean up after CBS Entertainments. . . . Does no one in television care enough to halt this corruption?[16]

Similar expressions of disgust were made in regard to *Who Bombed Birmingham?* (where the approach of the producers was later validated by the courts) and in relation to *Death of a Princess,* discussed in part two. However, both David Edgar (part two) and Derek Paget share a profound observation in regard to the overall criticism of docudrama. What they maintain, and I believe they are correct, is that many critics attack docudrama as a *form,* when what really disturbs them are the *opinions* being expressed. According to Paget, every TV system defines what constitutes the boundaries of the admissible and the inadmissible in terms of both *form* and *content.* According to the rules of the sixties, for example, *Culloden* was admissible, *The War Game* was not. Today, not many rules have been changed. It is just important to know what precise game is being played.

Given that the aim is to re-create history or political and socially important stories as accurately as possible, how can this best be done? Woodhead's method has been summed up by one of his scriptwriters, David Boulton, as follows: use "No invented characters, no invented names, no dramatic devices owing more to the writer's (or director's) creative imagination than to the *impeccable* record of what actually happened. For us docudrama is an exercise in journalism, not dramatic art."[17]

If we approve the method stated by Boulton and assume that it is bolstered by months of research, high-grade source materials (such as diaries and interviews), and meticulous verification of facts, the question remains, How do we let the audience know we have done all of this?

Ian McBride's answer is that you do not need to do anything specific. Instead, through time, the audience learns to trust certain organizations and certain program makers, much as U.S. audiences once trusted the implicit honesty of Edward R. Murrow and Walter Cronkite. A possible alternative answer is that given by Robert Vas in *The Issue Should Be Avoided* and by Jill Godmilow in *Far from Poland.* Both use signposting, which clearly indicates the source of what is happening on the screen. This technique is certainly feasible, though an alternative might be a form of filmic footnotes to go with the credits.

All of these discussions on the idea of docudrama and its forms and problems are timely and invigorating. However, one element is missing that, although not really necessary to formal criticism, should inform all serious discussion: the audience. Films are made for people—to be seen, enjoyed, and acted upon. Formal discussion of docudrama is all very well, but at some point attention must be directed to audience perception. Clearly, the sophistication level of the audience has changed immensely since Darryl Zanuck trundled out his biopics in the thirties and forties. As David Edgar once trenchantly observed in his article "Seeing Isn't Believing," viewers are not as befuddled as critics would make them out to be.[18] Most viewers do not for one moment imagine that there are clear windows on history. Nor do they generally confuse drama with documentary or believe that they are getting the only clear picture of a situation, a person, or a series of incidents. They are aware of the artifices of selection and imagined dialogue; and they understand well the concept of holding a particular, but well argued, point of view. And above all, they know that what they see is only a producer's vague approximation of what actually happened.

One can theorize away, but I suspect that the audience will continue to accept the best of docudrama as being an important force for good. They may grow more aware of its artifice, the means of selection, the biases, and the constraints—and all to the good. However, I believe that they will continue to see docudrama as a special genre, a tool that, when used well, provides some clear and necessary observation about the world, occasionally even stirring them to action. Here the last word can be left to David Edgar:

> As a writer about public life, I would defend dramadocumentary as a form in which important things can be said in a uniquely authoritative and credible way. But the form also needs to be defended because the presence of drama-documentary in the schedules is an active encouragement to the audiences to think critically and seriously about all the programs they watch.

Notes

1. Raymond Fielding, *The American Newsreel 1911–1961* (Norman: University of Oklahoma Press, 1972).

2. This is well illustrated at the start of HBO's *Stalin* (1993), in which unidentified footage from Eisenstein's *October* is freely mixed with genuine archive material.

3. See, for example, *Royal Flash* (London: Barrie Jenkins, 1970). George MacDonald Fraser began writing a series of humorous historical novels in the early seventies, using as his central character the bounder Harry Flashman. Flashman, of course, was already known to literature as the cowardly, bullying antihero who appears in the classic British novel *Tom Brown's Schooldays.* What distinguishes the Flashman series, besides their narrative force, comedy, and sex, is their meticulous regard for the details of nineteenth-century history.

4. Brian Winston, *Claiming the Real: The Documentary Film Revisited* (London: BFI, 1994).

5. Harry Watt, *Don't Look at the Camera* (New York: St. Martin's Press, 1974).

6. For further discussion, see the comments of Ian McBride in "Where Are We Going and How and Why?"

7. *Time,* 9 October 1989, p. 98.

8. For further discussion, see Bill Nichols, *Blurred Boundaries* (Bloomington: Indiana University Press, 1994).

9. See Seth Feldman's "Footnote to Fact," in *The Film Genre Reader,* ed. Barry Grant (Austin: University of Texas Press, 1985), 31.

10. *Journal of the Directors Guild* (March 1991): 10.

11. Quoted in Jeff Silverman, "Murder, Mayhem Stalk TV," *New York Times,* 22 November 1992, section 2, p. 28.

12. See Feldman, "Footnote to Fact," in *The Film Genre Reader,* for his discussion of attraction as being essentially narcissistic: "We are looking at something that is essentially part of ourselves. Furthermore satisfaction is derived from the communal sharing of an event and the mass catharsis inherent in jointly exposing social anxieties, experiencing the retelling of a familiar horror," p. 32.

13. *Vision,* April 1987, p. 6.

14. Walter Goodman, *New York Times,* 2 November 1989, section C, p. 10.

15. Brian Winston, "Documentary: I Think We Are in Trouble," *Sight and Sound* 48, no. 1 (winter 1978): 14.

16. *New York Times,* editorial, 31 October 1989, p. 14.

17. David Boulton, *Invasion: A Writer's Perspective* (Manchester: Granada Television Pamphlet, 1981), p. 8.

18. David Edgar, "Seeing Isn't Believing," *Sunday Times,* 22 August 1993, p. 21.

1

Hollywood and World History

George MacDonald Fraser

Half a century or so ago, when Ronald Colman and Clark Gable were giving new meaning to the mustache and half the civilized world yearned for Greta Garbo or Jean Harlow, while the other half gazed enraptured on Gary Cooper and Robert Taylor; when David Niven was an unknown extra being ejected from a Barbary Coast saloon, Buck Jones was still wearing that enormous hat, Fred Astaire was dancing the spirit of Wodehouse across the screen, and no one thought twice if John Wayne turned up as an ice-hockey player, or Humphrey Bogart as a Mexican bandit complete with accent—in those happy days, when the talkies were just a few years old, an interesting paradox was to be observed in the cinema.

Despite the coming of sound and a generation of actors and actresses who, unlike many of their successors, could speak clear and articulate English, it was still not enough for cinemagoers to be able merely to see, hear, and understand—they had to be able to read too.

Of course, this had also been vital in the silent days, when captions—like "And so her dark suspicions grew" and "All night long he wrestled with his Beast" and "Harness my zebras, gift of the Nubian king!"—were essential

---

From *The Hollywood History of the World.* Reproduced with permission of Curtis Brown Ltd., London, on behalf of George MacDonald Fraser, © 1988.

complements to the visual drama, but when motion pictures began to talk, there were those who supposed that the day of the written word was over, and not only in the cinema. My history teacher—and he was one who regarded motion pictures as the greatest disaster for education since the burning of Alexandria—saw the talking film as the final nail in the coffin of literacy. Why, he asked in despair, should his charges bother with reading, when that infernal silver screen talked to them?

He need not have worried. That flawed glory of the cinema, the costume picture, was going to demand a far higher standard of literacy from its viewers than ever the silent films had done. Rare was the historical epic of the 1930s that did not start off with a written prologue that might have taxed the comprehension of some of today's filmgoers. It usually began, portentously, with the words "In the Year of Our Lord," and then there would follow a concise summary of the War of the Spanish Succession, or the condition of the English peasantry in the twelfth century, or the progress of Christianity under Nero. And, by and large, they were not inaccurate. They and the films they introduced paid the audience the compliment of supposing them to have at least an elementary knowledge of, and interest in, times past, and with all their faults (and they were many) they took history seriously.

In view of some of the monstrosities that have been put on the screen in the past half century, that claim may seem bold. There is a popular belief that, where history is concerned, Hollywood always gets it wrong—and sometimes it does. What is overlooked is the astonishing amount of history Hollywood has got right and the immense unacknowledged debt we owe to the commercial cinema as an illuminator of the story of humankind; this even though films have sometimes blundered and distorted and falsified, have botched great themes and belittled great men and women, have trivialized and caricatured and cheapened, have piled anachron-ism on solecism on downright lie—still, at their best, they have given a picture of the ages more vivid and memorable than anything in Tacitus or Edward Gibbon or Thomas Babington Macaulay and to an infinitely wider audience. Nor have they necessarily been less scrupulous. At least they have shown history more fully than they are usually given credit for, as it was never seen before. For better or worse, nothing has been more influential in shaping our visions of the past than the commercial cinema.

For example, take a walk through the huge excavation of ruined ancient Rome, and consider that a tourist of two centuries ago could envisage the reality of the city of the Caesars only dimly, by reference to written accounts and a few highly imaginative paintings. But today all the world knows what it looked like, thanks to William Horning and Edward Carfagno and John de Cuir, among others. (And who outside the industry could identify them as cinema art directors?) Again, all the eyewitness accounts and historians' descriptions of Waterloo have less impact than Sergei Bondartchuk's breathtaking vista of the ragged British squares with Napoléon's cavalry streaming past them. When Samuel Johnson wrote *Rasselas,* he had no clear conception of what Abyssinia or old Egypt looked like; Cecil B. DeMille could have shown him, down to Cleopatra's hairpins, and parted the Red Sea for an encore. As James Thurber is alleged to have said of *The Ten Commandments:* "It makes you realize what God could have done if He'd had the money."

Of course, we know that no physical re-creation of the past can be wholly accurate; television reminds us of this regularly with its dramatized attempts to show us what we looked like (and did, and said, and even thought without apparently realizing it, God help us) in the 1930s and 1940s. And that is just the recent, visible past. This came home forcibly to me on a film location when I and a member of the cast, a former paratroop sergeant, labored in vain to make a modern actor look right in wartime battle dress. He was a splendid actor, too, of international reputation, but while we could crease his trousers with soap and put lead weights above his anklets and rest his hands just so on his pouches, we could not make him look or move like a soldier of 1944; he would have had to spend five years in the Second World War, we concluded.

Still, we got him reasonably right, and the director and the man's own acting talent did the rest; the result might not have satisfied Field Marshal Montgomery, but it served. Similarly, the re-creators of ancient Babylon, Shakespeare's London, and colonial Virginia do their best, and it too serves.

More or less, anyway. You cannot please everyone, not in the twentieth century. Where our ancestors gaped in awe at the magic lantern and the bioscope, we take a more critical view. We accept as a matter of course the technical miracle of the *Ben-Hur* chariot race, Sabu flying on the Genie's back, John Ford's aftermath of the Battle of Shiloh, and the huge spectacle of Cleopatra's arrival in Rome—and we are moved to mirth when she says to Caesar: "We've gotten off to a bad start, haven't we? I've done nothing but rub you the wrong way." Of course we are; we are only human, even scriptwriters.

This is only one of the pitfalls in the path of the historical filmmaker; more than ordinary films, they are liable to strike a false note. Those who make them know that, while millions of dollars' worth of planning and building, painstaking research beyond the dreams of many academics, and sheer technical brilliance can pass without much notice, one bad line (and it doesn't even have to be a bad line, it just has to sound amiss) or one visual anachronism, one piece of unhappy casting, one directorial slip, will have the customers falling about. There have been enough of these—as well as more culpable commissions of bad taste, willful philistinism, and sheer ignorance—to give costume movies, if not a bad name, at least a patronized and faintly derided status. My history teacher was reluctant to see *The Sign of the Cross* because he feared he might be offended by the sight of gladiators who chewed gum and talked like gangsters.

Without being unduly defensive on their behalf, one has to say that those who make historical films face hazards unknown to workers in other artistic fields. Take the novelist, pampered creature, in his or her one-dimensional world; the novelist can state simply that Sir Francis Drake rolled in and bowed to the queen or that Marie-Antoinette flung herself, sobbing wildly, on the bed, and that's it; the reader visualizes the scene. The filmmaker has to create it entire, from the coat of arms above the throne to the last diamond in the queen's ruff, and while cinema audiences contain mercifully few authorities on Elizabethan costume, they are well able to spot a wristwatch worn by a cutlass-waving pirate, a microphone boom reflected in a Roman breastplate, a zip fastener on a kilt, an uplift bra on a Byzantine bosom, or a Greyhound bus in the far background of a Western—all of which have happened, and no doubt there is worse to come.

Getting it visually right is one thing; it must also sound right, and historical films abound with instances when it didn't. This is a delicate area, since the writer is usually committing an enforced anachronism by writing in English, when the characters should by rights be talking Norman French or Latin. But it must be English, and acceptable in both North Shields and Wichita, Kansas, at that; so, given the task of constructing a conversation between King John and the abbot of Canterbury, the screenwriter must simply use his mother wit and sense of period, avoid anachronisms not only of fact but of usage, respect the author (if adapting a historical novel), and hope that the producers will cast George C. Scott or Charlton Heston or Oliver Reed, who will give it that indefinable thing called *style.* He or she must also bear in mind that, while there are mistakes that don't matter much (only a few experts are going to frown at the anachronism of the word *sabotage* in the mouth of Captain Bligh), there are times when strict accuracy can be fatal—let the script refer, quite properly, to an English public school junior as a *fag,* and no one in Wichita is going to hear the next line.

Which brings us to the subject which scriptwriters hate and movie buffs delight in—those famous lines that seemed all right when written in good faith and cold blood but were not. There is no insurance against them and no defense. Let the Lionheart's queen exclaim, "War, war! That's all you think about, Dick Plantagenet!" and the audience will erupt, and it is not a blind bit of use pointing out that Berengaria of Navarre probably said something very like that to Richard I, more than once. As who knows better than I, who coined the deathless protest: "But I don't want to marry the Queen of Scots! She's only six years old!" It may well have been a true reflection of the feelings of his youthful majesty Edward VI, but that didn't save it. The list is endless: "Take a letter. Mark Antony, the Senate, Rome . . ."; "This Tartar woman is for me, and my blood says, 'Take her!' "; "Delilah, what a dimpled dragon you can be"; and so on. We can console ourselves that the greatest screenwriter of all had clocks striking in ancient Rome and caused his Latin workingmen to talk like Elizabethan Londoners (and who knows that Burbage did not throw Hamlet's soliloquy back at him, swearing that he would sooner retire than repeat that in public. And how, exactly, would Burbage have phrased his rebuke to the unhappy playwright? There's an interesting exercise in dialogue writing.)

Such matters are the small change of historical filmmaking. Honest mistakes and follies happen; but what does one say to those more solemn critics who charge Hollywood with trivializing and distorting history, as well as with vulgarity, ignorance, bad taste, and all those other faults that my history teacher recited as, against his better judgment and with grave misgivings, he conducted us to the local cinema to see *The Sign of the Cross?*

Well, Hollywood is not a school for teaching history. Its business is making money out of entertainment, and history needs considerable editing and adaptation (which can, in some cases, justifiably be called distortion and falsification) before it is submitted to the paying public. This is something from which writers, directors, and producers have seldom flinched. In this they are not necessarily more culpable than many serious historians who, if they seldom deliberately falsify, are often inclined to arrange, shape, select, emphasize, and omit in order to prove a case, or confound a rival, or make propaganda, or simply present what they wish to believe is the truth. This, it seems to me, is a rather greater offense than that of the screenwriter who knows perfectly well that Charles Gordon and the Mahdi never met but who still makes them meet in the script. The screenwriter is not writing history but fashioning drama, and like Shakespeare before him he supplements fact with fiction as seems best to him. For me, provided a writer does not break faith with the spirit of history by willful misrepresentation or hatchet job, he or she may take liberties with the letter—but as few as possible.

My own impression, from a lifelong addiction to costume pictures and the history on which they are based (so far as I know it), is that Hollywood's liberties have been fairly venial and that its virtues far outweigh its faults. There have been glaring cases of distortion (the first two *Bounty* mutiny films come to mind), more often of trivialization and, most frequently of all, of harmless embroidery. Under the last heading, one may place the case of Josef von Sternberg and the vestal virgins, which is typical of good box-office (if not of good historical) thinking and is a common failing of costume pictures.

In the documentary *The Epic That Never Was,* which dealt with Alexander Korda's aborted production of *I, Claudius,* the costume designer John Armstrong described how he obtained from a Neapolitan statue authentic details of the dresses for vestal virgins, of whom there were to be six, the proper number, fully clothed. This was not good enough for the director, Sternberg. "I want sixty, and I want them naked," he told Armstrong, who obediently came up with costumes resembling bikinis under gauzy drapery. "It looked lovely," Armstrong conceded, "but it had nothing to do with the Roman religion." How far that kind of departure from truth matters is debatable; my history master might well have condemned it—but recalling his reaction to Claudette Colbert in *The Sign of the Cross,* I doubt it.

On a different plane, there was the experience of the late Alan Badel in a biblical epic. Going through the script, it seemed to him that unjustifiable liberties had been taken with Holy Writ; the words of Christ, in fact, had been rewritten. Badel complained to the director, high words ensued, minions ran to and fro, the head of the studio (one of the celebrated Hollywood moguls) was summoned, and finally the scriptwriter was asked to explain himself. And according to Badel, the poor soul leafed nervously through the script, compared it with a Bible, coughed, shuffled, and finally said: "Well, you see, Alan, we thought Jesus sounded just a bit cocky in there."

Plainly, it takes all kinds to make historical films; some have the passion of DeMille for accuracy, and some have not. I am no Egyptologist, but I am told that the research done for *The Ten Commandments* was so exhaustive that it eventually extended scholarship on the subject, and it probably did.

Longships built to scale with meticulous exactness for *The Vikings* were so successful that they astonished their builders by cutting through waves without pitching or rolling and were eventually sailed across the Atlantic. In both cases, the producers could have compromised, and probably no one would have been any the wiser; it is not strictly necessary to hunt out the details of Nelson's uniform from his naval tailors, or study the technique of stonemasonry in the twelfth century B.C., or scour medieval records for everything from recipes to hairstyles, but the fact that these things have been done as a matter of course should weigh for something with those who, misled by some of the film industry's wilder flights at history, mistakenly conclude that Hollywood could never care less so long as the money comes in at the box office.

It is worth remembering that the often-despised film moguls were the greatest patrons of the arts since time began; Hollywood employed more scholars and experts and diverse talents than any philanthropic or learned institution—and, incidentally, paid them better. They gave, and got, their money's worth, and in the process they built us old Baghdad, new and shiny, and the pyramids and the Colosseum; they refought Trafalgar and Thermopylae for our benefit and sent Christopher Columbus to the sands of Watling Island, Marco Polo to the courts of Cathay, Major Rogers to St. Francis, Rowan to Garcia; they sent Drake around the world and Stanley in search of Livingstone (to the tune of "Onward, Christian Soldiers," which hadn't been written then but sounded wonderful); they brought Clive and Zola, Lincoln and Saladin, Buffalo Bill and Catherine the Great, the duke of Wellington and Dick Turpin, Florence Nightingale and Calamity Jane, to life again; they showed us Argonauts and mountain men, Vikings and Jane Austen's ladies, gladiators and Roundheads, Chinese warlords and Pilgrim fathers, Regency bucks and Zulu impis. Really, it was the greatest show on earth.

Some of it was historical nonsense; most of it was not. If some of the images were blemished, they were better than no images at all. Samuel Pepys has given the most brilliant and finely detailed memorial of Restoration London that could be imagined—but imagine is the word; we must form our mental pictures from what he tells us and from artists like Peter Lely and Godfrey Kneller; is it sacrilege to suggest that *Forever Amber, Frenchman's Creek,* and *Hudson's Bay* add something worthwhile, if it is only a visual impression? All the world knows that when the Light Brigade charged in the San Fernando Valley, it was as the climax to a film that had no more to do with Raglan, Cardigan, and Balaklava than did *Little Women*—but even Alfred, Lord Tennyson might have had his imagination enlarged by the most spectacular re-creation ever seen of cavalry going neck or nothing into cannon fire. Bette Davis or Flora Robson could play only an imaginative personation of the great Elizabeth I, but each gave us something that the historian cannot. Personally, I always doubted that an army could be stopped by flashing polished shields until I watched it on the screen; I envisaged the Gordian knot as a vague tangle of rope until Richard Burton was confronted with something that looked like a spherical doormat. What the beginning of the Exodus was like no one will ever know—DeMille brought it to life. The sight of old Vladimir Sokolov perishing in the snow while Charles Boyer made sympathetic noises conveyed some sense of what the retreat from Moscow was like; the scene in which Jack Palance pulls on his glove while Elisha Cook stands wary and angry in the mud is art of a high order; it is also as true an impression of a Western gunfight as we are ever likely to get.

There is something else that the costume picture has done. I have lived long enough in the world of historical fiction to know how strongly it can work in turning readers to historical fact. Hollywood, by providing splendid entertainment, has sent people to the history shelves in their millions.

2

Clio in Hollywood

George F. Custen

> I have often thought that there has rarely passed a life of which a judicious and faithful narrative would not be useful. We are all prompted by the same motives, all deceived by the same fallacies, all animated by hope, obstructed by dangers, entangled by desire, and seduced by pleasure.
>
> —*Samuel Johnson*

> All history resolves itself very easily into the biography of a few stout and earnest persons.
>
> —*Ralph Waldo Emerson*

Richard Nixon, that most self-conscious of presidents, once remarked that he liked his movies "made in Hollywood." On the eve of one of the increasingly frequent escalations of the war in Vietnam, Nixon—who had built a career by attacking the ideological power of the media—sought reassurance for his decisions within the camp of the enemy. He screened Franklin Schaffner's 1970 biopic *Patton,* nurturing his dream of war while sitting in a darkened White House theater. This image conjures up one of Walter Lippmann's most pessimistic scenarios about the pictures in our heads created out of the mediated "pseudoenvironment" in which modern decision makers must dwell; even the president of the United States gets his scripts from Hollywood. Though the consequences of watching biopics are seldom as influential as they were in this instance for Nixon, most viewers, at least in part, see history through the lens of the film biography. In *Patton,* Nixon found a view of history that was congruent with his own. More importantly, Nixon's—and many Americans'—views of the world have been shaped, in part, by a lifetime's (and not merely a single) exposure to filmic representations of powerful individuals and the roles they played in history. A system of film production and distribution once upon a time created an environment in which film biographies were a common feature.

Released with increasing regularity from the earliest days of the cinema to the end of the studio era, the biopic played a powerful part in creating and sustaining public history. In lieu of written materials or firsthand exposure to events and persons, the biopic provided many viewers with the version of a life that they held to be the truth.

The biopic reached its peak—at least numerically—in the 1950s during the dying days of the studio mode of production.

From its cultural high-water mark in the William Dieterle–Paul Muni greatman cycle at Warners in the 1930s (the lives of Émile Zola, Louis Pasteur, and Benito Juárez), the biopic seems, since the 1960s, to have faded away to a minor form. Today, it is seen most frequently on cable channels like AMC or TNT, in a rare contemporary form like *The Doors* (1991) or *Sweet Dreams* (1985), or in intriguing transmutations of made-for-TV movies that cultivate a very different ideology of fame from their cinematic counterparts. What kind of lives did the biopic construct? Why did the biopic decrease in significance? What happened to the industry that nurtured this cultural form? What parts did these great lives on film play in shaping the audience's notion of the self? What kind of historical narratives were the studios attempting to fabricate in the production and distribution of the lives of the famous?

It has been suggested by François Truffaut and others that the Hollywood cinema was excessively obvious and that the cultural significance of genres like the biopic stood out with the clarity of cartoons, texts to be effortlessly deconstructed. Yet, as the recent debate over cultural literacy versus multiculturalism shows, to a large extent the purported universality of culture is constructed rather than spontaneous.[1] In order to understand the importance of this genre, we must come to see the films as the product of an organized culture of production. The contribution of these films to public culture and film culture alike can best be seen not through the analysis of individual works but through the constitution of a large body that forms a kind of supertext. Almost three hundred biopics were produced by the major studios during the classical period 1927–60. This body forms a code with distinctive components. The films were shaped by industrial practices that no longer exist, were nurtured by a star system that limited the specific shapes a life could take, and were sold to a moviegoing public through diverse publicity machines that created specific contexts for the reception of the great lives.

Rather than being obvious, the overall configurations of this group of films are, in many instances, unknown. With this institutional approach, the "obvious" honor of *The Life of Emile Zola* (1937) or the strenuous patriotism of *Yankee Doodle Dandy* (1943) attain a significance beyond the particular histrionics of a Muni or the unique charm of a James Cagney. The films form a tapestry whose narrative can be best appreciated by apprehending their place within the whole work. Through a close analysis of the machine that shaped the warp and woof by which the individual figures are woven, we are able to comprehend an identifiable historical pattern.

The biographical film (the *biopic*) routinely integrates disparate historical episodes of selected individual lives into a nearly monochromatic "Hollywood view of history." One way this integration occurs is through the construction of a highly conventionalized view of fame. These films build a pattern of narrative that is selective in its attention to profession, differential in the role it assigns to gender, and limited in its historical settings. Another way the Hollywood view of history is integrated is through the studios' strategic use of star images in the creation of the stories of famous people. Because I am interested in the codes formed by the overall Hollywood construction of biography, I examine these issues by looking at the patterns produced by all Hollywood biopics made during the studio era, 1927–60.[2]

Prior to television, and along with newspapers, magazines, paperback books, and radio, it was the Hollywood film that, attended with great regularity by a large part of the American people, shaped the public's perception of issues and set the public agenda on topics both important and trivial. Although there have been several studies, from all segments of the ideological spectrum, of the film industry as a producer of culture, none has investigated the code of the biographical film, its construction, and the particular worldview it creates when defining history.[3]

The film industry, as a manufacturer whose product is culture itself, has rarely been studied as an institution qua institution, one whose complex social organization possesses (and had to possess) rules for governing its seemingly naive cultural output. However, as Garth Jowett (1990:237) suggests, this previous trend—of slighting the institutional context of film production—has been changing. Movie corporations have made once-closed files available, and recent work by a number of scholars suggests that there is an increasing recognition in cinema studies, just as there is in communications, that texts must be studied as texts in action, in particular institutional settings, with specific audiences' responses.[4]

In the place of studies on how decisions were made to produce movies, anecdotal and mythological works bearing the imprint of the story lines of the films themselves functioned as a Hollywood substitute for a more historically grounded set of creation myths. Until recently, while there had been no shortage of glossy coffee-table books on the stars—of which the studios surely would have approved—there had been little serious scholarship on what anthropologist Hortense Powdermaker (1950) referred to as the "closed tribe" of Hollywood and its fascinating rituals.

One of the most interesting rituals to study is the construction of the Hollywood biographical film. In making the lives of the famous fit particular contours—and thereby controlling normative boundaries of actions and lives—these films cultivate the interests of their producers, presenting a worldview that naturalizes certain lives and specific values over alternative ones. Biopics also created a view of history that was based on the cosmology of the movie industry; in this world, key historical figures became stars, and the producers of these films often filtered the content of a great life through the sieve of their own experiences, values, and personalities. In this view of history, the greatness of the individual figure becomes that set of qualities that made a producer great or powerful in Hollywood rather than those traits that characterized the famous person in his or her own lifetime.

What Is a Biopic?

For my purposes here, a biographical film is one that depicts the life of a historical person, past or present. Biography is mediated through the creation of and competence in symbol systems, and the cinematic version of such mediation has antecedents far older than the film industry or even the technology of film. While undoubtedly people recalled tales of ancestors and other previous significant figures in their lives, the creation of notation systems (written language, iconic representations) more than the performance of a life through dance, gesture, or music created a sense of biography that located it in a particular permanent form. Biography thus arguably became the basis of the earliest forms of literature, for one of the oldest human impulses is to record for posterity something of the lives of one's fellows. This expression is found on prehistoric slabs and scraps of papyrus, and even, as we know, on cave walls.

So, too, is it found in the earliest works on film. Historical films, or rather re-creations of real events from the past, almost certainly were among the earliest genres of the cinema. In 1895, one could watch *The Execution of Mary, Queen of Scots* or shortly after, in 1898, view J. Stuart Blackton and Albert E. Smith's *Battle of Manila Bay* in a re-creation of this event that possibly was advertised as a record of the real thing. Sarah Bernhardt scored a major triumph in her 1912 performance of *Queen Elizabeth.* In Germany, Dimitri Buchowetski (*Danton* [1920] and *Peter der Grosse* [1922]) and Ernst Lubitsch (*Madame Du Barry* [1919] and *Anne Boleyn* [1920]) directed biopics of royalty, this focus being an early staple of the genre that would change by the 1930s. In France, Abel Gance commenced his film career acting in an early biopic, the 1909 production of *Molière,* and went on to direct the epic 1927 work *Napoleon,* as well as the less startling 1936 *Un Grand Amour de Beethoven.* Sir Alexander Korda, whose erratic career encompassed the roles of producer, director, and Svengali, helped cement a tabloid-inspired view of biography with *The Private Life of Helen of Troy* (1927), and, with more prestige, the 1933 *Private Life of Henry VIII;* one of the Warners' earliest commercial successes came with a biopic of the American ambassador to Germany, *My Four Years in Germany* (1918). The biopic, then, was a known commodity almost from film's beginning. Further, it had many variants—hagiography, psychological biography, autobiography—and was embroiled in the same controversies about truth, accuracy, and interpretation as its literary predecessors.[5]

Biography and the Recorded Image

In 1880, it became possible to reproduce halftone photographs, altering the content of newspapers as well as the picturing of the news. Readers, who heretofore had to content themselves with pen-and-ink drawings of the day's famous, could now see what such a person actually looked like. This expectation of seeing and not just reading about the famous certainly carried over into the cinema in two important ways. First, film—with its added dimension of motion and its narratization of images—created a most attractive forum for explaining the news or explicating past events within present-day frames. Second, pictures and their use in popular journalism transformed the very concept of fame. Leo Braudy, in *The Frenzy of Renown* (1986), argues that the possibility of reproducing an actual photographic image shifted the focus from perennial (one might even say societally structural) famous, like royalty and rulers, to a celebration of anyone in the news. As an early 1902 silent film, *The*

Capture of the Biddle Brothers (later made, in 1984, as a romance called *Mrs. Soffel,* with Diane Keaton and Mel Gibson), demonstrates, "headliners" from the print media became the subject matter of biopics, expanding the definition of this genre, which had previously centered on the doings of already famous, often lofty figures. In such a way, fame was democratized.

Sound film made possible another significant development in telling a life story; the broadening further still of biography, as the medium of mass entertainment, finally had the ability to fully narrate its own history of entertainment. From the 1940s on, biography came to mean not just what Leo Lowenthal (1944) dubbed "Idols of Production" or headliners (good and bad) but also and even particularly came to be associated with the entertainers themselves.

A biopic, then, from its earliest days is minimally composed of the life, or the portion of a life, of a real person whose real name is used. Other than this trait, the definition of what constitutes a biopic—and with it, what counts as fame—shifts anew with each generation. It is not that each generation creates or discovers necessarily new forums for fame; rather, certain careers and types of people become the prime focus of public curiosity in each generation. Moreover, the ways in which their lives are explained shift subtly, so that a life depicted in one way in 1930 might be a very different thing by the mid-1950s. Tracing a code for the biopic is an exercise in reconstructing a shifting public notion of fame.

Regardless of the surreal connotations with which Hollywood surrounded, say, Cleopatra, she was an actual living figure. Hercules and Salome, regardless of their physiques or number of veils, are probably figures of fiction. The point of such analysis is not the limited question, How "realistic" is Hollywood biography? The answer would surely be that Hollywood biography is to history what Caesar's Palace is to architectural history: an enormous, engaging distortion, which after a time convinces us of its own kind of authenticity. Hollywood biographies are real not because they are believable. Rather, one must treat them as real because despite the obvious distortions, ranging from the minor to the outright camp, Hollywood films are believed to be real by many viewers. They represent, according to Hayden White, not a concrete illustration of history, a literal recapitulation of physical cause and effect, but rather types of behavior and explanation that comprise the category "history": "Demands for a verisimilitude in film that is impossible in any medium of representation, including that of written history, stem from the confusion of historical individuals with the kinds of 'characterization' of them required for discursive purposes, whether in verbal or in visual media" (1988:1198–99).

While most biopics do not claim to be the definitive history of an individual or era, they are often the only source of information many people will ever have on a given historical subject. As John E. O'Connor notes, "However unfortunate, it appears likely that even well-educated Americans are learning most of their history from film and television" (1988:1201). Even at the height of its popularity, Lytton Strachey's 1928 book, *Elizabeth and Essex; A Tragic History,* was read by fewer people than saw the Strachey-inspired Bette Davis–Errol Flynn film, *The Private Lives of Elizabeth and Essex* (1939). Although most biopics make only limited claims to be treated as the final word on their subjects, neither are they meant to be ignored as useful historical materials. Unlike other films, almost all biopics are prefaced by written or spoken declarations that assert the realities of their narratives.[6]

In biopics, as I define them, the characters' real names are used. Thus, romans (or films) à clef—such as *The Greek Tycoon* (1978), a thinly disguised story of the Maria Callas–Aristotle Onassis–Jacqueline Kennedy affair; *The Rose* (1979), based on the life of singer Janis Joplin; or Warners' 1935 headliner *Black Fury,* a vehicle for Paul Muni based on the murder of labor organizer Mike Shemanski—although intriguing forms of creative bricolage, are not considered here. The fact that real names are used in biographical films suggests an openness to historical scrutiny and an attempt to present the film as the official story of a life. And, while such openness may indeed be a pose by a film's producers, it nevertheless is publicly presented as a natural state of film narration: Hollywood biopics are the true versions of a life.

Searching for the overlooked patterns that reveal the social order hidden beneath the doings of those heralded entertainers, scientists, artists, writers, inventors, capitalists, statesmen, politicians, and others, I also want to offer an explanation of why Hollywood, where the hero can have a thousand faces, should have constructed fame with such a limited, contorted profile. Following Emerson's dictum that all history "resolves itself very easily into the biographies of a few stout and earnest persons," the history of Hollywood has been reduced to the history of a few "great" (read larger-than-life) men.[7] While this corridors-of-power approach to history might be compelling as any Warners biography of the 1930s, it is also ideologically self-serving. The family resemblance between the chronicled histories of the Hollywood industry's founders and the famous figures frozen in black-and-white, ninety-minute narratives produced by these men, the boilerplate tales of immigrant pluck rewarded by a benevolent America, is a tantalizing but uncharted relationship.

Film and History

In focusing on the biopic as a kind of overlooked historical discourse, I am not claiming that the issues that adhere to film and its relations to history have not been considered. These issues are both large and, to an extent, largely unsettled. Because of this, the scope of any project purporting to deal with film and history as discourses must first lay out the terms under which questions about film and history might be asked.

Hayden White suggests that one must make a distinction between *historiography,* the representation of history by verbal images and written discourse, and *historiophoty,* the "representation of history and our thoughts about it in visual images and written discourse" (1988 : 1193). For White, film and video as branches of visual praxis are constituted by discourses that are "capable of telling us things about its referents that are both different from what can be told in verbal discourse and also of a kind that can only be told by means of visual images" (1193).

Much discussion of the biopic, as a kind of historical artifact, hinges upon some issue of how true it is and how the process of creating a film or video inevitably alters, in some way, the truth or accuracy of the telling of history.[8] Stated simply, one of the concerns of historians studying fiction film's relation to history is with what gets lost in the translation of the event from its verbal state to a visual/pictorial one; that is, how condensation and narratization alter the facts deemed "not essential" to the narrative to fit both a medium and the conventions of a genre (e.g., romance).[9]

This translatability problem—from event to its telling or describing—is unique neither to history as a kind of discourse nor to film as a medium. Since Plutarch, there has been an awareness that recorded or written history is a text that freezes the narrative in a particular, interested form. Biography, the isolation of a single life from the flow of history, can reduce the imputation of motive and the rendering of historical explanation to something even more facile, for the presumption that one can get inside the mind of another subject and mediate this incursion with a narrative explanation is a problem as old as literature itself. Reading the *Iliad* or the *Odyssey* illuminates how ancient a habit self-interested historical projection is; past generations, reconstructed by the present, are often seen as different, sometimes superior to the current crop of heroes. Homer, and writers ever since, have used tales of the past to score a point about the current inadequacies of a contemporary social group.

It is a particularly postmodern fixation, however, to be concerned with the processes of mediation as themselves being shapers of meaning worthy of separate study. The processes used and the materials that constitute recorded history are found to be far from transparent or neutral—ideologically, formally, and in other ways. Instead of asking what kind of clothing history's Muse Clio wears, contemporary practice prefers to disrobe her, deconstructing the fabrics used to weave the cloth that previously made up her transparent dress.

The larger issue surrounding the accuracy of historical representation, then, is not built solely upon pillars of facticity, legality, or any other single issue. Rather, the problem of encoding the historical narrative can be profitably addressed from a vantage point that incorporates many of these issues into a larger pattern. Communications might frame the issue of biographical mediation as one of translation of information, those conditions created when information encoded in one set of symbol systems is translated into another, partially different set of signs.[10] Since the very acts of daily interaction themselves are full of gaps, of poor translations, of approximations of "information" from one telling to the next, to assume that history (written on a larger scale than the information exchanged as part of the average human dyad) could avoid these issues that are present at the microlevel is both incredibly naive and severely limiting; for to frame the issue of historical representation solely as one of accuracy or truth is to overlook the social functions that might be performed by differential structurings of the historical discourse.

Recent feminist historians, as well as gay and lesbian archivists, have suggested that the very point of view represented by conventional history eliminates the perspectives of a sizable portion of its own subjects. History's pose of accuracy and its foregrounding of this issue as a litmus test in assessing different mediations of past events empower some groups (and some symbolic forms) at the expense of others. Alan Berube's *Coming out under Fire* (1990), a study of gay and lesbian soldiers during World War II, is a recent example of a history that conventional chroniclers had banished. Such recent excavation—often, of necessity, self-excavation—suggests that history as a process of mediation is far from disinterested, or complete. Rather, some historians accommodated and even encouraged the repression of minorities by not raising problematic, nonmainstream perspectives as part of their narratives. The history of sexual minorities, as well as other groups banished from conventional annals for many years, has only recently been recovered. To address history from the point of view of "accuracy" alone is to accept that such a condition exists and that it is disinterested rather than ideologically motivated.

There are those who would defend the position that research—historical or other—can get at the truth relatively untrammeled. Although anthropologist Margaret Mead believed that, given the proper training in observation, and with the use of certain techniques and equipment, an event could be filmed unaltered, there are few who would defend this essentialist position that the event, or its recording, exists in such a pure state. As White suggests,

> No history, visual or verbal, "mirrors" all or even the greater parts of the events or scenes of which it purports to be an account, and this is true of even

> the most narrowly restricted "micro history." Every written history is a product of processes of condensation, displacement, symbolization, and qualification exactly like those used in the production of filmed representation. It is only the medium that differs, not the way in which the messages are produced. (1988:1194)

All history, then, is a mediation, a set of discursive practices encoded in a time and often a place removed from their actual occurrence and thus subject to some degree of restructuring. To suggest, as Ian Jarvie does in "Seeing Through Movies" (1978), that film, biased toward description rather than analysis, lacks an adequate information load, in two hours, to do justice to most topics that can be done in print is to miss the point entirely. Rather than ask the question, How true is *I Wonder Who's Kissing Her Now* (1947) or *Wilson* (1944)? one might ask, What factors shape the construction of history in these particular mediations, and how are they similar to or different from other constructions of biography in film? In literature? In magazines? The patterns of these lives, the narrative and other devices used to construct these lives as parts of an institutional machinery of making film narrative, are of greater interest than the distortion of a single film, book, or folktale. I suspect that professional historians and film scholars have different ideas about what constitutes history and about the uses of film both as history and as a medium of communication. But there is a growing awareness that popular encodings of history—rather than those created for professional historians or film scholars—are powerful materials in building a consensus about what constitutes history and about what kind of history shall be constituted. To an extent, the memory of history many of us carry—if there be such a portable item as a collective memory—is a mediated one. Thus, both the coverage of history and its selective recovery through textbooks, film, and other media are important projects only just begun.

The Creation of Public History

Public history refers both to the product and to the process in which members of the mass public—the public at large—obtain their definitions of the symbolic universe from watching and talking about the communications media. Although the term is used to refer to history written "from the bottom up," it also conveys the idea that mass-media texts, and not other forms of historical narrative, are significant sources of history for large segments of the American population. Movies today are not the prime media agent cultivating historical images that they once were. In many respects, the enculturation function of movies has been co-opted by other media, notably television. However, film still exerts a powerful influence on people's notions of what counts as history, what properly constitutes a life. Today, because of their still-potent popularity and their apparent readability, films are an attractively persuasive source of information. The Hollywood biographical film created and still creates public history by declaring, through production and distribution, which lives are acceptable subjects.

In telling history through the individual life, Hollywood has had an enormous impact upon viewers' conceptions about the world. Sometimes this attempt at influence was intentional, as in campaign books studios distributed to exhibitors, exhorting them with a variety of strategies to exploit their audience before and after screenings. Biopics could be sold as educational, instructional materials. Some of this selling was actually sanctioned by various institutions with ties to educational systems. For many years, study guides for selected Hollywood films were published by *Photoplay Studies* and other corporations for formal instruction in history, drama, and literature in different public school systems.

A company called Pictorial Events Films, with the cooperation of Warners Studio, produced filmstrips of selected Warners films (among them William Dieterle's *Dispatch from Reuters* [1940]) for classroom and other showings, advertising, "By special arrangement, Warner Bros. make available for the first time a practical pretested plan to exploit motion pictures in classrooms and at large groups through the medium of especially prepared Pictorial Events Films." Included in this package, along with maps and charts used to illustrate key background points on the state of Europe in Paul Julius von Reuter's time, was a prewritten lecture for the teacher, with "Each shot . . . keyed by a number to a corresponding number on the text." These guides contained suggested lesson plans for the teacher to use after a film's screening; their focus ranged from cinematic questions to historical ones. And, by their use in classrooms, these films in particular, and film in general, were validated as legitimate carriers of the lessons of history or literature for viewers. These publications also contained information on the film's stars (though rarely on the screenplay's author), and this focus helped cultivate moviegoing and star worship as life-long habits.

Other forms of influence tied films in with other media in exploitation campaigns to maximize interest and attendance. Additionally, as Gaines and Herzog (1990) have noted, commodity tie-ins, in the form of clothing and cosmetics, helped exhibitors sell a film by keeping it in the public eye long after the duration of a screening. Thus, an exhibitor's campaign kit for MGM's *Tennessee Johnson* (1942) came with a copy of a telegram endorsing the film from the publisher of the influential *Parents' Magazine.* Exhibitors were urged, "Get cooperation of local Parent-Teacher organization to endorse picture to its membership," and, "Offer prizes for best reviews of 'Tennessee Johnson' written by history-class students under sponsorship of department head." The perceived historical value of these films, then, became a bargaining chip in the lucrative educational market.[11]

In addition to organized campaigns to integrate film content into the lives of young viewers via education, information gleaned from films by viewers finds its way into people's daily conversations after screenings. Such conversation has the general function of what Peter Berger and Thomas Luckman, in *The Social Construction of Reality* (1967), refer to as "reality maintenance"; topics initially raised by a film are broached in familiar settings in daily, nonaesthetic conversations with others. In *The Tacit Dimension* (1967), Michael Polanyi notes that with this kind of "tacit" knowledge, while eventually you could be conscious that you know a thing to be true, you are nevertheless unable to trace the initial source of such knowledge. For example, although it is possible that people's constructions about slavery are based on interpersonal communication or on books like *Roll, Jordan, Roll* or *Time on the Cross* or on a combination of interaction among different media and channels of communication, it is more likely that *Gone with the Wind* (1939), *Roots* (1977), even Ken Burns's recent PBS documentary, *The Civil War* (1990), are the sources of this information. Eventually, knowledge from different sources becomes merely what we know; the initial contact is indistinctly remembered or even falsely attributed to another experience. Such tacit effects of biopics certainly influence audiences as much as organized attempts to market, like some university in a frame, the films as valuable civics lessons.[12]

Film and Social Order

As George Gerbner and others, notably members of the Frankfurt school and more recently critical theorists, have observed, television, film, and earlier mass-communications systems cultivate the perspectives of the social order from which they spring. While much of the biographical doings in Hollywood films seem, from the professional historian's perspective, to constitute a slightly deranged form of dadaism, these films undoubtedly cultivated, for many viewers, images of what the life of, say, Madame Curie was really like. Not only did films order and in some instances create history, they also virtually defined for uninitiated viewers entire realms of endeavor and ways of being. For, as John O'Connor notes, "since the 1930s, film and television have become major factors in politics and culture. . . . some of the most important events of the past century took place before newsreel or television cameras" (1988:1201). In many cases, in seeing biopics, filmgoers were witnessing the first visual attempt to re-create a narrative that they knew of only from reports in school texts or newspapers. The re-creation becomes, de facto, the only version of history they will ever see.

While the obvious impact of *Madame Curie* (1943) may have been to tell viewers the story of the great scientist who discovered radium, it also posited a vision of what a scientist should be, how experimental method is applied to scientific discovery, and how a scientist should behave if the scientist is also a woman. Ex nihilo, these films told the tales of history's actors; yet, they also symbolically annihilated much of history by selectively eliminating certain activities, actors, and behaviors from the scripts of history. *Night and Day* (1946), the story of Cole Porter, is particularly instructive in creating a false history that systematically eliminates "problematic" aspects of a life from public consciousness. Porter's marriage of convenience to an older woman covers the fact of his homosexuality. By glossing over this critical aspect of Porter's life, sexual preferences other than those sanctioned by society and approved by the Hays Office are relegated to public oblivion, though, as often is the case, private channels arose to deal with what mainstream channels would not validate. Instead of proposing a subversive construction of marriage and sexual relations, *Night and Day,* with the full cooperation of the Porters, presents the myth of the devoted, supportive spouse of the (quasi-)isolated composer or artist, a human being presented as so special he or she can only be nurtured by one person who understands the nature of genius awaiting discovery. At another level, the distortion in Porter's life on film also naturalizes heterosexual marriage as the norm by eliminating other possible forms of relationship in the life of the artist. This attempt to "normalize" genius is a critical part of the construction of the well-adjusted, successful biopic hero. Each instance of biographical selection has this dual function: it *both* proclaims an episode as true while, as part of a larger pattern of a body of other films, it valorizes it as natural. In this world of created history, all acts of selection are value laden.

It is apt that Hollywood should give public figures the star treatment. Like figures in some festive holiday parade altered to fit this year's celebrity fashion, the set of filmic lives selectively unveiled before the public are changing spectacles, which are, in the long run, observable. There is a finite, repeated set of myths about what it means—signifies—to be, say, a statesman (but not a politician), a female entertainer—suffering through four reels of liquor and unfaithful men only, perhaps, to triumph at the end—or merely a famous person. It is possible that the model all professions conform to is one of fame and its relation to the ordinary individual. That is, what is operating in biographical films is the star system speaking of itself through its own contained, controlled means, animating its own values through the figures of a parallel world of stars. Here we have a world where we see history as the film industry, great men as the star system.[13]

Notes

1. Katharine Hepburn, herself a star of two biopics, in response to the question of how accurate the actors themselves thought the films were, suggested, "I think your common sense really tells you the truth about the amount of research; if it has been inadequate your visual sense and your hearing find it absurd and careless" (personal communication, 13 October 1989). Yet, a common sense that is itself shaped by the very forces of cultural construction that are hardly disinterested is not the natural lens it appears to be.

2. A saturation sample of all biopics would consist of 291 films. About half of these films are available on videotape.

3. The *Film Literature Index* has a lengthy section under "biography," but this subject heading refers to print narratives about the people who make movies and not the movies themselves. Although there are sixteen articles on individual biopics cited in *The New Film Index,* the actual films themselves, compared to other genres, have been largely ignored. There have been works that deal in part with the biopic. Nick Roddick's *New Deal in Entertainment: Warner Brothers in the 1930s* (1983) has two chapters that deal with foreign biopics and the studio's representation of American history. Robert Miller's *Star Myths: Show Business Biographies on Film* (1983) looks at popular entertainers; and in the coffee-table mold, George MacDonald Fraser's *Hollywood History of the World: From One Million B.C. to Apocalypse Now* (1988) has some relevant information on the accuracy of biopics, as does Michael Pitts's 1984 filmography on historical films, *Hollywood and American Reality: A Filmography of Over 250 Motion Pictures Depicting U.S. History.*

4. See, for example, Tino Balio (1985), Robert Carringer (1985), and Thomas Schatz (1988) for three recent works that place the meanings of film within the institutional contexts of their production.

5. One of the earliest controversies about the "accuracy" and the "ficticity" of biography concerned James Boswell's *Life of Samuel Johnson.* When first published, in 1791, it was deemed by no less an authority than the historian Thomas Babington Macaulay as a masterwork. Its author was considered the model for his field. Yet, from the 1920s on, with the publication of the voluminous Boswell diaries (the source material for the Johnson biographies), it became apparent that both the chronology of the life and some of the quotes attributed to Johnson, as well as the intimacy of Boswell with the great man, were in serious doubt. The issues surrounding Boswell's history as depicted in the *Life*—the accuracy of reproducing the past versus the author's taking a point of view, the view that biography is a

branch of history and not fiction, and making entertainment an incidental value second to accuracy—surround the lives on film as well.

6. In the purposive sample of one hundred biopics used for the content analysis [in Custen's book, *Bio/Pics*], 90 percent of all biopics were prefaced by a written, spoken introduction (in tandem or alone) that asserted the truth status of the narrative that was about to unfold.

7. Emerson echoes the sentiment of his contemporary across the seas, Thomas Carlyle, who, in his lectures "On Heroes, Hero-Worship and the Heroic in History" delivered in 1840 (and published in 1841), articulated the greatman thesis of history, suggesting that "in all epochs . . . we shall find the great man to have been the indispensable saviour of his epoch—the lightening without which the fuel would never have burnt."

8. It appears that early on Hollywood recognized that the construct "historical accuracy," detached from the context of the film industry, did not exist. Irving that (quoted in Leab 1990) noted, "if in telling a story, we find it impossible to adhere to historical accuracy in order to get the necessary dramatic effect, we do change it and we do feel it is the right thing to do." As Leab concludes, "Truth, accuracy, and a proper respect for history, then, have been routinely subordinated to the need for dramatic effect and even the whims of filmmakers." But, as the historian Pierre Sorlin (1990) suggests, it is important to keep in mind not merely the accuracy of a film but how this version was received by contemporary audiences. To this I would add the caveat that one must also look at how the film was packaged and sold—ironically or not—by the producing studios.

9. Daniel Leab cites Erik Barnouw on the epistemology particular media impart to history. Barnouw notes that "People who rely . . . on television for their knowledge of the past are dealing with . . . a situation where history is constantly being rewritten by the dominant medium to serve the purposes of the present" (quoted in Leab 1990:80). Barnouw's warnings about the organizational imperatives that shape TV programming hold true for film, magazines, radio, and other mass-based media.

10. Anthropologist Gregory Bateson (1979) and communications researcher Larry Gross (1974), as well as philosopher Ernst Cassirer (in *The Philosophy of Symbolic Forms*), have each noted that material originally encoded in one symbolic mode—gestural, spatial, verbal—is only partly translatable into some other, different symbol system.

11. Early studies of movie attendance patterns noted that children attended more frequently than adults, and young boys went more than young girls. The educational youth market, then, would be a highly valued slice of the mass audience. See "The Payne Fund Studies: The Effects of Movies on Children," in Lowery and De Fleur's *Milestones in Mass Communications Research: Media Effects* (1983).

12. For years, the telephone was called "the Ameche," a reference to Don Ameche, the filmic impersonator of the phone's inventor, Alexander Graham Bell. Such popular expressions illuminate the role film representation can play in shaping public perception of history.

13. For a broad cultural reading of what it means to be a star or celebrated person in contemporary Western culture, see Richard Schickel (1985) and Leo

Braudy (1986). Some of Braudy's notions are parallel to the ideas advanced here, namely that the state of being celebrated has superseded other kinds of achievement as a social index of worthiness. Obviously Leo Lowenthal (1944), or Walter Lippmann in his 1922 work *Public Opinion,* and Daniel Boorstin (1962), among other writers, have all focused on the metaphorical significance of celebrityhood.

Works Cited

Balio, Tino (ed.). 1985. *The American Film Industry.* Madison: University of Wisconsin Press.

Bateson, Gregory. 1979. *Steps to an Ecology of Mind.* San Francisco: Chandler Press.

Boorstin, Daniel. 1962. *The Image: A Guide to Pseudo Events in America.* New York: Atheneum.

Braudy, Leo. 1986. *The Frenzy of Renown.* New York: Oxford University Press.

Carringer, Robert L. 1985. *The Making of Citizen Kane.* Berkeley: University of California Press.

Gaines, Jane, and Charlotte Herzog (eds.). 1990. *Fabrications: Costume and the Female Body.* New York: Routledge.

Gross, Larry P. 1974. Modes of Communication and the Acquisition of Symbolic Competence. In *Media and Symbols,* edited by Donald Olsen. Chicago: University of Chicago Press.

Jarvie, Ian C. 1978. Seeing Through Movies. *Philosophy of Social Science.*

Jowett, Garth. 1990. Mass Media, History and the Development of Communications Research. In *Image as Artifact,* edited by John E. O'Connor. Malabar, Florida: Robert E. Krieger Publishing.

Leab, Daniel. 1990. The Moving Image as Interpreter of History—Telling the Dancer from the Dance. In *Image as Artifact,* edited by John E. O'Connor. Malabar, Florida: Robert E. Krieger Publishing.

Lowenthal, Leo. 1944. Biographies in Popular Magazines. In *Radio Research: 1942–43,* edited by Paul Lagerfeld and Frank Stanton. New York: Duell, Sloan and Pearce.

O'Connor, John E. 1988. History in Images/Images as History. *American Historical Review* 93, no. 5 (December):1200–1207.

Powdermaker, Hortense. 1950. *Hollywood the Dream Factory.* Boston: Little Brown.

Schatz, Thomas. 1988. *The Genius of the System.* New York: Pantheon.

Schickel, Richard. 1985. *Intimate Strangers: The Culture of Celebrity.* New York: Doubleday.

Sorlin, Pierre. 1990. Historical Films as Tools for Historians. In *Image as Artifact,* edited by John E. O'Connor. Malabar, Florida: Robert E. Krieger Publishing.

White, Hayden. 1988. Historiography and Historiophoty. *American Historical Review* 93, no. 5 (December):1193–99.

3

British TV Dramadocumentary: Origins and Developments

John Corner

The term *drama* can be applied in two rather different ways to documentary material, even if both ways are finally related. First of all, it can be used to indicate the exciting, intensive character of an event; and second, it can be used to indicate enactment (professional or otherwise, variously rehearsed or not) in front of the camera. The two usages are often in an awkward relationship with one another in everyday speech and in television (e.g., dramatic reconstruction is used to give a journalistic report a more "dramatic" character; our ideas of what is a "dramatic" event owe a good deal to film and television fiction). The way I am most concerned with here concerns enactment, the bringing to documentary work of the scripting, acting, and directional approaches of fiction. It is also possible to see the combination of dramatic with documentary approaches as being organized within the terms of one or other of two main kinds of "recipe." The approach of "dramatized documentary" begins with a documentary base or core and uses dramatization to overcome certain limitations and to achieve a more broadly popular and imaginatively powerful effect. The other approach, "documentary drama," is essentially a form of *play*, but it is a form that is seen to develop a documentary character either as a result of its scale of referentiality to specific real events (private or public or both) *or* because of its manner of depiction. These different reasons for making an attribution of "documentariness" to a play need to be kept apart in discussion.

In fact, quite apart from the general problem of critical subjectivity in using such classifications, maintaining a clear distinction between the two "models" becomes hard to do when confronted with certain examples (of which *Cathy Come Home* [BBC, 1966], is one). Nevertheless, the differentiation still seems to me to have analytic value, even where it is finally confounded.[1] We can apply it to the earliest television work to use a "mixed" approach.

Television Documentary and "Dramatization" in the 1950s

The "story documentary" was one of the forms used by the official film documentarists of the Second World War. Although there were stylistic variations between the films, the essential idea was to take a documentary theme (the submarine service, for example, or the nightly bombing raids of the Royal Air Force) and treat this by "particularizing" it around a story line with characters, which could be given an intimate rendering using the depictive methods of feature fiction. The result mixed informational throughput with narrative satisfactions, allowing for empathy with the main figures of portrayal, whose experiences and whose personal qualities were projected with far greater intensity and focus than more conventional documentary formats could have achieved. One can usefully talk here of the *proxemics* of the dramatization—its capacity to "bring us close" to the local human detail within the larger themes and sphere of action being addressed; this in contrast to the necessary and sometimes emphatically maintained "distance" at which a conventional documentary works, through its mixture of observation and commentary. Viewers were invited not to an exposition but to the witnessing of an "imitation of an action," to use Aristotle's classic phrase about the character of drama.

As with later forms of story documentary, the difference from the range of conventional feature fictions was discernible in a number of ways. Apart from the intermixing of the dramatic material with "actuality" sequences, perhaps the most obvious of these was the relationship between the story core of the film and the wider project of documentation. Although feature films (including wartime features) frequently provided a strong real-life context for their stories, the story documentary had an economy of depiction that required it continuously to register the nature of circumstances—both local and general—that were happening "to the side" of the main narrative. This might mean closing in to focus on particular procedural matters (aircraft bomb loading; the adjustment of course on a warship's bridge) or pulling back to look at the more general circumstances and processes of which the dramatized events were simply one part. The movement out from story to documentation and back (sometimes smoothly achieved, sometimes awkwardly) was nearly always of a kind that would be considered deviant within the conventions of realist feature filmmaking; there was simply *too much* time spent "out of story" looking at detail or establishing context. Only when one assumed an audience coming to the film with *some* expectations about being informed as well as entertained would the subsequent dispersal effect exerted on character interest and plot development be considered justifiable. I shall return to these points about the early story documentary later, since the precedent has exerted a considerable influence not only on realist tendencies in subsequent British cinema but on developments in television fiction.

The television documentarists of the 1950s were well aware of the story documentary mode, indeed many of them had worked on wartime productions themselves. However, their own use of dramatization was initially prompted by a different set of requirements. Paramount here was the need to produce documentary television about circumstances and processes that could not be filmed directly either because of restrictions on television access or because of the technical limitations placed on live broadcasting. Without the option of videotape recording and with the expense of location shooting on film, the obvious "solution" was dramatic reconstruction in the studio. Within these exigencies, the kinds of narrative intensity and explorations of person, action, and space available to the wartime film productions were simply not a possibility. In the more modest productions, the situation was in many ways akin to that of the 1930s documentarists, who had frequently resorted to "scenic reconstruction" (e.g., the cabin of a fishing vessel; the sorting office of a mail train) within films having no continuous dramatic diegesis. There was still the emphasis on the imitation of an action; the procedures of drama were allowing relations of proximity and offering an experience of witnessing. But the simulacrum was often a means of making up for the nonavailability of the original rather than a means of managing affective power and scopic field for full dramatic satisfaction. In her excellent account of BBC documentary production during this period, Elaine Bell notes the general character of this kind of studio-based work:

> Among topics dealt with in this period were hooliganism, borstal, drugs, working women, children in care, problems of youth, marriage and old age,

> prostitution, industrial relations and declining industries, while such series as *Made by Hand, I Made News, Pilgrim Street* (about police methods) and the much praised *Course of Justice,* which illustrated legal procedure by individual cases, were made. (Bell 1986:74)

Interestingly, Bell also notes how the BBC regarded this kind of work with some anxiety as to the status attributed to it by audiences. For instance, an internal memo notes with disappointment that an issue of the *Radio Times* had included a cast list for such a production, a practice its author thinks will "kill the reality of the programme." There was anxiety too about repeating dramatized documentaries. Whilst it was common practice for plays to be repeated live (i.e., the same cast going through the whole thing again in front of the cameras), it was thought that this might greatly reduce the status of documentary output. It is hard to credit the level of condescension toward the audience suggested by some of these attitudes. They indicate both a full awareness of the extent to which artifice has replaced reality in the production but a concern not to let this knowledge spoil the "illusion" for the viewer. In this early phase of engagement with the issues of creativity and truth generated by the "mix," there are clear signs of the themes that would become more contested and more complicated in later documentary and "realist" developments.

In a 1956 discussion, "The Story Documentary," Caryl Doncaster, an experienced television director of such programs, gives some interesting glimpses of the view from the production end. One section is worth quoting in full:

> The story documentary, however, has little in common with the straight drama, which depends for its effect on what the writer has to say, the strength of his plot with which he captivates our interest while he is saying it, and that "suspension of disbelief" which his audience must feel when watching, be it on the television set at home, at the theatre or in the cinema. The writer of the story documentary should never allow his own opinions on the subject he interprets to deflect him from impartiality. He must try to present each facet of the problem in true perspective.

As for plot, he is trying to present a cross section of life; therefore, what plot he uses must only exist to give shape and cohesion. He can never make use of deus ex machina, the happy ending, the numerous other theatrical devices that untie the knots. On the other hand, he is not trying to suspend the disbelief of his audience; for, through his technique both as writer and as producer, the viewer is presented with reality itself (Doncaster in Rotha 1956, cited in Goodwin et al. [eds.] 1983:8).

The self-denying character of the production ethos is here apparent, though we might wish to well think the claims about showing "reality itself" and the maintenance of a "true perspective," to beg several very large questions.

Related to the issue of artifice, its legitimacy, and its modes are the issues of generic distinction and generic blurring and therefore of audience perceptions and expectations. Even in the 1950s, a clear differentiation between what was and what was not dramatized could be hard to make. Bell cites the example of Maurice Wiggin, television critic of the *Sunday Times*. Wiggin had stated his dislike of the dramatized documentary method in terms that were to become familiar:

> The whole point of a documentary is that it is literally true. . . . If it is not literally true, it is not documentary but something else . . . a kind of play-writing. . . . We have had too much fact-based fiction cooked up in the studio and played by professional actors.

Later on in his article, he had contrasted such productions with a recent documentary about a London hospital at night. Of this he commented, "we saw the real thing, directly. It was more impressive than any documentary done in the studio." However, as Bell points out, drawing on other contemporary sources, this program

> was a "built OB" [outside broadcast], a totally scripted and rehearsed programme in which the people concerned were speaking lines learned by heart and performing movements worked out by the producer. The performers were actually playing the roles they played in real life, in the setting in which they actually worked, but nevertheless were acting in a scripted programme. (Bell 1986:76)

This raises the question of the different levels of fabrication that a production may employ, some perhaps being seen as more significant for the status of the program than others (the use of actors is clearly a major factor here). Wiggin may have been naive, but his wish to differentiate between studio-based, professionally acted productions and location-shot ones employing people in their "real" roles is not undercut by the example, even if the terms in which he expressed it are problematical. We can also see here how the notion apparently lying behind his comments, a desire for television access to a reality that is not only free of the studio and of professional artifice but also of *any* modification introduced by television's presence, connects directly with the later project of vérité.

The arrival of new technology in the form of lightweight 16-mm film cameras and subsequently of videotape removed most of the conditions that had made early dramatized documentary on television an expedient and popular response to limitations. Dramatization was no longer quite so "necessary" and projects of the kind described above were less frequently found in the schedules. However, as the wartime experience had shown, the dramatization of documentary material was still an effective way of performing certain communicative functions, of producing certain "effects," and new types of function and new depictive modes were to emerge. The problem of "access" did not disappear either, it simply moved to a higher level as television developed more ambitious notions about where it might go and what types of rendering of the real it might present to the viewer (see Kilborn 1994 on this point).

Documentary and the Realist Play

Dramatization of varying kinds continued to be used in documentary work, but there is no doubt that the return to prominence of dramadocumentary as an issue had a lot to do with developments in the realist play during the 1960s. To some extent following tendencies in literature and then cinema (charted in Laing 1986), a number of television playwrights became more concerned with using character and story to explore aspects of social change and social class. Plays were often based on intensive research, and their stories were given an extensive grounding in social circumstance, frequently realized in location shooting. Character and action were located in a contingent universe of work, home, and environment, which often departed from established dramatic conventions not only in the emphasis placed on "context" but also in the degree to which this context was "ordinary" and often "working-class"—introducing strong themes of class difference and class tension into the dramatic mix. There was, in much of this work, a "sociological" seriousness and commitment, which gave it, in some people's perceptions, a thematic proximity to documentary productions quite apart from questions of depictive style. In their earlier years, the hugely popular serials *Coronation Street* (Granada, 1960–) and *Z Cars* (BBC, 1962–65) were also seen to have at least an element of this documentarist ambition informing their construction.[2] In the case of *Z Cars,* this is immediately obvious in both theme and form; the series idea was actually developed by the BBC Documentary Drama Group (whose change of name from the Dramatized Documentary Group is significant; see Goodwin et al. [eds.] 1983:3).

Much of the debate through the 1960s and into the mid-1970s surrounded productions that, drawing on a variety of recipes for their "mix," offered radical, critical portrayals of contemporary British political and social life. These productions not only showed a convergence with the work of radical television drama noted above, they increasingly emerged from *within* this strand of work. Allowing for the caveats I have placed on the use of the distinction, one can say that here it was the drama that was increasingly given a documentarist articulation rather than the reverse. *Cathy Come Home,* about the housing shortage in contemporary Britain, is perhaps the most celebrated of the '60s' hybrids. *Cathy* is based on detailed research into the kinds of circumstances depicted in the film. It dramatizes these circumstances through the use of a single narrative concerning one "case"—fabricated from material drawn from a wide range of real cases and developed into a dramatic fiction. The portrayal of this constructed "typical" instance is grounded in the then-developing conventions of realist dramatic fiction, but it also uses a number of more directly documentary conventions, such as the use of anonymous "testimony" to camera, the use of expert and vox populi voice-over, the occasional use of a visual field and mode of cutting that imitate the modes of television reportage. The extent to which it circumscribes plot and character development in the interest of maintaining a connected thematic address to housing problems marks it out as "different," even for socially realist drama. The amount of research that informs its thematic aspects also suggests a documentary project, although, as such, it is invisible to the viewer. Finally, the frequent use of documentary conventions within the depiction itself, including voiced-over statistics and other information, seems to anticipate and encourage a level of documentary reading, without thereby deceiving the audience that it is watching actuality footage.

Yet, on the other hand, *Cathy* went out in the weekly *Wednesday Play* slot, is titled "a film by Jeremy Sandford" in the opening credits, uses an established actress as its lead, and includes a large number of scenes that, both in terms of the social space they explore (private encounters, arguments, lovemaking) and the mode of this exploration (close-ups, shot-reverse-shot sequences, continuity matches), draw on the language of realist fiction. Given all these factors, *Cathy* is something of a one-off event—a television "original"—in the development of British dramadocumentary, putting pressure on the conventions derived from both sides and, not surprisingly, acting as a frequent focus for debate about television's capacities as a medium not only for engaging with the real but, reflexively, with the dominant modes of its own representations.

Peter Watkins's *War Game* (BBC, 1965, not transmitted) is another highly original program that deserves mention here. This depiction of a nuclear attack on a British town was banned from transmission at the time (though distributed to certain cinemas) for reasons that have now been clearly established as having to do with the politics surrounding government nuclear deterrence policy.[3] As with so many other "controversial" dramadocumentaries, objections that were primarily about the substantive content and viewpoint expressed were strategically displaced into becoming objections about the unacceptability of the form itself. Thus disagreement over *issues,* risking an engagement around specific evidence and argument, becomes disguised as a fear about "deception" in communicative *style*. As we have already seen, this frequently involves considerable condescension toward ordinary viewers, who are often regarded as being at serious risk of miscognition and duping. *The War Game* is certainly a very disturbing film. Using a sort of time-capsule approach, it places the viewer as witness to catastrophic events in the future, as Britain enters a nuclear war. The passage from frantic preparation for possible attack through the strike itself and the resultant phases of physical, psychic, and social deterioration is depicted in a brilliantly edited mix of newsreel, vérité, and interview sequences. Continuity is provided by keeping the main focus on one locality. Unlike *Cathy, The War Game* contains few depictions that draw on conventional dramatic portrayal. Its entire visual and aural system reproduces the immediacy and rawness of actuality materials. In this respect, it is not so much a dramatized documentary as an imitation documentary. However, the work of the imitation draws upon historical and contemporary sources in order to put forward an argument about the "way it would be" were a nuclear conflict to occur. This use of a researched base—not to inform a propositional discourse of prediction but a dramatic discourse of imagined occurrence—lies at the heart of *The War Game*'s distinctiveness and power. Of course, as with *Cathy,* the program was freed from the normative constraints of "balance" affecting conventional documentary production and was able to organize its "imitative coverage" of future events around the implicit point of view that the nuclear deterrence policy was senseless and likely to end in disaster. In part it did this by showing the *horrific particularity* of a nuclear strike and by placing the viewer as a vérité observer of it, utilizing television's most potent ways of coding actuality (including present-tense reportorial commentary). This approach works on the assumption that, although people know such a conflict would be horrible, they can still be so "shocked" by looking at its specific manifestation as to be caused to reject their previous "abstract" acquiescence in nuclear deterrence policy. This "power of the particular" is a major factor in assessing dramadocumentary work for public profile and capacity to disturb.

In the mid-1970s, the public debate about hybrid forms flared up again in discussion of *Days of Hope* (BBC, 1975), a series of four plays by the writer Jim Allen about the working class and class politics from 1914 to the General Strike of 1926. The series was produced by Tony Garnett and directed by Ken Loach, the same team behind Sandford's *Cathy*. The depictive approach was grounded in dramatic realism. This was overlaid in certain scenes by a "documentary naturalism," which shot actions as if the camera were following them spontaneously (e.g., hurried and often awkward composition within the frame, adjustments of focus, and occasional "blocked" shots) and used dialogue that was only partly scripted, allowing for improvisation.[4] Certainly these codings of reportage (some of them comparable to devices used in *Cathy*) gave heightened immediacy values to the drama without encouraging the viewer to believe that they were, indeed, watching actuality. What seemed to have caused the "problem" was the coincidence of a sense of historical authenticity with a radical left-wing view of the politics of the period. Although the plays were conceived throughout in terms of narrative fiction, the tightness of their referentiality to certain real events, the emphasis they put on political and social setting, and then the radical interpretation they worked with caused some people once again to remark on the illegitimacy of mixed forms. A *Times* leader on the series noted:

> In a documentary political objectivity and historical accuracy are essential qualities; in a play they can have a depressing effect on the creativity of the author or producer. So it is important to retain a clear distinction in the mind of the viewer. (*Times,* 30 September 1975)

This ponderous advice was really unnecessary—it is very hard to imagine any viewer believing that the detailed rendering of often very personal events set in the 1920s was a "documentary" in *any* conventional use of that term. But viewers *were* presented with a critical treatment of political history surrounding and informing the personal story. Once again, anxiety over the substance of what was being "said" became displaced into claims about deceit in the "saying." As in the case of *The War Game,* the extent to which these complaints were made from a position of strategic bad faith should not be underestimated.

The mid-1970s also saw important developments at the other end of the spectrum from documentary drama, in Granada's Dramatized Documentary Department. Here, the emphasis was on the dramatic treatment of specific circumstances, involving the reconstruction of particular incidents from all available evidence, including tape recordings, court transcripts, other contemporary documents, and research with the cooperation of participants and witnesses. In 1970, Granada had produced *The Man Who Wouldn't Keep Quiet,* based on detailed documentation of a Russian dissident's imprisonment in a mental institution. With Leslie Woodhead as director-producer, it continued to do dramatized work on Eastern European themes throughout the decade, with perhaps the most notable productions being *Invasion* (1980—about the invasion of Czechoslovakia) and *Strike* (1981—about the Polish shipyard strike at Gdańsk and the development of Solidarity as a political movement). These productions drew extensively on dramatic imagination, but the degree of documentary evidence that went into the script and the tightness of relationship to real events and to real people gives them a distinctive character, more constrained in their use of conventionally dramatic language. (Woodhead has highlighted the prioritizing of documentary values in his striking comment, "we made bad plays."[5]) It is worth noting how the attempted "reconstruction" of specific real events in local detail continues to gives certain dramadocumentary projects a special sociodiscursive profile. This is in contrast to the more loosely referential "based on" formulas, which often attract playwrights, and the even looser relationship of contextual circumstances to historical reality in mainstream realist fiction. Of course, this is not to make any judgments about the "social truth" contained in a depiction, documentary or dramatic, but simply to note the different kinds of referential relation that are claimed, against which questions of "accuracy" may be raised, as well as questions of interpretative acceptability. ATV's *Death of a Princess* (1980), concerning romantic affairs within the Saudi Arabian royal family, is an interesting example of a reconstructive narrative using "modernist" devices to play off various accounts of "what happened" against each other. The program, press commentary on it, and the controversy it caused are well explored in Petley (1983).

In recent British television, documentary dramatization has used a wide range of styles. For instance, it has employed the model of the international thriller (as in Granada's *Why Lockerbie?* [1990] about the Pan Am aircraft bomb) and the disaster movie (as in the BBC's *Valdez* [1993] about the Alaskan oil spill). The dramatized use of the depictive codes of documentary, so evident in '60s work, has given way to more consistent and conventionally dramatic modes of portrayal, if with plot, characterization, and action constrained by informational and contextual requirements (Kilborn 1994 and Petley 1983 explore these shifts further). So, for instance, in *Shoot to Kill* (Yorkshire TV, 1990), a dramadocumentary about the operation of armed police units in Northern Ireland, although referentiality was established by a tightly specific indication of names, places, and dates, and although the drama opened out to include a whole range of "procedural" sequences in order to carry the indirect exposition, the depiction did not at any point "imitate" documentary portrayal.

It may be useful to conclude here by noting again the key issues around which the dramadocumentary issue has turned. These can be itemized as follows:

1. The "referentiality" issue. What tightness of relationship does the program claim with real events? Is it using a "based on" license or attempting (as faithful as possible) a "reconstruction"? "Based on" formulas can either allow dramatic transformations of specific events or, as in *Cathy,* allow the fictive construction of a "typical" case from research on real incidents.

2. The "representation" issue. How does the program look and sound? Is there an attempt to imitate the codes of documentary and thereby generate (if only "in play") reportage values? Is there a mix of dramatic with more conventional documentary material? What are the possibilities for "deception," for a viewer attributing an incorrect status to the depiction at any point?

3. The "manipulation" issue. This issue relates to the first two. The charge is made that viewers are encouraged to give truth status to unsubstantiated or purely imaginary elements and, furthermore, that the communicative, affective power of the dramatic treatment is likely to install accounts in the mind of the viewer with force and depth.

4. The "thematic" issue. In what way does the point of view given prominence in the program relate to "official" positions and attitudes? How is a debate of ideas set up within the program? As we have seen, behind some of the apparent concern expressed about hybrid forms lies the straightforward objection to views being aired that run counter to dominant dispositions and policies.

Perhaps the most important aspect of dramadocumentary as a controversial form, across its various manifestations, is the linking together of a "viewpoint" discourse with discourses of strong referentiality and of high imaginative potency. I have suggested that a distinction between the dramatizing of documentary accounts and the "documentarizing" of drama can be analytically useful, although I have also suggested that firm distinctions are hard to draw and that certain programs confound them altogether. As television's generic system shows an increasing tendency toward hybridization and reflexiveness, this blurring is likely to continue, but so is public debate about programs that combine dramatic with journalistic values in relation to sensitive political and social themes.

For the student of nonfiction television, one of the most engaging aspects of these formats is the way in which they pose more general questions about the transformative character of television-reality relationships. These questions concern presumed epistemologies, research and production methods, depictive forms, and modes of viewer engagement and understanding. The history of the more controversial programs also offers us a valuable insight into specific instances of the political and social formations within which television's "knowledge" is formed and distributed.

Notes

1. I first mooted this distinction in Corner (1979). Caughie (1980) uses a comparable differentiation and develops further the discussion of documentary drama.
2. Laing (1986) documents this for *Z Cars;* the social (and sociological) origins of *Coronation Street* are well explored in Dyer et al. (eds.) (1981).
3. See Arrowsmith (1981) for a perceptive study of the film. Tracey (1978) gives the best account of the behind-the-scenes events leading to its being banned.
4. Caughie (1980) brings this aspect out very well, along with its implications for viewer alignment and knowledge.
5. This is taken from the opening remarks of a talk given by Woodhead to students at Liverpool University in the spring of 1992, although he has used the phrase quite widely in interviews and writing.

Works Cited

Arrowsmith, S. 1981. Peter Watkins. In *British Television Drama,* edited by G. Brandt. Cambridge: Cambridge University Press, 217–37.

Bell, E. 1986. The Origins of British Television Documentary: The BBC 1945–55. In *Documentary and the Mass Media,* edited by J. Corner. London: Edward Arnold, 65–80.

Caughie, J. 1980. Progressive Television and Documentary Drama. *Screen* 21, no. 3.

Corner, J. 1979. Television's "Real Life" Dramas. *The Media Reporter* 13, no. 1: 3032.

Dyer, R., et al., eds. 1981. *Coronation Street.* London: British Film Institute.

Goodwin, A., et al., eds. 1983. *Drama-Documentary: B.F.I. Dossier 19.* London: British Film Institute.

Kilborn, R. 1994. Drama over Lockerbie. A New Look at the Drama-Documentary Debate. *The Historical Journal of Film, Radio and Television* 14, no. 1:59–76.

Laing, S. 1986. *Representations of Working-Class Life 1957–1964.* London: Macmillan.

Petley, J. 1983. Parliament, the Press and *Death of a Princess.* In *Drama-Documentary: B.F.I. Dossier 19,* edited by Goodwin et al. London: British Film Institute, 89–105.

Rotha, P., ed. 1956. *Television in the Making.* London: Focal Press.

Tracey, M. 1978. *The Production of Political Television.* London: Routledge.

4

Tales of Cultural Tourism

Derek Paget

"The cultural producer is keenly interested in the proliferation of wants which will lead consumers to seek out the commodities sold to satisfy those wants" (Terry Lovell).[1] When we are tourists (in the commonest use of the word), we go on "holiday" to new places, sometimes far-off and exotic. Once there, we may actually "work" quite hard, looking at the sights, checking off particularly famous corners of foreign cities in our itineraries, making sure that we have that all-important photograph of the view of or from a famous landmark or surviving emblem of historical significance. We may be overtly "cultural" as we trek round the Uffizi or the Louvre; we may be "historical" as we look over the pyramids or the Acropolis; or we may be happy to deep-fry in sun oil on "paradise beaches." What we are really doing of course, whether we are sun or sight worshipers, is *consuming* a very heavily marketed product, the benefits of which are much mythologized. It behooves us to consider this carefully, on the simple basis of suspicion: if someone's making a lot of money, isn't someone else being exploited somewhere along the line?

The First World is well attuned to the commercial activity of tourism and perfectly capable of ripping off fully as much as it is ripped off. Who, exactly, is exploiting whom in the Greek taverna on Rhodes or Corfu (intertextual

---

with the film *Zorba the Greek*)? It is difficult to say but quite likely that both tourists and "ethnic entertainment" understand each other. But Third World countries are different. Indigenous populations on Caribbean islands (those archetypal "tropical paradises") used to object quite strongly to being photographed by American and European tourists; they believed that part of their soul was being stolen in this act of appropriating their faces. The tourists laughed at the patent absurdity of this; they coaxed and cajoled, sometimes they even parted with money in their attempts to get these reluctant subjects into frame. Eventually, in most places, they have got their way, and market traders who trudge in from outlying parishes to set out the literal fruits of their labors now smile obediently for the importunate lenses of the tourists.

But the previous, apparently primitive reaction of the islanders had a point: photographs have a subject in more senses than one. The act of tourist photography converts indigenous *subjects* into consumed *objects,* objects to be possessed (at one remove, it is true, but possessed in important ways). The resultant objects are passed into a kind of currency back in the camera owners' home countries, where they become indicators of economic power, or sophistication, or of well-traveled knowledge of foreign lands, or of all these things in conversations and slide-viewing sessions. If the Grand Tour was an index of nineteenth-century sophistication, foreign travel is just as important now. Tourism is an expression particularly of American and Japanese economic supremacy. The heritage industry in the United Kingdom has recognized this very clearly; in the absence of competitive manufacturing industry, the Brits fall back on that which cannot be taken away from them—the past (or carefully selected versions of it). This is a commodity that sells particularly well to a nation, the United States, rather troubled by its relative lack of a past and ever eager to find it in Europe. The present U.K. government is even now seeking to hijack secondary school history syllabi for precisely this heritage purpose.

But there is a wider "cultural tourism," which takes consumers on a "trip" across the borders of *experience* (for the purpose of saying, We've *been* there!). Media tourists consume issues as if they were the sights of tourists' itineraries. In the wake of the urban riots of July 1981 (according to one apocryphal story), a social worker in Camden was suddenly contacted to provide a guided coach tour of poor districts of north London for the mixture of "professionals" who tended to form the "task forces" set up to advise the government. Although these people lived and worked in London, they stared with a mixture of horror and amazement at the conditions they needed a coach tour to learn about. Marie-Antoinette is alive and well and living in certain well-heeled areas of London? Some True Stories can be seen as coach tours for the privileged.

Cultural tourists, then, visit unfamiliar territory over which they hold economic power, and they go for specified periods in order to consume "ways of life" different from their own. Having done this, they can collect information; they can claim knowledge; they can make authoritative pronouncements about this territory. As with "real" tourists (who often claim to "know" foreign countries on the basis of short acquaintance), cultural tourists may well gain a particular experience that is of use and value; the problem is that they will often believe that this is all that is necessary. The necessity of setting "experience" into an overarching social and political context for observer and observed will not always be recognized. If knowledge and information have to be inferred from dramatic True Stories in a socially realistic mode, the claim for second-order experience (through the empathy of "involvement" with "characters" portrayed on the screen or stage) seems even stronger.

Cultural production of the tourist kind is so widespread that a full list of examples would soon become tedious. Almost every issue, every "problem," has been mediated through a True Story. Nuclear power and its dangers? See Mike Nichols's *Silkwood* (1983). Human rights in fascist dictatorships? There's Constantin Costa-Gavras's *Missing* (1982). In postcolonial situations? There's the Stephen Biko case and *Cry Freedom*. Apartheid? That had been a particularly hot issue in the 1980s. The horror of war? Such films are legion (pun intended). On U.K. television, the output of material dealing with Eastern European opposition to the USSR (and especially with the Polish trade union Solidarity) has been quite remarkable—a list would include *Three Days in Szczecin* (ITV, 1976); *Invasion* (ITV, 1980); *Two Weeks in Winter* (BBC, 1982); and Tom Stoppard's *Squaring the Circle* (ITV, 1984).

Of course, addressing such subjects as these is rightly taken as an index of the continuing "conscience" of the artistic enterprise. Without such efforts, society would be considerably diminished (if nothing else, they provide some insurance for the artist against charges of fiddling elegantly while the world explodes). But they are also potential salves to the conscience of the consumer, who can show by evincing a taste for such things that s/he is not solely interested in bread and circuses. Real tourists can (and do) justify themselves on the basis of the foreign exchange they bring to other countries and on the increased understanding they achieve and bring back with them. Cultural tourists frequently believe that their increased "understanding" is likely to contribute toward ameliorating problems. The more this way is specified, of course, the likelier this is to be true, but in most cases it remains at the level of unspecified (therefore vague) "consciousness-raising."

What is being marketed and consumed is an *attitude* of concern, a quasi-religious moral feeling partially assuaged at the point of production, which relies on the religion of fact to which I drew attention earlier. In many cases, cultural production may contribute as much to keeping a "problem" in place as it does toward shifting it. The crucial question is: What happens after a social problem has been elevated onto the arena of public debate? In the absence of real political will, shaped by collectivity rather than the "choosing individual," all the individual tourist can do is withdraw his/her support. Individually, you can only decline to holiday in Sun City, but you won't abolish it on your own—to do that, it is necessary to join an organized collective, which will take action.

The major interest for the student of cultural production is the means by which (and the means through which) mediation of problematical issues takes place. Like the Caribbean islander, many "subjects" are in danger of further impoverishment through the appropriations of institutionalized cultural production. This is especially true of that most consensual of mediums, television. True Stories are a necessary, but never sufficient, index of commitment in art.

Cathy Come Home

"When *Cathy* was written there was little information available in print. Now there is a lot. And there seems no end to Britain's housing crisis" (Jeremy Sandford).[2] The individualizing of issues through social-realism techniques has a tendency to scratch the cultural itch rather than treat the social inflammation, *displacing* rather than focusing issues and encouraging the tendency to "taste" issues touristically. The example of *Cathy Come Home* has often been used to demonstrate how a piece of cultural production can have direct influence on the events it treats. The first screening of *Cathy* in 1966 led, we are sometimes told, to the formation of the organization Shelter (dedicated to helping the poor with housing problems). Jeremy Sandford noted with pride that, "It is good to know that I have altered, if only by a very small bit, the conditions of life for others in my own society." But within a few years, he was saying the pessimistic opposite, as can be seen from the quotation at the beginning of this paragraph.

It is as well to be cautious in attributing any social change directly to a dramatic work; Shelter itself, as its founder, Des Wilson, has subsequently observed, would have been formed with or without *Cathy*. The teleplay undoubtedly contributed to a climate of opinion; in that sense, it did no harm and may well have done some good, but it was not *instrumental*. Stoke's local documentary *Fight for Shelton Bar* is sometimes held up as an example of what campaigning theater can achieve, but Peter Cheeseman is the first to acknowledge that it was the organized efforts of the workers that saved the local steelworks (for a pitifully short time, as it turned out). As has been remarked before, dramatic art can uniquely reflect and inflect, but real change is an altogether larger matter. Theater, film, TV, and radio can make a contribution toward change but only where a climate for change already exists. Why commentators on cultural production should want to claim more than this is revealing of them in particular and of society in general.

If *Cathy* is approached initially through formal analysis, it is clear even from the published screenplay that what John Fiske and John Hartley call "overlap in code networks" is a feature of the piece.[3] There are frequent occasions when a discourse more usually associated with other (nondramatic) kinds of programming is used to frame straightforwardly "dramatic" action. For example, about a quarter of the way through, a montage section described as "general shots of life in the area" (in which Cathy and her husband Reg live) is accompanied by Cathy's reflective voice saying:

> I fell for it, all the parts round here, these streets, they looked rough, and there was rats but life was quite good here. Some of the places was boarded up, with the upstairs windows empty, others was stuffed, crammed full with people and kiddies. Once I heard sounds coming out from one of the boarded up houses, sounds of a baby crying.

The "general shots" of working-class streets and houses have both a diachronic function (following, through time, Reg and Cathy's downward spiral in the housing market, which leads eventually to the pitiless "Part III: Accommodation") and a synchronic function (as ironic and simultaneous counterpoint to Cathy's hopeful monologue). This fragment is part of an extended voice-over and shot-montage sequence, following an extended meditation by Cathy on the significance of "love" and "nice surroundings" for a child. The voice-over commentary is more "commonly associated with news and documentary programmes"; in *Cathy,* it "is used to bring with it a sense of reality" (Fiske and Hartley, p. 64).

As well as being "straight" information, Cathy's words are also "artful": they have been composed to reflect the speech patterns of a representative working-class girl. The writer attempts the kind of replication that will convince at the level of factuality. Crucially, the sequence is presented as if it were part of a documentary. Carol White, the Cathy actress, used her technique as a performer to bolster this illusion. The concern is not whether working-class girls really speak like this but whether this speech pattern will induce the audience to believe. If it does, it inevitably supports the program's "truth claim" by reinforcing the apparent reality. True Stories routinely alter facts if it is thought "necessary" to the truth claim to do so, but any challenge to the citadel of believable behaviors is to be avoided.

In his personal memoir, *Asking for Trouble,* Donald Woods gives details of four "real" occurrences that were not included in Attenborough's film *Cry Freedom;* all were excluded because the filmmakers feared they would not be believed. "Sir Richard Attenborough explained that translating true stories into film involved not only the transmitting of true facts to the screen but facts that, no matter how true, would not *strain the credulity of the audience*" (pp. 8–9, my emphasis). The four incidents included one in which the fugitive Woods, waiting tensely for his passport to be stamped at the South Africa–Botswana border, has to wait while the official takes a phone call. Although Woods fears it might be the Security Police, it turns out to be the man's wife on the line with instructions about the household shopping! This would be "too much for cinema audiences to accept," thought Attenborough and screenplay writer John Briley. Woods concurred completely with this editorial decision because "anything which detracted from the credibility of the real story would be counter-productive, and because . . . much of the power of the *film* derived from the fact that it tells a true story" (p. 10).

It is instructive to observe which parts of stories are deemed truer than others. Attenborough's decision (at a professional level an entirely competent and understandable one) relates entirely to the fictional discourse of social realism, within which he and his film were trapped. His problem was not truth or otherwise but that intertextuality which is part of every sophisticated viewer's baggage—it is this that makes the "true" incident in question potentially "false." Anticlimactic phone calls at crucial moments in a realist plot are a too-good-to-be-true cliché because they seem to happen in every other film you see (though it's difficult when put on the spot to think of an actual example).

Sandford's first attempt at the subject that was to become *Cathy Come Home* was a radio documentary called *Homeless Families,* composed largely of montaged verbatim interview material. In *Cathy Come Home,* this provenance is evident not just in Cathy's own "shaped" voice-overs but also in the use of radio-style "wildtrack" voices on soundtrack, in which some of Sandford's original material was used. It is difficult to show any of this on the printed page; in a credit page note, Sandford says that he has added "some of the voices that were heard on wildtrack in the course of the film." A good deal of this wildtrack "consisted of the words of real people living in the various locations we shot." Reaction to the radio documentary was "virtually nil," Sandford tells us. But such "truth" as background, that was a different matter; the documentary reality in the (successful) film provides an authenticating device for the drama. Carol

White's performance as Cathy, location filming, the use of the soundtrack, the "real people" extras, shot composition and montage—everything in the project overlaps with a discourse of factuality deriving from the documentary.

Camera shots replicated newsreel camera techniques; in an interview, Sandford commented: "The newsreel cameraman who may have to run to get his effects brings a vividness to the screen that is often lacking in the overstylized and ossified techniques so often found in TV drama productions. Ken Loach wanted to get this actuality aliveness in and succeeded."[4] The key words in this account are *vividness* and *aliveness:* Sandford's understanding of the mediation of the issue of housing coheres around a concept of the observable "real." Just as bourgeois historians of the nineteenth century believed in E. H. Carr's "Ark of the Covenant in the temple of facts," so twentieth-century cultural producers tend "to pin their faith on actuality film" (McArthur, p. 28). Documentary devices generate *belief,* as do the writing and acting techniques of social realism (or such is the almost universal understanding).

But this capacity to inspire belief, which constitutes one of social-realist documentary drama's main truth claims, exists in a very narrow theoretical band. Social-realist drama's rapprochement with the recording documentary is relatively unproblematical; neither actors' realistic behaviors nor documentary's claim to reproduce reality are directly confronted (provided the film is competently done). There is intertextuality between the two codes but never a clash—they are never "competing discourses." There is a mutual complementing, which finally effaces difference. "Realistic" acting and "realistic" filming never call attention to themselves; they are elided, for all the world as if the one really were the other. At all costs, audience "credibility," once won, must never be challenged or strained.[5] This was the formal problem Attenborough had with the deleted larger-than-life elements of Donald Woods's escape. Besides the phone call, there was a border searchlight scene, like something out of a World War Two escape movie (Woods makes the comparison himself on p. 348 of his account); there was a (new) car, which inexplicably broke down; it was all much too good to be true. Like good tourists, movie audiences like to see new things (or, at the very least, old things in new packaging).

Sandford calls attention to Ken Loach's skill in doing the job of effacing difference; Loach has, he says "a wonderful gift for simplification," and the effect of his suggestions for change at early script meetings was "to give the story a more simplified or classical shape" (Sandford, p. 13). Sandford seems to mean here that Loach knew "shorthand" ways of conveying the fictional narrative and driving it along quicker. In the opening sequence of the film, for example, Loach simplified very specifically. In Sandford's original script, this section, about Cathy's arrival in London, was much longer, but Loach got it down to a slick linkage montage sequence in which Cathy is given a lift by a lorry driver, while in voice-over she looks back, older and wiser: "I was mad in a way in those days . . . suppose you could say I was bored, wanted a bit of adventure . . . some adventure" (pp. 23–24). The contrast is between a "then-Cathy" (stage direction: "freed at last from ties to her family, heart-whole, at the age of consent, but unconsenting as yet, exultant yet shy," p. 21) and a "now-Cathy" ("I was mad . . . in those days"). We see a pretty, careless Cathy obviously being fancied by the lorry driver; we hear the voice of a carefull Cathy. The meaning we are intended to construct is that, during the following hour or so, we will find out how the one grew into the other. This is the narrative dynamic of a piece of film fiction, which establishes very quickly the simple fact that Cathy has left home. In the original script, Sandford wanted to explore the leaving, but Loach understood, perhaps more clearly than the writer, that the film was to be about the housing trap and not about why young people run away to London. Time spent giving an account of the latter would mean time lost dealing with the more important former. So he has composed what Sandford rightly calls a "classical" series of opening shots.

If we compare this filmic opening with the first page of a naturalistic play like Henrik Ibsen's *Doll's House,* we can see in both how the need for "believable" exposition is met by the smooth deployment of a series of conventions deliberately intended to facilitate the flow of the narrative. In *A Doll's House,* we read class location and economic circumstance off the setting, time of day from the lighting, and time of year from the properties even before any character has had to speak.[6] In *Cathy Come Home,* a similar range of signifiers helps us to "read" the montage sequence and its accompanying voice-over; the sequence is unproblematical precisely because it is "classical"—it is like any number of other realistic films on television or in the cinema. The coding of this "shorthand" has some drawbacks, notably the "sixties-sexist" portrayal of Cathy. Why does she have to be "young, pretty, and with an air of excitement about her" (p. 21)? Sandford himself seems to feel vulnerable about this, because he is constrained to say in his introduction: "People often tell me that Cathy was too attractive—a girl as attractive as that could never have become homeless. This is nonsense. I would say that, on average, the girls I've met in Part III: Accommodation were more attractive than those outside, although I couldn't say why" (p. 13). This misses the point and is itself somewhat sexist in its chivalrous championship of "attractiveness," which is always only culturally relative and expressive of male dominance.

The point at issue is why a group of filmmakers should feel it necessary to portray an attractive Cathy in the first place and, by so doing, actively reject the possibility of telling the story of a notionally unattractive Cathy. The answer must surely be that, like the lorry driver in the opening sequence, the male section of the audience must be attracted to Cathy through desire (a common fate for the female at the center of play and film narratives and reflective of dominant patriarchal and heterosexist cultural assumptions). Sandford indirectly acknowledges this aspect in his courtly defense of the Part III: Accommodation female, a defense that partly "commodifies" her.

Cathy must now be read as a kind of "sixties icon." It is surely no accident that a Cathy-inflected pop song (the Beatles' "She's Leaving Home") followed the film in 1967. Now much anthologized in school poetry books, this song just about holds together a sad girl–happy girl opposition via the mix of sweet (Paul McCartney's voice) and sour (John Lennon's). What gives it away is its quasi-classical musical arrangement. Like "She's Leaving Home," *Cathy Come Home* has become both a cultural and a historical "monument." Both telefilm and pop song, with their versions of social conscience, have permeated the collective unconscious. Today, schoolchildren wrestle with the split narration of "She's Leaving Home" in English lessons, and a 1988 teleplay, *The Diary of Rita Patel,* is seen as a 1980s *Cathy Come Home.*[7] *Rita Patel* told a "based on fact" story about an Asian family suffering urban racial harassment. In spite of the invocation of *Cathy* (intended as glowing praise), *Rita Patel* did not gain anything like the attention in the 1980s that *Cathy* achieved in the 1960s, and one is forced to conclude that Rita's brown skin may have had more than something to do with this. Because a white audience is still the dominant one, cultural production is still limited in the way it feels able to address racial issues.

Keeping the Lid On

"The effect of *The War Game* has been judged by the BBC to be too horrifying for the medium of broadcasting" (BBC statement, 1965).[8] *Cathy Come Home* was not the only television True Story to become something about which it was necessary to have an opinion in the 1960s (even if one hadn't seen it). Peter Watkins's 1965 *The War Game* was even more interesting because, at least in the first instance, very few people were able to see it at all. Made in 1965 and finally seen on television in 1985, *The War Game* has been a cause célèbre for over twenty years. Its longevity as a site of controversy and conflict makes it highly suitable as a representative of those True Stories that have periodically disturbed cultural production and exposed contradictions within society. Lesser-known examples might include A. E. Harding's *New Year over Europe,* and the Theatre Workshop's *Last Edition* (a 1940 Living Newspaper, which caused Joan Littlewood and Ewan MacColl to be arrested and "bound over" because of the play's "unpatriotic" attitude to events leading up to the declaration of war). Better-known television examples include Antony Thomas's 1980 *Death of a Princess,* which so offended Saudi Arabia (with its reconstruction of an Islamic execution of an Arab princess and her lover for adultery) that a British foreign minister—Lord Carrington—even apologized to the Saudis about it.

The War Game challenged the postwar establishment orthodoxy of nuclear deterrence for the first time, and it continued to be an embarrassment for a considerable period (unlike *Death of a Princess,* which was controversial for a few months). Controversy of any kind foregrounds a particular cultural dilemma (or series of dilemmas); the nuclear deterrence dilemma has been both difficult to resolve and impossible to ignore. Societies will always have problems that are difficult to resolve, of course; the difference with controversial issues is that the unhappiness that exists as a result of particular problems creates a certain turbulence in society as a whole. This turbulence ensures that problems have the high profile of controversy and in turn ensures that they cannot be totally ignored. While some problems can be conveniently assigned to the margins on a permanent basis, others won't, as it were, go away. One site at which controversial problems tend to reemerge is cultural production.

The policy of nuclear deterrence has never been easy to "sell" to civil populations, and a "dialogue" concerning its morality and its viability has been going on ever since it was first promulgated. A myth of deterrence has been one of the main planks in power-wielding nations' "defense" and foreign policies ever since the onset of the Cold War in 1947. There has been an ongoing establishment interest in sustaining the case for deterrence, but there has also been an accompanying minority opposition to those policies, which in the United Kingdom has been manifested notably by the Campaign for Nuclear Disarmament, formed in 1958. *The War Game* can be seen as a product of that oppositional movement (as, indeed, can *Oh What a Lovely War*). The fact that the BBC, the institutional guardian of a hegemonically constructed "consensus" in the important field of broadcasting, could not countenance the transmission of the film in the 1960s tells us much about establishment fears concerning the level of civil acceptance of nuclear deterrence. This is often the fate of "sensitive" subject matter; you only know how sensitive it is when it gets suppressed.

The irony about *The War Game* was, of course, that it was not entirely suppressed: the initial furor was followed by institutional realization that withdrawal from the schedules was provoking too much attention (indeed, it all looked a little like censorship). This caused the BBC to allow a film made with their money, but rejected by them, to be shown to a handpicked audience on a restricted cinema circuit composed mainly of "art" cinema clubs and university film societies. The patriarchal presumption of the large-scale institution is revealed through such an action. *The War Game* was, as it were, "licensed" to be shown to those to whom it was thought it could do no harm; both the means of production and also the point of consumption were manipulated. The selected target audience was composed mainly of those already educated, or in the process of being educated, into the very social group empowered to make future censoring decisions. There was probably no need even to formulate such a policy of licensed transmission; it emerged as a "commonsense" solution to a thorny problem, a "reasonable compromise" in a tricky situation. It was, in other words, an *ideological* decision.

The cozy circularity of all this reveals that the harm feared was in fact to the system and not to the individual. Undeclared fears about the damage *The War Game* might do to the policy of nuclear deterrence (in terms of its attack on the credibility of that policy) were neatly diverted into declared fears about individual sensibilities—and thereby displaced. At the "protection of individuals" level, it was relatively easy to excuse the act of censorship. The extent of a hegemony's ability to introduce Catch-22 logic whenever push comes to shove is remarkable; this logic allowed you to watch *The War Game* provided you believed its case already, otherwise it was deemed "too horrifying." Like Charles Dickens's Mr. Podsnap, cultural watchdogs at places like the BBC are vigilant in excluding from mass transmission anything "calculated to call a blush into the cheek of a young person," but (again like Mr. Podsnap) they reserve the right to be the final arbiter on all "blush" factors. A large part of Peter Watkins's original aims and objectives in making the film were nullified at the crucial point of consumption of his film, which was intended as informational—it was meant to lighten citizens' darkness.

As ever, domination of the means of production (the BBC's ownership of Watkins's film through economic controls) provided ready tools of censorship, which are more dangerous because masked.

Neither is it just the U.K. establishment that is prone to such dealings. France was unable to cope with Marcel Ophuls's *Sorrow and the Pity* in 1969. Ophuls's film was different from *The War Game* in that it was a documentary proper, with straight interview material. It effectively deconstructed the French myth of the Nazi occupation (in which no one collaborated, everyone was a Resistance freedom fighter), declaring the hitherto occluded facts not only of a more widespread collaboration but also of infighting between different Resistance groups. Also made for television, this film too had to be shown first in cinemas, and it too generated terrific interest (especially amongst the student audience). Like *The War Game,* it promised to force an unpleasant subject into a very public forum. In the United Kingdom in 1965 and in France in 1969, establishment answers to the problems posed were the same. The policies of *minimum* visibility followed in France and Britain are a triumph of institutional craftiness, limiting damage while sidestepping the accusation of overt censorship. Whenever such things occur, it is vital to press the institutions concerned, both at the individual and at the collective level.

Another Sixties Icon?

"It is with the proliferation from the late '60s of dramatized documentaries . . . that the debate about categories and credibility really begins to bite" (Leslie Woodhead).[9] The eventual transmission of *The War Game* in 1985 does not mark the institution's coming to its senses so much as it does the release of the policy of nuclear deterrence from the "protected category." It was not, after all, as if there had not been periodic attempts to shift the film off the proscribed list during the intervening twenty years before it was at last released to a mass audience. The final decision was contingent upon shifts in global politics (which can be seen most plainly in the Ronald Reagan–Mikhail Gorbachev accords of the late 1980s). To put it bluntly, the film was no longer such an embarrassment; its transmission no longer mattered so much to the power elite.

The pre-1985 effectiveness of *The War Game* should not be discounted, however. According to the broadcaster Ludovic Kennedy, introducing the film on television in 1985, an estimated six million viewers worldwide had already seen the film. But this cannot make up for the fact that we will never know what its impact might have been had it been viewed by a mass (and partially uncommitted) TV audience in 1965. This fact was made that much more poignant by the evident "sixties-ness" of the film when compared to its modern equivalents, *Threads* and *The Day After*. *The War Game* is another icon of the 1960s, that decade now become so much the territory of the cultural tourist (after all, so much was going on then!). It is one of a trio of British documentary dramas that, made in the middle of the 1960s, constituted the (then) boundaries of the admissible and the inadmissible in terms of both form and content. *Culloden* (a Watkins film of 1964) and *Cathy Come Home* were admissible; *The War Game* was not.

Culloden demonstrated that formal properties alone do not matter in the last analysis; it is the attempt to force particular issues onto the public agenda that is crucial. The filmic techniques used in *Culloden* are similar to those used in *The War Game;* the real difference between the films lies in the comfortable remoteness of the historical period of the former and the altogether too close proximity of the issues and events portrayed in the latter. Slaughter of Scottish innocents of two hundred years ago, however realistically portrayed, can be easily coped with; the simulated incineration of modern citizenry was deemed more likely to be threatening to the young person, and the broadcasting Podsnaps acted quickly.

Both *Culloden* and *The War Game* were different from *Cathy* in their concentration on issues and events; they were less-individualized pieces of cultural production. Their classic structure was intertextual more with documentary filmmaking, less with socially realistic play making. They made heavier use of the *authoritative* (as against the *character*) voice-over and greater use of the "purely" informational insert (of statistics, maps, graphs, etc.)—all evidence of a documentary provenance. Voice-over provided a continuous editorial gloss on visuals, which were primarily illustrative and informational, as they tend to be in the documentary proper. The camera style imitated that of the actuality documentary; it was, as it were, 1960s state of the art. There was a good deal of that shaky, handheld camera work that is typical of "crisis" reports on TV news and was to become such a "real" feature of U.S. television coverage of the Vietnam War in the late 1960s. There was a consistent documentary correspondence between the commentary and the filmed subject, with periodic jump-cut shifts being sutured by the editorial voice.

To take an example: one of *The War Game*'s first visual subjects is a worried-looking black woman on a bus. Unlike the opening of *Cathy,* the sequence in which she features is not dramatic narrative; there is no dialogue, no character voice-over, no point-of-view shots. *Cathy* is the filmed equivalent of fourth-wall theater naturalism, with the audience unacknowledged; but the black woman in *The War Game* looks directly at the camera. The omniscient commentary's indexical utterance accompanying this image runs, "This woman has had to leave her husband." We are encouraged to "read" the sequence in the context of an earlier factual statement (which revealed that men over eighteen will not be evacuated in time of nuclear war).[10]

The black woman is, in other words, not an actress engaged in the job of characterizing but a documentary "specimen," designed to illustrate through representing. Because she is documentary object (and not *Cathy*-style "character" subject) she can look at the camera without disrupting any "illusion"; there is similarly no need for her to speak, she simply has to signify in ways determined by the editorial voice (hence the mournful look). We then see her descend from the bus in what we are told is a "strange town." The camera cuts to her just once more, after a white woman (a resident of the "strange town" because she is filmed standing at the threshold of "her" house) has said that she hopes no "coloreds" will be billeted with her. The word *colored* is itself an eloquent verbal icon of an earlier historical conjuncture, mobilized here to challenge the audience in one more way. The whole sequence centers *audience* rather than character.

The action that unfolds is similarly dominated by a commentary designed to inform and challenge those *outside* the action; this drives the film along and provides its distinctive dynamic. Unlike *Cathy,* where voice-overs and their accompanying visuals tend to be reflective moments sealed off from the narrative, *The War Game*'s voice-overs are not structural embellishments, they are integral to the structure of the piece—they give contextualizing information, they shift the scene, they explain. The point of identification is generalized and constantly shifting. There are, it is true, various figures who feature more than the black woman does (a police inspector, for example), and occasionally these figures are personalized to the extent of a name. But the audience is not asked to empathize with specific characters; the distinctive focus is not on *an* individual but on *individuals.* This is because the film's project is to demonstrate the likely plight of a generalized "people" in a nuclear war. People in general, and the audience by association, are involved in the deadly "game" of the film's title. The key player in *The War Game* is the *viewing,* not the "acting," subject.

The temporal sequence of *The War Game* is therefore not marked out by an individual consciousness but by the progress of nuclear attack. This too reinforces the powerlessness of people, totally at the mercy of the bomb and its subsequent effects. The film does not show the governmental decisions that led to nuclear attack, increasing the sense of powerlessness further; people accustomed to constructing themselves as active agents are shown in the process of becoming the things (the dead things) that are the consequence of "defense" policies allegedly framed in their interests. The inexorable advance of the attack is communicated by direct and indirect means (announcements from the voice-over commentary and montaged "radio announcements"). Visually, "realistic" camera work (like the evacuation sequence) is montaged with vox populi street interviews in which people from outside the drama say what they know about nuclear war and with rolling captions giving information.

Because the whole project of the film is not only to simulate but also to prophesy, many of the commentary locutions are conditional—"should *x* happen, *y* could/would follow." After the evacuation sequence, there is a freeze-frame of a man who has just been threatened with imprisonment if he continues to refuse to take his quota of evacuees; over the freeze-frame image, the commentator-narrator says, "Should Britain ever thus attempt the evacuation of nearly 20 percent of her active population, such scenes as these would be almost inevitable." The interaction between this conditional statement and the cinema verité camera technique has the effect of privileging probability over possibility. After all, we are seeing what purports to be a manifest "reality"; we are used to decoding images such as these as tokens of reality in our "readings" of the news and the documentary proper. The documentary image may depend upon a "constructed equivalence" between real subjects and film objects (Fiske and Hartley, p. 48), but for most viewers, the constructed equivalence of documentary involves the least problematical effort. Thus, although the words make a condition ("Should Britain . . ."), the images work with an apparent reality (which is "convincing").

The conditional element in the commentary is made more of a certainty by a quasi-academic "footnoting" technique, which again derives from the documentary. This culminates in a full list of sources given in a kind of visual bibliography at the end of the film. Precedents are continually cited in support of the credibility of the (fictional) visuals. A sequence following the air raid shows the burning of corpses, then the camera cuts to a line of bodies being covered with quicklime to prevent the spread of disease; the commentator says, "Everything that you are now seeing happened in Germany after the heavy bombing in the last war." Japanese precedents are offered later: apathetic survivors are depicted in abject misery, their morale nonexistent. "This happened," the commentator admonishes us, "at Hiroshima." But, like the Living Newspapers before it, authentication alone could not save *The War Game*.

Television's cultural centrality consists partly in its "good fit" with the way individuals perceive reality. Especially important is its apparently human field of vision; thus when we are told something could happen and we then see it happening before our eyes, we are less aware of the experience as mediation, and the overall effect is potentially very powerful—and convincing. The hijacking of documentary truth-claim techniques for advertisements (consider, for example, how the authoritative voice-over has been appropriated) has had the effect of nullifying some of the effects used in *The War Game* somewhat, with the result that the truth claim has now to be mediated in other ways. The conventionality of *The War Game* has only become fully apparent as its particular use of conventions approaches the level of cliché (i.e., with the passage of time). In 1985, the Mick Jackson–Barry Hines *Threads,* covering similar ground to *The War Game,* dispensed almost entirely with voice-over, preferring a teleprinter graphic to mediate basic information. In the early part of the film, the only voice-over (used during the opening credit sequence) gives an essentially poetic account of a society's interdependence; these are the "threads" of the title. The accompanying visual is similarly "poetic"—a spider spinning its intricate yet fragile web.

Direct looks at the camera were permitted in *The War Game* in a way that would not be possible in the discourse of "fiction film" favored by *Threads* and

The Day After. Looking at the camera, even more speaking to it, would unhinge the illusion in fiction film, much as direct address would disrupt the naturalistic stage play. *The War Game*'s use of interviews is interesting in this respect. Early in the film, street interviews appear to be "genuine"; a team of interviewer and crew seem to have gone out as a roving commission to find out what the public know about nuclear warfare. A familiar range of "truthful" responses result, the degree of self-consciousness before a camera (on the part of the filmed subject) being an index of their truth rather than their ineptitude (which it would signal if they were trying to "act").

Initially, it appears that there are two main uses of the interview in *The War Game,* one "straight documentary" and the other "dramatic." "Straight documentary" interviews stop people in city streets and ask questions like, "Do you know what strontium 90 is and what it does?" "Dramatic" interviews interrupt the action with more open questions. So, as the camera follows a Civil Defense volunteer leafleting a street of terraced houses, the off-camera interviewer suddenly says, "Excuse me, what are you doing here exactly?" The interviewee, acting startled, turns and replies. But the participants in "drama" sequences are in fact the same people as those used in "documentary" interviews. This is not to say that "genuine" interviews were acted, of course, because *The War Game* used a largely civilian, amateur cast (British Actors' Equity objected to this at the time the film was made). The point is that the "cross-coding" that occurs in *The War Game* reveals very clearly the "normal" degree of acceptable conventionalizing in television documentary modes. The whole thing can be faked very easily, and it is a mistake to suppose that this is an unproblematically bad thing.

Another interesting collision between the "could/might" and the "did/shall" constructions of the commentary occurs in the firestorm sequence. Firemen (the genuine article, the Kent Fire Service) are seen trying to cope with the firestorm, which is the second consequence of the bomb (the first being the horrific blast). We are told of the high temperatures in the eye of the firestorm (800°C), which convert into hot winds. The camera records the men being flung about by the force of the wind, which is also taking away their oxygen; it closes in on gas-masked figures so that we see their agonized expressions. "These men," we are told, "are dying both of heatstroke and of gassing." The shift to the present tense in the commentary is revealing, marking the moment the film transgresses the boundary between drama and documentary. If *The War Game* were the pure actuality of news film, this is indeed the tense that would have to be used.

Such transgressions have become increasingly problematical for filmmakers, partly because of the extent of the compromises forced on them. And yet one should not blame cultural producers for not fighting battles that are the proper preserve of more overtly political action. As journalist John Pilger recently observed, tinkering with the mechanisms of society in the 1960s "made Britain appear less divisive . . . which held great benefits for the ruling order, whose power it reinforced."[11] One can gauge something of this power through the changes wrought in cultural production since the Swinging Sixties.

Notes

1. Lovell, *Pictures of Reality,* 58.
2. Sandford, *Cathy Come Home,* 140. Des Wilson, founder of Shelter, pointed out in *I Know It Was the Place's Fault* (1970) that the problems raised by *Cathy* actually got worse in the four years after the play's transmission.
3. Fiske and Hartley, *Reading Television,* 64.
4. Goodwin and Kerr, 17.
5. David Edgar believes that "the factual basis" of documentary drama is what gives it "credibility" [see Edgar's chapter in part two of this book].
6. See Mayer (ed.), *Ibsen Plays: Two,* 23.
7. *The Diary of Rita Patel* was written by Carole Boyer, directed by Michael Jackley. John Naughton, of the *Observer,* described it as a *Cathy* for the 1980s. Like *Cathy,* it concluded with statistics (in this case of "racial incidents" in the Metropolitan Police area of London).
8. See Tracey, "Censored: *The War Game* story," 40. Tracey convincingly demonstrates the high level at which "refusal" of *The War Game*'s thesis took place.
9. From Leslie Woodhead's "Guardian Lecture" at the British Film Institute, 19 May 1981 [see Woodhead's chapter later in part one of this book].
10. Quotations from *The War Game* are taken directly from the film itself.
11. John Pilger, "Losing Freedom in the Fog," *The Guardian,* 10 December 1988.

Works Cited

Fiske, John, and John Hartley. *Reading Television* (London: Methuen, 1978).
Goodwin, Andrew, and Paul Kerr (eds.). *BFI Dossier 19: Drama-documentary* (London: BFI, 1983).
Lovell, Terry. *Pictures of Reality* (London: BFI, 1980).
Mayer, Michael (ed.). *Ibsen Plays: Two.*
McArthur, Colin. *Television and History: Monograph* (London: BFI, 1980).
Sandford, Jeremy. *Cathy Come Home* (n.p.: Marion Boyars, 1976).
Tracey, Michael. Censored: *The War Game* Story. In *Nukespeak: The Media and the Bomb,* edited by Crispin Aubrey (n.p.: Comedia, 1982), 38–56.
Woods, Donald. *Asking for Trouble* (London: Penguin, 1987).

5

Docudrama on American Television

Tom W. Hoffer and Richard Alan Nelson

In tight close-up, Hal Holbrook, portraying Commanding Officer Lloyd Bucher of the ill-fated USS *Pueblo,* dramatized the agony of capture and imprisonment in this Vietnam era incident. Much of this conflict and fixing of responsibility was not widely understood until the show aired because most of the facts were buried within hundreds of pages of hearing testimony and congressional reports. The two-hour dramatization of the *Pueblo* investigations isolated the crucial issues and presented them to a mass audience far beyond that which would have viewed even the fragmented TV news reports of the incident. This presentation of a real-life contemporary problem in dramatic fashion on television is an example of documentary drama, or docudrama.

In this chapter, we trace the antecedents of the docudrama and identify its evolution. We also examine its appeals, problems, and potential for public good.

In their pure form, as in the case of *Pueblo,* docudramas can be informative and yet entertaining in a way impossible for the traditional documentary. While the documentary per se is in many ways subjective, it still depicts in-

From the *Journal of the University Film and Video Association* 30, 2 (spring 1978).

dividuals and events as they actually occurred in real, nonmediated time and space. The docudrama, on the other hand, may provide *realism,* but the events portrayed are created and restructured (i.e., they are events that have occurred solely for the purposes of mediated communication). Therefore, a docudrama is a television re-creation based on fact even though it relies on dialogue, actors, sets, and costumes to re-create an earlier event.[1] The accuracy and comprehensiveness of such a re-creation—just like the documentary itself—can vary widely and is conditioned not only by intent but also by factors such as budget and production time.

In our own literature review, we have formulated nine distinct categories, ranging from the "pure" form, based on investigatory and trial records re-creating events in the lives of actual persons, as in *Pueblo,* to a form that utilizes historical personages or themes but that includes some fictionalization.[2]

Historical Antecedents

The idea of re-creating events for the camera is as old as the movies. As early as 1898, Spanish-American War "actualities" used faked re-creations of battles when the cameramen couldn't photograph the real thing.[3] In these early newsreels, audience deception was not the filmmaker's primary intent, although this practice would lead to greater manipulation in the future. At this time, however, filmmaking was still struggling as a penny-arcade amusement and was not commonly recognized as a journalistic medium.[4]

World War I accelerated the mixing of fictional elements with true-life situations, and newsreels as well as dramatic feature films from the European battlefields included heavy doses of re-created "realism."[5] Following the armistice, the Soviet regime's recognition that film could serve a propaganda function led to the development of motion pictures best exemplified by Sergei Eisenstein's *Battleship Potemkin* (1925). Despite the fictional centerpiece of the "massacre" on the Odessa Harbor steps, the film has a strong documentary-like quality in its depiction of events during the abortive 1905 uprising against the czar.[6]

Radio's Influence on Form

Even before regular network newscasting became a reality, the idea of dramatizing news by using actors to impersonate headline personalities had been demonstrated on radio in the *March of Time* and its predecessors.[7] As in the later film version by Louis de Rochemont, the object was not to mislead but to explain controversial issues. As Bohn and Lichty note:

> The creation of this style emphasized several distinct and unique techniques. The most notable, and at times, controversial, was the reenactment of events. This allowed the producers to select and arrange their material in ways best suited to the construction of dramatic narrative. The reconstruction of reality in journalism was not new, of course. What was new, however, was admitting this reconstruction and declaring it valid.[8]

Radio also served as the breeding ground for reality-based programs, such as *Gangbusters* (1935–40, NBC; 1940–48, Blue ABC; 1948–55, CBS; 1955–57, Mutual), *Famous Jury Trials* (1936–40, Mutual; 1940–49, Blue ABC), *The Big Story* (1947–55, NBC), *Dragnet* (1949–56, NBC), and many others, most of which were transplanted to television with varying degrees of success. These shows often relied on actual police, government, and journalistic case files. *The Big Story* (which also was aired on NBC-TV from 1949 to 1955) is among the more interesting in that it represented the beginning of "checkbook journalism." Reporters were paid five hundred dollars for stories based on their experiences, and the producers used actual persons and locales when possible. What differentiates a program like *The Big Story* from the later television docudramas is important to note. Crude by today's standards and hampered by low budgets, weekly serialization, and a thirty-nine-week production commitment, the producers exhibited the tendency to overlook factual details and to fictionalize when necessary to ensure an upbeat thirty-minute conclusion.

Biographical Motion Pictures

At about the same time, audiences were becoming conditioned to dramatic film re-creations of stories "torn from the front pages" of contemporary newspapers. Warner Brothers successfully exploited a gangster cycle with such films as *Little Caesar* (1930), *The Public Enemy* (1931), and their later imitators. Warners also followed with a line of distinguished biographical films, such as *The Story of Louis Pasteur* (1935), *The Life of Emile Zola* (1937), and *Juarez* (1939).

Other movements, such as the Film and Photo League, produced politically motivated "social documentaries" during the Depression years. These often re-created key incidents in anticapitalist labor struggles and also formed part of the docudrama tradition. Certainly the postwar "street films" of the Italian neorealist movement and the noir films of the late 1940s, such as *The House on 92nd Street* (1945) and *Naked City* (1948), contributed to the later development of television docudrama techniques.

Early Television

Early American commercial television naturally drew from the foregoing experiences and "models." But from 1948 to about 1969, the pure mixture of documentary and drama, usually in the form of historical or biographical "prestige" presentations, was not a major program type on the commercial networks.[9]

Armstrong Circle Theatre, beginning in February 1955, is generally recognized as the first continuing sixty-minute series to utilize the pure docudrama form. Unlike conventional fictional dramas, which utilized well-known actors, *Armstrong Circle Theatre*'s fact-based dramatizations focused on the story itself as the "star" of the program.[10] Executive producer David Susskind and producer Robert Costello set the guidelines for this unique format. Costello later discussed what they had in mind:

> We aim to combine fact and drama—to arouse interest, even controversy, on important and topical subjects. . . . We support them with authoritative statements by recognized leaders in specified fields. . . . We can't use an idea only or a news story only, we must also be able to present some potential solution, some hope for our citizens to consider, to think about.[11]

Despite the earlier radio and film influences on docudrama, the form did not immediately realize its full potential for public affairs. There are several reasons for this retarded growth. Certainly it has always been easier and cheaper to present fictional entertainment under the guise of realism than to attempt a meticulously factual re-creation. *Highway Patrol* (1956, Syndicated) and the later *Untouchables* (1959–63, ABC-TV) are police-style programs originally based on real-life occurrences, utilizing a narrative format and other documentary elements. But as they grew from their basic core of stories, it was necessary to invent new fictional plots or, as was the case with *Dragnet* (1951–59, 1967–70, NBC-TV), "change the names to protect the innocent." From a legal standpoint, the *Dragnet* credits also minimized lawsuits for invasion of privacy.

Additionally, the 1950s were not notable for the generation of much controversial or contemporary programming, despite the well-remembered confrontation between Edward R. Murrow and Senator Joseph McCarthy. Television was still a novelty, largely consisting of transplanted radio content and formats. The thrust in TV documentary followed later, after the payola and quiz scandals at the end of the decade. Interestingly, the program forms that would change commercial television were slowly incubating in public television.[12]

Impact of Public Television

The influence of public television (PTV) in putting new life into the docudrama form is important yet largely overlooked. Moreover, the aesthetic framework for combining documentary and dramatic elements was clearly worked out and nurtured in the noncommercial (often British) arena years before the form moved in large numbers to the American commercial networks.

The 1977 TV season on public television brought forward another "pure form" of drama and fact, which elegantly illustrated the potential for public affairs. *Eyewitness* was a miniseries of four one-hour newsmagazine programs taking contemporary issues and dramatizing them for a fuller analysis impossible with a strictly documentary presentation. Like *Armstrong Circle Theatre, Eyewitness* de-emphasized the role of actors to provide a clear analytical thrust.

Explored were such contemporary matters as the motives of four would-be or accused assassins (Lee Harvey Oswald, Arthur Bremer, Sara Jane Moore, and Sirhan Sirhan), an investigation of recent germ and drug experiments conducted by agencies of the U.S. government, and a second-by-second re-creation of a descending aircraft before it crashed, killing seventy-one persons. In the latter segment, viewers heard dramatized dialogue of the pilots and control personnel, based on actual tape recordings, while they watched the pilots in the cockpit. A split screen, with one portion showing a radarlike profile of the descending aircraft against the hilly ground, provided a useful perspective in understanding the pilots' behavior as they fast approached the ground. This series of four programs, entirely based on transcripts, personal journals, and other authenticated materials, was tied together by a narrator who provided additional information and a frame of reference for the contemporary issues presented.

The difference between this "pure form" of docudrama and the potential it has for dramatizing and analyzing public issues is probably best illustrated by comparing the two broadcast versions of the Karen Ann Quinlan case. In addition to the *Eyewitness* version, a docudrama special on NBC-TV called *In the Matter of Karen Ann Quinlan* was aired in September 1977. Brian Keith and Piper Laurie starred as Joseph and Julia Quinlan, the distraught parents of a twenty-three-year-old woman in a coma since 1975.[13]

In the *Eyewitness* version, viewers were eavesdroppers at the hearing where the Quinlans petitioned to have their daughter removed from a respirator. While the language, based on transcripts of the hearing, was emotional and Mrs. Quinlan was shown making an abrupt departure, obviously upset with medical descriptions of her daughter's vegetative state, the overall focus was on the issues involved not on the Quinlans. However, in the commercial network television version, laced with star personalities, an entirely new dimension to the case was projected. This dealt more with the parents' and family's reaction to the situation and their emotional struggle with moral and civil problems. Certainly the perspective in each program was valuable. But in terms of public affairs, the *Eyewitness* approach was a more objective handling of those matters. The *Eyewitness* version downplayed heavy emotionalism, which could prematurely obstruct an impartial analysis by the viewer.

Reality Is In

Given the "modeling" from public television and imported British programming (long rejected by the commercial networks as too narrow for their mass audiences), conditions in the commercial marketplace changed in the early 1970s. Conditions were positive for a revival of the docudrama but with a decidedly different emphasis. Previously, with the distinct exception of *Armstrong Circle Theatre,* the docudrama form largely consisted of historical and biographical re-creations. As the nation approached the Bicentennial, more of this content emerged, such as in *The Adams Chronicles* (January 1976, PBS) and *Decades of Decision* (March 1976, PBS), in which new detailed profiles of historical figures were presented.

At about the same time, the Watergate scandals and their aftermath began to attract continuing media attention. Similar long-term "events," such as the Vietnam War, also featured advocates and detractors manifesting continual challenges to establishment practices and spotlighting inner workings and corruption of higher levels of government. In all of these issues there developed a number of media "personalities" whose lives and policies were churned over in newspapers, magazines, and books. Thus, while one form of docudrama gave us our earlier history in analytical and interpretative fashion, a new form developed that treated recent events and the human or emotional side of newsmakers. (This emphasis was entirely consistent with happy-talk news and behind-the-scenes interpretations of "news stars" as reported in print publications like the *National Enquirer, People, New Times,* and *Rolling Stone.*)

Because of the impact that these current events had on most lives in the United States and the ability of television to transform small emotional moments into big ones, stories exposing behind-the-headlines decision making, as in *Raid on Entebbe* (January 1977, NBC-TV) or *Missiles of October* (December 1974, ABC-TV), attracted substantial audiences.

The exposition of our past also provided perspective for contemporary events, as in *The Andersonville Trial* (with a parallel to Vietnam, January 1973, PBS), *The Autobiography of Miss Jane Pittman* (with background to the civil rights movement, January 1974, CBS-TV), *Pueblo* (about individual responsibility in a system having organizational problems, 1974), *The Execution of Private Slovik* (questioning military justice, March 1974, NBC-TV), and *Farewell to Manzanar* (a detailed account of one Japanese family's wartime internment, March 1976, NBC-TV). Unresolved problems in American life and history led to aberrations providing "what if" resolutions, such as *The Trial of Lee Harvey Oswald* (September 1977, ABC-TV) and *The Court-Martial of George Armstrong Custer* (December 1977, NBC-TV).

Such re-creations now cut across TV, the stage, and the theatrical motion picture in a sort of self-fulfilling cycle. It is clear that the docudrama form has become an important factor in contemporary broadcasting strategy. In analyzing this phenomenon, several critics have remarked that this growth coincides with a decline in the number of network investigatory documentaries. For example, Gary Deeb, syndicated TV writer for the *Chicago Tribune*, writes:

> The TV news documentary, originally conceived by Murrow and Co. as a force for social good, is on its deathbed. . . . Not only are all four American TV networks deliberately slashing the number of hours devoted to documentaries, but all seem bent on keeping such telecasts away from anything more controversial than the pros and cons of traffic safety.[14]

At the same time, long-standing loyalties and patterns in the industry were weakened by ABC's rise to the number one network spot. In part created by their attempt to lure youth and new audiences through "stunting"—the practice of placing many specials and miniseries in the lineup—the door has remained open on all the commercial networks for increasing experimentation nurtured by a concern for maintaining audience flow to the networks in prime time.

For years, the staple of the industry has been the so-called habit series with self-contained episodes revolving around continuing characters. But beginning in the early 1970s, it was apparent that younger viewers were not as committed to program formats or even to TV viewing as were their parents. Coupled with higher production costs and the less-committed younger viewers, less new series programming was being produced, often twenty-six or fewer new episodes for an entire season.

In 1977, ABC experimented with the so-called third-season concept for spring replacements of failing series. Their willingness to cancel weak programs at this time further opened up the window for the docudrama, in the form of made-for-TV movies and miniseries. Since the initial made-for-TV film aired in 1966 (*Fame Is the Name of the Game*), their ratings track records and quality have compared favorably with regular series programs. For example, CBS's *Autobiography of Miss Jane Pittman* obtained a 30.8 rating and 47 share when it was aired on 31 January 1974. *The Execution of Private Slovik* generated a 25.7 rating and a 40 share later that year.[15]

Thus, the new docudrama form had strong appeals to several constituencies. For writers, they could espouse controversial ideas in relatively safe historical formats, just as many writers did in the American films of the 1930s. For producers, many contemporary docudramas were already presold by heavy news coverage of the events and the personalities. In a miniseries or a blockbuster-movie made-for-TV format, advertisers were attracted to such ratings successes as *Roots* (January 1977, ABC-TV) and *Washington: Behind Closed Doors* (September 1977, ABC-TV). For the audiences, there was a good story linked to nostalgia or an insider's view of newsmakers depicted in human terms.

Problems and Controversies

While the docudrama has the potential to educate and enlighten because it involves a re-creation of events, the form is also subject to potential abuse. Many of the contemporary docudramas have drawn at least moderate criticism for alleged inaccuracies. Some have even been accused of flagrant distortion.

For example, a former member of the U.S. Marine Corps fighter squadron VMF 214, in his analysis of the NBC-TV series *Baa Baa Black Sheep*, presented *TV Guide* readers with a "fact versus fiction" list, concluding that the whole series was as phony as a three-dollar bill.[16]

With regard to ABC's re-creation of the Harry Truman–Douglas MacArthur controversy, *Collision Course* (January 1976), Patrick Buchanan pointed out that MacArthur's alleged snub of Truman at Wake Island never happened.[17]

The wife of blacklisted broadcaster John Henry Faulk, in *Fear on Trial* (October 1975, CBS-TV), was falsely depicted as walking out on him before his libel suit went to trial.

In *Judge Horton and the Scottsboro Boys* (April 1976, NBC-TV), scriptwriter John McGreevy admitted to inventing dialogue, but a lawsuit against the network was dismissed because negligence had not been proven.[18] A docudrama on John F. Kennedy, *Johnny We Hardly Knew Ye* (January 1977, NBC-TV), was termed a "fairy tale" due to various inaccuracies and distortions, and critic Richard Reeves called it an "appropriate addition to the pseudohistory that is replacing documentaries on television."[19]

While the above sample of complaints about distortion, inaccuracy, or omission may seem endless, there is some small comfort in recognizing that such charges are not new to documentary filmmaking or electronic journalism. This does not excuse deliberate falsification, but there are some justifications for altering a setting or telescoping events given the limited time frame in which such re-creations must be depicted—provided, of course, that such changes do not materially distort the analysis or deliberately mislead the viewers.

The National News Council addressed the crucial area of potential distortion when "the needs of drama may tend to take priority over journalistic standards."

> The Council cannot, and does not wish to deprive television of this art form which has given rise to great plays, novels, and movies. Nor is the Council in a position, since it deals only with journalism, to pass judgment on particular docudramas. Nevertheless, because docudramas are a hybrid form—a mingling of fact, or alleged fact, and dramatic license—and because of the particular factors noted above in respect of television—the Council expresses its concern and urges that the television networks take this matter under serious consideration, going beyond mere routine disclaimers, to assure a proper regard for factual and historical accuracy.[20]

NBC-TV attempted to establish a special unit, under the direction of eighteen-year news veteran Robert "Shad" Northshield, to produce re-creations of stories that might otherwise have been documentaries. This noble effort, however, ended in November 1977 without one finished production because of threats of legal action by some of the real-life persons to have been depicted in the proposed *Buffalo Creek Disaster.* This was an uncompleted docudrama about six hundred community members in a West Virginia town who successfully sued a mining company after several dams it had built collapsed in 1972, killing 125 people.[21] After mining officials presented the network with a list of alleged errors and demanded changes in the first script, NBC decided to disband the docudrama unit. Thus, the out-of-courtroom re-creation presents very real problems for producers seeking to dramatize and document actual events yet avoid costly legal battles. This is one reason many docudramas are based on trial records, since such documentation is a defense in litigation for privacy or defamation.[22]

In addition to omissions, inaccuracies, and wholesale historical revisionism, the featuring of prominent entertainment personalities in roles of relatively unknown persons whose lives are subject to docudrama treatment is potentially misleading. Stars bring to these re-created roles wholly different characteristics and appeals generated through their entertainment experience.

Despite these problems and the potential for controversy, the docudrama form has considerable potential given today's competitive electronic and print marketplace. Television news, or documentary film for that matter, has seldom had the access at the "right moment" to events later deemed "newsworthy" in order to fully capture the story. Indeed, as Daniel Boorstin has written, much of our news is mere pseudoevent. The combination of dramatic and documentary forms offers a unique perspective on and analysis of both current and historical occurrences, attracting a much larger audience share when compared to the traditional documentary or newscast. And it should be emphasized that these are often "new" audiences who otherwise would not watch a documentary or theatrical presentation.

This new hybrid, as in *Pueblo,* can also illuminate and sharply focus on various political, economic, social, and military problems, placing a considerable burden on program producers who must be both professional and responsible enough to balance the need to generate audiences with the need for an accurate rendering of issues. While many docudramas will be burdened with this struggle to balance drama with documentation (or "actuality"), the potential social and political benefit to the viewing public justifies more careful exploitation of this important form.

Conclusions

1. The docudrama did not eliminate the documentary but when comparing the two forms, docudramas generally place more emphasis on personality and narrative. One continuing problem with this form is obtaining the appropriate balance between accuracy and fairness, on one hand, and dramatic embellishment on the other.

2. Docudramas that emerged on the commercial networks after 1970 were distinctly different from most earlier efforts, with the exception of *Armstrong Circle Theatre,* in that the newer programs concentrated more on contemporary newsmakers.

3. The antecedents to contemporary docudrama on American commercial television are found in public television and in American film and theater.

4. The role of public television in "modeling" contemporary docudrama has been largely overlooked. However, this influence is not clearly defined given the existence of a "pure" form of docudrama on the commercial networks in *Armstrong Circle Theatre* and the initial resurgence of the form presented in

British imports. Public television, however, was instrumental in utilizing trial records in re-creating dramas linked directly to contemporary events, such as *The Andersonville Trial, The Watergate Cover-up Trial,* and the *Trial of Inez Garcia.*

5. The revival of the docudrama on American commercial television was directly conditioned by public interest in newsmakers and the Watergate scandals, network experimentation to build mid-1970 audience ratings on prime-time TV, and the appeals inherent in the American Bicentennial.

6. While there will continue to be problems in accuracy, fairness, and interpretation, the docudrama can potentially serve as a catalyst in identifying public issues. Through this form, it is also possible to reach audiences far beyond those of the traditional film or television documentary.

Authors' Note

We wish to acknowledge, with grateful thanks, the following support: The Florida State University Foundation and President's Fund for financial help in part of this research; Dr. Donald F. Ungurait, Department of Mass Communication, FSU, for loaning us issues of *TV Guide;* Dr. David J. LeRoy, Department of Mass Communication, FSU, for advice and reference materials on TV audience research; and Ed Herp, director, WFSU-TV, and his staff for assistance in acquiring PTV materials.

Notes

1. This definition differs from that proposed by Edgar E. Willis in his *Foundations of Broadcasting* (New York: Oxford University Press, 1951), 101, where he describes a documentary drama as "a program presenting information or exploring an issue in dramatic fashion, with strong emphasis usually on the social significance of a problem."

2. The nine category types are (1) monologues that re-create events or lives of actual persons, such as *Clarence Darrow* (September 1974, NBC-TV); (2) event-oriented programs, such as *The Night That Panicked America* (October 1975, ABC-TV) and the six-part miniseries *Search for the Nile* (1972, NBC-TV); (3) biographical docudramas, typified by *Jennie: Lady Randolph Churchill* (October 1975, PBS); (4) docudramas with unusual topical or contemporary relevance re-created from events in the lives of actual persons, examples include *The Watergate Cover-up Trial* (March 1976, PBS) and *Victory at Entebbe* (December 1976, ABC-TV); (5) programs that re-create historical religious figures and themes drawn from religious writings; (6) shows drawn from historical or contemporary settings that do not identify actual persons by name were classified as "documentarized fiction" and separated out into this category as in *Washington: Behind*

Closed Doors (September 1977, ABC-TV) or *The Autobiography of Miss Jane Pittman* (January 1974, CBS-TV); (7) speculations about what "might have been" (such as *The Trial of Lee Harvey Oswald* [September 1977, ABC-TV]), are listed here because we consider these aberrations, since most of the program or miniseries is fiction and can never be verified; (8) programs that only partially re-create events in the lives of actual persons were categorized here; (9) this category, almost the flip side to category 6, includes "fictionalized documentary" programs like *Roots,* which have characters and events independently verifiable and real but embellished with a degree of fictional elements to assist the continuity and development of the plot; Alex Haley, the author of *Roots,* has called such a process "factionalizing" as distinct from "fictionalizing." The content analysis is the subject of our continuing research.

3. Clyde Jeavons, *A Pictorial History of War Films* (Secaucus: New Jersey: Citadel Press, 1974), 16. Pioneer filmmaker Edward H. Amet used detailed models in a bathtub to "document" the sinking of Admiral Cervera's fleet at Santiago. Spanish military archivists reportedly believed his statement that he "photographed the battle through a telescopic lens from six miles away" and as a result purchased a print of the film for their collection.

4. In *Mutual film Corp. v Ohio,* 236 U.S. 230 (1915), the court declared that "The exhibition of motion pictures is a business pure and simple, originated and conducted for profit . . . not to be regarded, nor intended to be regarded . . . as part of the press of the country or as organs of public opinion." Cited in Richard S. Randall, *Censorship in the Movies: The Social and Political Control of a Mass Medium* (Madison: University of Wisconsin Press, 1968), 19. The precedent stood until *Burstyn v Wilson,* 303 N.Y. 242. 101 N.E. 2d 665 (1951); 343 U.S. 495 (1952).

5. Leif Furhammar and Folke Isaksson, *Politics and Film* (New York: Praeger Publishers, 1971), 611.

6. See David Mayer, *Sergei M. Eisenstein's* Potemkin: *A Shot-by-Shot Presentation* (New York: Grossman Publishers, 1972); and Furhammar and Isaksson, 16.

7. See Thomas W. Bohn and Lawrence W. Lichty, "The *March of Time:* News Drama," *Journal of Popular Film* 4 (fall 1973): 373–87; Raymond Fielding, *The "March of Time"* (New York: Oxford University Press, 1978); Claudia A. Case, "A Historical Study of *The March of Time* program, including an analysis of listener reaction" (master's thesis, The Ohio State University, 1943); Lawrence W. Lichty and Thomas W. Bohn, "Radio's *March of Time,*" *Journalism Quarterly* 51 (autumn 1974): 458–62.

8. Bohn and Lichty, "The *March of Time,*" 379–80.

9. See Robert H. Stewart, "The Development of Network Television Program Types to January 1953" (Ph.D. diss., The Ohio State University, 1954); Robert Lee Bailey, "An Examination of Prime Time Network Television Special Programs 1948 to 1966" (Ph.D. diss., University of Wisconsin, 1967); and William Kenneth Hawes, Jr., "A History of Anthology Television Drama Through 1958" (Ph.D. diss., University of Michigan, 1971) for in-depth studies. While most of the early television anthology dramas, as compared to series, serial, or single-drama specials, were based on fictional writings and aired live, occasional docudramas were presented. Many of the historical plays of Shakespeare, for example, were

aired. *Philco Play House* was typical in that it occasionally showcased scripts based on the lives of famous persons, such as Vincent van Gogh, Ignaz Semmelweis, and Ann Rutledge. Although there were many contributing factors leading to the decease of live anthology TV dramas, the main reason was that its cost effectiveness in delivering viewers became increasingly uncompetitive in the late 1950s compared to other kinds of television programming. By 1958, they virtually disappeared from the airwaves, probable victims of the then very popular formula Western series. See Hawes, 33–34, 79, and passim. We should also note here the continuing use of biographical dramas on the long-running NBC series of specials, the *Hallmark Hall of Fame*.

10. See Myron Berkley Shaw, "A Descriptive Analysis of the Documentary Drama Television Program, *The Armstrong Circle Theatre,* 1955–1961" (Ph.D. diss., University of Michigan, 1962), 47–58. Shaw analyzed more than one hundred docudramas aired during the period. He identified *Portrait of America* and *American Inventory,* weekly half-hour programs telecast on NBC, as among the first docudrama series (p. 93).

11. Shaw, 64. This necessitated occasional telescoping of facts and changing of names. A. William Bluem in his *Documentary in American Television* (New York: Hastings House, 1965), writes: "However authentic *Circle Theatre* might have been, as a form it was really neither fish nor fowl. On the one hand, its commitment to the faithful duplication of events and people limited its freedom as drama; on the other, the use of actors and theatrical conventions deprived it of any validity as documentary. *Circle Theatre* failed to recognize that documentary and fictional drama not only cannot exist side by side in television, but can better strengthen and inform each other only when they do exist independently" (p. 193). There are, of course, exceptions, and Bluem's conclusions are by no means definitive. Besides those programs cited in the text above, one could point to distinguished series like *Profiles in Courage* (1963–65, NBC-TV), the British-made *Espionage* (1963–64, NBC-TV), and others.

12. Les Brown, "Public Broadcasting Serves as Incubator for Commercial Networks," *New York Times,* 29 March 1977.

13. Joan Kron, "As Karen Ann Quinlan Lives on in a Coma, a New Book and TV Film Tell Her Story," *New York Times,* 24 September 1977, p. 10.

14. Gary Deeb, "Documentaries More Timid," *Tallahassee Democrat,* 6–12 February 1977, p. 17. Other factors besides government and sponsor pressures are also contributing to what one critic has called "the disappearing TV documentary." Sander Vanocur writes in a *Washington Post* column (12 December 1976, p. E3), titled "The Disappearing TV Documentary: Is This Patient Worth Saving?" that "the problem is that the form of the documentary has not changed in 25 years. . . . Wedded as they seem to be to the documentary form of the earlier years of television, documentary-makers are losing their audience and impact." It should be noted that a docudrama on Edward R. Murrow that was to have aired on CBS was "axed" because it apparently painted an unflattering portrait of the network. See Gary Deeb, "Edward R. Murrow Film Axed by CBS Executives," *Tallahassee Democrat,* 19 February 1977, p. 11.

15. These are exceptional performances, but many do quite well. Docudramas have been especially successful when competing against reruns and summer re-

placements. And even though the absolute numbers of the typical made-for-TV movie may only be marginal, the "networks can charge sponsors higher prices because the long-form anthology attracts the best demographics (on the assumption that people who seek out TV movies are casual, selective viewers—not the kind who get hooked on series and watch them week in week out)." See "Golden Age of Movies Made for TV," *Broadcasting,* 27 January 1975, p. 24. See also "What's Behind the Decline," *Broadcasting,* 14 November 1975, p. 43; and "Why Is TV So Bad?" *Newsweek,* 16 February 1976, pp. 72–75.

16. Frank E. Walton, "'Baa Baa Black Sheep' Is Pulling the Wool over Our Eyes," *TV Guide* 25 (23 April 1977): 15–20.

17. Patrick Buchanan, "How History Was Distorted in TV Drama," *TV Guide* 24 (13 January 1975): A-5–6.

18. "'Scottsboro' Dialogue Invented," *Tallahassee Democrat,* 9 July 1977; "'Scottsboro' Film Libel Suit Against NBC Is Dismissed," *New York Times,* 13 July 1977.

19. Richard Reeves, "Kennedy Drama Turned History into Fairy Tale," *TV Guide* 25 (12 February 1977): A-6.

20. National News Council report, "Statement on Docudramas," in *Columbia Journalism Review* (May–June 1977): 85.

21. "NBC-TV Decides Discretion Is the Better Part," *Broadcasting,* 7 November 1977, p. 36. The network continued to contract for docudrama production with "outside" producers, but these producers had no significant news background.

22. General guidelines can be found in William L. Prosser, *Handbook of the Law of Torts* (St. Paul, Minnesota: West Publishing Co., 1971), but one should consult an attorney familiar with case law in particular jurisdictions since the law of privacy, for example, will vary from state to state. It is also advisable to carefully review recent cases concerning "public persons."

6

Brian's Song: Television, Hollywood, and the Evolution of the Movie Made for TV

Douglas Gomery

In November 1971, Richard Nixon reigned as president; the Vietnam War still needed to be unraveled; campus protesters still took to the streets; and Watergate lay in the future. What were Americans watching on television? *All in the Family* (CBS, Saturday, 8:00 P.M. EST) had surged to the number one spot, far surpassing its closest competition: *The Flip Wilson Show* (NBC, Thursday, 8:00 P.M. EST), *Marcus Welby, M.D.* (ABC, Tuesday, 10:00 P.M. EST), and *Gunsmoke* (CBS, Monday, 8:00 P.M. EST). Fifth in the overall ratings battle for that season (1971–72) was ABC's *Movie of the Week* (Tuesday, 8:30–10:00 P.M. EST). Movies had always been popular on U.S. television, but this was the first series of movies made for television to break into the top ten. These movies easily surpassed a long-running detective series, *Hawaii Five-O* (CBS), and two short-lived offerings on NBC, *Sarge* (with George Kennedy) and *The Funny Side* (with Gene Kelly as host) on Tuesday night. On 30 November,

---

From *American History/American TV: Interpreting the Video Past,* edited and copyrighted by John E. O'Connor, 1985. Reproduced by permission of John E. O'Connor and Douglas Gomery. Updated notes © Douglas Gomery, 1996.

ABC presented a little-publicized TV movie, *Brian's Song.* That showing achieved a 32.9 rating and a 48 share, the highest for any TV movie up to that date. More importantly for the profit-seeking networks, *Brian's Song* ranked tenth for any movie presentation ever on television. With *The Wizard of Oz* accounting for five of the top ten to that November night, *Brian's Song* rose to join *The Bridge over the River Kwai, Ben-Hur,* and *Born Free* to form TV's elite top ten movies. Quite an honor for a film with no stars or publicity hype.[1]

But why? Here was a tale of friendship between two running backs who played for the Chicago Bears. Brian Piccolo was white, slow, and small. Gale Sayers was black, fast, and correctly built to become one of professional football's greatest runners. The film focused on their differences as people: Sayers quiet and introspective; Piccolo merry, effusive, ever the clown. Their friendship began at the Bears' training camp in 1965 and ended with Piccolo's death from cancer in 1970. At age twenty-six, Piccolo left a wife and three daughters (the latter not seen in the film). Neither the film's undistinguished direction nor its open sentimentality seemed to diminish its popularity. The sum of the parts overcame any single drawback. This narrative situation, drawn from real events, seemed to have provoked—quite unexpectedly—a moment of memorable potency in the midst of the chaotic Vietnam-Nixon era.

The public's response to *Brian's Song* certainly caught television moguls by surprise. Quickly, awards and praise issued forth from all sides. *Brian's Song* won five Emmy Awards, including outstanding single program for entertainment for the 1971–72 television season. The Directors Guild honored Buzz Kulik. From nonindustry sources came a George Foster Peabody Award for outstanding achievement in entertainment and citations from *Black Sports Magazine,* the American Cancer Society, the National Conference of Christians and Jews, and the National Association for the Advancement of Colored People (NAACP).[2] Even President Richard Nixon jumped on board. "Believe me," proclaimed America's thirty-seventh president, "[*Brian's Song*] was one of the great motion pictures I have seen."[3]

With *Brian's Song,* the made-for-television motion picture came of age as an entertainment genre. Here we have a significant turning point in the history of United States television programming. Why did *Brian's Song* (and other movies specifically made for television) overtake Hollywood features in the ratings war of 1971? The answer takes us back to the origins of the American television industry, to the development of its business and programming practices. Most Americans are familiar with *The Late Show, The Early Show, Sunday Night at the Movies,* and other series that have turned television homes into cinema museums displaying the best (and worst) of Hollywood's creations. Nearly every one of the current "film generation" embraced the magic (and genius) of the American cinema through television. And throughout this era, the American television industry has prospered, becoming one of the more profitable of U.S. businesses. Consequently, we first of all need to examine the history and relations of two American businesses, one growing (television), one declining (theatrical motion pictures). Since we have precious little that qualifies as systematic history in this area, we should immediately begin to integrate the business history of television into a literature well synthesized by Alfred D. Chandler in his book *The Visible Hand: The Managerial Revolution in American Business.*[4]

The methods of business history alone cannot explain, however, the extraordinary popularity of *Brian's Song.* From a sociological perspective, television movies seemed to serve the need for topical entertainment in an era of instability identical to Warner Brothers' social films of the Great Depression. But why *Brian's Song?* What intersection of ideological forces produced its unexpected overflow of popular interest? All television programs, not just news shows, deserve to be studied as indicators of significant shifts in dominant attitudes, beliefs, and values. Like motion pictures from earlier decades, popular television represents the merger of art and industry, a mass spectacle. Understanding how hit shows reflect and/or shape the dominant ideology is a difficult task. New work in film studies provides us with a start. Thus, this chapter addresses two fundamental problems of television and history (business history, and television and ideology) through the genre of movies made for television and one product in particular, *Brian's Song.*

On the surface, the historical relationship between the U.S. film and television industries seems clear enough: the leaders of the film industry unilaterally opposed any interchange with the television industry between 1945 and 1955. Only after the movies had clearly surrendered their mass audience to television did the movie moguls consent to deal with their poor visual cousin. Such claims portray the chieftains of the motion picture industry as narrow-minded dolts.[5] I argue they were not. On only one level did they refuse to do business with television. Until the mid-1950s the major Hollywood studios did withhold feature films from television presentation—but for quite sensible reasons. From 1945 to 1955, even the largest television networks could simply not afford rents competitive with even a declining theatrical box office. During that decade, the chief operating officers of Hollywood's biggest concerns embraced (as it turned out incorrectly) the vast potential of revenues from theater and subscription television.

At first, Hollywood tried to purchase shares of major television properties. For example, Paramount Pictures owned parts of the DuMont network, KTLA (Los Angeles), a subscription television firm, and a theater television corporation. Fox also owned a subscription television concern. On the exhibition side, the United Paramount Theater chain (nine hundred theaters strong) acquired the American Broadcasting Corporation. For a variety of reasons, however (which would constitute another essay), the film industry never was able to gain enough power to challenge the radio, then television networks. All attempts at subscription and theater television during the 1950s proved unprofitable. But Hollywood was able to gain a foothold in the production end. As early as 1951, Columbia established a subsidiary, Screen Gems, to produce filmed material for television. Within four years, the major studios plunged headfirst into production. Warner Brothers, with *Cheyenne, 77 Sunset Strip,* and *Maverick,* led the way. Soon this relationship proved so profitable that Hollywood stuck to the business of supplying programs and/or studio space, while exhibitors turned to alternative investments.[6]

As this jockeying for power was taking place, feature film material was being shown on American television. Initially it came from abroad. In particular, the Ealing, Rank, and Korda organizations in Britain, which had never been able successfully to crack the U.S. market, supplied features as early as 1948. Undersized U.S. producers like Monogram and Republic came on board next. Although these two concerns and a dozen other competitors tendered more than four thousand titles, their cheap production values in Westerns (Gene Autry and Roy Rogers) and serials (*Flash Gordon*) only served to remind early television viewers of the vast storehouse of treasures still resting in the vaults of MGM and Paramount.[7]

To understand how and why the major Hollywood producers finally agreed to rent and/or sell their backtitles to television, we have to return to May 1948, when an eccentric millionaire, Howard Hughes, purchased controlling interest in the weakest of the major Hollywood companies, Radio Keith Orpheum (RKO). In five years, Hughes ran RKO into the ground. Debts soared past twenty million dollars; production fell by 50 percent; new activity neared a standstill. To appease minority stockholders, in 1954 Hughes purchased their shares for $23,489,478.16—in cash. (He wrote a personal check.) He then controlled a studio lot, stages, properties, films, and other assets. A year later, Hughes sold the whole package to General Tire & Rubber Company for two million dollars. At the time, General Tire controlled WOR-TV in New York and desired the RKO features for its proposed *Million Dollar Movie* series. Since General Tire did not want to enter the film production business, it quickly rid itself of all nonfilmic physical property. The studio lot, for example, went to a former RKO employee, then television's number one attraction, Lucille Ball, for her Desilu operation. It also peddled limited rights to 704 features and 1,100 shorts to C&C Television, Inc., for fifteen million dollars. Consequently, in July 1956, C&C auctioned rights to the RKO package to one station per television market for cash and/or "bartered" advertising spots. General Tire retained exclusive rights for WOR and other stations it owned. By July 1957, *Variety* estimated that C&C had grossed twenty-five million dollars in eighty markets alone.[8]

Such profit figures impressed even the most recalcitrant movie mogul. Within the space of twenty-four months, all the remaining major Hollywood corporations released their pre-1948 titles to television. For the first time, a nationwide audience was able to confront a broad cross section of American sound films and rediscover two decades of Hollywood pleasure production. All the companies were able to tap a new source of needed revenue at the nadir of their transition into the posttelevision era. Columbia, a minor studio, moved first. In January 1956, it announced a deal to rent pre-1948 features.[9] As a result, in fiscal 1955—an otherwise dismal year—Columbia was able to achieve a record five-million-dollar profit. Instantly this minor had become a major. Two months later, in March 1956, Warner Brothers sold its pre-1948 library of 850 features and 1,500 shorts to PRM, a Canadian-American investment company, for twenty-one million dollars. Suddenly it could record a fifteen-million-dollar profit. Twentieth Century–Fox upped the ante. It licensed its pre-1948 features for thirty million dollars (plus a percentage) to National Telefilm Associates. In August 1956, MGM topped the Fox figure. By distributing through a wholly owned subsidiary, on one day alone it completed contracts with CBS's owned-and-operated stations and seven other stations for more than twenty million dollars, the largest single day's business in MGM's history. More came through additional contracts.

Paramount held out the longest because it had large investments in subscription television. In February 1958—nearly two years after the deals of RKO, Columbia, Warner Brothers, Fox, and MGM—Paramount sold, rather than leased, its pare-1948 library to RCA, then a talent agency. At the time, the deal, worth fifty million dollars, surpassed all others. But because Paramount *sold* rather than leased its library, MCA made out far better in the long run. By 1965, MCA had grossed more than seventy million dollars and had not even tapped the network market. The excess profits MCA generated from leasing Paramount's pre-1948 features enabled it to purchase Universal and join the ranks of giant media conglomerates.[10]

From 1955 on, pre-1948 feature films functioned as a mainstay of off-network schedules. The networks only booked feature films as specials, not as regular programming. For example, during the 1956–57 season, CBS initiated its annual airing of *The Wizard of Oz.* By 1960 all three networks reasoned that *post-1948* Hollywood features could generate high ratings if offered in prime time. Before that could begin, the studios had to settle with Hollywood craft unions on residual payments. In a precedent-setting action, the Screen Actors Guild, led by Ronald Reagan, struck and won guaranteed amounts. Consequently, on 23 September 1961, NBC premiered *Saturday Night at the Movies* with *How to Marry a Millionaire.* The thirty-one titles shown in the series, fifteen in color, all were post-1950 Fox productions. All had their television premiere on *Saturday Night at the Movies.* Color films helped spur sales of RCA sets; then, as now, RCA owned NBC. Moreover, feature-length movies enabled NBC effectively to counterprogram proven hits on CBS (*Have Gun, Will Travel; Gunsmoke*) and ABC (*Lawrence Welk*). As was generally the case during the 1960s, ABC quickly imitated NBC's effort. A midseason replacement, *Sunday Night at the Movies,* commenced in April 1962. CBS, the ratings leader, did not feel the need to join in until September 1965. By then, the race was on. As early as the fall of 1968, the networks presented recent Hollywood feature films seven nights a week. By the 1970s, overlapping permitted ten separate "movie nights." In the long run, programming innovator NBC retained the greatest commitment to this particular programming form, probably because of continued corporate investment in colorcasting.[11]

This vast display of movie programming quickly depleted the stock of available first-run material. Although the total number of usable features had increased from three hundred in 1952 to more than ten thousand in 1964, growth then slowed to a trickle. Station managers began to wonder just how often they could repeat pre-1948 titles. The networks established a formula for post-1948 titles: show it twice on prime time and then release it into syndication. Not surprisingly, movie producers began to charge higher and higher fees for current theatrical products. Million-dollar price tags became commonplace. Soon network executives reasoned that costs had reached the point where it had become more profitable to produce and sell their own movies. Such a practice would reduce costs and provide a method for making pilot programs for projected series. Since at this time networks normally paid for part (or all) of the development of pilots, significant savings could be effected. And these made-for-TV features allowed the networks to test the ratings power of proposed series in order better to forecast success.[12]

The first made-for-TV feature as part of a regular series was presented on Saturday, 26 November 1966, by NBC, *Fame Is the Name of the Game.*[13] This "world premiere" resulted from NBC's contract with Universal to produce low-budget movies to be released first on television. These color films would, following network television airing, revert to Universal for domestic theatrical release (rare), and foreign theatrical and television release (common). In a short time, the number of made-for-TV features increased rapidly. By the 1971–72 season, when *Brian's Song* premiered, the networks had scheduled for the first time more made-for-TV features than theatrical products new to television. Again relative network power dictated who followed NBC's lead. In 1967 ABC reached an agreement with MGM for production of ninety-minute features. (NBC's television movies ran two hours.) Ratings leader CBS again trailed by two years.[14]

The rapid transformation to made-for-television movie programming took place because profits were higher than anyone expected. On the supply side, a television movie cost on average seven hundred fifty thousand dollars, about equal to the cost of four showings of a popular theatrical release. On the demand side, TV movies quickly proved they could attract sizable audiences and even at times surpass blockbuster features. Not surprisingly top network movie rating choices have included *Gone with the Wind, Love Story, The Godfather,* and *Ben-Hur.* More startling is the fact that *Ladies of the Night* (ABC, Sunday, 16 January 1977) vaulted to fifteenth place for all movies of any type ever shown on television. Others on the all-time top one hundred list include *Helter Skelter, Night Stalker, A Case of Rape, Women in Chains,* and *Jesus of Nazareth.* The only repeat case in the top one hundred has been *Brian's Song.* Moreover, this remarkable sports film achieved this honor in 1971 and 1972, when the made-for-TV publicity mill was only beginning to be set in motion. In general, ABC, which telecast *Brian's Song,* produced through its *Movie of the Week* the best ratings results. In 1971–72, for example, ABC gathered thirteen of the top fifteen telefeature ratings of the season. Barry Diller, then head of ABC's movie programming, parlayed that position into the chairmanship of a major movie studio, Paramount Pictures.[15]

Brian's Song was an altogether typical made-for-television production. Producer Paul Junger Witt had a connection with ABC through *The Partridge Family* series, first aired in September 1970. He hired William Blinn to create a script from Gale Sayers's routine autobiography, *I Am Third.* Witt also secured Buzz Kulik, a veteran television director. Kulik, a football nut, knew the Sayers-Piccolo story from the sports pages, saw it in the tradition of Howard Hawks as a love story between two men. At first there was a problem of casting, since in Hollywood there were few young male black actors with experience. Billy Dee Williams, then thirty-three, had been kicking around Hollywood and Broadway since age seven. His fame from *Brian's Song* shot him into major roles in Hollywood feature films—*Lady Sings the Blues* (1972), *Mahogany* (1975), and *The Empire Strikes Back* (1980). The latter made him a household name. Indeed, *Brian's Song* advanced many of its contributors forward several significant steps in their careers. Producer Paul Junger Witt went on to form his own production company, which turned out the controversial ABC comedy *Soap.* William Blinn wrote part of *Roots.* Kulik amassed a string of important made-for-TV movie credits, including *Babe* (1975), *The Lindbergh Kidnapping Case* (1976), and *Ziegfeld* (1978). Composer Michel Legrand earned an Oscar for *Summer of '42* six months after *Brian's Song*'s premiere. Jack Warden (who played George Halas) was nominated for an Oscar as best supporting actor in *Shampoo* (1975) and *Heaven Can Wait* (1978). But it was James Caan who benefited most. In 1971 his career seemed at a standstill. *Brian's Song* thrust him into the spotlight; *The Godfather* (1972) made him a star. Since then he has remained a major box-office attraction. Here was an early case of a television movie helping create a theatrical movie star. James Caan has not appeared in a made-for-television movie since *Brian's Song.*[16]

Brian's Song cost about four hundred thousand dollars to produce. The made-for-TV movie in the early 1970s had become what the B film was to Hollywood in earlier eras. Contending with restrictions on budgets, language and sex, ratings-minded networks, and a format demanding an opening "teaser" and six climactic "act curtains" before commercial breaks, creators had to work quickly and efficiently. The networks covered production costs in exchange for two runs. The producers then received 100 percent from syndication and worldwide theatrical rights. Production costs were kept to a minimum. Consequently, studio shooting constituted the bulk in most TV films. In *Brian's Song,* the considerable use of National Football League (NFL) film highlights of actual Chicago Bears games reduced costs. Shooting schedules averaged eleven days. With the air date known in advance, all preproduction work was completed in less than two weeks. That time included script revisions, selection of locations and crew, and any hassles over casting the stars. No time was set aside for rehearsals. The script served as the director's bible—"Shoot as written," as in Hollywood in the 1930s. Lighting was one parameter that clearly suffered, for it required too much time to light elaborate shots; all Hollywood agreed that the TV movie was a form for the close-up. Postproduction necessitated yet another week or two. In fact, that step was merely mechanical because so few additional takes were allowed, and only shots noted in the script were covered.[17]

If *Brian's Song* was a typical production, the public response was unprecedented. It proved to be the media phenomenon of late 1971 and early 1972, akin to *Love Story* of a year earlier. Columbia Pictures, for the first time ever, released the film to theaters after it was shown on television. This experiment was tried only in Chicago.

Perhaps too many had seen it already on television; and against major Christmas releases, *Diamonds Are Forever* and *The French Connection,* this TV movie could not even hold its own. The most unexpected success came in ancillary areas. Books dealing with Brian Piccolo became best-sellers. The original Sayers autobiography had been issued by Viking in November 1970. After the film's success, sales took off. The publisher, caught short, had to double the copies in print within one month.

Meantime *Brian Piccolo: A Short Season* by Jeannie Morris, wife of a Piccolo-Sayers teammate, was published by a small Chicago house to take advantage of the TV exposure. More than one hundred thousand copies were quickly sold, and Dell purchased the paperback rights for one hundred seventy-five thousand dollars, a sizable sum even by today's inflated prices. The phonograph record industry was also caught short. Michel Legrand's orchestral version shot into the top ten. Other artists quickly covered. Peter Duchin and Peter Nero produced versions for middle-of-the-road audiences; Hank Crawford created a soul version. This media blitz lasted only three months because the Hollywood publicity mill, caught unprepared, turned to other products. Yet the phenomenon has never completely died off. Throughout the 1970s, *Brian's Song* has continued to be shown on television, in syndication, and in classrooms and other social gatherings in 16-mm format. Uncounted numbers have seen it; few do not know of its reputation.[18]

The *Brian's Song* phenomenon points up the fact that in twenty-five years, 1946 to 1971, movies on television had traversed through four unique stages. First, the Hollywood studios tried to withhold their best films and pursue subscription and/or theater television. Then, needing the cash, they eventually agreed to sell and/or lease pre-1948 features and shorts to local stations. In 1961 the networks initiated stage three by beginning to broadcast post-1948 theatrical features in prime time. Such a strategy proved so successful that fees quickly escalated and inventories decreased to problematic levels. Thus in the late 1960s, the networks began to commission their own films. These made-for-TV features proved to be so popular that they rivaled the ratings power of even the most expensive theatrical products. Miniseries, novels for television, and docudramas came next. The 1980s will initiate movies made for pay cable. In October 1981, Alan J. Hirschfield, chairman of Twentieth Century–Fox, announced a series of original pay-cable movies. Costing about one-third the price of an average theatrical feature, each would be shown first on pay cable, then on over-the-air network television. Next would come foreign theatrical release. Worldwide syndication would terminate the revenue cycle. That same month, Home Box Office, a Time subsidiary, announced its first movie made for pay cable, *The Terry Fox Story,* the biography of another athlete who died young. And so the economic cycle continues.[19]

The made-for-TV movie has formed its own genre since 1966. This form seems to have fulfilled a particular cultural need: topical entertainment reaffirming basic values and beliefs. Here its function has resembled those Warner Brothers features of the 1930s so often utilized by historians to understand transformations in ideas and beliefs during the Great Depression. During the 1930s, Hollywood had to struggle in a moral and political straitjacket to produce acceptable social dramas like *I Am a Fugitive from a Chain Gang* (1932) and *Black Legion* (1936). Consider how historian Andrew Bergman describes these "topicals":

> Throughout the thirties, the Warner studios produced a number of films which dealt explicitly with aspects of social and political life Hollywood usually shunned. . . . [These] remain, without exception, fascinating documents, demonstrating both a gritty feel for social realism, and a total inability to give any coherent reasons for social difficulties.[20]

A similar situation has existed for TV movies. Pressures from advertisers, the Moral Majority, and the U.S. Congress limited what networks would attempt to present. Yet every executive knew that bizarre, topical films could attract large audiences. Their problem became how to make controversial topics noncontroversial TV movies—film that could titillate viewers without scandalizing them. Some public wrangling has always generated useful publicity. But too much could be disastrous. And there always had to be a modicum of stress on the positive. So for every *Roots,* there were dozens of films like *Can You Hear the Laughter? The Story of Freddie Prinze,* and *Dawn: Portrait of a Teenage Runaway.* Topical products *Helter Skelter, Dallas Cowboy Cheerleader, The Feminist and the Fuzz,* and *Raid on Entebbe* all reached the list of the top one hundred highest-rated films shown on American television during the 1970s. All emerged straight from the pages of a daily newspaper, the *National Enquirer, People,* and/or various features in broadcast journalism. Indeed TV-movie production schedules were so swift they could "scoop" theatrical fare. Some made-for-TV movies had completed their second runs before their more famous theatrical cousins had come to town.[21]

Television movies have excelled in telling small stories. Even in attempted extravaganzas or docudramas, the familiar elements of tight character development, the close-up, frequent interior shots, and repetitive dialogue help construct a particular form of narrative logic and style. As with Hollywood features from the 1930s, viewing could be interrupted and still be enjoyed because everyone was so familiar with the characteristics of the form. Film scholars David Bordwell and Kristin Thompson have described this mode as the classic narrative cinema. This formulation of storytelling on film depends on the assumption that action should result from individual characters acting as causal agents. Of course there can exist problems of nature and society. But these factors serve as catalysts or preconditions for narrative action. The story invariably centers on the difficulties of a small group of persons, their decisions, choices, and given character traits. So the hero or heroine has positive values and in the end wins (or loses gracefully). The villain has negative characteristics and fails in the end (or at least does not triumph). The plot moves on in a cause-effect chain as characters seek desired goals. When those figures with positive traits finally win out, we have the "happy ending."

In this classical narrative mode, according to Bordwell and Thompson, visual style is subordinated to a goal of effectively telling the story. So plot time omits all insignificant chunks in order to emphasize only the "important" events. The plot orders the story chronologically to tender the action most strikingly. If a character acts strangely, we soon learn why from (1) dialogue, (2) action, and/or (3) a flashback. Appointments, meetings, and "chance" encounters guarantee efficient character interaction. Motivation should be as clear and complete as possible. And all narrative puzzles must be closed at the finish. Leaving no loose ends, classical narrative films clearly seal up all questions or enigmas. We learn the fate of each major character, the answer to each mystery, and the outcome of each conflict.[22]

Although any subject is a potential candidate for classical narrative treatment, the more familiar the "story concept" the better chance it has to sell. Appropriately, for its *Movie of the Week,* ABC sought seventy-five-minute tales that could be comprehended in thirty seconds. In industry jargon, these were dubbed "concept" films. And of course this meant that these narratives could effectively be promoted in thirty-second commercials. In fact network "concept testing" involved interviewing target audience members (twenty-five- to forty-year-old white, urban Americans): Would you watch the story of such and such? If the answer was yes, then the narrative concept was considered. Sex and violence were euphemized while "social realism" was zealously touted. So controversies surface predictably each year, to be quickly forgotten by the next season. For example, today few remember that NBC's *Born Innocent* kicked off the 1974–75 season. That film, which chronicled the corruption of a teenager in prison, contained a graphic sequence depicting rape with a broom handle. Controversy was initiated; lawsuits were begun; ratings were high. And the studio developed a sequel, *Sara T.: Portrait of a Teenaged Alcoholic.* Indeed, for a time during the 1970s, treatments of rape and alcoholism provided the most popular controversial noncontroversial subjects.[23]

Brian's Song represents a classic narrative tale *TV Guide* efficiently summarized its essential narrative traits:

> A drama that captures the warmth of deep friendship and the horror of dying young. It's the true story of Chicago Bears running back Gale Sayers and his teammate Brian Piccolo, who died last year of cancer. Their training camp rivalries are traced and there's plenty of NFL footage, but football is incidental to the real story: a deeply moving account of the growing friendship between the Bears' first black and white roommates.[24]

Here, classic narrative cinema boils down the complex issue of race relations to competition between two individuals. Violence comes in an accepted form—professional football games. Sports fans, principally young urban males, already knew the ending. The concept of a friendship between men that is broken by death goes back to the origins of the American film industry. Indeed male "weepies" had been a staple of Hollywood's golden age. Consider *The Pride of the Yankees* (1942) or *Knute Rockne—All American* (1940). *Brian's Song* was a traditional story ripped from page three of 1970s sports pages. *Brian's Song*'s two central characters presented a vivid contrast. One was talented; the other tried hard. One was black, the other white. Football, as the *TV Guide* blurb indicated, simply served as a catalyst, a precondition for action. When both made the team and they became close friends, another enigma was needed. A clear villain emerged—cancer. But Brian Piccolo did not die in vain. Consider the final lines of voice-over narration in the film: "But, when they [his friends and family] think of him, it's not how he died that they remember but rather how he lived. . . . How he did live . . ."[25]

The lesson seems clear. Those who try hard and do their best in the face of adversity are life's true heroes. This is a "happy ending" in an otherwise very sad conclusion.

All techniques of camera work, editing, mise-en-scène, and sound were subordinated to the story. The plot, spreading over several football seasons, is easy to follow, since it always centers on the relationship between the two men. The film's structure, punctuated by five commercial breaks (two minutes each), conforms to an ABCC'B'A' structure. The opening (and closing) segment focuses on how the two men relate as they meet (and part). The contrast is vivid and striking. In the second and fifth segments, we learn how each handles adversity. First, Sayers helps Brian Piccolo simply make the team. Of course, All-American Sayers is assured of a place. Later Sayers learns to handle his friend's impending death and the frustration of not being able to do anything about it. The two middle segments also mirror each other. First, Brian assists Gale with the rehabilitation of his knee injury; then Sayers tries to help Piccolo with his physical problems. This process of rhyming constitutes a classical cinematic ploy and unifies differences in the story elements. From beginning to end, *Brian's Song* ceaselessly repeats itself, making it easy to follow and fulfilling yet another characteristic of the classic narrative cinema.[26]

On the level of film genre, *Brian's Song* sparked a resurgence of the sports biography. That category of narrative subjects had been important throughout the sound era. After *Brian's Song* came *Rocky* (1976), *Semi-Tough* (1977), *Slap Shot* (1977), and *Heaven Can Wait* (1978). In 1973 *Bang the Drum Slowly* earned sizable box-office revenues. It too concerned a dying athlete (here a baseball player) befriended by a superior teammate.[27] Yet on the level of genre, *Brian's Song*'s connections to the past were even more subtle than similarities in subject matter. Consider a long-standing character type film historian Russell Merritt has labeled "the bashful hero."[28] Since the 1930s, one durable male figure has dominated American cinema. Whether essayed by Gary Cooper, Jimmy Stewart, or Henry Fonda, all moviegoers are familiar with the character of the easygoing, stalwart young fellow who was suddenly entrusted with great responsibility. Armed with homespun shrewdness and a laid-back, laconic attitude, he (never she) subsequently overcame formidable adversaries. He was likable, tall, lean, and soft-spoken. But when the situation demanded, he became eloquent in a simple, straightforward way. Fame seemed to seek him out. By any film's close, he had emerged as the best at his calling. Success came to him, seemingly by chance.

The bashful hero was spawned in popular culture in the Progressive Era. The egalitarian philosophy of the progressives precipitated as an article of faith the ineffable wisdom of the common man. Merritt locates its origins in the movies in a variety of genres created before World War I. The drawling cowboy, bashful in front of women yet stalwart in the face of danger; the rustic country boy; the shy but creative Charlie Chaplin tramp figure—all began in motion pictures made near the end of the Progressive Era. But this figure moved to the forefront in the 1930s with the emergence of sound films. Merritt points out the importance of the character this way: "[The bashful hero] reassures us that we too could have enjoyed the same success in his shoes, if we only had the opportunity he had. His creators want to assure us that we are heroic, attractive people in our natural state."[29]

In an interesting twist, *Brian's Song* cast a black man in the bashful hero role. Gale Sayers is the easygoing, quiet young man who possesses homespun shrewdness. But he changes. When the film opens, we learn of Sayers's inability to speak before large audiences. Brian Piccolo must coach Sayers for a speech at a rookie-of-the-year award banquet. Yet when it becomes necessary,

Sayers can speak directly and to the point. Consider his terse but effective advice to Piccolo during their first training camp: "Try it going to your left. They don't look for a right-handed guy to throw going to his left."[30] All this changes when adversity strikes. Sayers takes charge. He *asks* to tell their Bears teammates of Piccolo's illness and presents a moving speech "from the heart." Later at another banquet, he informs the world of Brian's real courage in a touching address. Generally the bashful hero seems to be a gentle, nonaggressive man. Yet he thrives on adversity, drawing on a seemingly unlimited pool of talent. He then easily moves others to tears and action. Gale Sayers in *Brian's Song* exemplifies this tradition with his newfound power of public address; as Merritt notes, "the conversion scene itself, in which the hero converts skeptics into true believers, is a constant feature in films of this kind."[31] Sayers moves the audience in the film (and at home in front of the television set) to tears by telling the world of the true courage of Brian Piccolo. And many seemed to respond, signaling the film's extraordinary success.

Yet the figure of the bashful hero cannot completely explain *Brian's Song*'s popularity. Simply put, why did it touch such a wellspring of public sentiment on that Tuesday late in November 1971? What intersection of special themes produced such an outpouring of interest and praise? In short, the film reconstituted a potent mix of popular mythic material during an era when many Americans seemed confused about fundamental conceptions of race, sex, and economics.[32] Specifically *Brian's Song* reworked three basic thematic concerns: (1) relations between blacks and whites, (2) the proper roles for women, and (3) the image and trappings of big business in the U.S. economy. The techniques of mythologization in *Brian's Song* function in subtle and complex ways, even as the film's form and style remain simple and direct.

What was this era like? Historians are still working on that question. But at present certain generalizations do seem clear. The "seething sixties" still formed a part of viewers' memories. Richard Nixon had been in power for two years, trying to unite the country around new goals: "To a crisis of spirit, we need an answer of the spirit." Yet questions of race, the proper way to end the Vietnam War, protest, and law and order refused to go away. Who should run corporate America? Weren't all large cities falling apart? And the youth were on drugs and practicing free love. Religion seemed under attack, replaced by the new morality. The 1960s did not end on 1 January 1970. Questions and doubt seemed to plague Americans up and through the Watergate affair in 1974.[33]

All these uncertainties had seemed more pressing in the 1960s. Why? Partly because from 1963 to 1969 the United States experienced one of its longest periods of sustained prosperity. The 1970s changed all that. Depending on which economist or government expert one listened to, a recession or depression overtook the U.S. economy in mid-1970. Whatever the label, the situation became grave very quickly. Unemployment, especially for minorities and youth, surged upward. The overexpanded war industries were especially hard hit, reflecting the winding down of the American involvement in Indochina. Educated middle-class technicians and engineers suddenly found themselves out of work and competing in a glutted job market. Moreover since 1893 the United States had enjoyed a generally favorable balance of trade with foreign nations. In 1971 the dollars paid for international debt exceeded imports, adding to the domestic economic woes. Times were not good when *Brian's Song* was presented, and Nixon had chosen to do little to alleviate hard times until the 1972 election drew closer.[34]

A few sectors of the economy did continue to prosper. One was professional sports. The American Football League (AFL) and the NFL had just merged. Leagues in hockey, basketball, and tennis were created and/or expanded. By 1975 there were more than three times the number of professional teams as there had been a decade earlier. Sports truly became a big business. It rewarded its star performers as well as or better than some of the larger industrial corporations did their top executives. Teams annually mined newfound wealth from television. Far more people watched professional athletes on television than could have crowded into all of America's stadiums. For example, more than sixty-five million—the largest number ever to see a sporting event up to that time—looked on in 1967 as the Green Bay Packers beat the Kansas City Chiefs in football's first Super Bowl. Just about the time *Brian's Song* aired, the mania about pro sports was reaching the peak of its growth cycle.[35]

Yet *Brian's Song* was far more than a motion picture taking advantage of a popular fad. As recent work in film theory has demonstrated, it is far more interesting to learn what is systematically left unsaid in classical Hollywood films than to continue to probe for more surface themes. That is, ideas and beliefs more often are dealt with through what is left out, "structured absences." Seemingly marginal assumptions can tell us much about what people took for granted, their "lived relationships."[36] A complete analysis of *Brian's Song* would stretch far beyond the limits of this essay, but we can see in three specific ways how the film structured and simplified complex issues without ever directly "sending a message."

Race relations continued to be a festering issue in 1971. In October 1970, the U.S. Commission on Civil Rights reported "a major breakdown" in enforcement of civil rights. Public opinion polls showed that 78 percent of all Americans opposed the idea of busing schoolchildren to effect racial integration. And the North was rapidly replacing the South as the focus of violent confrontations over school integration.[37] In *Brian's Song,* direct presentation of these contradictions was glossed over. How? By reducing the issue to the most personal level. Could two players competing for the same job get along? Recognize that these were special men. Sayers was an All American, not an "uppity nigger." Here the use of the bashful hero mythos effectively stripped the Sayers figure of the threatening quality often associated with black men. He was portrayed not as loud, demanding, or assertive but as quiet and shy, simply wanting to fit into the system. Subtler touches underscored Sayers as a nonthreatening black. He was very well dressed. He showed up at the Bears' training camp in a spiffy blue blazer and a well-trimmed Afro haircut. No wild clothes or exaggerated hairstyle for this character. He looked white, even "higher class" than Piccolo. Moreover he had a beautiful house in what was shown to be an all-white neighborhood. Sayers's wife had straightened her hair and behaved appropriately "perky." She could be white too. Black children (suggesting the busing issue) were not seen, only referred to. In short, the Gale Sayers portrait fit conveniently into the superblack mold established by Sidney Poitier during the 1960s. He posed no problems. One can almost hear viewers saying: "If only all blacks could be like him, then there would be no problems." Left unsaid is any consideration of the societal implications.[38]

Yet contradictions do exist. Consider the use of deep-focus photography. Here, with a wide-angle lens and placement of figures and decor, a motion picture director can create an image in depth. It is not as frequently used in television as in theatrical motion pictures because of video's limited screen size. But in a confined space, there do exist a number of possibilities for action on two levels, foreground and background. For example, near the end of *Brian's Song,* Gale Sayers calls Brian Piccolo for one last time. Behind Sayers, we see his new black roommate. It would have been easier to frame a shot with no roommate, so are we to believe that all other players at Sayers's position were black? (A rule was laid down early in the film that players should room together by position, hence Sayers and Piccolo.) But we know from elsewhere in the movie and the history of professional football that other whites were available. For example, Ralph Kurek, a white, was mentioned several times in the film as the man Piccolo had to "beat out" for the job. Are we then to assume that the interracial roommate scheme worked only for Piccolo and Sayers? That would surely not contribute to a happy ending. And such an interpretation undercuts the otherwise optimistic portrait of race relations in the movie.

If race relations were presented in a simple but not always straightforward fashion, so was the world of professional football. In 1971 professional football in the United States functioned as a prosperous, growing big business with enormous player salaries, well-organized unions, and million-dollar television contracts. But in *Brian's Song,* that world was categorically denied. Football was reduced to a simple game, with just coaches and players. For example, early in the film, George Halas, owner and coach of the Chicago Bears, is shown as a single entrepreneur. He decorates his own office. Contract negotiations are done man to man, without high-priced lawyers. Players have no union or long-term contracts. Here is a world where all that counts is how one performs on the playing field. The best play; others warm the bench. *Brian's Song* omits all those characteristics sports fans have come to associate with professional football in its television era (post 1957). The George Halas figure states it directly in the film when he reminds Sayers that Piccolo cannot play: "I've had a policy on this team from the very start—the best player plays, no exceptions. And right now Kurek is the best player."[39] It's the outside world that is seen as unfair, either through racism (a societal problem) or cancer (a problem of nature). Cancer is the least fair because it is so random. There is no way one can compete against it. As such, cancer offers a counterweight to the film's portrayal of football.

Brian's Song portrays football as a mom-and-pop small-time business. But sometimes cracks show through. The producers made constant use of football replay films, some in slow motion, which visually reminded viewers of television's role in professional sports. Many sports contradictions are embodied in one character, J. C. At first this black man seems to be a coach. He lectures the players about their playbooks; he instructs Gale Sayers on the difficulties of the new roommate policy. Quickly we sense he is merely a player, presumably the captain. (Knowledgeable football fans recognized the reference to J. C. Caroline, a famous Bears defensive halfback.) But soon he is replaced by the "true leader," Gale Sayers. It is the latter who tells the team and the world of Brian Piccolo's death. Indeed by the end of the film, J. C. has become just "one of the guys." Certainly it was too radical an idea for J. C. to be a coach. All coaches were white. Gale Sayers was as close to becoming a leader as is possible for a black. As a bashful hero, he took on many of the characteristics of the white mythos. Even in this simple portrait of big business, whites ran things, and blacks worked for them. Like Jefferson Smith in Frank Capra's *Mr. Smith Goes to Washington* (1939), Sayers only assumes temporary power, and in the end the institution remains unchanged.

The least-complex mythic portrait involves the role of women. Although women's rights groups had made some progress by 1971, their victories had been small. Along with teenagers, women continued to be less trained, lower paid, and the last hired and first fired. In the world of *Brian's Song,* women became nearly invisible. This was a man's love story in which Sayers and Piccolo seem most comfortable together. So at the end, Sayers held Piccolo's hand (we even got a close-up of that image) and comforted him while their wives, the only female characters in the film, stood offscreen. The film closed with Sayers, not Piccolo's wife, Joy, declaring his love. *Brian's Song* is a throwback to the buddy films so common in the 1930s and 1940s.

The two principal female characters, wives Joy Piccolo and Linda Sayers, have been reduced to flat stereotypes. They literally appear first in the film as two-dimensional black-and-white images, faded photographs tacked on the walls of their husbands' common dormitory room. As extensions of their husbands, they quickly become best friends. They sit together at football games. They giggle in unison at their husbands' jokes. When "real" help is needed (Gale learning a speech, or needing rehabilitation), it is Brian who helps him. Characteristically, in the end Joy and Linda break down, unable to handle the situation. Even Brian Piccolo, as sick as he is, must comfort his wife. In sum, women play limited and traditional roles in this modern buddy film. It is interesting to note that many traditional black groups, like the NAACP and Urban League, praised the film. At least blacks were visible on the screen. No women's groups lauded *Brian's Song.* In no way can it be seen as a positive portrait of women.

In general, *Brian's Song* represented a major turning point in the economics of U.S. television by confirming the popularity of made-for-TV movies as an approved, respectable genre and thus breaking the ground necessary for *Roots, Shogun,* and other original works for television. Analysis of this particular film offers interesting examples of how social and cultural forces in the United States during the Nixon era were reflected in the mass media. Through TV movies, Hollywood was able to tackle social issues of race and sex in a controversial yet noncontroversial way.

A.R.

When I turned to Douglas Gomery for permission to use "*Brian's Song,*" he asked me if I would mind if he wrote an afterword, from the point of view of the nineties. I was delighted and extremely grateful that he was willing to put in the effort. His afterword rounds out what I consider to be one of the most interesting pieces ever written about American television.

Afterword to "*Brian's Song*"

It has been more than a decade since I published this article, and I must say that I am proud of how well it has held up. For this volume, I would like to place my essay in some historical context, arguing that *Brian's Song* set in motion general trends still with us and that it also sparked a continuing specific interest in docudrama as biography.

First, *Brian's Song* demonstrated that the TV movie belongs as a long form TV staple. Since its premiere, the movie made for television has successfully functioned as a predictable and expected part of the television landscape in the United States. In retrospect, *Brian's Song* surely pioneered the "disease-of-the-week" subgenre of the docudrama form; now regularly we expect disturbing stories of rape, stalking, kidnapping, and drug addiction as routine narrative cores, providing ammunition for those who loath TV to further denounce the medium. Still serious social commentary can be found, but more likely on Time Warner's TNT and HBO or Seagram's USA network. Here is where the Emmys now go. The major networks have turned to one-hour series, such as *ER, Chicago Hope,* and *The X-Files,* to comment on serious social issues.

Second, *Brian's Song* also unleashed the TV movie as biography, with example after example of the lives of Madonna and Mia Farrow, of Roseanne and former Mouseketeer Annette Funicello. Consider *Naomi and Wynonna: Love Can Build a Bridge,* broadcast as a two-part miniseries on Sunday, 14 May 1995, and Monday, 15 May 1995, on NBC—to high ratings during a key sweeps month. We find the story of how country music's most honored mother and daughter used singing to span generational problems and deal with a devastating disease (in this case hepatitis). Predictably part one told of their remarkable rise to fame while part two followed the struggle and stabilization of Naomi's disease. This story had been presold as a best-selling book, and while critics labeled it simply another bio-pix, fans tuned in in impressive numbers (just as fans of Gale Sayers and Brian Piccolo had done a generation earlier), and NBC turned to find more biographies for future sweeps screenings.

Both these trends underscore that *Brian's Song* still must be seen as a major turning point in the history of the TV movie. It made the genre respectable and created a form Hollywood still uses to tackle social issues in a controversial yet noncontroversial way. I believe that the genre characteristics I analyzed are still very much with us and will continue well into the next century. Thus my article deserves this new printing, and I thank Alan Rosenthal for including it in this volume.

Notes

1. Cobbett S. Steinberg, *TV Facts* (New York: Facts on File, 1980), 172, 181; Alex McNeil, *Total Television* (New York: Penguin, 1980), 31; Tim Brooks and Earle Marsh, *The Complete Directory to Prime Time Network TV Shows, 1946–Present* (New York: Ballantine, 1979), 419–20.

2. Other awards *Brian's Song* achieved include the following: Writers Guild of America Award; Golden Globe nomination; Golden Reel nomination; an "Eddie"

nomination by the American Cinema Editors; National Conference of Christian and Jews Mass Media Brotherhood Award "for Outstanding Contributions to Better Human Relations and the Cause of Brotherhood"; Congressional Record commendation as "one of the truly moving television and screen achievements in recent years"; American Cancer Society Special Citation. As of 1981, all fines of the National Football League go to the Brian Piccolo Memorial Cancer Fund. See Craig T. Norback and Peter G. Norback, eds., *TV Guide Almanac* (New York: Ballantine, 1980), 310–12.

3. *New York Times,* 28 January 1972, p. 91.

4. Alfred D. Chandler, *The Visible Hand: The Managerial Revolution in American Business* (Cambridge: Harvard University Press, 1977).

5. Gerald Mast, *A Short History of the Movies,* 3d ed. (Indianapolis: Bobbs-Merrill, 1981), 260–61; Robert Stanley, *The Celluloid Empire* (New York: Hastings House, 1978), 126–27; Laurence Kardish, *Reel Plastic Magic* (Boston: Little, Brown, 1972), 180–85.

6. Orton Hicks and Haven Falconer, MGM Television Survey: Interim Report, 29 April 1955, Dore Schary Collection, Wisconsin Center for Film and Theatre Research, Madison, pp. 1–8; Charles Higham, *Hollywood at Sunset* (New York: Saturday Review Press, 1972), 149; Michael Conant, *Antitrust in the Motion Picture Industry* (Berkeley: University of California Press, 1960), 109–10; Harvey J. Levin, *Broadcast Regulation and Joint Ownership of Media* (New York: New York University Press, 1960), 62–65.

7. Hicks and Falconer, MGM Television Survey, 8–11; Higham, *Sunset,* 107; *Broadcasting,* 17 January 1955, pp. 50–51; *Autry v. Republic Productions,* 213 F.2d M7 (1954), opinion; *Republic Productions v. Rogers,* 213 F.2d 667 (1954); Christopher H. Sterling and John M. Kitross, *Stay Tuned* (Belmont, Calif.: Wadsworth, 1978), 545–46.

8. Hicks and Falconer, MGM Television Survey, 14–25; *Broadcasting,* 28 April 1956, p. 96; Richard Austin Smith, *Corporations in Crisis* (Garden City, N.Y.: Doubleday, 1966), 64–66; *Broadcasting,* 15 March 1954, p. 65; *Broadcasting,* 19 December 1955, p. 40; "Coup for Teleradio," *Time,* 16 January 1955, p. 86; *Variety,* 1 May 1957, p. 50; Conant, *Antitrust,* 152; Gertrude Jobes, *Motion Picture Empire* (Hamden, Conn.: Anchor Books, 1966), 168–69; Donald L. Barlett and James B. Steele, *Empire* (New York: W. W. Norton, 1978), 165–70, 210.

9. The preponderant number of titles were restricted to pre-1948 titles because of union agreements.

10. *Broadcasting,* 2 January 1956, p. 7; Bob Thomas, *King Cohn* (New York: Putnam, 1967), 262–87; *Broadcasting,* 23 April 1956, p. 98; *Broadcasting,* 27 August 1956, p. 68; *Broadcasting,* 21 May 1956, p. 52; *Broadcast-ing,* 5 November 1956, p. 48; *Variety,* 5 June 1957, p. 27; *Broadcasting,* 25 June 1956, p. 48; *Business Week,* 1 September 1956, p. 65; *Variety,* 6 March 1957, p. 25; *Forbes,* 15 December 1957, p. 11; *Forbes,* 15 November 1965, pp. 24–28; Stanley Brown, "That Old Villain TV Comes to the Rescue and Hollywood Rides Again," *Fortune,* November 1966, pp. 270–72.

11. Hollis Alpert, "Now the Earlier, Earlier Show," *New York Times,* 11 August 1963, p. 22; "Over the Rainbow," *Time,* 25 August 1967, p. 60; Robert Rich, "Post '48 Features," *Radio-Television Daily,* 29 July 1960, p. 27; *Forbes,* 1 August

1960, p. 23; "Saturday Night at the Movies," *TV Guide,* 23 September 1961, p. A-9; John B. Burns, "Feature Films on TV," *Radio-Television Daily,* 30 July 1962, p. 32; *Variety,* 24 September 1980, pp. 88–89; *Variety,* 21 June 1972, p. 34; *Variety,* 20 September 1978, pp. 48, 66; McNeil, *Total Television,* 851; Cobbett S. Steinberg, *Reel Facts* (New York: Random House, 1978), 355–57; Brooks and Marsh, *Complete Directory,* 416–20; Harry Castleman and Walter J. Podrazik, *Watching TV* (New York: McGraw-Hill, 1982), 149.

12. Martin Quigley, Jr., "11,325 Features for TV," *Motion Picture Herald,* 18 January 1967, p. 1; Neil Hickey, "The Day the Movies Run Out," *TV Guide,* 23 October 1965, pp. 6–9; Avra Fliegelman, ed., *TV Feature Film Source Book* 13 (autumn 1972): 10–15; Walt Spencer, "Now Playing at Your Neighborhood Movie House: The Networks," *Television* SSV, no. 1 (January 1968): 49; Ryland A. Taylor, "Television Movie Audiences and Movie Awards: A Statistical Study," *Journal of Broadcasting* 18 (spring 1974): 181–82.

13. Several sources list Universal's *See How They Run,* telecast, 7 October 1964, as the first movie made for television. The distinction between that work and *Fame Is the Name of the Game* is that the latter was the first TV movie broadcast as part of a regular series. *See How They Run, Scalplock* (1966), and *The Hanged Man* (1964) were more like filmed specials. See Alvin H. Marill, *Movies Made for Television* (Westport, Conn.: Arlington House, 1980), 11–12; and Paul Michael and James Robert Parish, eds., *The American Movies Reference Book: The Sound Era* (Englewood Cliffs, N.J.: Prentice-Hall, 1969), 37.

14. Spencer, "Now Playing," 41; Henry Ehrlich, "Every Night at the Movies," *Look,* 7 September 1971, p. 63; Jack E. Nolan, "Films on TV," *Films in Review* 17 (December 1966): 655–57; *Variety,* 18 August 1971, p. 30; *Variety,* 14 June 1972, p. 29; *Broadcasting,* 15 January 1973, p. 37; Don Shirley, "Made-for-TV Movies: It's Coming of Age," *Washington Post,* 6 October 1974, pp. E:1–2; Douglas Stone, "TV Movies and How They Get That Way," *Journal of Popular Film and Television* 7 (1979): 147–49.

15. Dick Adler and Joseph Finnigan, "The Year America Stayed Home for the Movies," *TV Guide,* 20 May 1972, pp. 6–10; *Broadcasting,* 15 January 1973, p. 37; Roger Noll, Merton J. Peck, and John J. McGowan, *Economic Aspects of Television Regulation* (Washington, D.C.: The Brookings Institution, 1973), 67; Caroline Meyer, "The Rating Power of Network Movies," *Television,* 25 (March 1968): 56, 84; Jack E. Nolan, "Films on TV," *Films in Review,* 24 June–July 1973): 359; Caroline Meyer, "Series Movies: New Headache for Programmers," 25 January 1968): M-60; Shirley, "Made-for-TV Movies," *Washington Post,* 6 October 1974, p. E:3; Herbert Gold, "Television's Little Dramas," *Harper,* March 1977, pp. 88–89; *Broadcasting,* 25 September 1972, p. 61.

16. John W. Ravage, *The Director's Viewpoint* (Boulder, Colo.: Westview Press, 1978), 103–12; Ephraim Katz, *The Film Encyclopedia* (New York: Crowell, 1979), 191, 673, 708, 1208, 1236; Les Brown, *The New York Times Encyclopedia of Television* (New York: Times Books, 1977), 43, 477; Christopher Vicking and Tise Vahimagi, *The American Vein: Directors and Directions in Television* (New York: Dutton, 1979), 27–28; Leslie Halliwell, *The Filmgoers Companion* (New York: Avon, 1977), 119, 248, 410, 430, 548, 750, 771; Arleen Keylin and Christine

Bent, *The New York Times at the Movies* (New York: Arno Press, 1979), 89; Marill, *Movies,* 348; *Variety,* 8 December 1971, p. 34.

17. Martin Kasindorf, "Movies Made for Television," *Action* 9 January/February 1974): 13–15; Eileen Lois Becker, "The Network Television Decision Making Process: A Descriptive Examination of the Process Within the Framework of Prime Time Made-for-TV Movies" (master's thesis, University of California–Los Angeles, 1976), 19–96; *Variety,* 8 December 1971, p. 34; Gold, "Little Dramas," 90–93; *Broadcasting,* 27 January 1975, p. 21; *Broadcasting,* 15 January 1973, p. 36; *Broadcasting,* 7 August 1972, pp. 23–25.

18. Kasindorf, "Movies," 16–19; *New York Times,* 28 January 1972, p. 91; Gale Sayers with Al Silverman, *I Am Third* (New York: Viking, 1970); Jeannie Morris, *Brian Piccolo: A Short Season* (Chicago: Rand McNally, 1971); *Variety,* 15 December 1971, p. 29.

19. *Broadcasting,* 19 October 1981, p. 61.

20. Andrew Bergman, *We're in the Money: Depression America and Its Films* (New York: New York University Press, 1971).

21. Patrick McGilligan, "Movies Are Better Than Ever—On Television," *American Film* (March 1980): 50–54; Becker, "Decision Making," 41–54; Stone, "TV Movies," 150–55; John M. Smith, "Making Do—Or Better? The American T.V. Movie," *Movie* 21 (autumn 1975): 38–40; Bruce Cook, "Can Filmmakers Find Happiness on Television?" *AFI Report* 5 (spring 1974): 38–40.

22. David Bordwell and Kristin Thompson, *Film Art: An Introduction* (Reading, Mass.: Addison-Wesley, 1979), 50–59; Raymond Bellour, "To Analyze, to Segment," *Quarterly Review of Film Studies* 1 (August 1976): 331–54; Stephen Heath, "Film and System: Terms of Analysis," *Screen* 16 (spring 1975): 7–77, and *Screen* (summer 1975): 91–113.

23. Nancy Schwartz, "TV Movies," *Film Comment* 11 (March–April 1975): 36–39; Becker, "Decision Making," 57–125; Gold, "Little Dramas," 87–89; *Broadcasting,* 27 January 1978, p. 21; *Broadcasting,* 15 January 1973, pp. 40–45; Stone, "TV Movies," 154–57; Smith, "Making Do," 141–45; Cook, "Happiness," 42–46.

24. *TV Guide,* 27 November 1971, p. A-55.

25. William Blinn, *Brian's Song: Screenplay* (New York: Bantam, 1972), 118–19. All dialogue quotations were double-checked against a 16-mm copy of the film.

26. Other elements also help unify the story and develop its important themes. Obvious to all must be the theme music. The leitmotif is directly associated with death and dying. More subtle but just as effective is a motif of meeting and gesture. First we see Brian and Gale greet each other very formally by reluctantly shaking hands. As they become close friends, they "slap hands," a gesture of black origin. At the end, the two men gesture awkwardly. When Gale first comes to see Brian in the hospital, they must shake hands left-handed because of Brian's infirmity. In the death scene, they clasp hands for the first time. Here black and white are finally united, but only in death.

27. The theatrical film *Love Story* also influenced *Brian's Song.* Indeed, young people dying through no fault of their own has been a popular narrative structure

since the romantic period. See also Steinberg, *TV Facts,* 334, and James Monaco, *American Film Now* (New York: Oxford University Press, 1979), 7–10.

28. Russell L. Merritt, "The Bashful Hero in American Film of the Nineteen Forties," *Quarterly Journal of Speech* 61 (April 1975): 129–39.

29. Merritt, "Bashful Hero," 131.

30. Blinn, *Screenplay,* 25.

31. Merritt, "Bashful Hero," 134.

32. *Brian's Song*'s narrative and genre elements proved so powerful that no commentators seemed to notice the liberty the film took with the story (the intercut football sequences contain errors in matching costume and color) and fact (Piccolo and Sayers were not very good friends off the field; racism continued in their private lives).

33. John M. Blum, Edmund S. Morgan, Willie Lee Rose, Arthur M. Schlesinger, Jr., Kenneth M. Stampp, and C. Vann Woodward, *The National Experience,* part 2 (New York: Harcourt Brace Jovanovich, 1973), 758–92; Richard Hofstadter, William Miller, Daniel Aaron, Winthrop D. Jordon, and Leon F. Litwack, *The United States,* 4th ed. (Englewood Cliffs, N.J.: Prentice-Hall, 1976), 678–705; Samuel Eliot Morison, Henry Steele Commager, and William E. Leuchtenburg, *A Concise History of the American Republic* (New York: Oxford University Press, 1977), 715–45; Richard D. Current, T. Harry Williams, and Frank Freidel, *American History,* 5th ed. (New York: Knopf, 1979), 768–99.

34. Blum et al., *National Experience,* 804–5; Hofstadter et al., *United States,* 708–9; Current et al., *American History,* 817–18; Howard Zinn, *A Popular History of the United States* (New York: Harper & Row, 1980), 529–69.

35. Roger G. Noll, ed., *Government and the Sports Business* (Washington, D.C.: Brookings Institution, 1974), 1–32, 275–324; Walter Adams, ed., *The Structure of American Industry,* 5th ed. (New York: Macmillan, 1977), 365–400.

36. "John Ford's *Young Mr. Lincoln*" (a collective text by the editors of *Cahiers du Cinéma*), *Screen* 13 (autumn 1972): 5–15; Nick Browne, "The Politics of Narrative Form: Capra's *Mr. Smith Goes to Washington,*" *Wide Angle* 3, no. 3 (1979): 4–11.

37. Morison et al., *Concise History,* 740–44; Jerome H. Skolnick and Elliott Currie, *Crisis in American Institutions* (Boston: Little, Brown, 1970), 70–123; Hofstadter et al., *United States,* 707–8; Current et al., *American History,* 816–17.

38. The use of other filmic parameters reinforced this picture of race relations. Consider, for example, the use of camera work that created the motif of running. Sayers and Piccolo seemed always to be paired in training camp spring tests. Who was faster? Of course, Sayers, the superhero, always won, with Piccolo struggling close behind. But here the continuous use of a telephoto lens, squashing spatial depth, linked the two together as they ran. In one lyrical moment, coupled with slow motion, we see the two race through the park "for a beer." With a telephoto lens and slow-motion photography, they seem to run as one. Even though these two athletes compete, they are united.

39. Blinn, *Screenplay,* 52.

7

The Guardian Lecture: Dramatized Documentary

Leslie Woodhead

First—the bad news: "The so-called dramatisation or fictionalisation of alleged history is extremely dangerous and misleading, and is something to which the broadcasting authorities must give close attention." That alarm was sounded by the Lord Privy Seal Sir Ian Gilmour in the House of Commons on 24 April 1980. And the spring of 1980 was a rough season for drama-dockers across the land. The hunt was roused, you'll recall, by the uproar surrounding the transmission of *Death of a Princess* in early April; and within days, Dutch Muslim activists, Australian diplomats, and American State Department officials had joined British politicians and the furious Saudi government to generate what was arguably the biggest single row in television history. The curious fact was that, under all the immediate rumpus about whether princesses really hunted for boyfriends in black Mercedes and the wider concern for the effect on our future oil supplies, the row was really about the legitimacy of a television form.

Now you'd be understandably amused to find the aesthetics of the sitcom or the creative hazards of discontinuous recording in the single play surfacing

---

This is the text of a public lecture given at the British Film Institute, May 1981. Reproduced by permission of Leslie Woodhead, © Leslie Woodhead, 1981.

for debate on the Commons order paper. But the central thrust of the *Death of a Princess* affair was made quite explicit by Lord Carrington speaking in the House of Lords. Responding to a question about "the tendency of some television companies to present programs deliberately designed to give the impression of documentary based on fact," Lord Carrington said: "It might be as well for those who are producing these programs to have a good look at the consequences of what they are doing." Well, as one of those practitioners of dramadocumentary squarely in the foreign secretary's sights, I'm grateful to the BFI for giving me the opportunity of this Guardian lecture to prepare my defenses.

Actually it's not quite like that. At the risk of sounding perverse, I should say at the outset that I find myself in some sympathy with the minister and his parliamentary colleagues about some aspects of the current dramadocumentary boom. And I certainly share his conviction that it's an area where debate and self-examination are imperative. I also have a hunch that over and above the specifics of the dramadocumentary debate, the public unease has to do with the wider concerns of television's accountability and the contract with the audience. But I should add that I imagine I part company with the foreign secretary in believing that properly deployed dramatized documentary is a valuable television form. But more of that in a moment.

To be sure, there do seem to be an awful lot of the things about these days. Bewilderingly labeled as *dramatized documentary, documentary drama, docudrama, dramatic reconstruction, documentary re-creation,* and even, in a highly colored American variant, as *faction,* an example crops up somewhere most weeks. A vigorous academic tradition is already established, pursuing dramadocumentary fossils in Shakespeare, in Greek tragedy, and even in prehistoric cave paintings.

But however distinguished the claims for its pedigree, there is no doubt that the television dramatized documentary is a troublesome beast. For program makers, it's hard to get right and involves the wedding of some disciplines that are, on occasion, difficult to reconcile; for companies, it's uniquely time-consuming and alarmingly expensive; and for broadcasting authorities and now, it seems, governments, it inevitably raises questions about the blurring of fact and invention, the erosion of journalistic disciplines and the confusion of the viewing public. Only the other day, the director of the BFI suggested to me, with some kindness, that we dramadocumentarians were saddling ourselves with an impossible burden, charged as we were with responsibility for the resolution of fundamental debates about historical accuracy, imaginative truth, and journalistic credibility. It all seemed likely, he implied sadly, to end in tears. So why do it? Why unleash such an unruly beast at all?

Here I must at last declare a massive interest. As a full-time keeper of the bothersome creature with a unit at Granada specifically set up to make dramatized documentaries, I believe that it is worth all the aggro. It seems to me quite simply that the dramatized documentary does allow us to do some things on television we couldn't do any other way and to articulate some important and difficult themes and ideas with a vividness and clarity that couldn't be achieved by any other means. That's the commercial—the realities are, as usual, somewhat messier.

There is of course a basic and I think insoluble problem with definition. Dramadocumentary makers swap labels like cigarette cards, but the resultant sets are hopelessly ill matched. One of my colleagues has identified three major strands to the form, while another has isolated six varieties. Yet another has produced an intriguing analysis based on mathematical parameters of drama and accuracy. For my money, there are about as many valid definitions as there are dramadocumentaries. At the end of last year, I found myself on the British Academy of Film and Television Arts' platform for yet another dramadoc tussle with no fewer than seven distinguished program makers, all of whom could be considered employers of the form. You won't be surprised to hear that no two of us could agree on what it is. I find it much more useful to think of the form as a spectrum that runs from journalistic reconstruction to relevant drama with infinite graduations along the way. In its various mutations, it's employed by investigative journalists, documentary feature makers, and imaginative dramatists. So we shouldn't perhaps be surprised when programs as various as *Culloden* and *Oppenheimer,* or *The Naked Civil Servant, Suez,* and *State of the Nation*'s cabinet reconstructions refuse tidy and comprehensive definition. To a degree, I go with Jerry Kuehl, who said at the Edinburgh Television Festival during another hunt for the dramadoc: "The terminological confusion and the lack of common agreement about what a dramadocumentary is, is a sign of vitality." Since then of course we've also discovered that it can mean trouble. It's my feeling that much of that trouble grows out of those confusions about form and intention both in the audience and in the program makers.

For the moment, rather than make theological points around the formal issues raised by a comparison of, say, *Edward and Mrs Simpson* with *Three Days in Szczecin,* I fancy it might be more useful to try to locate the impulse behind the dramadocumentary form.

My own motive for taking up the dramadocumentary trade was simple, pragmatic, and, I suspect, to some degree representative. As a television journalist working on *World in Action,* I came across an important story I wanted to tell but found there was no other way to tell it. The story was about a Soviet dissident imprisoned in a mental hospital. By its very nature, it was totally inaccessible by conventional documentary methods. But the dissident, General Piotr Grigorenko, had managed to smuggle out of the mental prison a detailed diary of his experiences. As a result, it was possible to produce a valid dramatic reconstruction of what happened to Grigorenko and tell that important story. That pattern of motives and intentions seems to me to summarize why many dramadocumentaries get made—and also to indicate why they raise understandable doubts and reservations. The basic impulse behind the drama-documentary form is, I suggest, simply to tell to a mass audience a real and relevant story involving real people. The basic problem is how to get it right after the event.

My own priorities have remained obstinately journalistic, with a fundamental emphasis on detailed research, often extending to years of cross-checking and amplification, and on high-grade source material, such as tape recordings and transcripts. A preoccupation with accuracy of design and the employment of camera crews schooled in documentary rather than drama have sought to give our reconstructions a definition apart from that of established television drama.

At the same time, I'm conscious that I used the word *story* in talking a moment ago about the Grigorenko reconstruction. While it's an established journalistic shorthand, it's perhaps revealing about the dilemmas inherent in the narrative formulation of historical events. There is at the moment a revival of enthusiasm for the narrative mode in historical writing with historians like Emmanuel le Roy Ladurie in books like *Montaillou.* The gains in vividness over more austere and analytical methods is apparent, but it's clear that the form is better at answering "what" and "how" questions than it is at responding to "why" questions. Drama of course adds to the confusion.

From the fundamental requirement to re-create as accurately as possible using the techniques, forms, and values of imaginative drama comes the unease that many people feel for the dramadocumentary form. How are we to respond to this television mongrel—crossbred from the techniques of fiction and the factual claims of journalism and documentary? What level of authenticity is being offered, and how skeptical should we be about claims of accuracy? Does the blurring of documentary and dramatic values imply a dilution we should worry about? Is our audience confused?

Well, there is clearly potential cause for concern here, and not just to foreign secretaries. The modish boom in dramadocs over the last few years, fueled on occasion perhaps by fashion and a sense of where the big budgets may be buried as much as by a real concern with content, has led to some understandable unease. But I think that there's a lot that's positive on the dramadoc balance sheet, and I suggest that the debate over the form could prompt some long-overdue scrutiny of factual television in general and as a result, I believe, some refreshment of the contract with the audience. But for the moment, some history.

Dramadocumentaries have been made for British television since the early 1950s. From the start, practitioners have not lacked confidence in the originality and worth of what they were doing. Setting aside the fine tradition of film documentaries stretching back through Humphrey Jennings to Georges Méliès at the end of last century, one of the earliest TV dramadocumentary makers, Caryl Doncaster, claimed in 1951: "The dramatised story documentary is one of the few art forms pioneered by Television." It seems likely, however, that the initial motivation for that pioneering was in part sheer necessity.

At a time when television was almost exclusively studio bound and film was anyway limited to four-minute magazines on heavy 35-mm cameras with optical sound, one of the most effective ways of bringing documentary preoccupations to the screen was to offer them in a dramatized form, using an acted script based on thorough research. The same technique was used in the 1950s by Duncan Ross in his courtroom series *The Course of Justice* and by Colin Morris in carefully researched documentary plays about delinquent children, unmarried mothers, and strikes. But on the whole, in the apolitical doldrums of the late '50s, television was slow to follow up on the welding of documentary and drama achieved in wartime films like *Target for Tonight* and *Fires Were Started.* It's worth recalling that both *Coronation Street* and *Emergency Ward 10* were described as dramadocumentaries when they arrived in the early '60s. About the same time, Tim Hewat and his *World in Action* team enlisted the aid of actors to re-create incidents in journalistic documentaries like *The Great Train Robbery* and the Portland spy case. But for the most part, television journalists were preoccupied with the liberation offered by the new lightweight film equipment for observational documentary.

The frustration with existing forms was at that moment more apparent amongst people making television drama. And the conviction that there was a valuable tool for the expression of relevant concerns in the fusion of documentary techniques and imaginative drama was left to a new generation of program makers in the television drama of the mid '60s.

That fusion really came of age with *Cathy Come Home* in 1966. I would draw a distinction between the issues raised by documented drama like *Cathy* and the documentary that dramatizes real events. But the excitement and controversy surrounding *Cathy* uncovered many of the worries that have troubled critics of dramatized documentary. The program came from the drama department; and it's undeniable that until recently most of the heat in the debate about the confusion of categories has been centered around work with dramatic priorities rather than programs at the documentary end of the spectrum. Whether that's because drama people make better plays or because documentarians do better research is an open question.

Cathy Come Home was certainly a powerful piece of television, but as well as widespread reservations about the glamorization of the central characters, serious doubts were also raised by many people professionally concerned with social welfare about the program's accuracy. On its second showing, most of the documentary captions giving relevant statistics were omitted because of doubts about accuracy. Yet despite these reservations, *Cathy* was effective enough for its writer, Jeremy Sandford, to be able to claim that "as a result of the film and certain meetings we held afterwards, Birmingham and certain other towns ceased their practice of separating 3 or 4 hundred husbands per year from their wives and children." The underlying assumption that television drama should seek not only to reflect but also to change society has informed much of the most interesting work in the field of documented drama over the past decade, from *The Lump* to *Law and Order* and *The Spongers.*

It seems to me it's that assumption in the work of people like Tony Garnett, Ken Loach, and Jim Allen that has really caused discomfort rather than formal worries about the confusion of categories, which their programs often arouse. The implied worry, it seems, is that the forms and credibilities of documentary and news are being recruited to smuggle a political message. But it seems also that the worry is somewhat selective. As Ken Loach pointed out, "Criticisms about confusing fact with fiction are reserved by certain papers for political films, but ignored when Edward VII or Churchill's mother are romanticised and glorified."

There was one program of the late '60s that did, however, isolate the issue of confusing categories. *Some Women,* produced by Tony Garnett and directed by Roy Battersby, was a play by Tony Parker about women in prison. Parker had interviewed several women who had recently been in prison. Five actresses read and absorbed the original transcripts and, without a script, reenacted the interviews on location. Although intended as a *Wednesday Play,* transmission of the resulting film was held up for two years because it "blurred" the border between fact and fiction. It was eventually transmitted, without the *Wednesday Play* identification but with an explanatory introduction by Tony Parker, to enthusiastic reviews. In particular, Maurice Wiggin of the *Sunday Times,* while insisting that he was "always concerned about the tendency to smudge the distinction between fact and fiction," called the film "reporting raised to the level of art." He also warned would-be imitators to "ponder the indispensable integrity of the pioneer."

From the late '60s, program makers from the documentary side of the fence became increasingly interested in the possibilities of dramatization. There was, I think, at once some exhaustion with the conventions of current-affairs documentary, a frustration about access to a range of important stories, and a sense of the increasing complexity of relevant issues.

It is with the proliferation from the late '60s of dramatized documentaries impersonating real people in real events authenticated by journalistic sources, such as transcripts, tape recordings, and eyewitnesses, that the debate about categories and credibility really begins to bite. Some early examples established the guidelines.

In his reconstruction of the *Chicago Conspiracy Trial,* Christopher Burstall compiled his script exclusively from official court transcripts. Having spent a couple of weeks sitting in the Chicago courtroom for a *World in Action* documentary, I know how accurate Burstall's dramatization was, down to details of setting and wardrobe. For Granada in 1969, Mike Murphy made *The Pueblo Affair,* calling it "a compilation" in which every speech or statement was a verbatim transcript of an actual source. My own dramatized documentaries, like the film on General Grigorenko and others on a Red Guard trial during China's Cultural Revolution, the Szczecin dock strike, an investigation of the worst midair crash in history, and an account of the Soviet invasion of Czechoslovakia, have similarly been anchored in transcripts, tape recordings, and eyewitness records. I would argue that dramatized documentary of this kind, pursued for a specific journalistic purpose and maintaining journalistic priorities even at the risk of inadequate drama, does have a particular status. I would accept that, because of its special claims to accuracy, it also has particular obligations.

I'll return to those obligations in a moment. For now a preposterously small footnote about an ultimate theme—Absolute Truth. The debate about absolute truth versus mere accuracy is of course a favorite dramadoc pastime. I have a favorite Ernest Hemingway quote to contribute.

> A writer's job is to tell the truth. His standard of fidelity to the truth must be so high that his invention out of his experience should produce a truer account than anything factual can be. For facts can be observed badly, but when a good writer is creating something, he has time and scope to make it an absolute truth.

In fact, the Americans, who seem to have an enviable appetite for big questions, appear particularly exercised on this issue. I was reading the other day the transcript of a rather bizarre "docudrama symposium," where fifty Americans in the expanding docudrama business met for a truth-telling session in

California. In a stylish keynote speech, that improbable dramadocker Gore Vidal observed: "We don't go to Shakespeare for history. He is never true but he is always truthful."

Well, the superiority of absolute truth over mere accuracy doesn't need my recommendation. But that's surely more valuable as a corrective against arrogance than as a prescription invalidating notions of journalistic accuracy. "Getting it right" does have validity in journalistic terms, not against the standards of an elusive absolute "truth" but against standards of evidence as they might be understood in a court of law.

But this is of course where we came in. By its very nature, dramatized documentary makes special claims to accuracy, and such claims are often heightened by the deliberate deployment of techniques and mannerisms derived from factual documentary. And the context of television inevitably sets these programs in the territory of news and current affairs, creating an expectation of authenticity.

In his Edinburgh article, Jerry Kuehl argued, "There is a complicity between producer and audience which involves using dramatic criteria to judge truth or falsity." He further argued that no amount of underpinning by documentation, tape recordings, or eyewitness evidence can resolve the dilemma that dramatic artifice and selection employed by the producer crucially condition the material. As a result, no dramadocumentary can possibly live up to claims of accuracy, or rather and more worryingly, the audience cannot tell at what level of credibility to accept any particular sequence.

It's at this point that it seems to me that the thrust of objections to the dramadocumentary form cut deepest and pass on to embrace a debate about the nature and credibility of the whole range of factual television. It's also, I would argue, where dramadocumentary, properly pursued and signposted, can refresh that debate in an important way. For, if we accept that dramatized documentary can only be a subjective construct, we must allow that the same is inevitably true to some degree of current-affairs documentary and of news itself. Reading Tony McGrath's piece in the *Observer* about the dramatic contrivances of news crews in Belfast, and recalling an earlier piece about similar staging by American crews in El Salvador is merely a nasty illustration of what can happen when subjectivity goes sour.

It's of course inescapably true that, even after four years' research, *Three Days in Szczecin* remains a network of editorial judgments, ranging from where to select from nine hours of tape recordings to where to put the camera. But it's a defining strength of the form that it allows me to tell the audience about these conventions. When I make an observational documentary with many of the same editorial interventions, it's much more difficult both for the audience to locate the subjective content and for me to find a way to tell them about it.

To a degree, the demythologizing of factual television is already well established. The delusion of absolute objectivity is almost laid to rest, and television itself has in a small way begun the job of owning up about documentary and news to point out the inescapable subjective content in every camera movement and edit. The contrivances of the documentary maker have been rumbled, and there's a growing public awareness that the manipulative presence of the director is as significant in *Johnny Go Home* as it was in *Cathy Come Home.*

I'm not myself convinced that the viewer is as bemused by the professional capers of news editors and documentary makers as television academies would sometimes claim.

Our audience in 1981 is, I fancy, a good deal more sophisticated and suspicious than either broadcasters or authorities often allow. Few viewers of even the most convincingly mounted dramatization will mistake it for actual documentary or imagine that they have somehow been provided with a clear window on recent history. An audience will be aware that they are watching the producer's best approximation of what happened. But only last week I was reminded during a talk by Peter Fiddick of Huw Weldon's observation to program makers: "Never underestimate an audience's intelligence—or its lack of information."

I am myself convinced that makers of dramatized documentary do have a special obligation to let the audience know what they're up to—what's been called by one American critic "the right not to be deliberately misled." In any one program, it's likely that the material being dramatized will be derived from a variety of sources of varying status. It seems to me vital to signpost material to avoid as far as possible a confusion in the audience about levels of credibility. For *Three Days in Szczecin,* the central source was a smuggled tape recording of the crucial meeting, but alongside this, the writer Boleslaw Sulik also had scenes developed as a result of debriefing witnesses involving the imaginative re-creation of dialogue. We felt it necessary to indicate to the audience the differing status of this material.

And if I were making that film today, I would make even greater efforts to signpost those differences—on a continuing basis throughout the film. I'm now involved in developing a dramadocumentary investigation of the birth of Solidarity in the Gdańsk shipyards in the summer of 1980; and before moving from research to scripting, we're exploring ways of building into the form strategies to permit the continuous clarification of sources, and status—in effect to try to evolve a kind of "television footnotes."

During that American "docudrama symposium" I was talking about earlier, one contributor described the good writer of "dramatized documentary" as "a playwright on oath." But American critics have come to regard the docudrama form with intense suspicion, leveling charges of gross inaccuracy, willful distortion, and the reckless rewriting of history under the guise of authenticity.

Docudrama has even been branded unpatriotic. Given the glamorizations and confusions of television, like *Washington: Behind Closed Doors, Roots,* and *The Trial of Lee Harvey Oswald,* the mistrust is hardly surprising. Here, despite the recent claims of politicians, the form has had a less-tarnished career. For me it will remain a form of last resort, a way of doing things when conventional documentary can't cope. But rigorously pursued and properly signposted, I contend that far from muddying the television pond, while allowing us to explore some important and difficult themes, dramatized documentary can also provide a valuable opportunity to share with the audience a debate about some of the practices of factual television.

That said, it's worth remembering that the one British dramadocumentary almost exclusively concerned with exploring the idea of alternate realities, the power of myth, and the elusiveness of objective truth was a target for parliamentary abuse and diplomatic uproar. *Death of a Princess* vividly demonstrates what a hazardous and vulnerable form dramadocumentary is, even when pursued with such skill and intelligence. For me it also reinforces the crucial importance of fastidious labeling and signposting.

Anthony Smith's warning about the daunting precedents for the dramadocumentary debate was well taken. It is of course hardly likely that a handful of television makers will resolve the dilemmas that have plagued writers and historians over the last two thousand years. I keep on my office wall a quotation from Henry James that in times of confusion does at least serve as some kind of consolation. "The historian," James said, "essentially wants more documents than he can really use. The dramatist only wants more liberties than he can really take." I'm not quite sure where that leaves the worthy dramadocumentarian, but it's nice to know we're in good company.

8

Where Are We Going and How and Why?

Ian McBride

For many in England, the late seventies and mid eighties were seen, and are seen, as the golden age of dramadocumentary. And in this marriage of the fact and the drama, the reign of fact was absolute. In *Invasion,* for example, the Czech and Soviet Politburos are portrayed in all their pomp and glory, and it is clear that authenticity is the threshold, not the ambition. So every medal, every button, every military insignia is spot-on. Admittedly they were all facts that were relatively accessible, but the ring of authenticity was absolute. Alexander Dubek years later gave it unique validation. When he was interviewed for *World in Action,* he watched the scene with incredulity, and said: "Yes, it was just like that."

Was it really a golden age? If so, have we lost it? Where have we come to, and where are we going? And more importantly, like the questions posed in such films, how and why?

Those are the sort of questions I'm going to try to stimulate you with. First of all, can I thank David Edgar for inviting me and thank you all for turning

---

This chapter first appeared as a paper delivered at a conference on docudrama in March 1996, organized by the Department of Drama of Birmingham University, U.K. Reproduced by permission of Ian McBride, © Ian McBride, 1996.

out? A session labeled "dramadoc theory" sounds very cerebral for 9:30 on a Saturday morning, and I'm flattered—and unnerved—at seeing so many people here. But, a bit like the meeting before the first-draft script is commissioned, this session was hatched over a table in an Italian restaurant, and David's real brief followed that of any dramadocumentary filmmaker—"be authoritative, but be a bit provocative."

When you're sitting in the cutting room watching the rough cut of a dramadocumentary, the first thing that usually comes on the screen is a black frame with one word in small white letters: "disclaimer." It's usually referred to by the production team with typical irreverence as the health warning. It's written largely by the lawyer to the everlasting pain and disgust of the writer and director, and it's cared for and kept alive only by the executive producer, who as we all know has one eye on the film and one on the company and needs to prevent one frightening the other with the prospect of a clutch of writs. It is of course the paragraph that finally says that composite characters are portrayed and dialogue has been created, that the chronology has been changed—but that it's a true story.

Well, I'll give you my own disclaimer on this session now. After years in television, I probably am a composite character, and I may play fast and loose with the chronology. I'm distorting David's brief a little by seeking to be a little more provocative than authoritative. There are sometimes sessions at the Edinburgh Television Festival in which a captain of the industry gives what's called "a view from the bridge." Well, this is more informal and best regarded as "a view from the engine room." The thing that is good about engine rooms is that you hear at one remove what's going on up on the bridge, but you have a damned good idea of your own of what the ship is really doing.

I need to start with some delineations. Whenever you put the toilers in the dramadocumentary vineyard together, you seem to have almost as many definitions as individuals. I'm head of factual drama at Granada Television, custodian of the true story dramatized onscreen, and it's a broad slate. *In Suspicious Circumstances* revisits an atmospheric past as Edward Woodward intrigues the viewer by walking through period sets and examining the unknown quirks of a crime gone by; *Fighting for Gemma* confronts the present in full-blooded dramadocumentary to examine whether childhood leukemia can be shown to be linked to the nuclear industry; *The Trial of Lord Lucan* visits a "what if" future by pretending that Lucan is alive and well and available to the constabulary and putting him on trial, with the real evidence and a real jury.

The television spectrum is so wide. Much contemporary drama is as heavily rooted in fact as ever—whether it is implicit, as in *The Bill,* or explicit, it's worth recalling that both *Coronation Street* and *Emergency Ward 10* were described as dramadocumentary when they were born thirty-odd years ago. Many of you will notice that Kay Mellor's *Band of Gold* carries an acknowledgment to the working women of Bradford for the real firsthand research that has been carried out among the prostitutes of the north to deliver that authenticity and insight.

But when one moves into the "true story" the definitions are necessary. Derek Paget has written about "the promise of fact" and points out that a prior assurance of truth provides a cultural passport to credibility. When the filmmakers tell us "this really happened," they seize our attention and invite us to suspend more easily our disbelief in the performances that follow.

So let's mark out some territory. I believe there are two kinds of production currently paying occasional visits to our television screens that are sometimes loosely lumped together as dramadocumentary, and I'll return to that lumping together later and what I see as its dangers. There is dramadocumentary, and there is the dramatization based on a true story.

One of the early proponents of dramadocumentary, Caryl Doncaster, said in 1951: "The dramatised story documentary is one of the few art forms pioneered by television." Personally, I think it more likely that necessity, not creativity, was the mother of invention. Television was largely studio bound; film was limited to bulky 35-mm cameras with optical sound and four-minute magazines. To research a documentary subject thoroughly and to take it to the screen through an acted script was a very effective technique.

British television of the '50s showed little appetite for capitalizing on the potential of fusing the imperatives and techniques of documentary and drama, which had been achieved so well in wartime films like *Fires Were Started* and *Target for Tonight.* Again out of necessity, in the '60s the journalists occasionally picked up the tools—Tim Hewat and *World in Action* recruited actors to re-create incidents in documentaries on the Portland spy case and *The Great Train Robbery.* But documentary makers were by then largely enthused by new lightweight film equipment, which they wanted to use in observational films. It was a new generation of television dramatists who succeeded in fusing drama and documentary techniques in the mid-1960s, and we all know that a real television force arrived with the production of *Cathy Come Home.*

Cathy Come Home was of course a documented drama, created by dramatists, not a reenactment of real events—a powerful technique, which was to be followed honorably, for instance, in G. F. Newman's *Law and Order* or much later in *Tumbledown.* Most can be accurately described as dramatizations based on true stories: the emphasis on the dramatic priority and the stir that this drama provokes have long sat at the heart of the everlasting debate about whether the viewer is confused.

It came back to the documentary makers, the journalists, to develop the dramadocumentary in its very British form, the reenactment of events—the true, true story. Again I believe it was necessity, rather than free-flown creativity, that at least acted as midwife. (No doubt the form was alluring—how do you make a compelling documentary about homelessness to follow *Cathy Come Home?*—but as my colleague Alasdair Palmer, no stranger to dramadocumentary, wrote in *The Spectator* in 1995, truth may be stranger than fiction, but it also takes much longer and is far more complicated.)

The documentary makers' forays into dramatization were born as much of a need to gain access as a wish to experiment: a frustration with the limitations on their trade was as powerful as a wish to explore new forms. Lightweight equipment and the jet age had brought them access to stories and issues all over the world, it seemed. An audience less blasé and less well-informed than that of today would receive quite well documentaries and current-affairs films on issues in places they'd never been and were unlikely to be able to visit. And the filmmakers became adept at unraveling the issues of the modern world by focusing on the microcosm, especially by visiting the United States. An open society, few inhibitions about television and the camera, and people who talked well without need of subtitles. But the filmmakers were aware that this was an oversimplification of the world. Stories and issues were increasingly complex, and access to the really important stories was often totally denied to television, or at least denied in a form that was watchable and attractive to the viewer.

This was of course at its most acute in the closed countries of the world—behind the Iron Curtain, say, or in China. People like Leslie Woodhead became evermore frustrated at an impotence in treating issues as huge as the fate of dissidents in Soviet Russia while making films about the plight of tenants in squalid tenements in New York.

So for Woodhead and those who followed, the dramatized documentary was taken up in the fashion it has subsequently been described—the journalism of last resort. There was no way *World in Action* could go to Soviet Russia and film the trial and imprisonment of a notable Soviet dissident; no way in which the audience could get an insight into the manipulation and denial of human rights embedded in the society of a superpower. But when General Piotr Grigorenko's diaries were smuggled out of the Soviet Union and were painstakingly corroborated and double-checked, there was a way—reenact the events that have been documented; what David Edgar has eloquently described as joining up the dots in history.

Dramatized documentary in this form, anchored in transcript, tape recording, and eyewitness testimony, was aimed at delivering the audience a picture of the unglimpsed—philosophical and political issues as big as totalitarian oppression—with all the hallmarks of authority and credibility. The objective was clear: take the camera where the camera couldn't go, loosen wooden tongues, rehearse the evidence when the witnesses were all dead or too dutifully mute to testify. The risk of inadequate drama was traded for the particular status earned by those special claims to accuracy. I rather liked Ian Curteis's reference to Madame Tussaud's wax museum figures.

It's only right in that context to recall the restraints those program makers were working under, aside of their self-imposed austerity. Anyone who's been to a Chinese restaurant with Leslie Woodhead knows. For five years or so after he made a dramadocumentary on a Red Guard trial during China's Cultural Revolution, the routine was the same: introductions all round, to everyone in the restaurant. Mr. Woodhead was the director of the film in which the beaming waiter had starred, puzzled diners would be told. The desperate balancing act between the budget and the need for scores of extras meant Leslie had recruited every Chinese waiter within about seventy-five miles of Manchester.

But what probably brought the journalists and the dramatists together, whether in *Cathy Come Home* or *The Man Who Wouldn't Keep Quiet,* was the thought that television could not only reflect on the world but could perhaps change it. I believe that it is that feeling, of a potential for energizing change if only by informing the audience well about something others would prefer they remain in ignorance of, that has led or driven many of those in the field.

The other factor that unites dramatist and journalist is conflict, but in different places and on different levels. The dramatist needs conflict within a production; the journalist wants conflict to be created outside and by it.

The truth is that joining up the dots of history might have delivered varying doses of conflict within the drama, but too rarely did it provoke conflict outside. Dramadocumentary was fine, laudable even, when the location was the shipyards of Gdańsk or when Soviet tanks were rumbling through a Czechoslovakia simulated in Salford. It wasn't sort of subversive; the audience wasn't confused; no one was misled. I'm sure that it would be too simplistic to suggest that those in power have no problem with the dramatist or the journalist when they're trying to tell the truth about a regime or a political system that our establishment opposes. It's when the truth sits uncomfortably close to home, or to the perceived national interest, that the dramadocumentary begins to bite and the conflict really starts.

So to April 1980 and *Death of a Princess.* Within days of transmission, American State Department officials, Dutch Muslim activists, and Australian diplomats joined British politicians and an enraged Saudi government in denunciation. The row was ostensibly about accuracy—did princesses really hunt for boyfriends in black Mercedes?—but was of course really about oil supplies, arms deals, and lucrative trade customers. Sir Ian Gilmour, then Lord Privy Seal, voiced the concern in the House of Commons. "The so-called dramatisation or fictionalisation of alleged history is extremely dangerous and misleading, and is something to which the broadcasting authorities must give close attention."

So this was where the lode seam was. This was what energized this form. Take something really sensitive, something they didn't want you to know a lot about. Dig and dig and dig. Loosen those wooden tongues, liberate those mute witnesses. Join up the dots, but maybe in one of the darker corners of recent, very recent history. Keep it very close to home. Use the skills of some of our best dramatists. Transmit, and retire to a safe distance.

That was the spirit that brought us Michael Eaton's *Shoot to Kill* and Rob Ritchie's *Who Bombed Birmingham?*. The investigative journalist had grabbed hold of the form without apology and harnessed real dramatic talent to tell untold stories, to reveal. Why should only the devil have the best tunes, after all?

And the rows of course followed on cue: Margaret Thatcher told us after *Who Bombed Birmingham?* that WE—presumably as in grandmother—do not believe in "trial by television." At least one newspaper was moved to comment that television was the only place the Birmingham Six were likely to receive a fair trial. The chief constable of the West Midlands took the "princesses in black Mercedes" line and denounced the film as "shot through with half truths," an attack launched on the basis of the decor and layout of a room and the format of a meeting held therein to have been inaccurate. The rows did serve a constructive purpose—more than ten million people watched *Who Bombed Birmingham?,* nearly twice as many as had watched documentary after documentary I'd produced on the injustice. People knew much more of the whole picture; the issue then never moved off the national agenda, and the rest is real history.

And the rows didn't leave any of us squirming. The public service imperative—the journalistic validity—of these enterprises meant that no one felt uncomfortable in the arguments.

In the meantime, one of those other little accidents had happened. In a hotel room in the United States, on one of those empty evenings between business meetings, a woman channel hopped to PBS and landed on something strange. It was *Invasion.* The woman was English but had lived and worked in America for a long time. And she'd never seen anything like this on television. When the credits rolled, she made a couple of notes and picked up the phone.

The woman was Bridget Potter, then an executive vice president responsible for original programming with HBO Showcase. What followed was an alliance not only of function but of form. With Granada, and subsequently with the BBC, HBO set about eradicating the austerity of the programs and making them into full-blown dramatic films. In came the search for dramatic strength, if not perfection, in the script; the incidental music; the marquee names; the name talent and investment behind the camera; the filmic alongside the journalistic. There followed *Coded Hostile, Why Lockerbie?, Hostages, Valdez:* some of the best marriages we've seen between the journalist and the filmmaker.

A conference speaker mentioned talking with friends—viewers, punters!—about why they watched factual drama, and they said because it was important. I believe that some of the films I've just mentioned have delivered in that contract with the viewer. The transformation from the austere or puritanical to the relatively lavish television event has been made without breaching the fundamental contract to inform properly, to entertain, and not to mislead.

Which takes us to the two key issues raised by David Edgar—the intention of the program maker and the reaction of the audience. I believe that both have changed and continue changing, but I would differ with David on the significance of the points. I believe the biggest single factor in determining the current and future shape of dramadocumentary in British television is now the intention and agenda of the program *commissioners,* and the biggest single factor in *their judgments* is in their perception, or guess, at the audience's expectation.

The biggest shift in television—regardless of genre—has been from the power of the producer to the demand of the broadcaster. When Woodhead started work on *Invasion,* he did so because senior people at Granada were intrigued and arrested by guessing at events surrounding the Soviets' forced entry. "Make the film," they said, knowing that they would command its slot on ITV. They paid, and had to pay, only scant regard for the demands of their audience—if three million people watched it, three million people watched it. The contract with the audience was honored by quality—integrity—not quantity.

Today in ITV, that commissioning power is held not by producers but by broadcasters. And their preoccupations are with the size and shape of the audience: how many people are going to watch; what are their demographics?

That shift is mirrored in the preoccupations and standards of today's journalism. Inasmuch as I have approached my analysis from a journalistic standpoint, it's always worth keeping one eye on the mirror, to see where modern journalism is heading. Through history and across the range, to the heaviest of broadsheets, it has moved from the abstract and the philosophical to the human interest—the "people" story, long favored by television as the journalism of first resort. So we cover the war in Bosnia with stories about neighbors at war or the snatched meetings of separated families.

And so it now is with factual drama—the small people in the front of the frame play to illuminate the big issue at the back. In drama it was ever thus, and I don't have a problem with that. Sean Deveraux is murdered in the up-front story, and we gain an insight into the price of the arms trade; Gemma D'Arcy fights for life in the memorable scenes, and we grapple with issues of nuclear power, children, and leukemia. It may be condemned as "cultural tourism" and questioned as exploitative or manipulative, but the program maker has strong public service clothes to his or her arguments.

Without those clothes, the human interest story is naked when picked up by dramadockers, even when the journalists are among the most accomplished and the dramatist honorable. It is no coincidence that *Beyond Reason,* having been born at the *Daily Mail,* the slickest exponents of tabloid journalism, wandered through the marshes around the ocean of checkbook journalism, traduced some of the facts, intruded on the privacy and sensitivity of some of those portrayed, had no public service clothes, and was brought to the screen by one of the most commercially conscious of today's broadcasters; no coincidence that it led to a debate in the House of Commons, for the worst of reasons, to a thousand column inches condemning the form, to multiple complaints to the regulators, and to a reinforcing battery of new rules and restrictions on all of us.

As one very senior ITV executive told me recently: "We simply should never have made it."

We can still be in the golden age. That's up to us. What we really have to guard against is the journalist's imperative and the dramatist's vision being thrown by either the journalist's or the broadcaster's guess at what the audience wants and allowing that to become our sole determinant.

A cultural "market force," if you like, is capable of pushing a perceived appetite for human interest over the edge, shoving dramadocumentary out of any golden age into a rapid dishonorable discharge.

9

Lies about Real People

Jerry Kuehl

There's not much new to say about dramadocs, except that there seem to be more of them about these days, and they seem to be more popular than ever before. They've even invaded the wide screen. *Apollo 13, Ed Wood, JFK, Nixon,* and even the bizarre *Forrest Gump* are only the latest productions to have shown how popular this kind of visual history can be. I should lay my cards on the table and say straightaway that, since all such productions tell lies about real people, the current popularity of dramadocs means that more lies are told about more real people than ever before.

I'd better explain what I mean by a dramadoc, and I'd better explain what I mean by "lie." Dramadocs come in many forms; though they are marked by certain family resemblances. It would be nice to be able to say that in their "pure" form they contain distinguishing features, but there is no "pure" form. One of the very earliest was *L'Assassinat du Duc de Guise,* made in 1907 by the Paris company Films D'Art. The film was "based," as we would say nowadays, "on a true story of an episode from French history." Acting styles have changed, so we see the playlet as an over-the-top melodrama—although it was praised at the time for the sobriety of its performances—and we see it without dialogue, too, although its score was written by Camille Saint-Saëns. The scene, as filmed, shows actors pretending to be other people—identifiable other people; in other words, impersonators. The conspirator who plunged the knife, the false friends who lured the duke to his rendezvous, there they all are, gloating over their deed.

That's one kind of dramadoc: a mute representation of a well-known historical episode. This assassination creates serious problems, incidentally, for anyone trying to reproduce it faithfully. After all, we know only that the duke was stabbed, not where or how many times. But that is the one thing the camera cannot avoid showing unless cutaways are used (but they hadn't been invented yet) or unless the assassin masked his deed with his body (but for him to have done that, he would have had to mask the heinousness of his crime).

Georges Méliès's 1902 *Le Couronnement du Roi Edouard VII* is not an imaginative reconstruction of events in the distant past like the assassination of the duke. *The Coronation of Edward VII* is a meticulous reconstruction of a contemporaneous event. Today we would call it a collection of "edited highlights." Méliès took the best advice—Lord Esher's. The lord chamberlain, himself explained the finer points of the ceremony (although the king's indisposition forced the ceremony to be foreshortened—not for the first time life refused to imitate art). The scene was so contemporary, in fact, the program was made *before* the event took place so that it could be first shown the evening of the coronation, and its publicity carefully called attention to the fact that it was not the real thing. Here is what Méliès and his English collaborator Charles Urban said:

> Since the lighting inside the Abbey does not permit moving pictures to be made, and in order to give audiences the opportunity to have an idea of what this imposing ceremony was like, exactly as it was at Westminster Abbey, we have produced at great expense: Number 6815 Special: Reconstruction of the rehearsal of the Coronation of their Majesties King Edward VII and Queen Alexandria. Produced under the direction of C. Urban, London, and G. Méliès, Paris.

Here again, no sounds—apart from music—accompanied the images. Even so, the production exhibited many features common to dramadocs. Like *Apollo 13,* its producers boasted of their lavish budget. Like *Nixon,* they sought out the best technical advice; again, like *Apollo 13,* they apologized for their inability to film on location. Like everyone, their film was made for mass audiences. And like everyone, they got it wrong. The king saw the film, with the scenes omitted because of his illness, a few weeks later in the company of the producers. "What a wonderful machine the cinematograph is, Monsieur Méliès," he said. "It can even show things that aren't there."

Yet another kind of dramadoc features protagonists in real-life activities reenacting roles. Some years ago when a British television company, Granada, was concerned about human rights behind the Iron Curtain, it took up the case of the Sling family, one of the victims of the 1951 purge trials, which led to the death of Rudolf Slansky, the Czechoslovakian foreign minister, and of Otto Sling.

The film it made was called *Full Circle,* and the family, which had since taken refuge in the West, was persuaded to act out how they had been arrested. This too caused difficulties. Marian was alive, but Otto Sling was of course dead, and their two children had grown up. The secret police who arrested them came from Central Casting, and the jail to which they were taken was on the outskirts of London not Prague. Marian Sling herself had grown older in the meantime of course, but she was the same Sling—up to a point. She could no longer feign incredulity when the knock came at the door and could not have undone all that had been done to her in the intervening years, but given those restrictions she was the "same" Sling. Those who have seen the film might agree that she did not perform very well: she spoke English but rather woodenly, unlike her "husband," Otto, who was a professional actor. This might seem bizarre, unless we accept that what convinces us about performances is not what convinces us about real life. In other words, she was an inadequate performer of her own role; she could not convince us of her own ability to play herself with any conviction. The Sling phenomenon was true of those who had walk-on parts as well as those whose performances were the center of the drama, but this should not surprise us. Actors and actresses are prized for their skill at providing simulacra of real people, but a simulacrum is not the thing itself. It wouldn't make any difference, by the way, if Marian Sling were shoehorned into a "real" 1952 Prague townscape, with its shabby decor and its carefully preserved postwar Tatras and Skodas into which the victims were bundled. Authentic backgrounds, however carefully constructed, cannot help here, any more than they can in *Forrest Gump,* not because the decor is false but because the people are. Gump is a creature of the producer's imagination, just as Marian Sling is, twenty-five years after the event.

Is this judgment too harsh? Does Marian Sling have nothing in common with her own past? Nothing that's visible at any rate. She is like Forrest Gump, or rather Tom Hanks, only less skilled. The real-life baggage she carries is irrelevant to the "story" she has to tell. Like Anthony Hopkins in the role of Richard Nixon, she isn't even a very convincing look-alike. At least had cameras been around to record her being taken into custody in 1950 she would have looked the part, which is something Mr. Hopkins, for all of his skills as an actor, could never manage when asked to play Richard Nixon.

Falseness of gesture and falseness of appearance drive authenticity from docudramas. This is why those who admire these forms of dramatic life find the most trivial touches of verisimilitude so entrancing. *The Fall of Berlin,* a Soviet film of 1949, is monumental in its tackiness. It shows Adolf Hitler ostentatiously limping as a result of the July bomb plot the previous year, Joseph Goebbels ostentatiously limping too (as a result of his club foot), and Winston Churchill ostentatiously sporting a very large cigar, as if they all made up for the grotesque episode in which Joseph Stalin flies to Berlin to bless the union of Alexei and Natasha, the young hero and heroine. Anthony Hopkins has been praised for his portrayal of Nixon on the strength of his ability to mimic Nixon's tics and mannerisms, but reproducing mannerisms is only part of the story. Any professional impersonator can do that, although even they get it wrong. Not even Charlie Chaplin got Hitler right.

One of the areas where dramadocs fail most lamentably is in their treatment of dialogue. Solecisms, anachronisms, cultural idiocies of all sorts point to broader and more intractable difficulties. Since modern dramadocs rely on the *absence* of sound cameras capable of recording "original" events in the first place, you would think it would be vital to hear what was uttered as well as what was shown. But scripts are poor guides to what has been uttered. They do not show intonation or rhythm, nor do they show pauses or false starts. And when the language is not even that of the protagonists, as in the story of the Sling family, who spoke Czech, falsities are compounded. So the overwhelming proportion of dramadocs contain invented dialogue. I would prefer to call it *fanciful.* We're not left with much: actors who can't get it right even when the actors are themselves the protagonists; dialogues that don't get it right either, because they lack verisimilitude; decors that fail to convince because they're inevitably out of period. Yet despite these handicaps, dramadocs have never been more popular.

Perhaps it is not despite but because of these defects. Remember that dramadocs are stories based on real events but crippled by their lack of reality. They can never portray real events because, if they did, there would be no need for them. But if there were no dramadocs, what would be left? Just real events; in other words, fly-on-the-wall documentaries. This would lead straight to the conventions that have governed this kind of filmmaking since the days of Jean Rouch, the Maysles brothers, Roger Graef, and Frederick Wiseman. I say "conventions" because the fly on the wall is like a real fly, an irritating distraction—more likely to falsify whatever its ostensible subject may be than to enhance it. And anyhow, such shows are very unlikely to contain the dramatic punch that dramadocs need—the beginning, middle, and end so indispensable to their pace. Processes are not as lively as episodes. A further difficulty arises when the significance of episodes only reveals itself after the event. The Slings' arrest was a case in point: only their subsequent treatment by the Czech secret police and their flight to the West (and their continued faith in communism) made them worthy of Granada's interest.

It should be clear by now why I believe that dramadocs tell lies about real people. But let me spell it out: because they do not tell the truth. To say of something that it is the case when it is the case is to tell the truth about it. To say of something that is not the case that it is the case, or to say of something that is the case when it is not the case is to lie. Harsh words. Might it not be more prudent to be softer? To say that *Nixon* and *JFK* were "economical with the truth" by omitting lines of dialogue that threw doubt on Oliver Stone's doctrines? Or to say that tones of voice can't really be said to lie, although they may mislead or prevaricate? Or to say that invented lines of dialogue, though never spoken, were nevertheless "in character"? This is not where the problems lie: they lie in that, once an episode has been recorded on film, any attempt to reproduce that experience involves its perpetrator in deceit and dishonesty—in short, in lying about it. But what if that is exactly the point? What if doing dramadocs licenses the producer, in his or her view, to get the best of both worlds? To claim the power of the moving image without accepting the serious responsibilities that go with the job of being a visual historian. Once liberated from the necessity of telling the truth, imagination and fantasy can take free rein. They are limited only by the audience's credulity. Thus where Granada, still favoring dissenters, made a dramadoc about the 1968 Czech reforming Prime Minister Dubêk, the whole film was in English, except for the last scene. When the eponymous hero arrived at the opera, the "audience" sang the country's national anthem in *Czech.* Stalin could take off time from his busy schedule to fly to Berlin to review his troops and bless Alexei and Natasha. This may be uncomfortable for dramadoc producers who try awfully hard, but there is, to my mind, no fundamental difference between the lunacies of *Catherine the Great* ("You can't do that sort of thing. This is the eighteenth century") and the up-to-date inanities of *Nixon.* Earnestness of purpose is irrelevant when the difficulty is logical.

It's hard to predict what the sticking point for audiences is likely to be. They tend to be self-selecting anyhow, and their tolerance level is pretty high. Would *Ed Wood* have drawn larger audiences if it had shown the pornographic films to which he devoted his last years? Were fans of *JFK* offended by Oliver Stone's eccentric views about the president's not very ambiguous attitude toward

Vietnam? Professional historians, who make up an infinitesimal proportion of the audience for the film, weren't impressed, but they don't weigh very heavily in the scales.

It should be clear by now that the only thing that authentic moving images of representations of reality have going for them is their *authenticity.* So the only reason for preferring authentic images is that they're authentic. That clearly isn't enough for some spectators. Why should we prefer the authentic to the, well, what? Approximate? Uncertain? Mythic? I think the attraction of authentic images is, and can only be, that they are what they purport to be. Not everyone is impressed by this. Historians are interested in telling true stories about the past, and visual historians are interested in answering questions about the past with the help of moving images. Verifiable images are the bedrock on which telling the truth about the past is based. But not everyone is interested in the past or in telling true stories.

Now, there are many kinds of historians. A historian of drama may well be interested in the lives of actors and may well find Anthony Hopkins's portrayal of Nixon of interest as an example of his approach to a challenging role. But a historian of the Nixon presidency is unlikely to find anything at all of interest in Oliver Stone's cranky views, although a historian of popular culture might. But neither Hopkins nor Stone can add anything to our knowledge of the historical Nixon, Hopkins because he has nothing to say, and Stone because the source of his knowledge is Hopkins. Historians are concerned about the real Richard Nixon not about make-believe figures. This is what distinguishes real historians from those who only play at it.

We're getting at last to the heart of the problems. What is at stake is nothing less than the old, inconclusive struggle between those who are interested in history and those who are interested in fiction. Troubles begin and tempers rise when the two are confused. There is no need for this of course, but it would require a modesty on the part of fiction filmmakers that they seem unlikely to accept. All they need do is revive an ancient disclaimer: "Any resemblance between the characters portrayed in this film and any person, living or dead, is purely coincidental." That would disarm critics, including myself, but the cost would be very high. Who would go out of his or her way to see a film deal with an unnamed Southeast Asian country by explaining that an unnamed American "president" was preparing to withdraw his unnamed American advisers, when he was assassinated by a shadowy group representing powerful interests. Or flock to see a space capsule crippled by power failure. It would be honest, but I can't see it happening.

Part Two

Docudrama at Work: Practice and Production

Although there has recently been some growth in theatrical production, television is still—in the late nineties—the key medium for presenting docudrama to the public. This section looks at some of the implications and ramifications of that situation and, in particular, at the way a docudrama progresses through the U.S. system. Although it looks briefly at production parameters in classic and current Hollywood, the emphasis in the first half of part two is on the way power works within the commercial networks and on cable television. It examines the filmmaker's ability to tap into that power and the constraints that social, commercial, and advertising pressures exert on docudrama production, often leading to the submission to the lowest trends in public taste, or even to censorship.

I chose George F. Custen's "Hollywood and the Research Department" to open the discussion because he gives us a good understanding of some of the Hollywood rules for making biopics before the advent of television. What he clearly shows is that, while lip service was paid to truth and research, everything was subordinate to creating good mass entertainment, usually according to a Zanuck formula. If the truth was awkward, as in the case of Cole Porter's homosexuality, then omit it in favor of the "created" classic love story. Custen also reminds us how extensively the Breen rules and the production code worked against the interests of truthful biography.

Custen also makes us consider what, in the thirties and forties, constituted an acceptable life in Hollywood terms. Heading this category were great politicians like Abraham Lincoln and Benjamin Disraeli—after their biographies had been suitably sanitized by the scriptwriters. Also included in the list were approved writers like Émile Zola; scientists like Alexander Graham Bell, Marie Curie, and Louis Pasteur; musicians like Frédéric Chopin; and the occasional businessman-entrepreneur, like Cecil Rhodes. However, for sheer quantity, nothing could touch the number of films devoted to the careers of sports figures and entertainers, from Rocky Graziano and Knute Rockne to Glenn Miller and Al Jolson. For the most part, problematic and serious material was given a very wide berth, and one looks with amazement on a film like *Viva Zapata,* which seems to have defied the system.

Clearly, the main characteristics of biopics of the thirties were caution, safety, and "good taste." By contrast, the watchwords of the biofeatures of the last two decades have been controversy, outrage, and provocation. Part of this change is due to the abandonment of the code and a general loosening of cinema censorship. Part is due to the altered nature of the cinema audience and the total revolution in social and sexual attitudes over this period. And a good part is due to the rise of such directors as Sir Richard Attenborough, Oliver Stone, and Neil Jordan, who battle the system to bring to the screen their private visions of Gandhi's saintliness, JFK's martyrdom, and Michael Collins's heroism.

The breakup of old-time Hollywood and the abandonment of the old attitudes to screen biography are all part of a process of change that lasted more than twenty years. Warren Beatty's *Reds* (1980) is curious in that it marks the transition between the old and the new.

It is doubtful whether the subject of the film, John Reed—journalist, adventurer, communist, and Soviet lover—would have been acceptable in the thirties. And definitely not in the McCarthy era. By the eighties, after the sixties' turmoils and post Vietnam, a major political film could be contemplated with equanimity. It is clear, however, that Beatty cannot decide whether *Reds* is a love story and easy to do or a political story, which raises many more problems. There is still much old-time thinking in Beatty's approach. As a consequence, British left-winger and screenwriter Trevor Griffiths was dropped in favor of Hollywood old-time trustworthies Robert Towne and Elaine May. One suspects that ten years later Beatty might have stuck with Griffiths.

Though the feature cinema raises the most media comment with such films as *Malcolm X, In the Name of the Father, Nixon,* and *Amistad,* it is clear that by the late eighties it was television that provided the real base for docudrama. For example:

—Of the 115 movies shown on TV in the spring season of 1992, 43 were docudramas.

—In the fall, both the Frank Sinatra and the Jackson family miniseries drew the top audiences of the week, which meant audiences in excess of twenty-five million viewers.

—In the overall 1991 TV season, spring and fall, seven out of the top ten highest-rated movies made for TV were based on real-life happenings.

—In 1991 the *highest*-rated film was CBS's *Woman Scorned: The Betty Broderick Story,* about a woman who killed her ex-husband and his new wife.

—In 1989, the top-rated TV film was *Baby M,* based on the famous child custody case, while a miniseries about the Kennedy family outdrew first network broadcasts of *Robocop* and *Indiana Jones and the Temple of Doom.*[1]

The authors of the three chapters that make up the middle of part two explore the above phenomena and deal with the growth, spread, direction, and limitations of U.S. television docudrama. They illustrate very clearly how films move through the production system and what elements are at work in their selection, funding, and presentation to the public. (It is helpful to read the chapters in conjunction with Douglas Gomery's comments on *Brian's Song* in part one.)

In the first of the three essays, "Making *Bitter Harvest,*" written in the early eighties, Todd Gitlin analyzes the making of *Bitter Harvest* and examines the workings of the system in great detail. What is supremely evident from Gitlin's analysis is that in TV network docudrama the guiding principle is safety: stay with the bland; and whatever you do, don't offend the affiliates and the advertisers or the audience. Thus he writes, "The soapbox is forbidden furniture. This convention of the small, restricted, realistic story has ideological consequences. It has the effect of keeping the show compact, narrow, simplified." This is a long way, indeed, from Woodhead and the attitude to docudrama in the United Kingdom.

When Gitlin wrote his essay, U.S. television docudrama was dominated by the three big commercial networks. Since then, as Gomery remarks, serious, quality docudrama "can be found, but more likely on Time Warner's TNT and HBO or Seagram's USA network."

Thus working hand in hand with both the BBC and Granada TV, HBO has, over the last ten years, coproduced some superb docudramas, such as *Why Lockerbie?* and *Dead Ahead: The* Exxon Valdez *Disaster*. Nevertheless, as Betsy Sharkey shows in her piece, "*And the Band Played On:* Searching for Truth," HBO can also exhibit a certain awkwardness when confronted with controversy.

Randy Shilts's book on the AIDS epidemic first appeared in 1987 and evoked interest from ABC and NBC. The first soon passed on the project, and an option was taken up by NBC. This option was later dropped when it became apparent to NBC that you couldn't make a film about AIDS without also making it about gays. Betsy Sharkey shows how HBO eventually took over the project and pushed it through a stormy and difficult production process to a final triumphant screening.

And the Band Played On produced a good rating for a serious film but nowhere near the ratings of something like *Diana: Her True Story*. Now, popularity and high ratings are, in reality, the things producers dream about and for which network executives are willing to kill. The hunt for the best-selling docudrama formula obviously figures high on their list of priorities. Sometimes the hunt reaches the height of the absurd when we see different networks issuing films on the same subject within weeks, if not days, of each other. For example:

—Liberace died from AIDS in February 1987. In October of the same year, ABC presented *Liberace;* in that same week, CBS played *Liberace: Behind the Music*.

—On 27 May 1992, Carolyn Warmus, a twenty-eight-year-old former Westchester County teacher, was convicted of the murder of her lover's wife. Early in September 1992, ABC aired *A Murderous Affair: The Carolyn Warmus Story*. Three weeks later, in October, CBS broadcast *Dangers of Love,* exactly the same story from a slightly different point of view.

—The ultimate absurdity took place in 1993 when all three networks featured dramas about Amy Fisher, the media-dubbed "Long Island Lolita."[2]

This race for the best-selling formula doesn't just embrace aging music stars, nubile murderers, Marilyn Monroe, and the Kennedy clan. It hunts around the world's disasters, the political arena, the gossip columns, and even has the audacity to pry into palace bedrooms. In 1992, the British royal family, working through the travails of what Queen Elizabeth II called her "annus horribilis," also became prey to the hunt for ratings. This time all three networks had a go. What we eventually saw, in order of broadcast, played out over a few months were

—*Fergie and Andy: Behind the Palace Doors* (NBC);

—*The Women of Windsor* (CBS);

—*Charles and Diana: Unhappily Ever After?* (ABC); and

—*Diana: Her True Story* (NBC).

The most dramatic illustration of a producers' feeding frenzy may be the 1994 media pursuit of the story of Nancy Kerrigan and Tonya Harding. What was understood very quickly was that nothing could be more Hollywood than the story of a beautiful skater whose "Olympic dreams were nearly shattered by the henchmen of her fiercest rival."[3] The story had greed, a beautiful heroine, and appropriate villains. More than forty companies vied for the rights, with producer Steve Tisch making an alleged million-dollar deal with Nancy Kerrigan. This rush to pay was itself beautifully satirized in the media-reflexive HBO docudrama *The Positively True Adventures of the Alleged Texas Cheerleader-Murdering Mom.*

Looking for the right story has become big business. A few years ago, a local newspaper reporter might pick up a small-town scandal that would eventually be spotted by a writer or producer. Thus the idea for *Bitter Harvest* was sparked when director Richard Friedenberg read an obscure story about poisoned cattle in the magazine *Country Journal*.[4] Today that all seems ancient history. In the place of hit-and-miss spottings, we have specialized services, such as Los Angeles–based Industry R&D (IRD), which was established in 1992 to search for sensational tabloid news.

Discussing this phenomenon in *Entertainment Weekly,* Dana Kennedy wrote:

> IRD has a network of 500 sources who tip off the agency to local stories and make what IRD executive Tom Colbert blithely calls "victim referrals." The good stories are then funnelled to IRD's 17 clients—an eclectic bunch including five movie-of-the-week companies, one police show, one hard news client, and three ABC newsmagazines.[5]

For a final look at U.S. docudrama, I decided that I needed to confront the subjects discussed above, that is, popular taste and checkbook journalism, and found the perfect answer in Jeff Silverman's "Murder and Mayhem Stalk TV." The article was written in 1992 but is as relevant today as then. Little has changed, and if anything the public's passion for courtroom dramas and teenage murderers may have increased.

However, it is not enough merely to discuss the overall system, its workings, its possibilities, its constraints, and its basis of popular appeal. It is also important, in order to understand docudrama, to examine the creative process itself and the actual people whose vision inspires the form. The last four chapters in part two, mostly about British filmmakers, deal with the writer's and the producer's purpose, style, belief, and method—in short, what to say and how to say it.

In the second half of part two, I have chosen to lead off with David Edgar's "Theater of Fact: A Dramatist's Viewpoint" because his essay represents the clearest exposition I have come across of how a writer confronts the form. Edgar is also interesting on the evolution of docudrama and its problems and purposes, but above all his writing provides a superb and witty intellectual statement of the writer's position. He is harsh on critics and believes they totally misunderstand how docudrama writers work. He also discusses the movement in England away from Woodhead's journalistic approach in favor of a more classically dramatic form. He is generous toward audiences and finally defends the form because of its capacity to show us *how* certain important things occurred and to tell us that in a uniquely credible way.

Edgar is what we might call a concerned dramatist. As such, he follows in a long line of British TV writers from Peter Watkins and Tony Parker to Rob Ritchie, Michael Eaton, and others. By concerned I mean playwrights who are conscious about using the form for social enlightenment and the public good rather than for just entertainment. Jeremy Sandford fits directly into that category and is noted for having written the most famous British TV drama of the sixties, *Cathy Come Home*. The authors of many of the chapters in this book comment on the film, and a number of years ago I interviewed Sandford himself in *New Challenges for Documentary*.[6]

As Paget points out in part one, tremendous difficulties arise when docudrama challenges establishment orthodoxy. *Cathy* merely challenged the gray men and the faceless housing bureaucrats and was therefore acceptable. *The War Game,* for its part, crossed the line. It offended too much standard thinking and became ideologically unacceptable and unbroadcastable (at the time). Clearly there are dangers in writing the "concerned" play and rocking the boat. As Rob Ritchie, the author of *Who Bombed Birmingham?* cynically put it, "You know you are successful when your play never gets rebroadcast."[7] Such was the case with *Who Bombed Birmingham?, Shoot to Kill* (about police cover-ups in Ireland), and *Hostages* (about the Beirut hostages).

The case of *Death of a Princess,* written and produced by Antony Thomas, provides a good example of how diplomatic and commercial pressure is applied to a docudrama that rocks the boat. This film was based on the 1977 execution of a Saudi Arabian princess and her lover—and presents an extremely negative picture of the way the Saudi aristocracy and elite behave. When Saudi Arabia protested to the British government, questions were asked about the film in the House of Commons. Again the protest was against the form of the film. But it was easy to see that the anger in reality arose from the political opinions expressed and the damage done to British business interests.

Before its American broadcast on public television in 1980, Lawrence Grossman, then president of PBS, was told by the State Department that the film would offend Saudi Arabia and its presentation should be reconsidered. Clement Zablocki, chair of the House Foreign Affairs Committee, was blunter: he spoke of a substandard film wasting public money—a scarcely veiled hint to PBS to avoid antagonizing its funding source.

This pressure from the federal government was then supplemented by pressure from Mobil Oil, a coproducer of Saudi oil and a major contributor to public television. Mobil's strategy was to run advertisements in a dozen newspapers asking PBS to reverse its decision and to "exercise judgment in the best interests of the United States."[8] To the credit of PBS, most stations went on with the broadcast; a mere six declined to air the show, of which five were in North Carolina.

Over the years, the problems raised by *Death of a Princess* have caused it to become one of the most widely discussed docudramas ever made. In fact, six authors in parts one and two discuss or mention it in passing in their chapters in this book. However, I thought the time had come for Antony Thomas himself to speak about the film, its evolution, and its problems, and I subsequently specially interviewed him in Jerusalem for this book, "*Death of a Princess:* The Politics of Passion, an Interview with Antony Thomas."

After talking to Thomas, I became even more interested in the way a writer's work evolves. To satisfy that curiosity, I started interviewing a number of docudrama writers in depth. I wanted to see how they work, what their difficulties were, and how—in general—they approached this peculiar subject of fact fiction. Together the interviews ranged over twenty hours—too much for a book of this size. In the end, I made a short selection for my chapter, "Writers in Action: Ernest Kinoy, Michael Eaton, Michael Baker," from my discussions with those three very different but highly talented writers. Although abridged, the three interviews show how playwrights confront theory and how docudramas evolve in the real world.

I chose to conclude part two with the views of a producer because very often this is where the best ideas are generated, in the minds of people like Leslie Woodhead, Ian McBride, Sita Williams, Peter Goodchild, Colin Callendar, and a host of others. Above all, I wanted to show how producers and writers interact in the creative process, and I found that this was well illustrated in an essay by Irene Shubik.

Shubik is a highly esteemed British producer, probably best known for her work on the *Rumpole* series for Thames TV. She also devised the series *Jewel in the Crown* for Granada, after producing the award-winning pilot film *Staying On* by Paul Scott. However, originally Shubik cut her teeth on that respected BBC institution the *Wednesday Play,* where she was responsible for helping create some of the finest reality-based dramas seen in the United Kingdom, such as *Edna, the Inebriate Woman,* and *Chariot of Fire.*[9] In "Tony Parker and the Documentary Play," Shubik discusses her relationship with writer Tony Parker, one of the pioneers of the hard-hitting social-problem television drama. Parker's plays do not fit the classic docudrama formula. They are not reconstructions of clear historical events but—like Sandford's plays—take their meaning and power from the thoroughness of their research, their relevance to contemporary social issues, and finally their dramatic hold on the viewer. In the end, they too become part of the ongoing question, what is docudrama?

Notes

1. The examples cited are taken from Alan Rosenthal, *Writing Docudrama* (Boston: Focal Books, 1995), 10.
2. Ibid.
3. Quoted in Rosenthal, *Writing Docudrama,* 26.
4. Todd Gitlin, *Inside Prime Time* (New York: Pantheon, 1983), 167.
5. Rosenthal, *Writing,* 26.
6. Alan Rosenthal, *New Challenges for Documentary* (Berkeley: University of California Press, 1971).
7. I heard this remark during a private conversation with Rob Ritchie at the Birmingham seminar on docudrama in 1996.
8. Most of the incidents cited here were either told to me by Antony Thomas or verified by me when Thomas allowed me to go through all his press cuttings and letters related to the film. These cuttings included advertisements from American newspapers, correspondence, and a number of public articles by Antony Thomas himself.
9. The work of Dennis Potter was also featured widely on *The Wednesday Play,* which was also the original showcase for Jeremy Sandford's *Cathy Come Home.*

10

Hollywood and the Research Department

George F. Custen

> Let's agree on one thing at the start, boys. I don't think anybody cares about the facts of my life, about dates and places. I'll give you a mess of them, you juggle them anyway you like.
>
> —*Larry Parks as Al Jolson, talking to a group of screenwriters in* Jolson Sings Again

> As long as we are going to make the Joe Howard story more realistic in its foundation, although we intend to tell it in terms of humor, we should therefore adhere to some of the facts. . . . Now I don't mean to say we should follow his life, or anything like it, but whenever we can use a similar locale without destroying our own story we have created, we should do so.
>
> —*Darryl Zanuck to George Jessel, 11 October 1945, regarding* Hello My Baby

What was the role played by the studio research departments in constructing a life? Every studio had access to historical material, but to view facts as the sole basis of a biographical script is to ignore the many different factors that shaped what could constitute a cinematic life. Historical accuracy was one possible frame to place about a movie. Other issues were powerful determinants of what the final shape of the life might be.

Involved in the making of any biopic were problems of censorship, problems of casting and star image, and a host of legal issues surrounding the depiction of a real person. Most importantly, a powerful influence on the final shape of a biopic was the producer's own strong vision of what a proper film of a life might be. In the end, because of the interaction of specific instances of these four general factors—censorship, casting, legal issues, and the producer's conception of what a life should be—and further, because the film industry as a producer of culture was in each generation reinventing itself in response to extracinematic factors, a life on film tended to reference not historical texts but the almost hermetic systems of reference established in previous films.

Thus, the references used to construct *The Story of Alexander Graham Bell* were not contemporary accounts of Bell's life or interpretations of what the new invention meant for the nation. Instead, *Bell* was based upon previous Fox hits, only some of which were biopics, like *Drums along the Mohawk* (1939), *Suez* (1938), and *In Old Chicago* (1938). Bell, like other characters in biopic fiction, is made, like Mary Shelley's creature, of bits of previous incarnations of already-lived lives. Because of this ritualistic use of intertextuality, a similar shape to fame, something like an ideological taxonomy of fame, became the norm for making the cinematic life of a great man or woman. Thus Leo Braudy's observation that fame did not consist of a great or noble action but rather the reports of such action is nowhere more true than for biopics, where a hit life was constructed out of resurrected hit movies.

Research Departments and Their Bibles

Since the 1920s, and in some instances even earlier, film production companies' research efforts in narrative, costume, decor, and manners and mores had been organized as separate but integrated departments within the motion picture corporation.[1] The idea of research was present very soon after the movies established themselves as corporations with intensive divisions of labor. All the major studios maintained fully staffed research departments as part of their operating machinery. Many films had reason to make use of these research facilities. For example, fictive films like *Meet Me in St. Louis* (1944) might make use of information on interior decoration, architecture, fashion, or music of the period in creating sets, costumes, and script. Because the historical component of biopics was a commodity used to differentiate it from other studio fare, however, the research involvement in these films was always significant. This was the case even after the script had been approved for production and, sometimes, even after a film had been shot and was ready for release. Because the research for a typical film was so extensive, often filling several volumes, the organized materials were often used in publicity campaigns to help sell a film. At times, the very fact of extensive research was itself a selling point, as historicity via extravagant research efforts became, along with the presence of a well-known star or a famous director, a quality to exploit.

Once a story had been given the go-ahead and moved from the development phase into actual production, the job of the research department really started. Set and costume designers would want visual information on period details; actors would want information on the biographee to assist them in makeup and characterization; casting would need pictorial information on all the historical figures in the script; the director and producer would want both general and specific information on the settings in which the life would unfold; and the legal department would need a list of all characters in the film, preferably accompanied by signed release forms from living persons insuring their permission to be depicted in a movie version of a life.

To assist filmmakers in these undertakings, the researcher first turned to the studio's own libraries. The Warners library alone contained almost ten thousand books, as well as vast amounts of pictorial material assembled for previous films. Additional volumes could be borrowed, as needed, from area public libraries, special collections at libraries outside Los Angeles, from private universities, or, in rare cases, could be rented from private collections. Generally, one person from research would be assigned to a picture for its duration. However, on prestige productions, or on productions in which difficulties arose or in which specialized knowledge was required, more than one person might be assigned to a film. For example, Warners' prestige production *All This and Heaven Too* had three researchers (Hetta George, Jean Beck, and Augusta Adler) assigned to it, all overseen by department head Herman Lissauer, Ph.D. They worked a total of eleven weeks. And, although principal photography for the film was completed on 20 April 1940, research personnel nevertheless continued to work for another week on problem areas of this project.

The research for the Bette Davis vehicle was done simultaneously with research on other films. In preparation at the same time as *All This* was another biopic, *The Lady with Red Hair* (1940), a vehicle for Davis's sometime nemesis and costar, Miriam Hopkins. To meet the research demands of these two projects, the department would weave in and out of historical periods, now concerned with French legal procedure of the 1840s, now interested in acting conventions of the nineteenth-century New York stage.

Although these research teams were occasionally augmented with information gleaned from outside experts or consultants in specialized fields or were, from time to time, forced to defer to the studio legal department, the range of questions the department was expected to answer on their own was truly astonishing. By the 1920s, the procedures necessary to ensure a smooth-running operation had been institutionalized, and these departments had become supremely adept at fielding questions. And, because of the cultural weight accorded film as a pretelevision source of public history, studio research departments were perceived as quasi-public repositories of knowledge to which viewers wrote for advice on noncinematic matters, such as etiquette or interior design.

The overall job of the department was to answer specific questions from writers, directors, art directors, producers, and other personnel concerning any and all aspects of production. The reason behind the existence of such an extensive research machine is far from clear, however. As part of the complex division of labor that characterized the producer-unit mode of production Bordwell, Staiger, and Thompson (1985) suggest was the norm in Hollywood during this period, the labor of research had what might be called an instrumental function. But a description of the department's goals in these terms alone—research departments were part of the chain of production—avoids larger issues, namely why studios should be concerned with facticity at all and how this concept was operationalized by studio research personnel. The ideology motivating the large range of research requests was rather more complex than this research-as-work approach would suggest.

There were competing and contradictory expectations from different personnel as to the purpose of the work that went into the massive research guidebooks (the "bibles") assembled for each film. These bibles were of the utmost importance to a film, for they represented, during all phases of production, the shared basis upon which decisions pertaining to historical accuracy were made.[2] Carl Milliken, Jr., eventual head of Warners research in the 1950s, described the significance of these bibles for an in-house publication, the *Warner Club News:*

> Because the information must be chiefly pictorial, there is prepared on each picture, a compilation of pictures usually referred to as the "bible." The department copy of this material is bound in a large volume as a permanent record of the work done on the picture. Copies of the pictures applying directly to their phase of the work are sent to the various people that are directing work on the picture—the producer, director, art director, property

> casting, makeup, wardrobe, etc. The complete compilation is usually so impressive that the publicity department sends a copy to New York for use in exploiting the picture. (1940:3)

The heads of research themselves, with their staff of in-house experts assembling these bibles, seemed to be after a linear, factual account of a famous life: getting the chronology straight, getting the characterizations accurate or at least recognizable, getting accurate pictures of the costumes and reliable accounts of the mores of the period as described by various reliable primary and secondary sources. They fully expected that their research findings, housed in these bibles, would be used by all film personnel in their various capacities in making a biopic. This use of the bible was standard operating procedure at all the studios, as the directive on the cover of Fox's bible for *Cardinal Richelieu* suggested: "These notes should be read in advance of production as they are designed to give ideas for set dressing, props, modes and manners, [and] business."

Like other contributors to the filmmaking process at a well-organized studio, the researcher had specific tasks to do and standard operating procedures with which to accomplish his or her assignments. However, years of working in a fact-dominated environment must have left a mark on those in the research department, and, as in other professions, researchers internalized a set of work values that were specific to their corner of the lot. A "researcher's culture" arose, complete with its own values and hierarchies, and part of this culture undoubtedly was a particular slant on how directors and producers could best use their skills in making a biopic. When researchers' advice was ignored or some imaginary line demarcating fact from fancy crossed, given the power structure at the studios, the responses of the personnel in charge could be quite harsh.

I do not wish to give the impression that the members of the research staff were, like the dictionary compilers of Howard Hawks's *Ball of Fire* (1941), intellectuals from Central Casting, superannuated creatures holed up in a dark room in pursuit of a truth detached from the realities of the world of moviemaking. Researchers, as part of the community of commercial filmmakers, were tolerant of the conventions of poetic license used in constructing narratives for biopics. If they had been around a studio lot long enough, they also should have been well versed in the analysis of the structure of Hollywood power and on their own limited role in influencing what appeared on the screen. In most cases, the director and/or producer or the studio's head of production set the tone for how much energy would be expended for research on a given picture. Because their relationship to the labor of making a cinematic life was different from that of producers, however, they held different values. At times their tolerance was stretched too far by the depiction of history in a script. And, although it was not the research department's job to advise the producer on what standards of realism should apply in a biopic but merely to present him with the requested facts, pride in their work and a sense of the contribution they could make forced them at times to violate the standard operating procedures of supplying answers and instead to confront a particularly flagrant violator of the standards of fact in the biopic.

The Producer's Culture

With their energies divided among the forces of censorship at Production Code Administrator Joseph Breen's office, the legal department's fear of litigation based on either invasion of privacy or libel, and the campaigns to be mounted for publicity and ticket sales, producers, often balancing the demands of competing priorities, were far more pragmatic than researchers were. Experience in the past had told them that getting the facts straight was merely one consideration to be weighed against many other variables in determining what aspects of a person's history would become part of a celluloid life.

A clear picture of the different values producers and research personnel held on the facts in a biopic can be illustrated with the Warner Brothers biography of Cole Porter, *Night and Day*. Porter himself was as successful a businessman as he was a composer. He had, through protracted negotiations with Jack Warner, raised the asking price for the Warners' rights to use thirty-eight of his songs in a film based on his life to three hundred thousand dollars. Well aware of the conventions of show business biographies and experienced in financial negotiations concerning artistic properties, Porter, in order to make a more commercial film, was willing to sign away certain of his biographical rights. To this end, he and his family, including his wife and his mother, signed release forms so that Cary Grant and Alexis Smith could impersonate them in a film that bore only the most superficial resemblance to their actual lives. Porter's contract stipulated that

> it is understood that Producer in development of the story . . . upon which the photoplay shall be based shall be free to dramatize, fictionalize, or emphasize any or all incidents in the life of Seller, or interpolate such incidents as Producers may deem necessary in order to obtain a treatment or continuity of commercial value. (USC, Warners Collection, *Night and Day* file contract, p. 6)

Porter realized that the events in his life were not necessarily the same as a story of his life. The direct remuneration and untold free publicity such a film of his life would generate were worth the distortions of the strange concoction that was eventually made.

Normalizing Genius

Every life presented scenarists and producers with different kinds of problems in narratization. These problems could concern condensation of events, censorship, legal entanglements with surviving relatives, and, absorbing all of these considerations, Hollywood's shifting conventions on what constituted a life worth depicting. In the Porter case, there were more than the usual number of obstacles to overcome. Warners' solutions to these problems illustrate the machinery of studio production at its most characteristic.[3]

Porter himself seemed as adept as any Warners writer at constructing the narrative of his own life. Although he and Linda Lee Porter, his elegant wife, were publicly associated with the glamorous world of opening nights, Porter was also part of a less public, often covert world. Porter was gay in an era when public acknowledgment of homosexuality was, in most instances, not possible. While every member of a minority group has his or her life mediated through the perceptions of mainstream culture, sexual minorities present different problems of representation, both in movies and in their own presentation of self in everyday life. Unlike many ethnic, national, or other minorities who can't "pass" because of certain physical characteristics, the gay man or lesbian can, if he or she so desires, adopt the various public postures associated with heterosexuality. Thus Porter carried on a very active gay life in private, while his public life as a married cosmopolite was much chronicled in gossip columns. His wife, Linda, was, according to Lawrence Bergreen (1990), a lesbian. Although aware of his gay life, Linda had reached a mutual accommodation with her husband vis-à-vis his (and presumably her) sex life. Simply stated, Porter could act on his gay desires as long as he publicly played straight. Charles Schwartz, a biographer of Porter, notes that Linda Porter's main concern about Cole's gay life was "that if word got out to the media of how he was carrying on, it would be terribly damaging to his reputation and career" (1977 : 176). Having constructed a front of heterosexuality in his real life, for Porter aiding Warners in perpetuating this artifice was, from his established perspective, in his best interest. Porter bought into the values of the culture that repressed him and other gays and lesbians by energetically putting up the front of heterosexuality and marriage, the values of the world of the Breen Office. Films like *Night and Day,* and men like Cole Porter, merely reinforce a kind of sexual hegemony through their willful banishing of gay elements from their respective scripts. Thus, a history the movies won't make (that of the Cole Porter whose witty songs of "Love for Sale" could have referred to his taste for male hustlers) becomes a nonhistory that is relegated to a kind of symbolic netherworld of alternative, nonmainstream sources. For Hollywood as a sustainer of the social status quo, the first problem of picturing a life, then, might be to eliminate those areas that the culture tells us should not exist.[4]

The second problem of a life is dealing "properly" with the elements that *are* deemed worthy of existence. Porter's marriage to the older, wealthy Linda Lee was hardly the stuff of other Warners biopics of this period. Full of periods of estrangement due to his extramarital affairs, his marriage would be unfilmable were the facts ever brought to the attention of the Breen Office. Of course, since homosexuality (section 2, subsection 4 of the 1934 Production Code) was so far beyond the pale of discussable topics in the 1940s, the nature of the marriage never surfaced as a debatable issue. Nevertheless, while his marriage was a fact, its cinematic depiction—deemed a necessary part of the great-life package—was pure Hollywood.

Additionally, Porter in his social attitudes was not the lofty, benevolent individual that a great man, in the mold of George Arliss, was supposed to be. As Charles Schwartz has suggested in his biography of Porter, Porter was more than a bit of a snob and at times even quite bigoted. Although born in Peru, Indiana, he did not identify with middle America but with the New York–Paris–Beverly Hills axis. He was not Will Rogers. On the surface, Porter's life was hardly the stuff of inspiration for movie audiences.

The Porter life, or rather a story based on a life, had much that could be inspiring. In addition to the wealth of words and music that were strong selling points with various sheet music and record tie-ins, there was Porter's very real courage in overcoming a crippling riding accident that in 1937 left him, at age forty-five, nearly paralyzed and in excruciating pain. Here, then, in Porter's fight to resume his life and career in the aftermath of his accident, was a Zanuck rooting interest. And, if this particular angle was not enough of a lure for audiences, Warners could—and did—invent other attractions.

A memo of 7 July 1943, to production head Hal Wallis outlined a strategy:

> The life of Cole Porter can be a "wholesome" story. It is the triumph of the hick. It will be doubly amusing because he triumphs as a sophisticate. . . . Mr. Porter's life, though rich in incident, follows a simple, straight story line.
>
> My talk with Mr. Porter convinces me he will show a very cooperative attitude. He recognizes the plot needs of movie entertainment and agrees to interpretations that will assist the picture's box office.

The memo further suggests guidelines that would help the film's box office. Certain facts of Porter's life would have to be rewritten. Porter had inherited a sizable fortune from his grandfather, and prior to his success as a composer he had, supported by his grandfather's and his wife's money, led a somewhat frivolous life. The average viewer, it was reasoned, would hardly find these circumstances—inherited wealth and the seeming absence of a work ethic—congruent with American values. By foregrounding Porter's struggles and physical tragedy, rather than his rather freewheeling lifestyle, and by redefining his relationship with his wife to conform to existing norms of glamorous heterosexual romance, the film could be inspirational. *Night and Day* became the wholesome story Wallis foresaw, the tale of a fellow who, given the gift of music (which he generously shared on the Warners soundtrack) nevertheless created (with the aid of his adoring, loving wife) his greatest work in his triumph over pain. Charm and surface had been transformed into character and depth, and marginalized sexual behavior, first eliminated, was then reclothed in the appropriate costumes.

Researchers assigned to *Night and Day* were less interested in the value of Porter's life and more concerned with getting its facts in the proper order. Only if the order were so shuffled as to be virtually entropic would this disturb the values of the researcher. The head of research, Herman Lissauer, focused his skills not on the amorous numbers in Porter's love life but on the chronology of the hit Porter songs that were to appear in the film. In a memo of 20 April 1944, he noted, "A great many songs are out of their proper dates, and I am sure that this is unavoidable as our script is written. However, some of the songs are ascribed to periods so far away from their correct dates it is inevitable that both audience and critics should see the discrepancy right away."[5] In *Night and Day,* the title song appears some fifteen years ahead of its actual composition. But this chronological gaffe was an intentional strategic gamble; Warners traded off the few people who might spot this slip for the role the song played in motivating Porter's love for his wife. In the film, then, he is shown composing the song at the front during World War I, musing about his absent love. His heterosexual romantic desire motivates the specific composition, nicely normalizing the composer, enabling audiences to view the song as a valentine to marriage and love.

In addition to chronology, since many of the participants in the Porter story were living, a number of the research questions were integrally tied in with legal considerations. To assist producers in understanding possible legal problems, Lissauer, as was common practice on biopics, supplied the legal department with a list of all characters in the script, identifying them by their status as fictive or real and, if real, living or dead.

For example, in *Night and Day* the character of Carol Hall, even though given a false name in the script, is identifiable as Ethel Merman. Since American law forbids the unauthorized depiction of persons without their consent, regardless of how flattering the portrayal, the appearance of Carol Hall, easily recoded as Merman, was, noted Lissauer, a problem. Further, she is shown making unreciprocated (and invented) advances at Porter, a complication different from the mere unauthorized use of a person's image.

Similar issues adhered to *The Lady with Red Hair,* the story of the divorced Mrs. Leslie Carter (played by Miriam Hopkins) who, having lost custody of her only child in a scandalous divorce (in 1889), takes to the stage as a means of obtaining the money to win back custody of her son. Arriving in New York chaperoned by her naive aunt (Laura Hope Crews in a repeat of her Aunt Pittypat role) unknown, untrained, and unaware of the ways of the theater, she succeeds in gaining the backing of the theatrical genius of the day, David Belasco (Claude Rains). After monumental battles of ego and under the tutelage of the acerbic Belasco, Mrs. Carter triumphs as an actress.

Here, the potential legal problems were twofold. First, David Belasco's heirs, having read the script for the film, did not like the depiction of their famous relative as a rather charming but shallow applause milker who hitched his wagon to the star of Caroline Carter. Unable to disprove the Belasco family's allegations, and fearing a lawsuit, Warners was forced to make some minor changes to please the impresario's surviving family.

Major changes, however, had to be made to accommodate surviving relatives of Mrs. Carter's first (divorced) husband, Leslie Carter. They objected to the unsympathetic depiction of their relative as the cause of the divorce, and Judge Frank Loesch, the Carter family spokesman, wrote Warners attorney Morris Ebenstein that the script libeled his clients Leslie Carter (d. 1908) and Leslie's sister (d. 1933) and that the truth of the Carter divorce, contra the *Lady with Red Hair* script, was that Mrs. Carter's romantic attachments, and not the behavior of Mr. Carter, were the grounds for the granting of the divorce. Although the original script had the wronged Mrs. Carter driven from her own home by an indifferent husband and the machinations of a jealous sister-in-law (it was, after all, allegedly based on Caroline Carter's diaries), creating audience sympathy for the divorced Caroline, the Warners had to bow to the truth of the divorce trial record—and the fear of a lawsuit—and eliminated Mr. Carter as a character from the script. The film thus was reframed as a valiant divorced woman's battle to regain her self-respect and the love of her estranged son after a humiliating and highly public divorce trial. In the modified script, Caroline Carter takes to the stage to defend her honor and make money to win back her son. And, in a scene in which we witness the fusion of jury and audience metaphors, Caroline, on the opening night in her old hometown, wins back her estranged friends in her original community through her acting, followed by a scorching speech from the stage apron. Breaking the barriers established by the proscenium—and those established by class and characterization—Caroline Carter directly addresses her former social contacts, now members of the audience who have come to judge her. Arguing for the virtues of motherhood and American fair play, she scores a personal triumph, as well as a professional one, when a member of the audience seated in the cheap seats turns the tide against the snobbish wealthy audience members who have come to scorn her. As in so many other films that suggest entertainment is truly democratic because it is judged by "the people" (e.g., *The Great Caruso, Yankee Doodle Dandy, Oh, You Beautiful Doll*), the applause of the audience, first started by average and not wealthy audience members, signals their surrender.

After years of experience at biopic research, Lissauer had become adept at anticipating such legal complications and had worked this angle into the normal research procedure for a biopic by notifying the producer of potential trouble with the facts of a life as depicted in a script. In this way, approaches to editing a life became institutionalized procedures at the studio.

Of equal weight to these legal issues were the typical research minutiae on which these departments thrived. Thus, for *Night and Day,* there was a twenty-six-page research inventory of requests, ranging from the correct placement of the Yale insignia on a megaphone to a 31 May 1945 request as to the year electric Christmas ornaments were first used. A good deal of research attention was given to material that would be used by other departments to create a factual mise-en-scène. These facts—like the historically accurate Christmas decorations—would be mixed with the other rearranged facts that constituted the film's narrative. It could be argued that research supplied the raw materials that would then be rearranged by a host of architects for legal, moral, economic, and aesthetic reasons. The resulting structure, at times, bore only a faint resemblance to the initial blueprint. It was not uncommon, then, to have invented characters moving implausibly, without a trace of irony, through historically accurate sets. The research for any given film was both ubiquitous and submerged, carefully attended to and willfully ignored.

For the producers of biopics, historical accuracy was not the foremost concern. While well aware of the role history might play in these films (Zanuck, for example, could be most articulate on poetic license in Fox biopics), for the most part producers were more concerned with crafting a film narrative that would win audience sympathy, thereby selling tickets. For producers, historicity and accuracy were attractive as long as they remained selling points.

Notes

1. See Brown (1973) for an early account of the organized research efforts, particularly in the art department, for D. W. Griffith's monumental film *Intolerance* (1916).

2. The very choice of the term *bible* used to describe these guides suggests their authoritativeness when it comes to interpreting questions of fact and history in the biopic.

3. Sometimes obstacles to portraying a biopic life could come from forces outside the producing studio. This occurred with Fox's film on the life of Stephen Foster, *Swanee River*. After Hedda Hopper had suggested, in her column of 4 September 1939, published in the *Washington Post* and other papers carrying her byline, that the film would portray Foster as "inebriated in nearly every scene," letters lamenting this possible denigration of Foster poured into Fox from shocked educators and sundry Stephen Foster societies. After years of "laundering" lives to fit the studio's and the Motion Picture Producers and Distributors of America's concept of public morality, in this instance, readers at the Breen Office merely cautioned Fox to follow the guidelines used to depict the use of alcohol in any film (section 1, subsection 4 of the Production Code) and, despite proposed boycotts, no changes were made in the film script.

4. This fact of Porter's life—his homosexuality—illustrates the difficulty of doing institutional histories of film based on written material alone. Simply stated, that which can't be discussed or written about ceases to exist as archival data. These "holes" in the language—the refusal to commit to writing about certain practices parallel similar gaps in the subject matter of the film life. The author is forced to use secondary material and, interestingly, material often not deemed officially appropriate for serious academic study, like Kenneth Anger's hugely entertaining *Hollywood Babylon* (1975). Often only in such nonmainstream media sources can banished or taboo behavior be chronicled at all. Academic standards of proof can be as repressive as the culture they seek to illuminate.

5. One reason researchers were convinced that some semblance to the actual chronology of a life should be maintained was the mail they received from viewers who attended to such perceived factual errors. It was not uncommon for vigilant viewers to write to research departments and point out mistakes that marred their enjoyment of the film, and studios expected mail from "specialists" who, with their trained eyes and ears, would pick out problems average audience members might ignore.

Works Cited

Bergreen, Lawrence. 1990. *As Thousands Cheer: The Life of Irving Berlin*. New York: Viking.

Bordwell, David, Janet Staiger, and Kirstin Thompson. 1985. *The Classical Hollywood Cinema: Film Style and Mode of Production to 1960*. New York: Columbia University Press.

Brown, Karl. 1973. *Adventures with D. W. Griffith*. Edited by Kevin Brownlow. New York: Farrar, Straus and Siroux.

Milliken, Carl. 1940. Information Please. *The Warner Club News* (June).

Schwartz, Charles. 1977. *Cole Porter: A Biography*. New York: Dial Press.

11

Making *Bitter Harvest*

Todd Gitlin

If an idea rings bells for subordinate and chief alike in a network-TV movie division, then they go after producers and writers to write scripts. Ninety percent of the time, though, producers and agents pitch their ideas first. Either way, the network has the upper hand. It knows what it doesn't want even if it doesn't know what it wants. Producers have to tailor their pitches to the standard conventions, and eventually the script has to match the network's version of the dramatic verities—characters should be simple and simply motivated, heroes familiar, stories full of conflict, endings resolved, uplift apparent, and each act should end on a note of suspense sufficient to carry the viewer through the commercial break. Wherever the idea originates, the development and approval process is the same. Aspiring producers and writers learn that it makes sense to arrive for the pitch meeting with appropriate article or book in hand, certifying that the project comes already equipped with mass popularity and significance.

When a project snakes its way into a producer's hands from more obscure sources, it is harder to sell, though not impossible. When the project is out of the ordinary and the sell is harder, then the television–industrial complex must come into play, and personal connections count all the more heavily. The disposition of a single executive or a star might make all the difference. The production company has to have a solid track record. The paradox is that, when all these usual elements are in place, the product stands a chance of being unusual. A case in point is *Bitter Harvest,* a 1981 movie made for NBC, based on the actual poisoning of most of Michigan's cattle by a mispackaged chemical and loosely derived from the 1978 book of the same name written by a Michigan farmer, Frederic Halbert, and his wife, Sandra.

Bitter Harvest starred Ron Howard, one-time child star in *The Music Man* and the long-running *Andy Griffith Show* and later a teenage star in *Happy Days.* Howard played a farmer whose cattle sicken, whose child develops rashes, and who gradually, against the lassitude and callousness of the state's health bureaucracy, traces the illness to a toxic fire retardant, polybrominated biphenyl (PBB), that had been mistakenly mixed into cattle feed. More children and adults sicken; the state still refuses to quarantine the poisoned cattle or ban their milk. Finally, to alert the populace, the farmer kills his own cattle. The show drew a good Nielsen rating of 18.0 and a handsome 29 percent share of the viewing audience, although promotion had been botched and major affiliates in Philadelphia and Dallas didn't carry the movie at all. It drew four Emmy nominations. The writer won a Writers Guild of America Award, among others, for his script. Yet the picture came within inches of not getting made.

Bitter Harvest began with an earnest, unflashy young man named Richard Friedenberg, who had directed, among other films, a feature called *Grizzly Adams* he thought so contemptible that its enormous box-office success filled him with disgust. He had also directed on television for a while until he lost interest, whereupon he decided to see if he could write. In his diffident way, Friedenberg admired Italian neorealism, especially Vittorio De Sica's *Bicycle Thief* and *Umberto D.,* from which he extracted the idea that TV movies could tell small personal stories that revealed the larger society. Like most young Hollywood writers trying to get noticed, he wrote "spec scripts," scripts on speculation, and sold nothing. "I have a totally uncommercial mind," he says, and so he was unemployed for months on end. Whenever he came up with an idea, his agent told him, "Forget it," and Friedenberg started looking for a new agent.

Friedenberg was a loner, a conscientious objector to the Hollywood glad-handing circuit; and he had the odd habit, from a Hollywood point of view, of reading a magazine called *Country Journal,* where one day in early 1979 he noticed an article about a Michigan farmer, Ric Halbert, who had campaigned to get the state to do something about his poisoned cattle. To Friedenberg this sounded like a television story, a large issue on a small scale, but his old agent was as usual less than enthusiastic. Friedenberg liked the Michigan idea well enough to try it out, among other ideas, on a sympathetic agent named Norman Stevens.

Any television deal brings a producer, a writer, and often a star into conjunction with an executive, often through the mediation of an agent, and all at the right time. Accidents happen, yet even accidents have a history; happy accidents happen to people who get into the right places often enough at the right times. Friedenberg's new agent happened to intersect with a bright young producer, Tony Ganz, who had been to Harvard, worked in documentaries on PBS's *Great American Dream Machine,* and then gone to work for a successful producer named Charles Fries at the Metromedia conglomerate. When Fries went off and set up his own company, Ganz went with him as a producer. Charles Fries Productions became one of the pillars of the TV-movie business and over the years sold some forty movies to the networks.

In the spring of 1979, just as the Love Canal chemical dump was becoming national news, Three Mile Island was stopping the national heart, and *The China Syndrome* was growing into a national media event, Charles Fries happened to go to a meeting that Fred Silverman also attended. Within Fries's earshot, Silverman turned to Norman Lear and said that the Love Canal story was interesting and that someone should do a movie of the week about it. The next day Fries sent a note to Ganz and Malcolm Stuart, his partner in the Fries Productions Development Department, repeating this conversation and saying, "Is this of any interest to you? See if you can follow this up."

Ganz knew barely anything about Love Canal, by his own account, so he did some research that convinced him Love Canal "wasn't the right story, but a story about chemical pollution seemed like an exciting idea." He began talking to Hollywood agents, writers, and New York agents who handled new nonfiction manuscripts. After several months of looking, he had failed to find anything that lent itself to the dramatic boundaries of a small-screen movie. "One day—this is where the accident happened—" he recalls,

> I went into Malcolm's office, and he was on the phone, so the man who was sitting in his office had no one to talk to until I walked in, and his name was Norman Stevens, and he was Friedenberg's agent—I guess he had just signed him. None of this would have happened if Malcolm hadn't been on the phone, because I would have asked him what I was going to ask him and left. Stevens said, "What are you looking for?"—typical agent kind of question—and usually the answer to that question is "Jesus Christ, anything I can, anything that's interesting that I can sell." But in this case I had a better answer.

Ganz told Stevens he was looking for something like Love Canal.

The next day, Friedenberg was in Stevens's office reeling off a list of possible story ideas. Halfway through the Michigan cattle story, Stevens stopped him. "Hold the thought," he said. Stevens picked up the phone, dialed Tony Ganz, and set up an appointment.

Ganz didn't treat his first conversation with Stevens all that seriously until Friedenberg came in and told him Ric Halbert's story. Then he paid attention, for he heard Friedenberg tick off what he thought were the hallmarks of a workable story: character, visible consequences, visible accomplishment, and the symbolic accoutrements of a morality tale. "I thought it was one of the best stories I had ever heard, period," Ganz says.

> It had at its center a character, which was crucial and something that was missing in most of the other stories that I had heard. They tended to be group efforts at stopping chemical dumping, and that sort of thing. And there was a victory involved, but it wasn't too pat—I mean, it was a sort of hollow victory, or Pyrrhic, in the end. Nine million people were contaminated. There was just this guy, who at least sounded the alarm, and made certain connections that everyone else refused to believe in. And it had strong central characters. And it was in the middle of the country which is a landscape that appealed to me.

Ganz has his own recombinant repertoire of movie precedents.

> It was the same landscape as *Friendly Fire*. I didn't think *Friendly Fire* was a masterpiece . . . but I loved the way it looked, and I loved that it wasn't New York or Los Angeles or on either coast. I went to school in Vermont, so I knew cows a little, and I liked cows. They're big, stupid, and dumb. They're sort of like us, in fact. They do what they're told. They don't fight back. In the end, they go into the pit, and they get slaughtered, which is what we're doing to ourselves. The cows also made visible the effects of the poison. In most of those other stories no one really gets sick. It's an *it,* in the water table, or where there's radiation leaking from a *China Syndrome* plant, and you can't really dramatize it. The cows got sick, and you had to take them out back and shoot them, just like in *Hud*. It was a terrific story. It just all worked.

The idea went first to CBS, where executives passed, saying that the *Lou Grant* series had already done an episode on the PBB poisoning; they didn't want movies to duplicate series. *Bitter Harvest* then went to ABC, where an executive said she liked the story but, after all, the switch of the fire retardant for the cattle growth additive was an accident, so where was the drama, where were the good guys and the bad guys? Reasoning of this sort has the effect of prohibiting TV movies from depicting the social structures that make accidents routine, even, paradoxically, predictable. A company that permitted the two chemicals to be packed in similar sacks, one pile next to the other, could not be held accountable by a dramatic form that refused to recognize the normality of evil.

NBC, the third buyer in town, was widely believed to be so overloaded with commitments and so short of capital that there seemed no sense pitching to them. The idea of *Bitter Harvest* therefore languished for several months. Then it received the blessing of the Hollywood gods, who move through revolving doors.

One of Ganz's producer colleagues at Fries Productions was an experienced TV hand named Irv Wilson, a magnetic, gregarious man who had shuttled through every cranny of the TV business, from ad agency to Universal Studios to talent agency to the NBC Programming Department. In fact, Irv Wilson had helped pioneer the development of TV movies at NBC. He was not always averse to TV fluff. He owned up to having devised *The Harlem Globetrotters on Gilligan's Island* during his second tenure at NBC, and while he was there NBC aired *Enola Gay,* a romance about the bomber mission that dropped the atomic bomb on Hiroshima. But Wilson was possessed of an uncommonly active social conscience. Born into a Depression-era working-class family in the Bronx, he had been instructed by the social-problem movies that Warner Brothers produced in the thirties and forties. He had worked for Henry Wallace in the presidential campaign of 1948. Although Wilson was no longer committed to any particular political position, he did think television entertainment had a responsibility to be more than entertaining, at least some of the time. While still with Fries, Wilson bought his *Los Angeles Times* one morning and read the first in a series of articles called "The Poisoning of America." "It was incredible," he recalls, "and Tony came in one morning, and we were talking about it, and he said he had met a writer who had a story that he had heard, Richard Friedenberg, that was a true story, and he thought it was fantastic. I said, 'Gee, you ought to do something about that.'"

Then Fred Silverman tapped his old friend Irv Wilson to run NBC's West Coast Specials Department, which was to include whatever Wilson could pass off as "a special movie." As soon as Wilson told Ganz about his impending move, Ganz enlisted him for an unusual sort of pitch meeting at NBC with an executive named Dennis Considine. "Dennis," as Ganz put it later, "was in the curious position of being pitched to by the man who was about to be his boss, and he knew it. So at the end of [Friedenberg's] telling the story, he looked at

Irv and said, 'Well, what do you think?' And Irv said, 'I think it's great and we should buy it.' I had never been in a meeting like that; it was really fun."

Wilson was sold by the time he got to NBC, but NBC was piled high with movie commitments that extended back years. Ganz kept calling Wilson, and Wilson kept saying, "Someday I'll get it through for you," but right then NBC was only making movies to fulfill existing commitments. There was no money for new deals. Six more months passed. Dick Friedenberg gave up for the second time and busied himself with other futile projects. But Wilson was biding his time. Then *Time* magazine came out with a cover story called "The Poisoning of America."[1] As Wilson remembers it, "On the cover of *Time* was a guy being swallowed up by this crap in the ground. And I showed it to Brandon Tartikoff, and he says, 'All right, write the script.'" Wilson was sure that the *Time* cover had made the difference.

Ganz and Friedenberg were jubilant, but almost immediately they had to worry about possible network censorship. As soon as NBC headquarters in New York learned of the project, they "red-flagged" it as a possible legal risk. Ganz didn't know how seriously to take New York's concern, but he decided to test the waters. He called up an NBC attorney named Barbara Hering, whose job was to inspect movies based on fact for potentially litigable issues. He found Hering to be, as he put it, "at once supportive and pleasant and, on the other hand, guarded and realistic that it was not going to be an easy project." Ganz made an astute decision. He decided to level with Hering.

> If you're too careful in the beginning and you write a sort of compromise script keeping one eye open for legal problems, you won't even get to test the legal problems. So I said to her, "Look, it seems to me, unless you disagree, that we should just proceed now as best we can, being somewhat careful but writing the story as it happened." And she said, "Yes, do it that way, and then let me see it."

Ganz was still apprehensive about how to handle the company, the governor, and the Michigan bureaucracy but decided to save his worries for later. "It is impossible to get reliable, consistent answers from anybody about what you can and cannot do. So if you react too soon you could be reacting to the wrong thing."

Instead of handing in the usual first or second version, Friedenberg and Ganz were inordinately careful and handed in a fourth or fifth draft. NBC program executives waxed enthusiastic, asking them only routine questions about dramatic structure: What was the proper balance between the time before and after the farmer ascertains the source of the illness? Couldn't there be more scenes between the farmer and his wife? "They asked a lot of questions," Ganz recalls, "and I think without exception they were questions that we had asked ourselves and tried eleven different ways."

Irv Wilson knew, meanwhile, that success would depend on the hero's appeal and had for a long time been thinking about Ron Howard, a surefire TV draw. Wilson later thought his major achievement at NBC was to have nudged Ron Howard's career toward serious drama. The first movie Wilson had pushed through at NBC was *Act of Love,* a movie about euthanasia committed by one brother on another. He had persuaded the producers that Ron Howard had just the kind of likable image to sweep the audience into sympathy. And—all-important to getting a movie about euthanasia made—NBC had commitments to Howard.

Now Wilson saw Howard as box office again: "The first time I met him I loved him, because he reminded me of today's Jimmy Stewart. Every Frank Capra picture you want to make, you could recast Ron Howard, and it's smashing, because he is the all-American boy who is so pure and so fucking honest, and good, and decent." *Act of Love* should have been depressing, by TV standards, yet it garnered high numbers, a 21.7 rating and 35 share. So in the case of *Bitter Harvest,* Wilson's argument for Ron Howard met no resistance. "Jimmy Stewart could have played that part, right," Wilson said. "*Bitter Harvest* was a Frank Capra movie," one idealistic, responsible man against the system. Karen Danaher, a forceful and socially conscious former junior high school teacher and TV newswoman, whom Wilson had brought into the NBC Movie Department, had the same feeling. "When I read the script," she says, "I knew we had to get a TV star that people could trust." When Ganz saw a cassette of Howard's dramatic performance in *Act of Love,* he was convinced. Wilson fired the script off to Howard, and he was sold on it immediately. So the *Time* cover made possible the writing of the script; the script garnered Ron Howard; Howard sold the show. For the smaller part of Howard's farmer neighbor, NBC brought up Art Carney, another piece of offbeat casting. Carney was expensive, but the network was willing to spend the money for what, in effect, was insurance. Howard's agreement, and Carney's, neutralized the opposition of the affable and cautious Perry Lafferty, NBC's West Coast senior vice president for programs, who reported directly to Brandon Tartikoff. "I had a lot of reservations about it," Lafferty says, "because I didn't know whether the audience would be interested in such a disagreeable subject. It's got Ron Howard and Art Carney, and you can make a good promo on it and take a good ad. But for me, I thought it was very tough, and material that I've heard about before." Novelty that was *too* novel was out of bounds; novelty not novel enough was stale. "You've had the chemical wastes and all that stuff over and over and over. I didn't think it was going to be that big a ratings-gatherer." Lafferty had often been a conservative voice in high NBC circles; he had resisted *Hill Street Blues* as well. This time he was overruled.

From then on, *Bitter Harvest* went through the network screening process without much tampering. Ganz remained apprehensive, but Hering was satisfied. "They really did a first-class job on the hard facts," she says,

> whether there had been real negligence bordering on reckless negligence in the factory, which led to the mix-up; whether the Agriculture Department had really been bound down by red tape, or whatever the cause, but failing to do what was necessary to take strong steps to stop a problem that was clearly very serious. All of those things were very, very heavily substantiated. You get into charges like that, and you have to worry a little bit, because you're making serious claims against important institutions and organizations. If justified by the facts, the program performs a public service, but if the facts are not as portrayed, the possible undermining of the public's faith in their institutions would be not only unfair to the institutions but a real disservice to our audience. It's not the same when the story is about a guy who is truly anonymous, in that he might be any one of hundreds of people, and whose story, however interesting, is simply personal.

A few changes were dictated for legal reasons. For one thing, Fries Productions' insurance company demanded that the name of the state of Michigan be taken out. Ganz wanted to keep Michigan, for verisimilitude's sake, but NBC backed the insurance company, and Ganz went along. Michigan became "the state." Later on, Ganz regretted the sacrifice of realism. But it could equally well be argued that the very generality of "the state" made the story more universal and more powerful. This poisoning did happen somewhere, but it could have happened—it could still happen—anywhere. The names of the Michigan Chemical Co. and Michigan Farm Bureau Services, Inc., the companies responsible for the chemical switch, were also changed, but this was Friedenberg's doing. Even the earliest outlines Friedenberg had worked up for Ganz had used the pseudonym United Chemical. Ganz felt no particular moral outrage toward these particular companies. After all, they had paid millions of dollars in claims. So he did not care about this change, any more than he cared about the change in the farmer-hero's name from Ric Halbert to Ned DeVries. Such changes are standard in the movie-based-on-fact format. They afford legal protection and may even contribute to the movie's aura of familiarity. If the audience knows that a character is no more than "based on" a living person, the character comes closer to Everyman. The farmer Ned escapes from the singularity of Ric Halbert and is pulled closer to Ron Howard playing Ned, and therefore to Ron Howard, the trustable, Jimmy Stewart–style actor.

Hering intervened on only one script issue. Late in the movie comes a scene in which Ned tries to alert another farmer, a tense and conscience-stricken man who has unknowingly—or so he says—sold his poisoned milk on the market. The farmer pulls at his son's hair to show Ned—it is a wig. There are bald patches all over the child's scalp. Barbara Hering questioned the accuracy of this vignette. "If the bald patches and wig were true, they could be shown; but not otherwise." Ganz was also asked not to linger on this shot, "because," he was told, "we are not out to scare people needlessly." No matter. Brief as it is, the moment in the film when the farmer pulls away his child's hair remains shocking. Real people were really hurt. That was what happened when Michigan was poisoned.

As the script went through refinement after refinement, though, one potentially troublesome line kept nagging at Ganz. When Ned finds out the nature of the toxic chemical in his cattle feed, he races home, triumphant, to tell his wife about PBB. "What on earth is that?" she asks. In early versions of the script, Ned answers, "It's a fire retardant. It's used for TV sets so they don't burn up." Ganz knew that RCA, which owned NBC, also manufactured television sets. "I knew NBC would say something." He consulted with friendly West Coast programming executives. Although Barbara Hering had never flagged this line—it was a problem of corporate public relations, after all, not the law—one executive feared that someone above Hering in the New York chain of command might raise a fuss. Knowing that the red flag of controversy was already flying over the project, and not caring exactly what PBB was used for, Ganz decided on discretion–self-censorship, some might call it. "I was concerned," he said afterward, "that something like that could blow the whole goddamned project." At a late stage of the script, he changed the line to: "It's a fire retardant. They put it in plastics or something."

Another political point flattened during the shooting was a borderline case that couldn't be laid at the door of the network—or, for that matter, the audience. Dr. Freeman, Ned's medical angel, testifies before a state committee in favor of a cattle quarantine. In the middle of a long speech about the effects of PBB—about its permanent presence in the bodies of those who eat the meat or drink the milk from the poisoned cattle, about effects that might even skip a generation—the script had Freeman say, "And don't think it's an isolated case. There are thirty-five thousand other chemicals out there that are unsafe, and they're being spilled and dumped and buried all over the planet." During the shooting in the dairy country of northern California, at the last minute, Tony Ganz and the director, Roger Young, decided Freeman's speech was too long—almost a minute and a half. These lines seemed to them the most expendable. "We didn't want to get didactic," Ganz said. "It seemed too much a documentary statement. We felt that, given the reality of that little courtroom in that little town, nobody was thinking about anything but the nightmare of one particular chemical." Friedenberg agreed. To him the issue mattered so little, in fact, that, when I asked him about it just after the shooting, he couldn't remember whether the line had stayed in or not. But Richard Dysart, the actor who played Freeman, was disturbed about the cut. He thought this was the one moment when *Bitter Harvest* generalized from PBB to make a larger point about the chemical industry. Freeman was speaking directly to the audience. After the cut, was the story of PBB narrowed into a single dreadful exception, "an isolated case"?

Ganz and Friedenberg thought not. They believed they made the larger point by hewing close to the story of PBB. They adhered to the prevailing aesthetic of small scale, in which the general point is inherent in the particular, and indeed their claim cannot be dismissed out of hand. True, any cut, in a literal sense, changes the meaning of the whole. To make this simple point is my bias; it is the bias of all close readers of texts, especially those who claim to ferret out the traces of political censorship or the virtues of political expression. But I confess I am not altogether convinced by the literal-mindedness of such criticism, especially as it bears on a medium that rushes lines past us at an irreversibly fast pace. Lines that break radically with the expected level of discourse might be more memorable, therefore more effective, especially when they come from the authoritative Freeman; or conceivably a general message buried amid the specific, in the context of the small-scale story, goes by so fast as to be lost with or without such individual lines. The tools for assessing the effects of lines are too crude to tell us anything.

Whatever the effect of this or that line, it is clear that Ganz, Friedenberg, and all other "docudramatists," simply by accepting the conventions of their form are committing a kind of self-censorship. Television docudrama abhors what it considers polemic, didacticism, speechifying. Convention clamps a tight frame around the story. It doesn't want the larger public world leaking in. The soapbox is forbidden furniture. This convention of the small, restricted, realistic story has ideological consequences. It has the effect of keeping the show compact, narrow, simplified. Indeed, coherence is defined as narrowness, and not just in the thinking of the writers but audiences, too. It is the dramatic aesthetic that prevails in this culture. Such conventions are shared, not imposed. When they are shared long enough and deeply enough, they harden into the collective second nature of a cultural style. True, against restriction there arises a counterconvention based on audience identification with the normal. If Ron Howard is Everyman, and if his fictional state is Everystate, and if Ron Howard's cows and child and neighbors are at risk, then in imagination everyone is at risk. But there is still a difference between saying that PBB is in the body cells of virtually everyone in Everystate and warning that there are thousands of other dangerous chemicals—that PBB is, in a way, Everychemical.

Bitter Harvest further restricts the meaning of the problem of chemicals. What, after all, is the source of Ned's troubles? It is expressed most pointedly in NBC's promo, where the voice-over says breathlessly, "And now: Ron Howard in *Bitter Harvest,* the true story of one man's triumphant battle against the bureaucracy. His cattle were dying and no one would help."

This accurately defines the movie's main line of tension: Ned's care played off against the heedlessness of the agricultural bureaucrats. The state is no true guardian of bucolic peace; from the opening shot—acoustic guitar and flute sounding a sweet, wistful melody over a shot of Ned and his wife feeding their calves from giant baby bottles—we understand that Ned is that guardian. Later, when the cattle start drying up, Ned gets the bureaucrats to conduct tests, which come out negative. The bureaucrats outrage Ned by suggesting that he is guilty of bad management. These unkind and uncaring men claim knowledge and impugn both his skill and his care. But Ned has been to college and can't be so easily intimidated. He fights to reclaim his title to both knowledge and care.

The question the movie poses is, Who really knows and who really cares? When Ned presses the agricultural inspectors to undertake further tests, they protest that they aren't a research laboratory. In other words, they really aren't in the business of knowing. He has to shame them with direct evidence. He trusts his intuitions about his cattle and his methods; while bureaucrats play by the book, the farmer and lover of animals is the real investigator. Persistence leads Ned to direct action. Behind a wall in his barn he finds a pile of rats that have died from eating his feed; and when the bureaucrats continue to put him off, he dumps the rats onto their conference table. Ned's devoted search for the truth pays off when he shames a state technician into performing one more test. This gives him the data to find help in the person of Dr. Freeman, the good scientist freed from bureaucratic fetters, the crusty spirit of truth seeking incarnate. In the end, though, even antibureaucratic truth seeking proves insufficient, and Ned has to take direct action again. The cost is terrible, all those cows shot down; but even at this traumatic moment Ned demonstrates he is closer to the cows than any remote bureaucrat.

The written text ("crawl") and simultaneous voice-over that follow give Ned credit for a victory but indicate that bureaucrats will still be bureaucrats:

After Ned DeVries killed his herd, public pressure forced the state to start testing livestock for contamination. Over five hundred farms were closed. Thirty thousand cattle were driven into mass graves and slaughtered. It was not until two years later, in 1976, that testing was finally begun on state residents. Ninety percent of the people tested showed levels of PBB. Another year passed before a law was enacted to eliminate all contaminated meat and milk from the marketplace. It is now estimated that eight million men, women, and children carry the toxic chemical PBB inside their bodies.

Ned expects the state to help; he is a citizen, and he feels entitled to public health. When the bureaucracy derails his rights, he crusades. But never in *Bitter Harvest* does he couple his fury against the state with any comparable attack on the company. There is one scene in which he joins a state team investigating the factory where the PBBs were substituted for a cattle feed additive. Ned shows disgust, but he never takes up the cudgel against the company. He claims no entitlement against the private economy. The corporate decisions that produced PBB and similar chemicals, the mentality that relies on them, the slack shop-floor conditions that permitted such substitutions are never mentioned; by the convention of the hero-centered narrative, the corporate bureaucracy remains invisible.

Ned, and the movie, accept the political-economic division of labor: the company should manufacture; the government should regulate. This keeps the movie on the normal side of American ideology—yet without making it conservative, as Americans measure the term. The corporation is more forgotten than forgiven, while the most visible blame is the government's for not regulating well. Although Ned is a lone hero, his rugged individualism departs from the kind celebrated in the speeches of Ronald Reagan. In fact, *Bitter Harvest* cleverly turns the Reagan view of the world on its head. In Reaganism, "bureaucracy" and "regulation" are inseparable evils. In the movie, bureaucracy, not regulation, is to blame. Ned shows that the public urgently needs regulation, while bureaucracy obstructs it. Citizens then have to act to force the government to live up to its legitimate calling. If this sounds familiar, it is not only the Frank Capra formula of the thirties but also the crusading image that brought both Jimmy Carter and Ronald Reagan to power. All hail to the outsider who takes up the call to clean the Augean stables! The hero's foray into politics brings about the public good. In that sense, *Bitter Harvest* was deep in the grain of American political mythology.

If the forte of everyday American screenwriting is the short, flat line, *Bitter Harvest* put it to good use. The movie was movingly understated, sharply directed, and well photographed (including a lovely sequence of the live birth of a calf)—in short, one of the best of its breed. Shot in a breathtakingly intense and underaverage eighteen days, on a budget of $1.8 million—at the low end of the TV-movie range—it didn't look as if it had been prefabricated on the back lot. On the weakest network, even without two major affiliates, Philadelphia and Dallas–Fort Worth, the show won its time slot handily. As a rural show, it had the advantage of a lead-in from a rural series, the popular *Little House on the Prairie* (from which, significantly, it lost no audience). It beat out *M*A*S*H* and *Lou Grant* on CBS and another serious movie on ABC.

Under such conditions, an above-average share might have suggested that Americans were concerned about major social issues and interested in straightforward dramatic representations of likable Americans grappling with them. Yet *Bitter Harvest* made barely a ripple on network consciousness. The day after it aired, I overheard one ABC executive say to another, "They claim this *Bitter Harvest* was high [i.e., clear and simple] concept. What high concept? All it was was a bunch of sick cows." Robert Greenwald, an independent producer who was pushing hard to make a CBS movie about Love Canal, grumbled that the networks would attribute *Bitter Harvest*'s success to Ron Howard, period. The networks were more comfortable drawing negative conclusions from the ratings failure of a run of social-issue movies than taking the chance of offending their nervous affiliates or advertisers or any other powerful institutions or blocs of viewers. Only an executive with conviction would have bothered to use the success of *Bitter Harvest* to fight such a drift toward the bland; and politically committed executives, even politically interested ones, were rare. Indeed, within a year of going to New York as NBC's senior vice president for programming, Irv Wilson was on his way back to Los Angeles as an independent producer, and by then the projects he was pitching were less political than ever before.

The reasons were a little obscure, but constant frustration was certainly one of them. Wilson's imagination didn't usually transcend the normal TV-movie conventions, but one project he pushed at NBC was an uplift story called *300 Miles for Stephanie,* based on a true story of a Hispanic policeman in Texas, father of a mortally ill little daughter, who decided to run three hundred miles to declare his faith. Wilson wasn't religious, but he liked the fact that the movie was going to star Hispanic actors exclusively. At a certain point, he sensed that the other executives, including Fred Silverman, were stalling.

> I screamed at Fred and everybody else. I said, "If you don't order this movie, they're going to burn the building down. If I was a Mexican, I would bomb this fucking building, because we're doing shit for any of these people. It's our

responsibility to do it." Then I knew that I was in big trouble, because I had a big mouth, and they don't want anybody rocking the boat.

When less-passionate executives than Wilson feel twinges of social conscience, they can buy indulgences with heartwarming stories of non-Hispanic people struggling to overcome handicaps: affliction stories, the kind of movies that one industry influential calls "cripflicks." As one network executive points out, "The networks are always mistaking real social issues for little human-condition stories." For weeks, whenever I told executives I was trying to understand how television dealt with social issues, they proceeded to tell me about movies dealing with alcoholism, cancer, drugs, crippling illness, death, and dying. Writer-producer Carol Evan McKeand (*The Waltons, Family, Second Family Tree*) said she had judged the 1980 television-movie entries for the Humanitas Prize, a high-prestige Hollywood award: "They were all about death and dying." If the preferred stories give us "deviants" at all—homosexuals, criminals, fundamentalists, people of color—the principal attitude they recommend is mild tolerance, which is the cement of a plural order that can't abide basic criticism for fear the fragile cultural balance will tip and the mythological national community decompose.

Network pressure against a political definition of social problems is automatic—so automatic that executives don't construe it as pressure at all. Not only is "innovation" clamped within the iron embrace of the little personal story, but even that category is routinely depoliticized. I mentioned to CBS's Jane Rosenthal, for example, a story the *Los Angeles Times* had been following for several days. A black Pasadena, California, couple wanted to adopt a sixteen-month-old white infant they'd cared for since she was three months old. A court-appointed psychologist said that the child, whose natural mother was of Armenian descent, should be given to an Armenian couple, that she would have a hard time if brought up by black parents. This seemed to me ideal material for a TV movie: potentially gut-wrenching conflict on a small, family scale. I asked Rosenthal whether this was the sort of story that would be suitable for CBS. Without missing a beat, she replied that CBS had in development a story about a child whom a court wants to take from its deaf parents. "It has similar kinds of elements," she said. "We've sort of done the adoptee story, where the court's trying to take the child away. It just sounds like we've seen it before."

Note

1. *Time*, 22 September 1980.

12

And the Band Played On: Searching for Truth

Betsy Sharkey

About twenty-five minutes into *And the Band Played On*—HBO's film about the early years of the AIDS epidemic—a choreographer played by Richard Gere looks out the window of his doctor's office at a gay Halloween parade in the street below. He sees men in skeleton costumes and one dressed as the Grim Reaper. He does not see any groups of men dressed as women. But there were drag queens in the parade scene when it was originally filmed.

The deletion of those images and other similar ones were at the heart of a clash over the emphasis of the two-and-a-quarter-hour film, which had its premiere on HBO at 8:00 P.M. on a Saturday. The central issue was how the gay community would be portrayed: dark and blunt, even if that perpetuated some negative stereotypes, or less confrontational and thus more palatable to both heterosexual and homosexual viewers. Those involved say Hollywood's own ambivalence about homosexuality played a part. In the end, the softer image prevailed. As a consequence, a scene in a gay bathhouse was made shorter and one in which a bookstore owner explains the use of amyl nitrite, or poppers, was cut.

With great difficulty and after six years of controversy, *And the Band Played On* finally made it to the screen with a star-studded cast that, in addition to Mr. Gere, includes Matthew Modine, Ian McKellen, Lily Tomlin, Alan Alda, B. D. Wong, Anjelica Huston, Phil Collins, Steve Martin, and Swoosie Kurtz. The project had three directors and provoked a furious debate not so much about AIDS but about the nature of docudrama, how truth is determined, and whose right it is to decide just what truth is. The issue often comes up in connection with docudrama, but it has been argued most fervently when recent, historical events have been dramatized, as with the films *Mississippi Burning* and Oliver Stone's *JFK.* The literal truth (whether two people ever actually met or had a particular conversation, for instance) is one consideration; a broader truth (what a particular group of people were like at a particular place and time, perhaps) is another.

Like Randy Shilts's book of the same title and on which it is based, the movie *And the Band Played On* attempts to expose the deadly role that inaction and infighting among government officials, blood banks, the scientific community, and segments of the gay community played in the early spread of acquired immune deficiency syndrome. The director, Roger Spottiswoode, believed that the film would be as much a social statement as a dramatic work. It was he who wanted the controversial images to remain. Mr. Shilts thought they should go, and at least one gay rights advocate threatened to mobilize protests if the scenes weren't pulled.

The screenwriter, Arnold Schulman, who wrote twenty drafts of the script, is brutal in his assessment of the production's troubles. "I lived through every issue we dealt with in the movie—egos, greed, politics," he says. "It was a nightmare."

The flurry of interest in turning *And the Band Played On: Politics, People, and the AIDS Epidemic* into a movie began soon after the book was published in October 1987 and appeared on best-seller lists. Mr. Shilts, a correspondent for the *San Francisco Chronicle,* was inundated with movie offers.

"There was that first blast of publicity over the worst stuff, that got a lot of movie interest," says Mr. Shilts. "We were offered one million dollars by a Japanese company to do the Patient Zero story. That was my first condition—no Patient Zero film." (Patient Zero was the name given to a French Canadian flight attendant identified by the United States Centers for Disease Control and Prevention [CDC] as the center of an early cluster of men who contracted AIDS.)

That fall, when television producer Aaron Spelling was home with the flu, a friend sent him a copy of the book and he became interested in adapting it.

Another producer, Edgar Scherick, had read it in manuscript and was also intrigued. "It was a very rich, but very segmented tapestry," says Mr. Scherick, "one that did not appear to me easily rendered to the screen. There was, however, a lot of heat on it."

Mr. Spelling went to ABC, where he had a long-term relationship, but the network passed on the project. Mr. Scherick quickly secured the rights, pitched the book as a miniseries to NBC, got approval to proceed, and hired a writer.

The story was not an easy one to tell, particularly for a medium that relies on a mainstream audience and corporate advertisers rarely known for embracing controversy. Although Mr. Shilts's book deals exhaustively with the science and politics of the disease, homosexuality is clearly the subtext. Any adaptation would likely require an examination of how the sexual practices of some gay men affected the early spread of the virus at the beginning of the 1980s, while Mr. Scherick was interested in exploring the idea that AIDS had emerged "at the height of the gay liberation movement." NBC, he says, had other ideas. (NBC cites its legacy of dealing with AIDS in made-for-television movies, from *An Early Frost* in 1985 to *Roommates,* scheduled for broadcast in the spring of 1994.) "It became apparent that they wanted to make a picture about AIDS," says Mr. Scherick, "but not about gays." When it came time to pick up the option in late 1989, NBC also passed. The project slipped into limbo.

"Then a crazy thing happened," says Mr. Spelling, whose company bought another that had options on many things, and on the list was *And the Band Played On*. HBO had also become interested. Robert Cooper, president of HBO Worldwide Pictures, saw in the book the prototype of what he believed an HBO movie should be.

"It was clearly unique," Mr. Cooper says. "And the story was provocative because it looks at so many constituencies and spares no one." He sent the book to the screenwriter, Mr. Schulman, whose credits range from *Goodbye, Columbus* to *Tucker*. Halfway through the book, he signed on.

The Format: Detective Drama or Documentary?

As the '90s dawned, Mr. Schulman was beginning the script. "There were about twenty different ways to go," he says. "Everyone agreed that we didn't want to do another *Longtime Companion*. This was not just one circle of friends affected by AIDS, but the world."

The decision was made to tell the story from the point of view of Don Francis, an epidemiologist with the CDC. Dr. Francis, played by Mr. Modine, a central figure in Mr. Shilts's book, was one of a handful of people who pushed for early intervention against the disease, which destroys the immune system. Such a focus was also more comfortable for the network, suggests Mr. Shilts. "Clearly, HBO believed the way to a mass audience was to have them see the story through the eyes of a heterosexual," he says.

HBO saw *And the Band Played On* as a detective story to be unraveled one thread at a time. So Mr. Schulman set about constructing the narrative around the roadblocks CDC researchers ran into in the search to identify, then prevent and treat AIDS. The first draft was sent to Mr. Shilts for review. He sent back pages of suggestions. The exchange became an integral part of the process over the next three years.

"He'd tell me things that might be offensive," says Mr. Schulman, "even though many of the lines were from his book." The dialogue between the two often became one of semantics—why the term *sexual orientation,* for example, would not offend and *sexual preference* would. "I thought you could change a line here and there and make a difference," says Mr. Shilts. "But when a scene is played out dramatically it has so much more impact."

The project had no director until Joel Schumacher, whose films include *Flatliners* and *Falling Down,* became interested. "I assumed," he says, "that because this was HBO and the script was based on reality that an army of lawyers had checked the facts in the screenplay." But as he began talking to the real people portrayed, he found a great degree of dramatic license. At the end was a tender scene between hetero-heroic Don Francis and one of the Cassandra-like gay activists, Bill Kraus," recalls Mr. Schumacher. "And Bill Kraus is dying." When Mr. Schumacher learned that Mr. Francis had never met Mr. Kraus, much less been at his deathbed, he did some rethinking.

"I came to a kind of confrontation with myself over this whole docudrama situation," the director says. "I'm not sure I'm meant for it. I don't understand where the line is. This work was going to be a strong indictment of many people. How would I explain what parts to believe and what not to?" The tortured story of those years, he argued, didn't need additional drama. "I told HBO, 'I will give you a year of my life—free,'" he says. "Just give me two researchers, and I will travel the world and interview everyone who is still alive who is connected to this."

Mr. Schumacher said he envisioned following in the documentary tradition of the critically acclaimed PBS production *The Civil War.* HBO didn't agree, and the two parted. Mr. Schulman, who had been continuing to revise the script, learned through a newspaper item that the director had left.

The difference between literal truth and a larger truth seemed largely in the mind of the beholder. The screenwriter says: "There were hundreds of characters in Randy's book, so fictionalization was necessary at times. But we did not falsify any facts." Although Don Francis found his character evolving into "a cross between a saint and Don Quixote," as he puts it, he generally concurs with Mr. Schulman's assessment." There were many things that happen in the script that indeed did not happen, so I am talking to people I never really talked to," says Dr. Francis, who now works at Genentech, a California biotechnology company, to develop an AIDS vaccine. "What Arnold did was to accordion this stuff so the truth is there, but it is not in fact what happened."

In the fall of 1991, Richard Pearce, the second director, signed on. "There were still some concerns about how to tell a story that would be true to the facts and also be as dramatic as possible," recalls Mr. Pearce, whose films include *The Long Walk Home* and *Country*. He and the screenwriter further pared the script and began casting. "I knew that without stars attached to a project, it could sit for months," says Mr. Pearce. When Paramount Pictures approached him about directing *Leap of Faith,* he accepted.

The Casting: Star Needed, Must Be Major

It was 1992 before Mr. Spottiswoode, who is perhaps best known for the 1983 movie *Under Fire,* was signed as the next director. He decided the script needed still more work. "There were wonderful things in it," says Mr. Spottiswoode. "I just didn't know how to make Dick's version work." After six more drafts, casting resumed. But the script floated around Hollywood for months without a serious nibble from performers. By fall the situation was critical. "Roger told me that HBO wouldn't green-light the movie without a major star," says Mr. Shilts.

About that time, both he and Mr. Spottiswoode attended an AIDS fundraiser in San Francisco. Neither had a specific part in mind when they collared Richard Gere as he was slipping into his limousine at the end of the evening, "Roger is a friend of mine," says Mr. Gere. "When he and Randy told me they couldn't get *The Band* financed without a star, I told them I didn't have time for one of the larger parts, but maybe a cameo." Ed Limato, vice chairman of International Creative Management, has been Richard Gere's agent for more than two decades. He had never recommended a television project to his client. "But Cooper came to me," recalls Mr. Limato, about the HBO executive, "and said, 'This thing is falling apart. Richard says he doesn't have time, but if he will do it, we'll make it.'"

Mr. Spottiswoode had also approached Matthew Modine, Mr. Limato's client at the time as well. Within a week, both actors had been signed, as had

Whoopi Goldberg. "Once we had Richard and Matthew and Whoopi," says Mr. Shilts, "other actors starting calling to volunteer."

Mr. Gere took the part of the gay choreographer with AIDS, a composite character loosely based on Michael Bennett, the creator of *A Chorus Line,* who died in 1987. When Ms. Goldberg, cast as Dr. Selma Dritz of the Bureau of Communicable Disease Control in San Francisco, developed a respiratory infection, Lily Tomlin stepped in. Mr. Shilts suggests that the casting difficulties underscore Hollywood's ambivalence about homosexuality. Indeed, the pivotal role of gay rights advocate Bill Kraus went to British actor Ian McKellen, who is himself a gay rights advocate.

"Homophobia is so inbred in Hollywood," says Mr. McKellen. He points to one particular scene and its impact on the film's texture. The scene was meant as a snapshot of the domestic life of a typical monogamous gay couple. Kraus is returning from a long trip and greets his lover, Kico, played by B. D. Wong, with a brief hug and kiss. "At the time, an HBO executive told me he was frightened by this display of affection," recalls Mr. McKellen. "'Gross' was the word used. I did not agree." Mr. McKellen argued that an audience who had watched characters dying for an hour would not change the channel because of a homosexual kiss. The scene did not make the final cut.

Postproduction: Conflict over the Final Cut

Filming ultimately began in November 1992 and ended in January 1993, over its six-million-dollar budget. By the time the film was complete, $8.7 million had been spent.

"Roger had shot it in a very darkly personal way," says the film's editor, Lois Freeman-Fox. "It had this documentary, realistic feel to it. HBO thought it was too dark. I think they didn't want to trust Roger's vision." HBO generally defends its position throughout the fracas and attributes the conflicts to what Mr. Cooper summarizes as "just creative differences."

As the film moved into postproduction, the uneasy relationship between HBO and Mr. Spottiswoode intensified. HBO brought in a supervisor whom Mr. Spottiswoode stopped allowing in the editing room. Tensions were such that HBO executives began holding postproduction meetings with the producers, but without Mr. Spottiswoode.

Nevertheless, by early April 1993, Ms. Freeman-Fox felt they were close to a cut that satisfied HBO's concerns. When a disagreement erupted over Mr. Spottiswoode's desire to show the film informally at the Cannes Film Festival, a memo from the director charging the network with censorship was leaked to the press. Later Ms. Freeman-Fox watched, stunned, as a police officer came into the editing room and walked out with a copy of the film. A month later, Bill Couturie, who produced the 1989 Academy Award–winning documentary about AIDS *Common Threads: Stories from the Quilt,* got a call from HBO asking him to recut the movie, acting as a consultant.

"I didn't want to do it," he says. "I would be taking someone else's work and making changes." But Mr. Couturie knew Mr. Shilts and called to ask his opinion of the film. "Randy had some serious problems," recalls Mr. Couturie, "and he thought the gay community would too. I agreed." Both men believed that there was an underrepresentation of positive images of gay people and too many negative stereotypes.

"I didn't want it to seem that Roger didn't shoot a wonderful film," says Mr. Couturie. "He did. But the overriding reality of the AIDS epidemic in the U.S. is that, because of homophobia, we let Pandora out of the box. That to me was so much more the issue than whether or not the film included bathhouses or anything to do with the gay community."

It was decided that three controversial scenes be cut or shortened. Two others, however, involving Patient Zero, remained the same. Additional documentary footage of government officials was intercut throughout the film. To balance a strong gay character against a strong straight character, new scenes were added to expand the part of Bill Kraus, while some scenes featuring Don Francis were trimmed.

On reflection, Mr. Spottiswoode believes there was a genuine disagreement on how best to tell the story. "The moral of Randy's book was that because you can't prejudge the future, what you have to do is tell the truth," he says. "I felt that was our job, to portray what really happened." What he ran up against, he thinks, was another valid point of view to which he could not reconcile himself.

"It's the idea that, if the past carries images that would fit people's preconceptions and prejudices, reproducing that will reinforce their worst instincts," he says. "I don't think I made a film that did that."

Mr. Modine, for his part, describes the controversy as a schoolyard spat that nevertheless resonated with many issues Mr. Shilts explored in his book. "If there is any hope for us, it is that we'll be honest about our past so that we can learn from it," he says. "You can't be politically correct about history."

13

Murder and Mayhem Stalk TV

Jeff Silverman

Judge Sol Wachtler may have stolen the spotlight for a few hours, as the story of his arrest on blackmail charges unfolded, but Amy Fisher remained the media's darling of distress. Still, the media-in-heat madness that swelled the sordid saga of Ms. Fisher didn't begin with her love for Joey Buttafuoco or with her shooting his wife, Mary Jo, or with her membership in the local chapter of an after-school call-girl club. It didn't even begin with the first howling headlines of her adventures. No, credit the genesis to a Nassau County, New York, policeman who, either by cultural osmosis or the luck of the draw, was savvy enough to speak Hollywoodese precisely when the focus was on him.

"Why did she do it?" reporters were asking, shortly after Ms. Fisher's arrest in May 1992. Detective Severin had the answer, deconstructing a complex scenario into a oneline insight obvious enough for network moguls to grasp. The Fisher-Buttafuoco fiasco, he surmised, was "a near-*Fatal Attraction*."

The sound that was then heard was the riff books flipping open. After all, the 1987 film *Fatal Attraction* grossed more than three hundred million dollars worldwide. In Amy Fisher, there hung a tale with not dissimilar elements, and it was true.

Suddenly, Ms. Fisher, then seventeen years old, was a scalding hot property, complete with a catchy nickname—the Long Island Lolita—and a high-concept pitch. In quick succession, the tabloids (both electronic and print) sounded red alert; producers inched their doomsday clocks toward midnight; and lawyers, anxious to round up the unusual suspects, took the offensive, locking their radar onto their targets. There were rights to be acquired and deals to be made.

The Fishers reportedly collected eighty thousand dollars from KLM Productions for film rights, which they used to cover their daughter's bail, and the Buttafuocos got between two hundred thousand and three hundred thousand dollars from Tri-Star for the rights to their story. KLM's version will appear on NBC, Tri-Star's on CBS. As a result, three networks will have docudramas. (ABC is to start filming its version, *Beyond Control: The Amy Fisher Story,* 23 November 1992 in Vancouver, Canada; it is based on news accounts and court records and stars Drew Barrymore.)

Television, of course, has long harbored a special place in its heart for criminal activity, dangerous obsessions, and sociopathic behavior, and it's willing to pay well for the opportunity to turn true stories with those elements into movies. The three traditional networks rely increasingly on such high-profile, true events (the stranger the better) to anchor their movie lineups. But something seems to be changing in the kinds of stories television is looking for (from disease-of-the-week movies to victim pictures), as well as in the stampede to acquire rights to a subject. The explosion in tabloid television and expose-all talkathons is partly responsible. So is the fierce competition between the networks to satisfy the fickle needs of an ever-shrinking audience.

The Stories: Riding the Tabloid Trail

"Murders, rapes, kidnaps, and batterings are the rule of thumb for the traditional networks in movies and miniseries," says former ABC president Fred Pierce, now a producer, "and the source materials are now easier to come by. Access to real-life situations has become quicker because of the explosion of magazine shows and local newscasts and video cams and satellite feeds." The stories are more available. "Frankly," he continues, "I think it's a little less challenging than to sit down and come up with a story on anorexia or an interesting social issue, but these kinds of stories draw ratings."

They do indeed. ABC's September 1992 broadcast of *A Murderous Affair: The Carolyn Warmus Story,* starring Virginia Madsen as a teacher convicted of killing her lover's wife, had the fifth largest audience of any program that week.

A Woman Scorned: The Betty Broderick Story, with Meredith Baxter as the emotionally battered mother of four and murderer of her former husband and his bride, was so successful (CBS's second-highest-rated movie of 1991) that a sequel was done. *Her Final Fury: Betty Broderick, The Last Chapter* was broadcast on 1 November 1992.

Before the 1992–93 season is out, networks will have focused on such true-life subjects of madness, mayhem, and disaster as

—The Oakland fire (ABC), the 1989 San Francisco earthquake (NBC), and Hurricane Andrew (NBC);

—Dr. Margaret Bean-Bayog, the Harvard psychiatrist alleged to have seduced a young patient who later committed suicide (NBC and ABC);

—Blanche Taylor Moore, the pious poisoner of two husbands and a boyfriend in North Carolina (NBC);

—Carolyn Sapp, the Miss America involved in an abusive relationship with former New York Jets running back Nuu Faaola (in which, in one of television's more imaginatively titillating casting coups, NBC actually hired Ms. Sapp to play herself);

—Eileen Franklin, the California woman who woke up one day to the sudden recollection that her father had murdered her best friend some twenty years earlier (NBC);

—Aileen Carol Wuornos, America's first convicted serial killer without a Y chromosome (the story, *Overkill,* was broadcast 17 November 1992 on CBS; the Courtroom Television Network will broadcast excerpts from the trial tonight [22 November 1992]);

—Wanda Holloway, the Texas woman who was alleged to have hired someone to kill Verna Heath, the mother of her daughter's principal rival for a spot on the school cheerleading squad (ABC, HBO).

So much for family values.

The Rationale, Part 1: Truth and Morality Plays

"I suppose these are as hard and difficult times as ever, and people are looking for windows into behavior," suggests John Matoian, CBS's senior vice president for movies and miniseries. "Hopefully, from these kinds of stories, they'll gain insight, and I hope—and this will sound naive—that these movies will explain events that could have been prevented, had someone stopped them before they went too far." In his view, the subgenre of true-life, high-profile crime stories is something of an update on the old concept of morality plays. "In every one of them, the perpetrator is found, sentenced, and not let go.

That's the basis of classic drama. I'm not saying that we're doing Shakespeare here," he concedes,

> but these stories do have similar themes running through them. After all, what was *Hamlet* but a story about a family in which one brother murdered another so he could marry the widow, and the son found out, and everybody ended up dead? Naturally, the networks would call it *Fatal Doings in Denmark: The Hamlet Tragedy.*

To perk Mr. Matoian's interest, true-crime stories must pass a two-part litmus test: "First, does it explore a facet of our lives that asks a question people would be asking or exploring?" In Betty Broderick's case, the question is, What is emotional battery? "Second," Mr. Matoian continues, "is there some insight into the event itself? The 'Oh, my God!' moment that has caused the kind of intrigue or notoriety that has been attached to the event, that makes the story more than just a retelling? These aren't just stories about someone who picks up a gun."

On Sunday, 29 November 1992, in *A Mother's Right: The Elizabeth Morgan Story* (ABC), for instance, Bonnie Bedelia plays the Washington plastic surgeon who hid her daughter in New Zealand and went to jail rather than allow her former husband to have visitation rights. Dr. Morgan said the little girl had been sexually molested by her father.

"Domestic violence stories in which someone acted on their darkest impulses have a catharsis to them," says Judd Parkin, Mr. Matoian's counterpart at ABC. "How can a man murder his family? How can a man molest his child? How do people act on their darkest impulses? These are questions that go beyond everyday experience. This may sound pretentious, but these are the questions that the Greeks were dealing with." Too bad Euripides is no longer available for quick rewrites.

If Mr. Matoian and Mr. Parkin are navigating the high road in their rationales, film director Michael Ritchie casts something of a colder eye in his observation. "Voyeurism," Mr. Ritchie insists, "has replaced drama in American life, and everyone in America seems to be willing to participate in the circus."

The director of *The Candidate, Downhill Racer, Semi-Tough,* and *Diggstown,* Mr. Ritchie is so fascinated by the various phenomena surrounding these television movies (and the media frenzies that have become part of them) that, after a twenty-five-year absence from the small screen, he is returning to explore them through the Wanda Holloway story. He is the director of HBO's black-comedic, tongue-in-cheekly titled *The Positively True Adventures of the Alleged Texas Cheerleader-Murdering Mom,* which is scheduled to have its premiere in early 1993. One thing that will dramatically separate the HBO movie, starring Holly Hunter as Wanda Holloway, from the rest of the pack is that its makers have promised it will take no creative liberties. "Every TV docudrama says it's based on a true story," Mr. Ritchie explains. "We're not saying it's 'based on.' We're being outrageous by saying it is absolutely, positively the true story: hold onto your hats for the craziest ride through the truth that's ever been done on television. There's a sense of sophomoric glee in our take on this."

Docudramas may be a form in need of send-up, but something else is different about this project. The film is turning its cameras on the media's role in hyping the story and the maneuverings required to obtain the rights from the people involved. ABC did a more traditional version of the story, *Willing to Kill: The Texas Cheerleading Story,* starring Lesley Ann Warren and Tess Harper, which was broadcast in early November 1992; and that, too, will come under HBO's scrutiny.

Originally, the networks passed on the project. "They felt there was no payoff because there was no murder," says Mr. Pierce, the film's executive producer. *True Adventures* found its payoff elsewhere. "Our third act becomes the feeding frenzy of the media," says Jim Manos, the producer. "Everything is inextricably tied. We're all part of it. We all feed off each other. We all perpetuate these situations. We are all somewhat obsessed by the media, being in the media light and the Warholian sense of fame." Mr. Manos even plays himself in the movie. So does the writer, Jane Anderson.

The Rationale, Part 2: Just Like the Folks Next Door

Why do Americans continue to invite electronic characters into their homes, characters they would probably cross the street to avoid? Perhaps it's because, until the moment they crossed society's lines of conduct, these people could have been the next-door neighbors. Hannibal Lecter could have been. Amy Fisher is.

With the proliferation over the last few years of television tabloids and talk shows eager to explore every anomaly of human behavior, these stories have become, well, eerily familiar. They have put us on a first-name basis with whichever Amy Fisher happens to crop up at the moment. In a sense, these tabloid shows have become the farm teams for prime time. "We're in the era of *Hard Copy,*" says Mr. Parkin. "There are so many reality-based shows that it's difficult for us not to pay attention to them. They have such a high visibility factor. Once a story has made the rounds, it has a presold awareness that's impossible to create even with a best-selling book."

Nevertheless, Mr. Parkin, for one, would like to steer his lineup more toward issue films than true-crime stories. Last year, two fact-based pictures, *Broken Cord,* about fetal alcohol syndrome, and *Something to Live For,* the story of Alison Gertz, a heterosexual woman with AIDS, did quite well in the ratings. And this year, the three major networks have more life-affirming, true headline stories on their schedules, like NBC's *Who Will Save My Life: The Anissa Ayala Story,* based on the leukemia victim whose parents conceived another child in hopes of that child being a bone-marrow donor.

"A *Something about Amelia* doesn't have to be ripped from the headlines to hit a nerve with audiences," says Parkin, referring to ABC's 1984 groundbreaking tale of incest. "Still," he adds, "TV tends not to lead but to follow. Audiences like true crime. And when we see something that works, we continue doing it."

The Rights: To Have and to Rip Off

"It's an experience. A bizarre one." Verna Heath, Wanda Holloway's intended victim in the Texas cheerleader to-do, is anything but happy. She is sitting in Michael Ritchie's air-conditioned trailer on location just outside Pasadena, California, which is doubling for her daughter Amber's gymnastics center. She has been watching Hollywood tell her tale, and she is not pleased by what she has seen. "They told me I would have real input in this movie," she says angrily, "but I haven't. It's like our life has been taken away from us. I don't feel like I'm in control, and I don't like that." When dealing with Hollywood you takes your money and your chances.

Technically, filmmakers don't buy anyone's rights to do a story, as long as they confine themselves to public domain materials, like newspaper accounts and court documents. "Once you are entered into court transcripts," says Mr. Matoian, "you are fair game." By buying rights, though, "you get insight into the story," says Mr. Manos, the producer. "They give an opportunity to begin telling the story. If you're careful and legally within your bounds, you can then write what you want to write." But it would be wrong. Says Mr. Parkin: "If there are victims, we always want their cooperation. If they don't want their stories told, their wishes should be respected."

In the days after her story broke, Ms. Heath fielded, by her count, fifty-six sugarcoated phone calls from producers, and the tabloids camped out on her doorstep. *A Current Affair* tried wooing her into an exclusive interview with flowers; when she demurred, they simply hid a microphone and camera and filmed her anyway.

"This has been the most stressful time of my life," she says. "I've had to deal with people I didn't trust, people who wanted my rights to make their movie.

They only want rights so you won't sue them. I'm angry at a system that took over my life." Of course, by agreeing to a deal, she became part of that system.

Mr. Manos was fascinated when he first came upon the improbable saga of the Holloways and the Heaths in the newspapers almost two years ago. Three days later, he was in on the chase, ensconced in the Holiday Inn in Channelview, Texas, fifteen miles or so west of Houston. Before leaving New York, he had contacted Troy Harper, Ms. Holloway's former husband, who had been quoted in news reports. In the end, Mr. Manos made his deal, for more than one hundred thirty thousand dollars, with Mr. Harper, his daughter, Shanna, the cheerleader wanna-be for whom a mother would kill. (Under the old Son of Sam laws, overturned by the United States Supreme Court in December 1991, Wanda Holloway could not receive money for her version of the story.)

"They became extremely quick learners," says Mr. Manos, "and very savvy to the whole business. It's funny and also part of the story: the education of Hollywood hype."

Producers are amazed and amused at how quickly, and eagerly, the uninitiated jump into the game. Earlier this year, Gross-Weston Productions, producers of the Emmy-nominated *Billionaire Boys' Club* miniseries in 1988, obtained rights from several families for *Firestorm,* a movie based on the devastating Oakland fire (to be broadcast on ABC in early 1993). "When word got around [about] what we were doing," says the producer, Ann Weston, "we got barrages of phone calls. 'Do you want my story? It's better than the one you bought.' Soon as they heard we were making a movie, every Tom, Dick, and Harry wanted to cash in."

More fascinating to Ms. Weston was how quickly the principal characters they contacted surrounded themselves with agents and attorneys seeking figures well beyond the Hollywood norms of twenty-five hundred dollars for an option on story rights, against thirty thousand to fifty thousand dollars if the movie gets made. "It's like you call someone in Appalachia," she says, "and they've never heard of Hollywood, but a week later they've got an agent and want ten million."

Ms. Heath didn't want ten million dollars; she just wanted what the other family got, sort of the way Wanda Holloway wanted for her daughter what Ms. Heath's daughter had. When it became clear to her that the producers of the HBO movie were ready to go ahead without her cooperation, she agreed to participate for fifty thousand dollars. All it has bought her, she says, is aggravation.

Call it Fatal Aggravation.

14

Theater of Fact: A Dramatist's Viewpoint

David Edgar

It's a truism that the one-time broadcast, original television play is always an endangered species; the irony of the early 1980s is that the target has shifted. The most poisoned darts are now aimed not so much at the "obscure" *Second City First* or the "obscene" *Play for Today* but at manifestations of the only single-play television form that is unique to the medium: the form known variously as *fiction, dramatic reconstruction, documentary drama,* or *drama-documentary.* This form has always had its critics, of course: Mrs. Mary Whitehouse cut her teeth on *Cathy Come Home* and *Up the Junction,* but the debate over Antony Thomas's *Death of a Princess* took matters to a different plane. This had partly, of course, to do with the perceived threat to our trading and diplomatic links with Saudi Arabia, and most interesting it was to see how those conservatives who fervently believed in freedom of trade as a precondition of freedom of expression tended to support the former over the latter when the two conflicted. But the importance of the affair to the makers of drama-documentary was that the film provoked many critics to express their strong reservations not just about *Death of a Princess* but about the form as a whole.

Two extremely distinguished commentators expressed their reservations good and early: immediately after the Saudi storm broke, Sir Ian Gilmour, then the Lord Privy Seal, told the House of Commons that "the so-called dramatisation or fictionalisation of alleged history is extremely dangerous and misleading, and is something to which the broadcasting authorities must give close attention." His view was echoed by Lord Carrington in the House of Lords, who warned that "it might be as well for those who are producing these programmes to have a good look at the consequences of what they are doing" (he was responding to a question about "the tendency of some TV companies to present programmes deliberately designed to give the impression of documentary based on fact"). Others quickly entered the lists as well; reasonably representative were Geoffrey Cannon, writing in the *Sunday Times* and Richard Gott in the *Guardian*.[1] Cannon's basic argument against dramadocumentary was that the "known facts" of contemporary or recent history can and are subject to "elaboration and embroidery" and, indeed, that "TV drama-documentary may deliberately stray away from truth for dramatic impact, and to feed the audience's predispositions or prejudices." Richard Gott's article began as follows:

> Well, what is it? Fact or fiction? History or current affairs? Scarcely a night goes by nowadays without Edward VIII, the Reverend Jim Jones, Winston Churchill or some other famous or infamous figure from the recent past, appearing on the television screen. Significant episodes in their lives are then presented in fictitious form ("artificial, counterfeit, sham"), or, rather, in a mishmash of fact and fiction and producer's whim. It is a profoundly unsatisfactory development in the use of television.

Gott then went on to accuse television producers and writers of usurping the function of historians, claiming to explain "what actually happened" in history, a role for which they are neither qualified nor competent, rather than pursuing their proper role of "illuminating the human condition" through the creation of imaginary characters in invented situations.

These are serious arguments, which deserve to be taken seriously. They are, however, based on severe misconceptions about history itself and the playwright's relationship to it; and I use the word *playwright* rather than *producer* or *director* deliberately, because it is my view that dramadocumentary is, primarily, not a journalistic but a dramatic medium, like soap opera, tragedy, and farce, that has been developed by writers in response to the changing world about them and that it should be defended as such.

The first and glaring problem with Gott's and Cannon's critiques of the form is one of definition. Richard Gott, for example, confines himself to the discussion of plays that present the actions of famous or infamous real people, living in the recent past, in fictional form. This definition would indeed take in most of the programs we would recognize as dramadocumentary, but it would also encompass almost any biographical film set in the recent past, from *Lawrence of Arabia* and *The Dambusters* to *Funny Girl.*

Geoffrey Cannon divides the form into two, distinguishing between faction (of which he gives *Roots, Holocaust,* and *Washington: Behind Closed Doors* as examples), and dramadocumentary, which he describes as a form dealing with "matters of social and moral concern." It is obvious that the latter definition could happily embrace almost every serious play ever written; but even the former group of plays have in common only that they deal with real historical events and use a mix of real and fictional characters—which might just about let out *Funny Girl,* if we define "historical event" in a way that excludes the Ziegfeld Follies, but would include most biographical war films and stage plays as various as Berthold Brecht's *Galileo,* Terence Rattigan's *Winslow Boy,* and George Bernard Shaw's *Saint Joan.* And a third commentator, Robin Sutch, replying to Gott's piece in the *Guardian,* went so far as to give the historical plays of Shakespeare and Aeschylus as examples of ancient precedents of the dramadocumentary form.[2] And it's worth pointing out that, apart from Cannon's subjects of social and moral concern, none of the above definitions would cover programs that most people would instinctively view as being dramadocumentaries but that do not include real people as characters, like *Law and Order,* two of the four episodes of Ken Loach's *Days of Hope,* and, indeed, *Cathy Come Home.*

It is of course true that dramadocumentary makers themselves have extreme difficulty in defining the beast they are riding. But it is also clear that the above definitions won't do and that pointing out that they won't do is more than a debating trick, because no definition of the difference between, say, *Churchill and the Generals, Three Days in Szczecin, Colditz,* and *Henry V* will do unless it takes into account the dramatic and ideological purposes of playwrights and the artistic and social contexts in which they work.

It seems to me obvious that, however inspirational the process of literary creation may be, most playwrights draw most of their subject matter from sources outside themselves; and when critics like Richard Gott complain that, by re-creating historical figures rather than creating imaginary characters, writers are displaying a lack of creativity and imagination, they are themselves displaying not a little ignorance about the process of making plays. It is, however, clear why this misunderstanding occurs; it has to do with the differences between writing plays about public and private life.

When playwrights write about a private theme—about, say, domestic life or romantic love—their models in real life are cloaked in anonymity; the real families or couples on which the play is based are unlikely to be known to its audience. If, however, a playwright chose to write about a battle, it is likely that an intelligent audience would pick up pretty quickly whether the story was based on the Peloponnesian Wars, the Battle of Trafalgar, or the Siege of Leningrad. Put another way, it is a shocking but true fact that, in France alone, literally millions of love affairs were commenced, enjoyed, and concluded between 1958 and 1969, and the playwright interested in the sexual habits of the French during the first decade of the Fifth Republic would be able to base a plot on any number of them.

The source material for a play about political leadership in France during that period is more limited, and it would be a perverse writer who did not consider including, in such a play, a tall, long-nosed statesman with a marked distaste for Anglo-Saxon countries and a liking for grandiose political rhetoric. And similarly, if I wanted to write—and as it happens, I once did—a play about electoral malpractice in a large English-speaking democratic state possessed of sophisticated surveillance technologies, it would be pretty coy not to set that play in Washington, D.C., during the Nixon presidency. It is true, of course, that some plays about public life have created their own allegorical world or have used an incident from the past to illumine the present (Max Frisch's *Andorra* is an example of the former technique, Arthur Miller's *Crucible* of the latter). But by and large, plays about public life have tended to be based on real and recognizable public events, either contemporary or historical. What sets dramadocumentary apart from the mass of public plays is not the employment of facts but the theatrical use to which those facts are put. In dramadocumentary, I believe, the factual basis of the story gives the action of the play its credibility.

Most good plays say things about human relationships and human society that are challenging and surprising and disturbing to their audiences; and all writers of such plays want to convince their audiences that they are right to be so challenged, surprised, and disturbed. Sometimes—in absurdist or symbolic drama—the power of a playwright's metaphor will be proof enough that his or her bleak (or euphoric) view of the universe is credible. But, for most of us, it is necessary to establish a bedrock of material (or a dramatic style) that is recognizable to the audience and gives what follows its legitimacy.

For example, John Hopkins's classic quartet of television plays, *Talking to a Stranger,* presented an unwelcomely bitter view of family life. What gave those plays their power—to shock and to convince—was that the characters' day-to-day behavior was terrifyingly recognizable, when set against our own lives and the lives of people we know. In the same way, Eugene O'Neill's *Long Day's Journey into Night* is incomparably superior, in its perception, its power, and its capacity to disturb, to anything O'Neill had written before precisely because the desperate and magnificent agony of the Tyrones is shown to us, initially at least, through the most trivial (but universal) of domestic conflicts: over mealtimes, table clearing, and drinks before dinner. Similarly, the conclusions of the plays of Shakespeare are often more radical and challenging to our assumptions about the world than anything written before or since. But the fact that Shakespeare's plays employed recognizable forms—tragedy, comedy, *historical* drama—provided a bedrock of shared assumptions on which he could build his vision of the human condition. Without that bedrock, the sense that the writer has won his or her spurs, the audience can shrug off the playwright's conclusions as bearing no relationship to the real world.

Playwrights writing about public life in the contemporary world are in a different position, both from the writer of domestic drama and from Shakespeare. We all have experience of the subject matter of domestic drama—we have all lived in families, grown up, fallen in love, and fallen out of it again; we can all judge our own experience against plays that present these activities to us. In public plays, however, there is no guarantee of any shared experience of the subject matter. Plays about war are presented on British stages and British television to audiences who now, by and large, have no knowledge of soldiering. Plays about the workings of one particular political party will be performed or broadcast to audiences consisting, in varying and unpredictable proportions, of members of that party, members of opposing parties, or members of no party at all. Further, there are no longer any cinematic forms that retain the universally accepted power of, say, tragedy or the historical epic. And, of course, we live in an age in which any unifying belief or set of values—which means any generally accepted set of criteria for judging human behavior—are absent.

I think that the theater of fact, the documentary theater, was created to give credibility to the playwright's analysis of the incredible happenings of our time. (The theatrical form of dramadocumentary predates the television form, but, in my view, it is on television that the form has reached maturity.)

One of the best examples of stage dramadocumentary is Rolf Hochhuth's play *The Representative,* written in the early 1960s. Hochhuth wanted to write a play about men of power and the terrible contradiction they face in balancing political expediency against moral principle. He decided to set his play not in the far or mythical past but during the Second World War. The context of the play's story—the Holocaust—was then and is now well-known. But Hochhuth's central incident—the refusal of Pope Pius XII to break the Vatican's concordat with the Third Reich in protest against the mass murder of the Jews—was not well-known at all, and Hochhuth's representation of the pope's actions provoked bitter controversy when the play was first staged. It's my belief that Hochhuth's statement about the Holocaust and the resistance to it would not have been nearly so powerful if it had not exposed an event of history about which his audience knew little or nothing. His act of documentary revelation performed, in his play, an equivalent function to that of the peripeteia of Greek tragedy: the sudden, unexpected, and shocking reversal of fortune that captures and freezes the themes of the play as if caught in a sudden shaft of bright light. The scene with the pope in *The Representative* is in fact a reversal of *expectation,* both about the character and about the type of play we are watching; and the credibility it gives to Hochhuth's message is not about the following of agreed and accepted constructional rules but about evidence.

This is a completely different use of historical fact in drama from that of Shakespeare in his history plays. Shakespeare drew stories from a variety of sources to explore the theme of kingship, including ancient Roman, recent British, and mythological history. I don't believe, however, that the fact that the plots of *King Lear* and *Macbeth* were drawn from mythology and those of *Henry VI* and *Richard II* from relatively recent history make Shakespeare's use of his source material substantially different. In all these cases he was writing tragedies; in no case was he revealing anything his audience couldn't have known. In one case, *Richard III,* he made a play of great dramatic power out of a set of facts that were almost certainly completely untrue.

In contrast, documentary drama relies on its facts being correct. The moral core of Rolf Hochhuth's second play (*Soldiers,* a critique of allied civilian bombing in the war) was undermined and destroyed by the historical untruth of an important though secondary incident in the play. Similarly, the power of *Cathy Come Home* depended on the fact that its thesis—that British cities suffered from wretched and inadequate housing at a time of presumed general prosperity—was timely and true. Without that fact, *Cathy* would have been little more than a sad anecdote of an inadequate family destroyed by an indifferent bureaucracy. In reality, of course, the play changed the way we think about housing. I think it changed the way we think about other things too—like the inner city, the role of the social services, and even the political system. Jeremy Sandford used his factual base in order to give dramatic force and credibility to a much wider theme.

It is, of course, precisely this *use* of factual material to sustain a thesis that provokes so much concern and criticism. As Leslie Woodhead of Granada Television's dramadocumentary unit argued in his Granada lecture, "the underlying assumption that television drama should seek not only to reflect but also to change society has informed much of the most interesting work in the field of documented drama over the past decade," citing the work of Tony Garnett, Ken Loach, Jim Allen, and G. F. Newman and pointing out that "the implied worry . . . is that the forms and credibilities of documentary and news are being recruited to smuggle a political message."[3] Certainly this worried Paul Johnson, in a piece commenting on *World in Action*'s reconstruction of the cabinet debate over the 1981 budget: for him, dramadocumentary deliberately blurs the fact/fiction distinction "for tendentious purposes, often in pursuit of partisan political ends. . . . The object, quite brazenly, is to influence opinion on contentious matters."[4] The same point was made by Geoffrey Cannon in his post-*Princess* piece in the *Sunday Times:*

> What I found disturbing about Ian Curteis's two recent dramatised reconstructions *Churchill and the Generals* and *Suez 1956* was that, in both cases, Curteis—as he stated openly and honestly—had a thesis about Churchill and about [Sir Anthony] Eden (put simply), that they were liable to states of mind approaching dementia, and he used known facts to demonstrate this thesis. . . . And while his thesis is—as far as I know—consistent with the facts, other interpretations are equally consistent.[5]

The problems with these arguments are several. While few people would justify the deliberate falsification or invention of incidents to support a vacuous historical argument (it is right that the film *The Deer Hunter* was criticized for apparently inventing its central metaphor of a group of Vietcong guerrillas forcing their American captives to play Russian roulette), accusations of political bias have a tendency to be oddly selective (no problems, as Ken Loach points out, "when Edward VII or Churchill's mother are romanticised and glorified"). Further, as Leslie Woodhead argues, even the makers of "real" current-affairs and news programs are at last owning up about "the inescapable subjective content in every camera movement and edit" and the fact that "the manipulative presence of the director is as significant in *Johnny Go Home* as it was in *Cathy Come Home*. But even more interesting, from the dramatist's point of view, is Richard Gott's unflattering comparison between the "amateur" writer of dramadocumentary and the professional historian.

In his witty and wonderful book *What Is History?,* Professor E. H. Carr takes much pleasure in exposing the nineteenth-century view of history as a collection of objective facts that it is the historian's task merely to discover, separate from speculation, and reveal. In reality, as Carr points out, it is a subjective value judgment that Caesar's crossing of the Rubicon is an important historical event but that millions of other peoples' crossings of that petty stream—in both directions and for reasons doubtless important for them—are not matters of any historical importance. Similarly, almost all our knowledge of Greece in the period of the Persian Wars is not objective knowledge at all, because it emanates exclusively from a small group of rich people in the one city of Athens. Further, our view that the medieval period was a time of great religious commitment might well have been influenced by the fact that almost all the contemporary chroniclers of that period were monks. And, finally, even those documents precisely designed to be pragmatically factual—minutes of meetings and so on—reflect the interests and prejudices and self-view of the person by whom or for whom the documents were written.

Professor Carr gives the example of the papers of Gustav Stresemann, the foreign minister of the Weimar Republic, which were published after his death in 1929 in three massive volumes, which concentrate almost entirely on Stresemann's successful diplomatic dealings with the West. This, as Carr points out, itself distorts history, as Stresemann in fact devoted a lot, even a majority, of his time to the pursuit of a much less successful policy toward the Soviet Union. But the point is that, even if the published selection were complete or accurately represented the whole, then the minutes of Stresemann's meetings with, say, Soviet Foreign Minister Georgi Vasilievich Chicherin would tell us not what actually happened but only what Stresemann thought had happened, or what he wanted others to think, or wanted himself to think, or (most likely of all) what his secretary felt that he might want to think had happened. And Chicherin's records of the same conversation would doubtless look very different, but they would be strikingly similar in one respect: they would be highly contentious, tendentious, and politically partisan.

But it is useful to take this example even further. Suppose that historians had available to them, which is not the case, both sets of minutes, Stresemann's and Chicherin's. I suspect—and I only suspect, because I'm not a historian—that they would look at those two accounts in two ways. First, the historian would set them against other facts, and if, for example, it was found that either statesman had said something he knew to be untrue, then he or she might conclude that the person was being cunning, devious, or at least excessively cautious with the other. Second, the historian might set the documents against what could be discovered about the characters of the two men from other sources: what their relatives, friends, and acquaintances said about them.

What I suspect the historian would not do—because it would be a most unscholarly procedure—would be to set these two men's recollections of this one event against the behavior of the historian's *own* relatives, friends, or acquaintances, or even against the behavior of him- or herself. It is *that* knowledge, knowledge not just of human behavior but of the skills necessary to communicate that knowledge to others, that is the treasured possession of the creators of dramatic fiction. They do it all the time. And, in particular, they have throughout the ages developed ways of showing the kind of behavior that tends to occur at meetings between the representatives of suspicious and hostile countries; of demonstrating the gap between what people say, what they mean, and what they subsequently do. A historian can say, of course, and back up the assertion, that a king claimed to be wise, just, and merciful when he was actually engaged in bumping off all his opponents. But only a dramatist can demonstrate how that hypocrisy manifests itself in the human soul: the self-deception, the paranoia, even the glorification of deceit that go on in the minds of men and women whose public and private faces are at war. (And in this context, I have always thought it significant that the soliloquy and the aside have been such enduring devices in the playwright's armory; they are, of course, devices precisely designed to show the gap between what someone says and what he or she thinks and feels.)

What I am saying is that dramatic fiction can uniquely illumine certain aspects of public life; and the dramatic power of dramadocumentary lies in its capacity to show us not that certain events occurred (the headlines can do that) or even, perhaps, why they occurred (for such information we can go to the weekly magazines or the history books) but *how* they occurred: how recognizable human beings rule, fight, judge, meet, negotiate, suppress, and overthrow. Perhaps the simplest example of the achievement of such an effect is in the actual physical reconstruction of a public event: trials, for example, can be comprehensively reported, but nobody who watched, say, the reconstructions of the *Gay News* blasphemy case or the Chicago conspiracy hearings could fail to take away from those experiences not merely a richer sense of atmosphere but a profounder understanding of the processes by which men and women advocate, defend themselves, give evidence, and pass judgment. There are many other public processes ripe for such treatment; I have recently been (for the first time) in trade-union negotiations and was deeply impressed by the gap between the public image of such events and the reality. I am sure that when negotiators have behind them millions or thousands of manual workers (as opposed to our couple of hundred stage playwrights) matters feel a little different; but I'm equally sure that all negotiations ultimately come down to spatial relationships, time of day, length and structure of the meeting, and basic states of mind, like tiredness, irritation, and impatience (on the one hand) and confidence, bloody-mindedness, and a functioning sense of humor (on the other).

The group of dramadocumentary makers to have applied such principles to their craft with most consistency and rigor has been the Manchester-based Granada unit, under Leslie Woodhead. In one sense, it is somewhat paradoxical that this group should have sought to apply what are (I have argued) essentially dramatic criteria to their work, because, as Woodhead explained in his Granada lecture, he entered the field at precisely the opposite corner.

For Woodhead, the priorities have remained "obstinately journalistic," with an emphasis on exhaustive research and cross-checking, "and on high-grade source material such as tape recordings and transcripts." But I would argue that the *results* of Woodhead's painstaking work have been increasingly dramatic, in the technical sense of that word. In the General Grigorenko dramadocumentary (titled *The Man Who Wouldn't Keep Quiet* and scripted by Woodhead himself in 1970), the "dramatic" element of the production consisted (by and large) of visual evocations of Piotr Grigorenko's protests, arrests, trials, and incarcerations; hardly a word (apart from an explanatory commentary) did not originate in Grigorenko's own diary. In Granada's second dramadocumentary treatment of Eastern European resistance (*Three Days in Szczecin,* scripted by Boleslaw Sulik and broadcast in 1976), the main action (the historical meeting between Polish Communist Party leader Edward Gierek with striking shipbuilders in 1971) was based on an actual tape recording of the proceedings but was amplified and fleshed out by the memories of strike leader Edmund Baluka (by then an exile in England). Baluka's reminiscences (as an openly acknowledged source) allowed Sulik and Woodhead to go much further in re-creating not just the facts of what was said and who said it but how the listeners reacted, inside and outside the meeting hall. *Three Days* was indeed a remarkable representation of an extraordinary historical event; it was also a peculiarly authoritative play about how meetings occur.

Woodhead's most recent dramadocumentary was *Invasion,* scripted by David Boulton and shown in 1980. The program fitted neatly into Granada's dramadocumentary criteria: it showed events (surrounding the Soviet invasion of Czechoslovakia) that could only be reconstructed; it was based on rigorous research. But for the viewer, it was a play, in which recognizable human beings negotiated, discussed, argued, lost their tempers, kept their cool, supported and betrayed each other. Two examples may suffice: at one point in the play, a friend sends in beer and sandwiches for the Czech Politburo, by now effectively imprisoned by the Soviet invaders. After several moments of agonizing indecision, the Czechs choose to offer part of their meal to the nervously polite Russian soldiers guarding them. Similarly, later on, another imprisoned Czech leader discovers that he and his Polish guard were members of the same unit in the International Brigade in Spain, and they swap reminiscences until the irony of the situation becomes too much for them. These are not just anecdotes, bits of what journalists call "color." They may not be the usual stuff of historical scholarship, but they are absolutely the stuff of history.

No one would argue, however, least of all David Boulton, that his play was impartial. It was written from the point of view of the liberals on the Czech Central Committee, and doubtless the conservatives in the Soviet leadership would regard these events in a very different light. Further, the play was largely based on the recollections of one person: Zdenek Mlynar, part-author of the Action Program of the Prague Spring. But, again, the program makers were completely honest about this fact, and Boulton began his play with a shot of the real Mlynar standing next to the actor playing him on the Austro-Czech border and reiterated the point frequently by using Mlynar's own recollections, in the past tense, as a commentary on the action. The viewers were therefore completely aware of the perspective from which the events were being seen; they could judge, for instance, Boulton's dramatization of Mlynar's initial refusal and subsequent agreement to sign the Soviet-drafted communiqué that sold out the Prague Spring against the fact that the scene was based on Mlynar's own recollections.

E. H. Carr argues that, in reality, the historian is a kind of protagonist in the history he or she is writing. In *Invasion,* the protagonist was Mlynar, with a little help from David Boulton. In other plays, however, the playwright him- or herself becomes a central character. As I have pointed out, writer Ian Curteis has been particularly berated for his treatment of Churchill and Eden; Geoffrey Cannon was concerned that "millions of viewers will continue to see Churchill and Eden through Ian Curteis's eyes."

Now, I am sure that Curteis (who always insists that his works are firmly labeled as plays rather than dramadocumentaries) feels that he has found the truth about his subjects and hopes that others will agree with him. I'm not sure that I do, but I am sure that I find Curteis's vision revealing about both his and our attitudes, in our own time, toward these two important figures in our national mythology; in the same way as I find the novels of Evelyn Waugh perceptive, although I am not a High Tory, and the plays of Shaw instructive, although I am not a Fabian either. But the important point is that, like David Boulton, Ian Curteis writes plays in which people are shown doing things that human beings do, and we are able to judge the quality of the writer's vision by the simple method that we unconsciously employ whenever we watch a piece of dramatic fiction—by asking the basic question as to whether it is credible that people should behave like this, setting what we see against our own experience of human affairs. And in the case of Curteis, there are two bonuses: we have our own knowledge or even experience of the Suez crisis and the Second

World War as yardsticks, and we can also judge Curteis's Eden and Churchill against other dramatic representations of the two men on stage and screen. With that armory of weapons of judgment, one may respectfully suggest that if viewers do indeed continue to see the two statesmen through Ian Curteis's eyes it is because they have judged his perception to be keener than the alternatives on offer.

And in this context, I can mention a case from my own experience. I can, perhaps, lay claim to having been the writer of the purest dramadocumentary ever written, because in 1974, during the Watergate crisis, I edited the White House tape transcripts into a forty-five-minute television play, in which every word spoken onscreen had been actually spoken in reality, and we had the transcripts to prove it. But, in fact, of course, the play was bristling with impurities: the whole process of making it had consisted of value judgments, from my judgments about what to put in and leave out to the director's judgments about what to look at and the actors' judgments about pace and inflection and gesture and mood. And those judgments—about how the words were said and why and with what relative significance—added up to an argument, which was that Richard Nixon was progressively deluding himself about what he was doing and that, when he said he didn't know things that he did know, he wasn't pretending but concealing the memory from himself. And although I think we were right, it is equally possible to argue that Nixon knew exactly what he was doing and was deceiving everybody except himself. But I'm sure that our act of turning those documents into drama, of showing one way in which those words could have been spoken by real human beings, had the effect of deepening our audience's understanding of those extraordinary events; and it may even have proved, for those who disagreed with our interpretation of the events, that they were right and we were wrong.

The threat to dramadocumentary does not just consist of critical attacks from critics, pundits, and ministers of the Crown. In November 1980, the Broadcasting Act became law, and with it, the provisions for the setting up of a Broadcasting Complaints Commission (BCC) came into effect. Broadcasters had been acquainted with the baleful nature of this body a few months earlier, when lawyer Geoffrey Robertson had addressed the Edinburgh Television Festival on the subject of the BCC:

> In the short space of three hours, the Commons Committee on the Broadcasting Bill approved the construction of a special court to judge radio and television programmes: the Broadcasting Complaints Commission. It will comprise "three wise men" with no media links, appointed by the Home Sec-

> retary, to "adjudicate upon complaints of unjust or unfair treatment . . . or unwarranted infringement of privacy." Replete with a staff of "officers and servants" paid for by a special levy on broadcasting companies, it will sit in secret to consider complaints from individuals (alive or dead), companies, clubs and foreign countries. It will summon broadcasting executives, call for correspondence, and hand down judgements which must be published in any way it directs.[6]

Acting without even the right of appeal, the BCC has the potential of being a mighty force for censorship, particularly in the form of self-censorship before the event. As Robertson pointed out:

> The BCC, as it has emerged from this process, is no longer an exercise in accountability. It is an exercise in control. It will become another means of levering television and radio into a strait-jacket which could never be contemplated for newspapers, books or plays. It is not an effective method for securing a "right of reply" for persons whose actions have been distorted, and its function is far removed from the desirable end of providing a speedy correction of untruths. It is, in effect, a court, whose case law will impinge on the way television programmes are made, the nature of subject-matter selected, and the techniques used for bringing history, drama and current affairs to life on the small screen.

The implications for historical plays and dramadocumentary are indeed awesome. Even after the government amended the provision that would allow the relatives, friends, and admirers of the dead to complain on their behalf (the Richard III Society?), the present procedure would allow the Saudi government to complain about *Death of a Princess,* the Soviet leadership to demand reparation for *Invasion,* and veterans of the ATS, a British women's wartime army, to prevent a second showing of Ian McEwan's *Imitation Game.* Doubtless the social service ministries would have had a high old time with *Cathy Come Home* and *The Spongers* (and the Police Federation with *Law and Order*) as well.

Not surprisingly, the BCC has the support of Mrs. Mary Whitehouse.[7] And the ubiquitous Paul Johnson has applauded the commission as "an element of salutary terror" to be wielded against the "new breed of young, radical producers and directors, some still in their twenties, who are without scruple in their pursuit of what they believe to be higher causes."[8]

As long ago as 1951, dramadocumentary maker Caryl Doncaster stated that "the dramatised story documentary is one of the few art forms pioneered by television." It is important that the form be defended for that reason alone; but there are wider implications. Through all the criticism of dramadocumentary runs a single thread of assumption: that while clever, educated people are able to recognize and judge a thesis when they see one, ordinary television viewers can somehow be duped into accepting an argument as objective fact. As it happens, the so-called cheap popular newspapers are full of letters from people who are highly critical of television programs that do not live up to the virtues that their makers claim for them, whether those virtues are those of entertainment or of historical truth. But even if it could be proved (and I doubt it mightily) that the majority of viewers really will take at face value anything that is pumped out at them, then it is an extraordinary indictment not of *dramadocumentary* but of the rest of television, that it is so uniform, so uncontentious, and so bland that it has bludgeoned its audience into a state of passive acceptance of everything they see.

As a writer about public life, I would defend dramadocumentary as a form in which important things can be said in a uniquely authoritative and credible way. But the form also needs to be defended because the presence of dramadocumentary in the schedules is an active encouragement to audiences to think critically and seriously about all the programs they watch.

Notes

1. *Sunday Times,* 13 April 1980; *Guardian,* 6 August 1980.
2. *Guardian,* 26 August 1980.
3. Typescript of "The Granada Lecture: Dramatised Documentary," delivered at the British Film Institute, 19 May 1981.
4. *Listener,* 19 March 1981.
5. *Sunday Times,* 13 April 1980.
6. *Listener,* 11 September 1980.
7. Letter to the *Listener,* 15 January 1981, and elsewhere.
8. *Listener,* 1 January 1981.

15

Death of a Princess: The Politics of Passion, an Interview with Antony Thomas

Alan Rosenthal

Antony Thomas's *Death of a Princess* reconstructs a journalist's investigation into the death of a young Arab girl. Though its first broadcast generated what is possibly the biggest row ever in the history of television, the original incident had passed almost unnoticed by the world.

On 15 July 1977, a royal princess and her lover were publicly executed in Saudi Arabia. It took six months for a British newspaper to identify the victims and their crime as adultery. Later a British carpenter, who'd been working in the Gulf, claimed he'd photographed the double execution. Soon another witness entered the scene, a German nanny who claimed to have been a family friend and known the princess well.

As more and more conflicting stories appeared in the press, a major debate opened up in the British Parliament. When the debate and criticism threatened a major diplomatic confrontation with the Saudis, the British foreign secretary apologized to them for his former condemnation of the execution.

At the time of the debate, Antony Thomas was regarded as one of the most noted and probing documentary directors working in England. In 1977 his three-part series on South Africa had won him the highest British television award of the year. More important, in 1974 Thomas had also made three films exploring the Arab world, so that the story of the princess was to fall on fertile ground. *Death of a Princess* is, in fact, based on Thomas's own six-month trail through four countries, as he tried to explore and understand what happened to the Arabian girl and why.

It took some while to settle on the form of the film. Doing a standard documentary was ruled out because of fears expressed by various interviewees. The originally scheduled writer favored a straight drama. Executive Producer David Fanning, from coproducing station WGBH Boston, argued for a documentary drama because "it combines a rigorous concern for facts, that characterizes the best of journalism, with the narrative thrust and dramatic strength of a screenplay." Docudrama won.

In the film, Antony Thomas becomes the journalist, Chris Ryder (played by Paul Freeman). The story begins at a London dinner party where the question of the princess's fate and what it represents is raised. The action then moves through different locations as the quest for truth goes on. The carpenter recalls the Saudi execution (actually staged in Cairo) in grim detail. The nanny Elsa Gruber (played by Judy Parfit) tells us about the private life of the princess. We visit the school she was supposed to have attended in Beirut. We see the civil war in Lebanon and visit clubs where Arab oil millionaires dance. An elderly Arab princess describes how rich Arab women go looking for sexual outlets by trailing men in their chauffeur-driven Mercedes. Someone else accuses the Saudi government of having taken fifty rebel air force officers up in a government plane and then throwing them to their deaths.

All of this is woven in and around the princess's story. The complete truth about her is never learned. It appears that she bungled her escape plans and was killed on the orders of her grandfather, but much remains unclear. The story of the princess is almost incidental to Thomas's plan. What he is really attempting to do is investigate the social pressures, ideals, and strains of a modern Arab society. It is a society whose inner workings (at least in the late seventies) were mostly hidden from Western eyes.

The central theme of the film and the dilemma of the Arabs is laid down in one of the first scenes, when an Arab professor asks, "How much of our past must be abandoned and how much of your (Western) present is worth imitating?" The issues then discussed include the force of Islam and its relationship to a royal house described by one character as "an autocratic regime having nothing to do with Islamic thought"; the general behavior of women and their place in Arab society; the civil war in Lebanon; the Palestinian morass; and the question of honor in society and family relationships.

Thomas covers a vast canvas, and his projections have a *Rashomon* quality. Was the princess merely a party lover, or was she a rebel who absorbed the passions of the Palestinian freedom fighters? Was she content with the veil or fighting for a new pure Islam? In the end, it doesn't matter because it is the deeper issue of cultural conflict that stays with us.

When *Princess* was finally transmitted in England by ATV Television on 9 April 1980, all hell broke loose. The Islamic Council of Europe attacked the film, saying, "It has angered the entire Moslem community in the United Kingdom . . . and the British Government cannot escape its responsibility for its ugly conspiracy to discredit the Royal family." When the Saudi Arabian ambassador protested the film, the British foreign secretary sent a personal message of regret to King Khaled. This in turn caused various British members of Parliament to attack the apology. As Labour M.P. David Winnick remarked, "It is undignified to see the Foreign Secretary apologize to a reactionary State."

The furor deepened when Penelope Mortimer, Thomas's first script colleague, wrote a letter to the *New Statesman* magazine on 18 April. Mortimer claimed a deep involvement with the film (denied by Thomas) and damagingly stated that, "with the exception of three people and a family, every interview and every character in the film is fabricated." She also added that no real effort was made "to check information about the domestic life of the Princess, and the man hunting." What the charges implied, in short, was that *Princess* was a work of fiction masquerading as documentary truth.

David Fanning answered the charge a week late, and Thomas discusses this at length in my interview with him. However, controversy over the film increased when it was scheduled for American broadcast by PBS. Five stations belonging to South Carolina public television, as well as stations in Houston and Los Angeles, refused to show it. The Saudi Arabian ambassador protested to the U.S. State Department about the pending broadcast. Representative Clement Zablocki of Wisconsin said the decision to show the film was ill advised. Mobil Oil, which funds much of PBS, called the film "A New Fairy Tale." It also ran huge newspaper advertisements, which quoted Mortimer's "fabrication story" and urged PBS "to exercise responsible judgment in the light of what is in the best interests of the United States." The ads did not mention Mobil's economic interests in Saudi Arabia. In spite of the pressures, Lawrence Grossman, then president of PBS, decided to go ahead with the broadcast.

After the Mobil ads appeared, Mortimer herself seems to have had second thoughts. Thus she wrote to the *New Statesman,* "By fabrication I meant manufacture or construction. If I had meant invented or forged I would have said so." Fanning and Thomas had won a victory but at tremendous personal cost.

Apart from the political hullabaloo and the question of documentary truth, there was also considerable personal fallout from the film. Following the broadcast, a number of Egyptian actors were placed on a veritable Arab "blacklist" and had their films boycotted in Saudi Arabia, Iraq, Sudan, Abu Dhabi, and Oman.

Most of the issues raised by *Princess* are still very much with us today. Of these the most important is freedom of speech. In 1998, freedom of speech and freedom of subject choice in broadcasting are still under fire in too many places. Here I include the Western world, not just the Middle East. One wonders whether *Princess* could be made today. I have my doubts. Thomas managed to say what he wanted and go on living a normal life. Salman Rushdie has not been so lucky. The situation is not good, but with awareness and action there is hope.

Since finishing *Death of a Princess,* Antony Thomas has made *The Most Dangerous Man in the World* (1982) and two programs on the Christian Right in the United States, *Thy Kingdom Come* and *Thy Will Be Done* (both in 1987). In 1992 and 1993, he also made two films for HBO on the quest for eternal youth and group prejudices in America. In 1996 he published a biography of Cecil Rhodes, the South African entrepreneur and statesman, and also wrote a nine-part TV series on Rhodes, which was broadcast by the BBC in the autumn of that year.

This interview was done with Antony Thomas in Jerusalem in 1993 and marked the beginning of a wonderful friendship.

Rosenthal: Death of a Princess tells a specific story but also describes the problems within a culture. How did you get involved?

Thomas: The newspaper reaction to the original story was sensational but didn't really affect me. It was a tragic story, and I didn't want anything to do with it. Then in London I met a very highly placed Saudi gentleman and was given an extraordinary version of the girl's death. It was a version that beautifully expressed the Arab dilemma and had a great deal to say about the democratic nature of our justice. It was a fine, wonderful, classic romantic story. I believed what I heard, and I knew enough about the Arab world that the story connected. And I thought I could tell that story as a drama. I had a lot of leads from that first meeting. I was told that the princess had been to school at the Arab University of Beirut, and I was determined to put flesh on the story, travel through the Middle East and find out as much as I could about her. And I would do a drama, a rather conventional drama on the life and death of an Arab princess, because I felt I had an awful lot to say on that particular story.

Rosenthal: Who backed you, and how did you put substance on your research leads?

Thomas: I presented the idea to ATV, a member of the British Independent Television Network. They were interested in it and off I went, only to discover the research was utterly baffling. I discovered very early on that many of the elements of the story I'd been told were simply not true. The most solid lead I had been given was that the princess was supposed to have met her lover at the Arab University of Beirut. So I felt I should begin there, in Lebanon, and find people who had known her, who had taught her, and her classmates. I also had a lead outside Saudi Arabia, a German woman who had been governess in the household of the princess's grandfather and who knew her personally. However, she was very complicated and legalistic, and it was going to take weeks before we had an agreement and would talk to me. So I thought I would go to Lebanon first and check everything out there. I also thought I should talk to some Arab women about some of the finer details of life in Islamic society, what it means to be a woman in an Islamic society. Then came the shock. After two days in Lebanon, I discovered part of this wonderful dramatic story was nonsense. The girl had never been to the Arab University of Beirut.

However I soon discovered something else very interesting: that the girl had become some kind of mythological figure in the Arab world. Everybody talked very passionately about her, even people who had never known her. She had become both a personal symbol and also a political symbol, and everyone was adopting her to their cause. Thus for a Palestinian family that talked to me about her, she had become a freedom fighter. This ability in the Arab world to deal in myth, hearsay, and legend found strong material in the story of the princess. I was slow to realize this but after a while began to see the importance of all these elements in the story.

Rosenthal: How far did you let people know what you were doing? And were you sure from the start it would be a docudrama or were you thinking of a more conventional form?

Thomas: I think *Princess* would have made a marvelous documentary film based on a journey to discover the truth, where everyone has their own version of who this girl was, depending on who they were themselves. However, when I then started recontacting my interviewees and said, "I'm thinking of a documentary and want you to repeat what you said to me," almost without exception they said, "Are you mad? We are never going to appear on film making these statements about Arab society and womanhood in Saudi Arabia. It's impossible!"

Then I moved to a second stage, which was to say, "Well, what if I dramatize this journey?" I questioned everyone I had interviewed and asked them whether, if I used their exact words, they would trust me to create a character who is completely different from themselves, exists in a different context, yet speaks those exact words? The permissions were given, and they formed the basis for the film. I took the interviews, I cut some of them down, but I was very careful to retain their essential sense as in the original.

Rosenthal: You were doing your research in Beirut in the middle of a civil war. You must have had many conflicting feelings.

Thomas: To be in Lebanon at the time of the war was very difficult. And I felt very uncomfortable sitting in this hotel and pursuing some personal obsession while a war was going on. I remember looking out of my bedroom window and across the street onto an apartment block. There was an old man sitting on a balcony lit just by oil lamps, and we made eye contact. And on his face there was such a mark of suffering and tragedy. I felt very uncomfortable. What the hell right did I have going there doing what I was doing? But in a way, it's a little experience like that which is argument for dramatized documentary. We can show those little subtle moments and observations that we remember that don't have a place in normal documentary. It's these very small, subtle moments that one can go back and re-create.

In Lebanon I had a feeling of intrusion, but Saudi Arabia was different. The subject was enormously sensitive, and there was no way I could interview someone and just say, "I am here to ask you about the death of this princess." Unless I knew the interviewee personally, I would always talk about the general political situation in Saudi [Arabia] and about Islamic law and so on. And then, in the most offhanded way possible, I would say something like, "And what about the story of the princess?" "What story?" And I'd say, "You know, the one that was executed." I would make it seem a little parenthetical thing that I was adding as an afterthought at the end of the interview. I had to go through that charade every time.

Script to Film

Rosenthal: Was it difficult translating your research into a script?

Thomas: It was the easiest script that I ever had to write because it simply followed the progress of my journey, and it wasn't necessary to reorder the time sequence. I transcribed all the interviews, and then the only creative thing I did was to say, "Well *X* is a housewife, I'll make her a journalist. *Y* is a journalist, I'll make her a teacher." After that it was just a matter of making sure I'd created the right recognizable context for the person.

The first draft I did contained everything. Then David Fanning and I would read the lines and try to feel the point where the attention dragged or the argument stopped being clear. So we were continually cutting and trying to get down to the essence of the drama. It wasn't like the normal way you handle a dramatic script. We weren't changing structure or adding new scenes for old. It was very different.

Rosenthal: I understand ATV didn't cover all the budget. How did you raise the rest? And, to deal with what seems the basic problem, how did you find an Arab location for such a potentially controversial film?

Thomas: It had a ludicrous budget by modern standards, two hundred fifty thousand pounds sterling. That was ten years ago, and we had to make a drama with forty-five speaking characters in three countries: England, Lebanon, and finally Egypt, where we did the major part of our shooting. ATV gave me half the money, and I raised the other half in two days in MIFED, the international film market, where everybody buys and sells TV ideas.

The big problem of course was finding an Arab country that would let me film the script. That was really tough. I tried everybody; I tried everyone from the Iraqis to the Tunisians to the Algerians. All these countries have got censorship departments, and I had to be very up-front with them. They were all very polite. The Algerians even told me that they applauded the sentiments of the film, but no one wanted to get into a political hassle just to help Mr. Thomas make his film. Finally the Egyptians agreed to let me do the main filming in their country. I guess the deciding factor was their anger at the Saudi rejection of their stand in the '78 Camp David talks with Israel. Lebanon was no problem. It was a country without a government, and you just went in and filmed. As for Saudi Arabia, I had some establishing material that I had shot there previously. Not executions but long shots and general street scenes and atmosphere.

Rosenthal: How difficult was it casting your Arab characters?

Thomas: There's no structure in the Arab world. There's no simple casting book like *Spotlight.* In fact, a good Lebanese friend of mine said, "You are about to do the most foolish thing in your life. You want to make a realistic film, and you are using Arab actors? You don't understand just how far that is from Arab acting tradition. You'll become a laughingstock. You are going to produce something so unreal that it will be the end of your career. You'll never get a job again."

Nine weeks before we were supposed to start shooting, I was introduced to this man who was supposed to be the biggest casting director in Egypt. We spent hours talking about every character. He took notes, supposedly knew exactly what I wanted, and we agreed I would come back two weeks before shooting to make my final selection. Well, eventually we came back to this famous casting director, and what did he have? Three Polaroids of his sister, her friend, and somebody else. That was all—and we had to cast forty parts.

So David Fanning and I did everything. We had all sorts of dinners with radio people and film directors. I described every character, and they gave me names. It was frantic. Every day people came pouring into our rooms for preliminary casting. Some thought it was some big Hollywood-type film, and my room was crowded with flowers from actresses who'd sent a bouquet ahead for these parts and sent a bouquet ahead for Mr. Thomas. Then lots of people sent me these sepia photographs. I'd see a handsome man with a Ronald Colman mustache looking about thirty, and then a man of eighty would arrive. It was an absolute scramble, and we were still casting during filming. In fact, when we started we only had half our cast.

Rosenthal: How did you feel about doing drama since all your previous experience was in documentary?

Thomas: Actually it was incredibly easy. I was trying to get as close to reality as possible, and it is simply the story of a man traveling through the Arab world meeting and interviewing people. Now, one of the things that breaks reality is too much choreography within the space, which comes from the tradition of theater. My rule was that nobody moved unless there was a dramatic reason to do so, because when you interview people you sit side by side, except for when you answer the phone or make coffee. You don't conduct interviews in a highly choreographed way.

My guiding principle was not technique in a theatrical sense but reality, and directing actors toward that end was terribly exciting. It meant draining away all preconceptions and histrionic qualities and bringing it all down to real speech and a truthful reality. Many of the actors, particularly the Arab actors, told me how exciting this was. It was the first time they had been given a chance to attempt realism, and they did it very well because they were talking about things they felt and which concerned them. Their training made them act way over the top, and my purpose was to drain that out of them and recapture a truthful quality and a certain stillness.

As for Paul Freeman, who plays the journalist, he had maybe the hardest job, and he did it marvelously. All he does is say "yes" or "no" and ask the occasional question, yet he brings life to it. The idea was that this traveler should have no context. We wouldn't know whether he was married or single. He's almost a half shadow, and that's not a pleasant demand to place on an actor.

Rosenthal: Tell me more about how the actor's roles would sometimes reflect their lives.

Thomas: In the film, a girl who is supposed to be a teacher represents radical Islam. Now, the film was made before the Khomeini revolution. So it was possible to be very idealistic about what Khomeini stood for, because nothing had been seen in practice. And the girl herself really believed in all those future possibilities. She read the script, became tremendously excited, and the words really became her words.

Rosenthal: It's very hard for anyone coming from England or America to imagine the hassles working in Egypt. I would imagine the difficulty with casting was just the beginning.

Thomas: You're right. We faced enormous problems of organization. The telephones didn't work. To call actors, you had to send runners off across the city and all that kind of difficulty. We were often working inside, and because of the lights and lack of air-conditioning the heat was unbelievable. And because the government had the script, we were always frightened that pressure from the Islamic fundamentalists would start to build, and we would be thrown out of the country without completing the film. We were really terrified of that since there had been a number of hostile articles in the Islamic press as to what we were doing, or what they feared we were doing. So we lived on our nerves. At any moment something could explode.

The most difficult day was the day we shot the execution. The budget was tight. We had to shoot a complex scene, and we had 250 extras that we could only afford for one day. We were working under incredible pressure in the fierce heat, and the crowd was starting to get very tense and uncomfortable. The princess was going to be shot and her lover executed with a sword. The scene was very disturbing to the Egyptians, and on the first few takes there were lots of gasps and exclamations of shock. Then we set up for the final shots where the square empties after the execution. Of course, once a square drains, it's a hell of a business to get everyone back in position. We did the shot, the square drained, and just before we wanted to cut, a lad comes in in motorbike gear and leather jacket, stands in front of the camera, and waves. I said, "For Christ's sake, you killed the shot." The crowd was upset, didn't quite know what was wrong, and before I knew what had happened had turned around and had started to lynch this man for destroying the shot. I tried to separate them, and finally a very bloodied motorcyclist hobbled out of that square.

Rosenthal: You mentioned there was one scene where the censor interfered.

Thomas: The censor was present during most of the shooting, and I couldn't persuade her to pass some of the lines in the first or second scene where we hear the princess's side of the story. She was adamant that the lines couldn't be filmed, and we argued and argued. The lines were essential for understanding the story, and without them the scene at the dinner party wouldn't play. The way I eventually got these lines was by taking advantage of the fact that the censor had tummy troubles that day and was a frequent visitor to the lavatory. So while she was out, we shot the vital lines.

Reactions and Anger

Rosenthal: The film is superb in its depiction of the life of the princess, Arab society, and the conflicts in the Arab world. However, the film itself seems to have been overtaken by all the governmental and political furor around it. Did you have any sense that the film would engender such an uproar?

Thomas: When the film was cut and had a rough premix, I wanted to show it to one of the senior men who had originally given me permission to shoot and make sure he was satisfied. I also wanted to show it to the cast in case any of them wanted to remove their credits or felt nervous about being associated with the film. But I had no idea what the reaction would be when they saw the whole film. In the end the cast were wonderful and said the most flattering things about what the film represented. Then I showed it to the senior man who had given me the first permission. He was very flattering and said he only wished that an Arab director had had the courage to make it. I then asked him if he was concerned about possible Saudi reaction, and he said, "Mr. Thomas, they are far too sophisticated to publicize your film by creating a fuss." So I went back to London very relaxed and wrote a memo to Lord Windlesham, who was the chairman of ATV, and for whom I had created problems in the past. This time, I told him, we could relax. And then the storm broke.

The prepublicity had unfortunately been rather sensational and had alerted the Saudis, who were trying to stop the transmission. But it went ahead. The following day, I expected the reviews to be on page thirteen or whatever, but they were front-page. Most were marvelous, but there were a few which were very disturbing. The reactions from some papers, like the *Daily Express,* were frankly racist. There was a vicious cartoon about Arabs tempting to stifle us British. "This is a democracy," the papers said, "and didn't the WOGs know that we had the right to show what we wanted to show."[1] I was very offended by that line and knew it was going to lead to serious trouble, but for the moment I could cope with the reactions. Then two things happened that made everything much worse. To explain that I need to backtrack a bit.

When I thought that this film was going to be a Joan-of-Arc drama, I'd approached novelist Penelope Mortimer to write the script. Penelope came with me on the research but was very resistant to the way I saw the story in the form of a journey. She thought it should be pure drama, and the direction I was going was doing her out of a job. Then she compromised and agreed to write the first draft, but it really wasn't terribly suitable. I thought we had an amicable understanding. I apologized for changing direction, for bringing it back into documentary, which wasn't her area, and we parted as friends.

Then I got a warning signal a week after the film was shown, when she wrote critically about the film in an English paper. I was confused because she had congratulated me so warmly during the previews, saying how right I was and how wonderful the film was. When I phoned her she apologized but a week later wrote her famous letter to the *New Statesman.* The first thing the letter did was more or less reveal who one of our characters was, which was extremely unfair because it caused that person a lot of problems. She also claimed that the film and the interviews were a fabrication. That was all that was needed. It gave ammunition to all the enemies of the film. The letter was used by the Saudis. It was also material for the politicians who were against the film, because now the issue was *fabrication,* instead of the democratic right to show the film, come what may. When I came back on the attack, Penelope recanted, but by then the beast was out of the stable, and I had to defend myself all over the place.

Two weeks after the transmission of the film, the Saudis broke diplomatic relations with Britain and our ambassador was expelled. I knew the consequences would be terrible, and then the heat was really turned on. One reviewer who had written a most complimentary review suddenly recanted. The foreign minister got in there and fought really dirty. The government's view, as put by the Foreign Office, was that the film must never be shown again under any circumstances. It must be buried and forgotten. With Miss Mortimer's help, they were now attacking on this moral front. When the British Film Academy wanted to show the film, they were subject to unbelievable pressure to abandon the screening. When it was invited to the Edinburgh Television Festival, again there was this pressure, and armed guards arrived at the viewing, which made everyone nervous and uncomfortable. They were there "in case there was a riot," because feelings were said to be so strong. Of course, there was no riot. It was all nonsense. People just came to watch the film.

Then the whole issue came up [over] the showing of the film in the U.S. On this matter, the Carter government behaved extremely responsibly, not like the British government, which got down on its knees and used every dirty trick to stop the screenings. The U.S. government said to the Saudis, "If there are things in this film that are inaccurate, then you must send us a list of these inaccuracies and we can make a judgment." The final list that the Saudis sent was crazy. It contained complaints that the robes the Arabs were wearing in the crowd scene were too dirty, and so on. There wasn't a single point of substance. Then the government said, "You are welcome to sue the people, and you've got all those channels, but this is a democracy." And because the Americans behaved so calmly and responsibly the film was shown.

Meanwhile, David Fanning and I were doing various radio and television interviews, and on one of them we faced Congressman Zablocki. He was going on about this ghastly film and what a disgrace it was, and what an insult to Islam and the Saudis. After a commercial break, David said in a very polite way, "Congressman Zablocki, can I just establish one thing? This awful, dreadful film that shouldn't have been made, have you actually seen it?" There was a long pause, and then Zablocki said, "No, but a friend of mine in Milwaukee has." And I felt that that really was an extraordinary comment on the level of some of the other stuff.

Problems of Dramadocumentary

Rosenthal: Many people dislike dramadocumentary. They feel, amongst other things, it plays fast and loose with truth. In your film, you make certain strong accusations or assertions. One concerns the way the Saudi princesses conduct their sex lives. Another accusation concerns the way the CIA acted in Arabia and the way Arab air force officers were thrown out of planes. Are there any major points or incidents in your film that were not based on fact?

Thomas: All those scenes you mentioned were reported to us as factually true, either by people who claimed they had directly witnessed them or claimed a close relationship with somebody who had. None of our statements stood without a hell of a lot of cross-reference. The film was about people's distortion of the truth, so we weren't going to accept as fact merely what one person told us. Nothing appeared in the film without the kind of meticulous cross-referencing such as one does in a documentary investigation. Of course all the hostile newspapers all seemed to concentrate on the business of "the sexual pickup road." Well, there *was* a pickup road, and the cars cruised it, and the women went looking for men. Now, one particular paper said that the road scene was unprovable and appalling, and so on. Yet, six months later, the same newspaper published its "exclusive revelations" about the pickups. Evidently *Princess* had been conveniently forgotten.

Rosenthal: There have been a number of articles in recent years that have talked about Arab stereotyping in the media. Have you been attacked at all on these grounds?

Thomas: No, and I would have been very hurt if anyone had done that. The people we see in the film are based on my friends and contacts in the Arab world. They are the foreground characters while the princess is really background. The people are highly informed. They speak English. Obviously, it was a journey through the Arab middle class, but none were stereotypes. Perhaps it could be regretted [that,] because I don't speak Arabic, I couldn't conduct my investigations in the backstreets and meet peasants and ordinary people. It was a very upper-middle-class view of the Arab world. Again, I think it could be fairly said that I chose a sensational event, a public execution in a town square, which is untypical of the Arab world.

Rosenthal: How do you feel looking back on the film after ten years and in a post-Khomeini era? Did it have a radical effect on your career?

Thomas: As far as the political message of the film, it strongly endorsed a radical Islam that went back to the teaching of the Koran and had nothing to do with the Saudi royal family. In that structure, Khomeini was regarded as a revolutionary figure who was going to clean up the regime. I guess what has happened subsequently has made that aspect of the film seem rather foolish.

On the other question, I thought I would be labeled "too hot to handle," but that didn't happen. I didn't know the U.S. well then, but I soon discovered that a controversy like that gives you a cachet. I didn't suffer professionally, but I did suffer personally. I was very battered by the sheer strength of the assault after the showing. It took a long time for me to calm down and get into another subject.

Note

1. The crude and derogatory term *WOG* is an abbreviation of a British army expression for an Arab, literally "Wily Oriental Gentleman."

16

Writers in Action: Ernest Kinoy, Michael Eaton, Michael Baker

Alan Rosenthal

A few years ago, when my interests started moving from documentary to docudrama, I decided to do a book about the work of the docudrama scriptwriter. In thinking about the subject, it seemed to me then, and still does today, that the task of the docudrama writer is even more demanding than that of the normal scriptwriter.

The task is like boxing with one hand tied behind your back, and the rope that binds you is called "truth." In my mind, docudrama appears as a minefield full of high explosives and rare treasures. To reach the rewards, you have to be prepared to live dangerously, and at every step you have to recall the sign over the entrance: "Watch the Facts."

While preparing the book, I interviewed about twenty writers over the course of a year. What I wanted to know was how they could create imaginative drama when their hands were shackled by the necessity of accuracy. So I put to them question after question, such as, "Do you think it is permissible to stray from reality, rearrange lives, simplify facts, and assign new motives to characters?" The answers, of course, were absolutely fascinating and formed the underpinning for what eventually came out as *Writing Docudrama.*[1]

What follows in this chapter are extracts from three of those research interviews: Ernest Kinoy, Michael Eaton, and Michael Baker. They are severely shortened, as sometimes the interviews went on for a few hours, but taken together they help to explain a little of the mysterious process of writing.

Ernest Kinoy, who leads off the chapter, can almost be called Mr. U.S. Docudrama. A warm, outgoing man, he started his career with NBC radio after the war. Very quickly he moved into television and was soon writing for *Playhouse 90,* the *Alcoa Show, Desilu Playhouse,* and a dozen other shows, including *The Defenders.*

A list of Ernest Kinoy's scripts would take up pages, but his work includes the first two hours of *Roots,* the feature film *Buck and the Preacher,* and docudramas about Abraham Lincoln, Edward R. Murrow, Chernobyl, and Skokie, Illinois.

What I tried to elicit from Ernie (who over the course of a few months became a good friend) was not just the mechanics of writing but the atmosphere in the networks over the years. In this respect, Ernest Kinoy's comments make an interesting supplement to the views expressed by Todd Gitlin in writing about *Bitter Harvest.*

Ernest Kinoy

Rosenthal: The Defenders was one of the best of the early TV series. What were the rules of the game and the procedures for a writer?

Kinoy: They did the first "Defenders" as a two-part show on *Studio One.* Reggie Rose wrote, but E. G. Marshall wasn't in it; it was Ralph Bellamy. It was a two-part legal thing, and they did the unusual thing of having as adviser Jerry Lightner, who was an attorney at the criminal bar, so that when they did something it was right.

That was supposed to be a pilot, but it languished on the shelf until there was a congressional investigation of where television was going. And there were hearings here in New York with questions like "Where is TV drama going? What's happening?" They were already starting to cry and moan. And then the hearings continued in Washington, and either William Paley or Frank Stanton was called on to testify, and one of the congressmen was belting him with "Why are there so many cheap comedies from the coast on film? Where is all the drama? What happened to *Playhouse 90?* Where's *Studio One?*" And he said, "Well, as a matter of fact, we have this marvelous program we are going to put on by the producers of *Studio One* and *Playhouse 90,* and it will be on very soon." And then after testifying he called up and said, "For God's sake, take that thing off the shelf and get it going." And that's how *The Defenders* got on.

Now, I had worked for the Producers for a long time and think I did the second one, and later on I did between six to eight of them a year.

Rosenthal: What was the time span in writing them? How were they blocked out? What were the vital ingredients?

Kinoy: Well, let me give you an example from the second one. About that time there had been a thing in the news that Robert Moses had gotten into a confrontation with some housewives who were demonstrating in Central Park. They wanted a playground built on a parking lot, or something like that.

So I came in and talked to Reggie, who served as story editor the first year, and said, "Listen, I've got an idea for this thing. Here's the issue. There's this Robert Moses type, this arrogant public fellow, and he's up against the housewives, and it gets to be a legal case as to whether they can do their thing." And he would say, "That sounds interesting," and you would do a short treatment.

From the beginning, at least in the ones I did, you were leaning on a legal issue. The key that you started with was mostly a legal issue, though sometimes it was a joke or a funny interrelationship of people. You'd start from that legal issue, and then you would say, "How the hell am I going to get characters into this?" and you would develop a two- or three-page treatment.

Rosenthal: Let's go more into the question of legal issues. You're a writer, not a lawyer like John Mortimer, who writes *Rumpole of the Bailey,* and yet you're dealing with a very complex and specialized area. How do you manage?

Kinoy: It would be often based on what was in the newspapers and the issues were very clear. We did things on civil rights issues and many things like that.

I was very fortunate because my brother happens to be a very prominent lawyer in civil rights and constitutional law, and I could always get advice and information from him. Several times I took cases he was interested in and switched them around and started with that.

We did one, for example, where they were developing a technique of how to get a case out of the states' courts. If they could prove that the state-court system was totally corrupt and unreliable on the issue under question, then maybe a constitutional way could be found to switch it to the federal courts.

Now that was the technique which they were using in certain civil rights cases, and I did a show on *The Defenders* about using just such a technique, and the network was very edgy. The show itself was about some northern Yankee–type deer hunters who get into trouble in a southern town. The next year, we did one with James Earl Jones about a demonstration outside of a construction site for black employment.

Each show usually took about a month to write, but if necessary you did it in less. They were written much closer to their airing deadline than is the custom now. And the difficulty is that that time lapse now gives executives the time to do creative thinking, which can be deadly to the show. But in those days, once the network approved the outline, it went so fast into production that they didn't have much time to complain.

Rosenthal: You were doing these interesting, complicated, sometimes highly political programs at the height of the McCarthy era. Then came all the blacklisting, firings, and writing under pseudonyms. Did either you or any of your friends write under different names, and how did the executives react?

Kinoy: I don't think anyone on *The Defenders* was affected. Not because they wouldn't hire him but because it just didn't turn up. But there was a very popular program on the networks at that time which was made in England called *Robin Hood* with Richard Greene, and it was written almost entirely by blacklisted American writers under other names.

I also remember a very funny situation when David Susskind hired a lot of blacklisted people in one way or another. He was putting on *The Bridge of San Luis Rey,* and he started from the script of an actress who I believed he was having an affair with at the time. And it was god-awful impossible. So he called Walter Bernstein seven days before they were to start rehearsals and said, "Walter, please, Walter!" So Walter totally rewrote *The Bridge of San Luis Rey,* and it went on very nicely.

A couple of months later, I happened to be out in Hollywood talking to a big-league producer and he takes a phone call. And as the call goes on, he is getting into all kinds of trouble and getting very upset. The call has to do with another project, but suddenly he turns to me and says, "You fucking New York writers. You get me into terrible trouble." I said, "What's the matter?" "Well," he said, "I hired this writer, with this marvelous credit who did this great show, and the script is shit." I said, "What writer did you hire?" "Well," he says, "the one who, er . . . did *The Bridge of San Luis Rey,*" and he tells me the name that went on it. And I start to laugh like hell, and I said, "Didn't anybody tell you? Walter Bernstein wrote that script."

Rosenthal: In the early sixties, you yourself wrote a script about the blacklist. How did it all start?

Kinoy: It was called *The Black List* because we had decided the time had come to do a script on the subject, and it was a great issue. There were a lot of possible topics, but we wanted to choose a story that would be very typical of what was happening.

At the time I said, "It's easy to do something about the star who's blacklisted, because the star who's blacklisted goes to Broadway or to England. It's terrible, but he's not dead. What's possibly more interesting are the cases of the middle-ground actors, ordinary working actors and writers who, when they were blacklisted, nobody came around, as they did to Dalton Trumbo begging him to work under the table, because who needed this guy anyway? Without the blacklist, they were marginal or just making out.

So we invented an actor, Jack Klugman played him, who had a small part in a film. Then what we went into was a legal situation, the equivalent of the Johnson intrusion and the *Counter Attack* battles, where the newspaper lands on this guy and gets him fired. He goes to the lawyer, and they discuss under what circumstances can they fight the situation. So the theme was what constitutional and legal basis can we have for bringing some kind of a suit. On the emotional side, it dealt with the point that this guy is now selling shoes. He was an ordinary working actor at best, but having been blacklisted, he was really lost. And the ending was not a happy ending. They have a case, and it may eventually get to the Supreme Court, but in the meantime this guy is dead. He's finished.

Rosenthal: Let's take it from there. We're dealing with the blacklisting of the fifties. Regarding the screenplays you've written, have there been many cases where you've written something but the network or the producer get cold feet because of the politics involved?

Kinoy: Many times. In recent years there has been, however, an interesting development. But let's go back a moment. During the McCarthy times, there was specific political concern, and what you had was self-censorship, where no one ever presented something controversial, something which they knew might be turned down.

I can remember in the late fifties doing a little thriller for a summer show of Chrysler's which was based vaguely on something that had been in the newspapers. It was about kids being lost in a cave. And what happens is that two preadolescent kids go off by themselves and another little kid tags along, and all three get lost in a cave. Now, their parents are upset and are at the police station.

In the story, the youngest kid who tagged along is black and the others are white, and it all takes place in California. This wasn't a story of active racism, but the point was that, when the parents converge on the police station, they don't understand that the three children were together. If they had, they would have been able to find them, through reasons I no longer remember. But the point was, because one of the children was black, nobody assumed they would be together.

So there it was, a fairly simple story, but I remember being asked to come out to the Coast where a woman took me out to lunch at Romanoff's. This indicated right away that something was very wrong. So just to prove my independence, I ordered scrambled eggs, to indicate that I wasn't taken in by Romanoff's. She then explained that there was just a little trouble, and would we mind if we made the little kid a Mexican. They could not tolerate having a black child as the issue. So I said, "The plot will only work in Brownsville, Texas. It won't work anywhere else. Well, maybe in San Diego. But nowhere else in the United States will anyone understand what it's all about." Then she said, "Well, if you won't do it, we're going to do it anyway. We're going to make the changes." So I said, "Well, take my name off." And I took my name off the show. Here was a case of a reluctance to deal with black Americans in a situation which wasn't at all confrontational.

By the early sixties, this had turned around. In the McCarthy era, there was a specific political objection to anything that was tainted with communism or the faintest communist ideology. But since then, the networks have done over the years very political things: *The Day After, Skokie,* and so on. However, the curious thing that's been happening is that they've been dropping projects not because they are afraid of a congressional investigation but out of exaggerated caution and cowardice.

What you get these days is that the networks will start or approve a project and part of that starting of the project comes from self-delusion. They think, "Boy, wouldn't it be marvelous," and then they start a whole project on some fascinating historical issue or political issue. So they get you going and you do a treatment, and sometimes you even do a screenplay, and then they chicken out. The fellow who had the authority to get the treatment done does not have the authority to spend the money, to make the film and actually do it.

For example, I did a piece for the producer Stan Margulies. Stan had an idea. He'd run into an organization of veterans of the Tuskegee airmen. In the Second World War, the army was totally Jim Crowed, and black soldiers were basically kept in menial tasks. The army was very reluctant to put them in combat units, though there were some and in the air force they were absolutely out in anything flying or to do with the technical side. Eventually they were politically forced to break that up, and an experimental unit was set up to train black pilots at Tuskegee. And, as you can imagine, a lot of fascinating things happened, and eventually their graduates went over to Europe and served with great acclaim. And Stan thought how the whole thing started would make a very interesting story.

Anyway, we got the approval of the Tuskegee veterans, and I met with a bunch of them, and we prepared a whole script. It was a very popular genre situation. It was the equivalent of five people getting together to go to West Point and things happen. They have all kinds of adventures, and they're five different kinds of people. So in its form, the Tuskegee piece was straightforward popular entertainment. Very good, I thought.

It was submitted to CBS around the time of Reagan's election, and CBS dropped it. Why? Well, the inside reports we had were that CBS said, "We don't think our audiences will be interested in any story about black people." And they dumped it.

Now, I happen to know some of the inside story because an old friend of mine, Roy Campanella, Jr., who was a director and editor, was out there sitting in some of these meetings with CBS. Now, he's black, and I think he left CBS over that issue because he was furious about it. So that was an example of self-censorship by the network, not because they were afraid that a congressional committee or someone else would attack them but because they were afraid to take a chance.

In and around the same time, Malcolm Stuart, a producer from the Coast, called me and asked me whether I wanted to do the story of [Alfred] Dreyfus. I said, "Sure. Great. Why not?" and we went to talk to the NBC executive.

This is now modern times, remember. The Second World War is over. The Holocaust is there, and we know all about that. So it's clear we can't and don't want to do it the way Hollywood did it in passing, in the thirties, in a film on Émile Zola. In that film, there is no audible mention of the fact that Dreyfus is a Jew. The only time you see it is when the French generals are looking for a scapegoat, and they take a close-up of the record, and there's the name "Alfred Dreyfus" and at the end it says "Jew." And if you were reading real fast you could see it. Then a voice-over says, "Oh! How did *he* get on the General Staff?" That is the extent of the mention of anti-Semitism in the old Hollywood film.

With all this in mind, I said to the executive, "If we do it, we can't do it that way." And he said, "Of course not. We want it tough and hard. We want the whole thing." So we went away and we prepared the treatment and they OK'd the treatment.

I think all this must have been around the time of Watergate, and what was so fascinating is that there were so many parallels. There was the enormous cover-up by the French military, and it really resembled Watergate. There was even the case of Colonel [Ferdinand] Esterhazy, who was blackmailing one of the General Staff who had set up Dreyfus, wanting to meet with one of the colonels who'd arranged the cover-up. They agree to meet but they're both nervous so they agree to meet at night in the woods, and the second colonel comes in drag dressed as a woman of the streets.

So there were all sorts of resemblances. And the material was marvelous. We used some material of Hannah Arendt on Dreyfus, where she almost attributes the rise of Nazism to the Dreyfus case and analyzes the role of the Church in the whole affair. We looked at all that and the role of the French rightist parties, and we did the whole thing.

And Dreyfus is not the hero of this thing. His brother is, as well as the attorneys and [Georges] Clemenceau. So we did the whole thing. Then it gets handed in, and my producer calls and says, "You've got to come to a meeting at NBC with Bill Storke." I go and Storke was very upset and troubled. "What's the matter," I said, "not dramatic enough?" "No, no. Dramatically it's very exciting. But tell me," he said, "does it have to be so Jewish?" and the network dropped it. Now, they never said that's why they dropped it, but they were concerned it wouldn't play in Peoria.

I did a script on the Miranda decision. It was an interesting case because as far as I could see the original Miranda was as guilty as hell. Now, the cops didn't beat him up—they tricked him, and they got the confession. But they were reasonably respectable guys. So I wrote the script, and the comment related to me by the producer was, "I'm not interested in the Miranda decision. Personally I don't care who gets convicted. Get the criminals off the street, and if innocent people go, the hell with it." That was the quote from the network executive. In other words, what he was reflecting was the attitude of the Reagan administration and that's where they thought their audience would be. So they dropped it.

Rosenthal: About four films, including one scripted by you, were eventually made about the Israeli raid on Entebbe, in 1976, when Israeli commandos freed over one hundred hostages being held by Arab and German terrorists. In going in, what struck you as the most compelling side of the story?

Kinoy: I thought the interesting thing was not the raid but the emotional and political conflict which the whole thing engendered. And on a few points I had something of a go-round with David Wolper, who was producing the film. For example, one of the things I'd found out and wanted to use was that on the plane, in the sweltering heat, with the Germans walking around with their hand grenades, the crazy Israelis are getting into big political arguments with the terrorists. I remember one guy told me he had rolled his sleeve up to show his concentration camp number to the German terrorists, while another got into a big argument with the Palestinians, and the Palestinian says (or at least this is how I worded it in the script), "I'll tell you what's wrong with Herzl. Back when he was saying there should be a homeland he didn't understand my great-great-grandfather was already living there." In other words, I told Wolper that to make it work you've got to give the Palestinians a chance to say what they've got to say.

Now, Wolper didn't want to do that. He was upset about the thought of having that kind of thing in. But I put my foot down and insisted. "Look," I said, "the odds are people are going to see it and end up where you want them to, but it will be false if these things aren't in. For one thing it happened. For another thing it's marvelous dramatically, this argument between a concentration camp survivor and a Palestinian terrorist.

Rosenthal: Let's turn to *Skokie.* One key thing interests me here: your method of interweaving fiction with reality.

Kinoy: In *Skokie* the obligation was to be absolutely true to what was going on legally in terms of the court battles, and we had to be very true about the position of people. We had to reflect what people really did and thought. Now, the fiction came in through the Danny Kaye family.

Here I wanted a family where you could show a number of things about Holocaust families and their children that you wouldn't and maybe couldn't find in one real family. And there were problems. I had to make the daughter fairly young, a sixteen-year-old teenager, whereas the daughter of a Holocaust victim would almost certainly be post college age.

Here, in this central family, I added in a lot of things from all sorts of sources. For example, there has been a lot of work on the conspiracy of silence between the survivors and the next generation. So I arranged the family so that could be explained as well. In other words, I wanted a script where you could discuss some general issues besides just the Nazi march on Skokie.

The fictionalization is not really fiction in the sense of dealing with nonrealities. What I was trying to do was create a composite family that would allow you to focus on some very trying and difficult issues.

One of the difficulties was that the Skokie case legally was very complex. There were at least five separate cases on various aspects of the issues, and you couldn't cover them all. What you had to do was pick very carefully because there was no way that you could cover the issues in all of them. But at the same time, you couldn't ignore them. What you had to do was find a way through it all that gave the essence of what was going on and along the way mention what was going on in that case over on the side and so on. The idea was that you haven't by omission falsified anything, but by selection you have found a line through which you demonstrate what were the essential conflicts and problems of that situation.

Then we had another problem. When I first did this I used false names. You do this in order to protect the original person and keep some privacy. But CBS now has a special department of paranoids and lawyers on these docudramas. They had been very badly burned by some mistakes they had made in the past and been sued successfully on a number of occasions. So they go over all these things very carefully.

However, after the Gwen Davis case (she was a novelist in California), they came back and said, "You've got to use everybody's real names." We said, "That's interesting. That's not what we used to do." But they said, "Don't argue. That's the way it's going to be. You have to use everybody's real names." Buzz Berger, who was active producer on the show, said, "Well, with this we've got to get releases from a lot of people, and it will make it very difficult." Then I said, "But there is no real name for this composite character. He's a fictional character." So they said, "All right. You can use your fictional name for him, but you have to use the real names for everyone else."

At that point, the lawyer for the ACLU [American Civil Liberties Union] in Chicago, whose aunt used to call him up from Florida and tell him he was anti-Semitic, called us. He was Jewish but had represented the Chicago Nazis on the freedom of speech issue and had consequently gotten into a lot of trouble. He spent two or three years going around having debates with people and being beaten by the Jewish community. Anyway, he said, "I've had it, and if you use my real name I'll sue." So CBS said, "OK. You can use a make-believe name for him."

This left us with the strange situation where at this point we had some characters totally fiction, some real with false names, and some real with real names. Thus the mayor's name is for real, as is the name of the guy from the B'nai B'rith in Chicago. As for the Nazi, nobody was worried about him as by this time he was in prison for child molestation. With Arieh Naor we used his real name, and he was furious because the actor playing him wore a beard and he doesn't have one. I had one character there who was the young woman in the Jewish Defense League who was a very loudmouthed young woman in reality. And I can't remember why, but we didn't use her real name either. Of course, a lot of this discussion is real nonsense because often the name, whether true or made up, never shows up on the air at all. It only appears in the script.

Michael Eaton: Writing *Shoot to Kill* and *Why Lockerbie?*

Michael Eaton is one of the most prolific TV dramatists working in England. His scripts include *Flowers of the Forest* (BBC, 1996), *Signs and Wonders* (four-part drama for BBC2, 1995), and *Fellow Traveller* (HBO Feature, 1989), which won best screenplay, British Film Awards. Like *Fellow Traveller,* both *Shoot to Kill* and *Why Lockerbie?* deal with human weakness, intrigue, evasions, betrayals, and death. At the time of our interview, Michael Eaton was working on a feature script about the enigmatic Irish hero Roger Casement, who was hung by the British in the First World War.

Rosenthal: Who initiated *Shoot to Kill?*

Eaton: Shoot to Kill was based on a very big British news story. In 1982 there were three incidents which took place in Northern Ireland. What happened was that within the space of a month an armed military unit, the Royal Ulster Constabulary, ambushed and fired on people who turned out to be unarmed. Several of these people also turned out to have absolutely no connection whatsoever with paramilitary Irish republican groups. Now, for each of these incidents, the police produced a plausible cover story as to what had happened and why they fired. However, one of the policemen involved was taken to court and told what actually happened.

Now this caused a great scandal because the police authorities were obviously telling one set of stories, whereas it seemed that the reality was very different. In the end, an inquiry was launched headed by John Stalker, assistant chief constable of the Greater Manchester Police. His brief was to go over to Northern Ireland and examine these three incidents.

Instead of doing a quick in-and-out whitewash job, Stalker and his team actually dug into the incidents and found out what was really going on. As soon as this started to be somewhat threatening to the RUC, a whole series of incidents took place which effectively disabled the inquiry and removed Stalker from it. To this day the findings of the inquiry have never been implemented in any court of law.

It was a well-known story, and Peter Kozminsky, a documentary director with Yorkshire Television, had been researching the subject for quite a while in order to do a film about it. However, it soon became apparent to Kozminsky that the conventional documentary format wouldn't work because (*a*) a lot of people wouldn't talk or cooperate with the media on this, (*b*) some of the most important players were dead, and (*c*) a number of people would only talk off the record. So rather reluctantly, I think, Peter gradually came to believe that the only way to tackle the subject was through drama.

Meanwhile, Stalker's own book had come out, and Peter and Zenith [a production company] were negotiating for the film rights. They then asked me whether I was interested in dramatizing the book. My response was that I didn't want to write a film just centered around one policeman. I thought that it was as important to make a film about everything that led to the inquiry as it was to make a film about the inquiry itself. Then Peter and Zenith decided they had enough sources already, particularly as John Forburn, Stalker's second in command, decided to cooperate as a major consultant. So after a few more discussions I said, "Yes, I'd like to do it."

Rosenthal: Can you tell me about the process from research to script and the various approaches that went through your mind?

Eaton: The research had been going on for a couple of years before I came onboard. There were also transcripts of three separate court cases that one had to wade through. While I was writing the first draft, there was also a researcher who could be directed by myself or Peter to check out further information and find more leads. Peter and John Forburn were also fleshing out and criticizing the material we already had. So when I first started I was already on top of the story, but new material and comments were continuously pouring in.

The problem was then to immerse yourself in the material so that you knew it backwards and come up with a convincing structure in order to tell the story in the most dramatic way. And that's the key word: *structure.* Let me give you an instance of this from *Shoot to Kill.*

I thought this was a story that was absolutely amenable to dramatization. It had a strongly defined set of conflicts. It also had a very clear narrative position in that the main characters move from one status, through conflict, to a different status at the end. But nevertheless you were faced with questions of how to make everything work, because it was really two stories. There was the story of a set of crimes, and the story of the *investigation* into those crimes, and the solution of the crimes. And I wanted to tell both stories.

When I came into the project, we discussed whether we could deal with the incidents that sparked off the inquiry by *flashback.* In other words, as the inquiry team learns what actually happened, so does the audience. That approach had the value of bringing the inquiry onto the stage right at the beginning. It also allowed audience identification with defined protagonists, Stalker and his team, with whom we can share the revelation of this information.

But to me there was one great argument against using this structure. It seemed to me that if the audience knew anything at all about the incident it was that Stalker was *unsuccessful.* They knew that he was taken off the inquiry before it was finished and that the story didn't have a Hollywood upbeat ending, where the forces of good triumph and the forces of revelation win out. So I knew, as it were, that there was very little suspense to this story because everybody knew the ending.

The way I wanted to do it—and it sounds very simple but has great structural implications—was to present things chronologically, whereby we see each of the incidents carried out by the RUC, and we present them in a way that later forensic evidence, produced by the inquiry, says that they actually happened. And we also see the police construct a cover story in order to give out to the press what *they said* had happened.

So the audience knows what *really* happened and what the police *said* happened. So when the inquiry comes on the scene, the audience knows more than the investigators. And to that extent, I think, one has created a situation of suspense because, as we see the first faltering attempts of the inquiry to get the truth, the audience knows when they are going in the right direction and when they're going in the wrong direction. Yes, the audience knows where the story is going to end, but giving them facts which the inquiry doesn't have involves them, I believe, much more centrally in the dynamics of the investigation.

Now the impact of this on structure was that the inquiry didn't start till about an hour and twenty minutes into the program. And that was a problem worth considering. Stalker and his team are the main protagonists, but we don't see them till we are well into the show, which is an extremely *unconventional* thing to do. But that also made me argue for a two-part drama rather than a one-part, because we deal with the incidents in the first part and the inquiry into those incidents in the second.

With the Pan Am story, *Why Lockerbie?,* I was faced with a different set of structural problems. It was also a story that didn't have a central protagonist. There were several people who potentially arose to play that role; but as real life doesn't follow the rules of drama, they soon found themselves out of the picture.

There was, for example, a man called Fred Ford who had the job of beefing up Pan Am's security. He was the perfect dramatic protagonist. He would be the man in the story you made up who would fight the bureaucracy, the institution, and sacrifice his own career and domestic life so that the truth will out. In reality, the moment he started blowing the whistle on what was happening he was fired! He would have been the perfect protagonist but was kicked out at the end of act one.

The real question was finding what the story was and how to structure it if we didn't have a good central protagonist. I looked at the material, and it struck me that it wasn't really a story centered around characters (because there's not one character who stays the whole course) but a story about two institutions. It was a story about an international airline with weak security and an international terrorist organization. The way I would then tell the story would be to look at those organizations from the top to the bottom, from the boardroom to the people who sit by the X-ray machines and examine your luggage, and from the people who go around the world looking for sponsorship for acts of terror to the soldiers who carry the bag with the bombs in them.

Rosenthal: You've told me you do various outlines for your docudramas. What purpose do they serve for you?

Eaton: Unlike fictional narratives, real life doesn't have a clear beginning, middle, and end. Given the jumbled mass of material, facts, and people in the story, you have to make decisions [about] where the story starts and where the story ends—and decisions [about] where the necessary expository elements from the back story can be brought in. The purpose of the outline for me is not to do a scene-by-scene breakdown. It's really a way of arguing for your approach to the material. The fuller scene-by-scene breakdown is useful because it allows everybody to agree [on] what's going to be in the story and what's left out.

Rosenthal: Docudrama has often been criticized for its invented situations, invented characters, and "creative" dialogue. What's your feeling on dialogue, and how do you cope with legalities?

Eaton: As a dramatist, I write the dialogue for these films, but I write it on the basis of the most important source material. We know a secret meeting took place. It was a meeting between certain people, and we know who those people were. We know what the agenda of the meeting was and what arguments various people at the meeting would have brought out. We know what actions arose from that meeting taking place, and therefore we are in a good position to decide which perspective and point of view was dominant.

Ideally I would like to be able to talk to everybody who was present at the meeting, but that's rarely possible. Sometimes we can talk to one or two and get their memories and perspectives. If we are lucky, we can report on the minutes of the meeting, but rarely do we get a tape transcript of what each individual actually said. So it's incumbent on me as a dramatist, taking that source, taking the journalistic information that we have, taking the public record that exists about the meeting, to finally put words into people's mouths. It's an area open to criticism, but I don't see a real problem with it.

While writing this form of drama, I'm in constant contact with lawyers acting on behalf of the TV company making the film. I'm sending them scenes, giving my sources, and informing them what lines are taken as verbatim record, and what ones I'm inventing on the basis of various sources. And the lawyers in turn are informing me what I can and can't do.

Rosenthal: Two final questions. What are the kind of stories that appeal to you? And what responsibilities, if any, do you have to the audience?

Eaton: The kind of docudramas I like to write are those that take us into institutions that we don't know a lot about. I want to explore the way ideas work in our society and the way ideas are mediated through institutions. And it seems to me the conventional documentary can only go so far in showing the actuality of those issues and also the responses. Those are the kind of docudramas that attract me as opposed to the very personal based emotional stories that tend to be the hallmark of U.S. TV docudrama.

As regards the audience, my view is that there is only one way these programs can work, and that is if we—the writers and producers—can establish an unspoken pact of trust between ourselves and the audience. Clearly docudrama is hedged around with all sorts of moral and ethical dilemmas, and I think one has to say to the audience, "Trust me. I'm not sensationalizing. I'm not making things up when I don't have any evidence to do so. I'm not trying to gain your sympathy for certain characters when they don't deserve it in order to make a neatly scripted drama. Trust me!" In terms of audience objectives, I think that's my main endeavor.

Michael Baker: The Writing of *Dead Ahead: The* Exxon Valdez *Disaster*

Michael Baker's early background was in BBC documentaries, and the discipline of nonfiction research obviously plays a key role in his dramatic writing. Besides docudramas, such as *Exxon Valdez* and *The Rothko Conspiracy,* Baker has also written a considerable number of original TV dramas and various TV adaptations taken from the novels of Ruth Rendell or based on the adventures of Agatha Christie's Hercule Poirot.

I chose to speak to Baker about his film on the *Exxon Valdez* oil spill because it seemed to me such a hard subject to dramatize. Unlike many other headline stories, there were no clear villains and heroes, no obvious thrust or narrative line, no clear conflicts, and no clear climaxes. I couldn't see where a writer would begin, but over the course of a few hours and many drinks Michael showed me how he managed to solve the script problems.

Rosenthal: Is there any one essential thing that guides you in writing docudrama?

Baker: I think research is the absolute key to dramadoc. I know in some places the writer doesn't always do the research.

You're given the *research,* and then you have to make do as you will. But I would say nine times out of ten, if you can, you should do most of the research yourself, because my philosophy of working is to get the journalistic values right first, and then decide what is the dramatic story that I'm going to create out of all this. There is a very practical reason why it should be in that order, and that is a legal one.

There are often many legal pitfalls you have to be aware of. Usually by the end of the process you've got lawyers crawling over the script, and if you haven't got the journalistic values right in the first place, you've got the most almighty mess you have to unravel. And it could mean the loss of whole scenes, which would be catastrophic at a late stage. So in that sense, I think the research is paramount.

Rosenthal: How did you set about writing *Exxon Valdez?*

Baker: The BBC approached me to write it. They themselves had been approached by HBO, who I think in turn had been approached by an outside company with the idea. Altogether research and writing took over a year. I wasn't initially expected to do the research. The BBC had a researcher onboard, but there was a difficulty of how much time he could spend on the project and releasing funds. They were only contracting him for a few weeks at a time. Anyway, it became more and more apparent to me that it was such a huge subject that I would have to do much of the research myself. And that's the best way of writing for me.

Rosenthal: Did you have any guidelines as to the way the film should be approached or structured? Or was it a case of do the research, and then we'll think about it?

Baker: Not really. I think all they knew was that this was an incident that had made a big impact in the U.S., and they somehow wanted to re-create the story. But they didn't know how. I knew that you couldn't do the whole thing. I knew you had to somehow zero in on various aspects, though I had no idea what those things would be until I'd got into the subject.

Of course what you find when you are researching a big story like this is that your perspectives are constantly changing. So if it becomes a question of whether you do the research first and then call a halt to write, or whether you research and write simultaneously, it's difficult to say. The research and writing is normally a complementary process all the way through. In the case of *Exxon,* we did most of the research and then we wrote. Then we went back out to Alaska and saw more people. And that changed my ideas about the whole thing. So it was very much a multilayered process.

As the research went on and on in Alaska, Texas, Washington, et cetera, I gradually met the real people involved in the story. A lot of them had retired, and I struck lucky on a number of cases where they had left the company and could speak more easily. And that was a very crucial thing. Because it became more and more apparent that the story we were going to do was certainly not the environmental story, because I'd watched maybe twenty documentaries about the environmental story, so there was no point in doing that. And that's another thing. I think when you are doing these things, you should always go for an angle that couldn't be done in any other way; otherwise, why are you doing this as a drama? What is the point in doing it as a drama if you can do it as a documentary? It sort of shores up the ground on which you are working if you can find that philosophical raison d'être. It's a good question to have in your mind when you start out: "Why am I doing this as a drama?"

Soon it became apparent to me that the real story we were looking at was the political story behind the disaster—the backsliding, the cock-ups, the government trying to renege on its responsibilities, in other words, a fairly explosive story in journalistic terms but also one that would be very dramatic if you could carry it off. Dodgy legally, but that was probably a price worth paying for a good film.

Rosenthal: You've done the research. You've got a mass of notes. Ideas and approaches are forming in your head. Where do you go from there? Did you write a treatment?

Baker: Yes. My first consideration was how to present the story as a drama.

The first treatment was almost just looking at the story as a whole. It was a very long thing in which I picked out salient sequences and scenes for a possible drama. What would be the entertaining scenes. What would be revelatory. What were the little details that were funny or gripping or made you laugh or cry. It was at that kind of level. In other words, I was looking for what was dramatic about this story without attempting to find the kernel we needed or the key line that would take us from beginning to end.

Then the treatments that followed were largely a process of whittling down the length and getting it into a shape, and I think that is probably what a treatment is for—to find your shape so you can start writing your scenes.

Rosenthal: You obviously had a variety of stories you could have followed and paths you could have gone down. You had so many choices of where to take the film. Can you tell me more about that and the choice of key "interesting" characters?

Baker: For a long time we were interested in a fisherman. We thought maybe he was going to be a focus of some tension.

There was also a guy called Kelly, a member of one of the communities on the sound, who almost single-handedly launched a kind of wildlife rescue operation which had run into the most appalling bureaucratic obstructionism, as a result of the government's arm's-length approach to the spill. And I began to wonder if maybe we could reduce our canvas and look at the story through a Kelly story. Or maybe we should do the captain's story.

And one by one these story possibilities were jettisoned for one reason or another. Kelly's story was too environmental. It also posed problems of filming wild animals. From the beginning we knew we would use archive for the spill.

We knew you couldn't re-create the spill, so we knew we were into using real archive.

So gradually a number of stories got jettisoned. The captain's story we jettisoned pretty early on partly because there wasn't really a thread all the way through. I mean, he got taken off the ship, and then he was out of the story until he came to trial. So there was a huge blank unless you wanted to deal with a story before the crash. Structurally it couldn't have worked. Also I always felt that the captain's story was dodgy morally because it was very unclear as to his guilt. He got off at the trial and legally he was innocent, but it was quite clear that he'd been drinking. He got off on a technicality, and ultimately on appeal he was acquitted on all counts, but it was pretty clear from talking to people that he wasn't drunk but had been drinking against the rules.

Rosenthal: Can you tell me more about finding the story and finding the conflicts? Are you aware of looking for these things, or has it become an automatic process for you?

Baker: I suppose it's rather automatic. You assume there will be conflicts. The story followed conflicts. So it wasn't as if I had to look for it. It was very obvious just looking at the facts that everybody had been in conflict. What we were trying to find was the *right* conflict. Also a conflict which wasn't black and white.

I was very concerned all the way through that we should present a story in which human beings were presented with a crisis and we could see what would happen to them. And most of the time they fucked up. The bottom line of the whole *Exxon Valdez* story was "give human beings a crisis and they'll fuck it up."

For me it was not so much a search for conflicts but, because the story was such a sprawling one, much more a search for *characters* who could carry the audience through from the beginning to the end. And of course once you had found those characters, you were automatically making a selective process.

But it had to be the right characters. It had to be the right *spread* of characters to give you enough of the whole story. You couldn't be really playing around with a character who was only a sideshow to the main attraction.

And I didn't really want these people to be heroes. I wanted them to be human beings you could sympathize with, people whom you in the audience would root for but who were also fallible faced with this crisis. I now suspect that in the end product these people, especially Dan Lawn, is a bit of a hero, perhaps more than I would have liked.

In the end, it became apparent to me that Dan Lawn and Frank Araossi, the Exxon executive, who were on different sides, would provide the axis on which the story would hang. They were both characters who, though having different agendas, had a lot of affinities. They were both isolated in their own camps and were both basically trying to do good jobs.

Rosenthal: Can we talk about structure? It seems to me the beginning is fairly obvious. You need to show the beauty of the location and the surroundings and go on quickly to the ship and the disaster. But how do you round off a film like this with no natural ending?

Baker: The end was always a problem. There was no end in the sense that the story went on and on. They were still cleaning up even when I went back. I eventually decided there had to be a very early cutoff point, and the cutoff point would probably be within days of the spill. As it happened, it turned out to be eight days.[2] I also knew that Araossi had been called back a week later and that later on Dan Lawn had been fired. We had problems all the way through. Everybody had a different opinion as to what the end of the film should be and at what point to end it.

Rosenthal: In the end, your visuals bring out the environmental disaster very strongly. This is the first time we really look at the cost. Before we just knew the oil was spilt.

Baker: That idea of an ending came quite late. But once we knew the *opening* would be the sound and its beauty, it became clear that the story would be enveloped, or would have bookends. We see the pristine sound at the beginning, the tarnished sound at the end. But that was quite a late decision.

The first script I wrote was just the taxi coming into the bay, the sound in the late evening, and the impressive circle of mountains around the bay at night. But we couldn't square the beginning with the end. And it was because we were having problems with the end that we thought of the envelope idea. What you're seeing in the archive all the way through is the gradual tarnishing and destruction of the sound. It is getting worse all the way through, till you have Dan Lawn filming on the island where you see all the dead and dying ducks. So that then became a very legitimate part of the story. And we thought, let's begin with the wonderful unspoilt beauty of the sound and end it with the destroyed sound.

Rosenthal: Can you tell me about the different versions of the script—what was added, what was lost at different times?

Baker: I said earlier that I thought the story would hang together because of the fishermen. The fishermen were locals. Their livelihood was under threat, and when they saw nothing was being done they rushed in. So there was an obvious dramatic logic to their story, which I thought maybe we could harness. And there were a lot of people, myself included, who hung on to that story for a long time.

The problem was that the fishermen's story was in a way too close to being an environmental story. It also clashed with the Dan Lawn story, which was more political and stronger. Dan was a public official trying to do his job, thwarted by the very people who should have been backing him.

One of the interesting things to me is the way in which real events are often incompatible with dramatic reality. On the night the tanker ran onto the rocks, there was a meeting in Valdez of the subcommittee of the Valdez council. The committee had been set up some months before because a number of people in Valdez had begun to get very concerned about tanker safety in the sound, and the committee was saying everybody is getting complacent and lax, and inspections of the terminal weren't being done properly. Then one of the woman council members gave a talk and ended it off by saying, "Gentlemen! It's not a question of *if* we are going to have a major spill but *when.*" And of course a few hours later the *Valdez* ran onto the rocks.

Initially everybody thought, "Great. This happened the very same night." But when you think about it, had you kept that scene in, it would totally have undermined what was to come. And people wouldn't have believed it.

Notes

1. *Writing Docudrama* (Boston: Focal Press, 1995).
2. The film is split into days, showing the progression of the crisis.

17

Tony Parker and the Documentary Play

Irene Shubik

No world could be further removed from the private, interior mental landscape of David Rudkin's plays than that of Tony Parker. Parker has been described by Anthony Storr in the *Sunday Times* of 15 February 1970 as "Britain's most expert interviewer, mouthpiece of the inarticulate and counsel for the defence of those whom society has shunned or abandoned." A totally self-effacing writer, his world is one of pure external observation—journalism of the highest kind. An analysis of his plays, produced on *Wednesday Play,* shows their genesis and their reception by audiences and critics.

Parker had started out as a businessman (who also wrote poetry), working as a publisher's representative. Then, in 1953, the Craig-Bentley case happened. Two boys were charged with the murder of a policeman; the younger, who had fired the shot, was too young to be executed; the older, Bentley, was just old enough and was hanged. So deeply disturbed was Parker by this that he wrote to the Howard League for Penal Reform asking what an ordinary person could do to change the penal system. Their only suggestion was that he should become a prison visitor, which he did. Later, learning that prison visitors must

From *Play for Today: The Evolution of Television Drama.* Reproduced by permission of Irene Shubik, © Irene Shubik, 1975.

not associate with prisoners once they have been discharged (a time when they probably need the most help), Parker became a voluntary associate—a person who offers friendship and practical help to discharged prisoners.

Parker not only began to "associate" with prisoners, he began to write books about them. All his books have been built up from painstakingly accurate research and hours of interviews with actual prisoners, many of whom he has known for years before the actual interviews are recorded. So great a respect has the Home Office for his books that he was granted by them the unique privilege of living for three months in Grendon Prison to record conversations with anyone, staff or prisoners, with whom he wanted to talk, without censorship—an experience recorded in his book *The Frying Pan.*

I first met Tony Parker when I bought his book *The Unknown Citizen* for *Story Parade.* I had commissioned the adaptation of the book from Philip Broadley, a friend of Parker's. Broadley had hinted to me that Parker might be interested in trying to write a play himself. When I started producing *Wednesday Play,* it occurred to me that the time was ripe to approach him. Whether he would be capable of writing in dramatic form or not one could only ascertain by taking the risk. Certainly the material he had at his fingertips would be eminently suitable for television. It was a risk worth taking. One knows and expects on such a program that there will have to be a certain failure rate with scripts. In Parker's case, it was a risk that more than paid off.

By the time he came to see me in April 1967, Parker had five books to his credit: *The Courage of His Convictions* (1962), a study of a professional criminal; *The Unknown Citizen* (1963); *The Plough Boy* (1964), based on the Clapham Common gang murder case; *Five Women* (1965), a portrait of five women criminals; *A Man of Good Abilities* (1966), the fascinating life story of an elderly compulsive embezzler. All the books had, of course, been built up from hours of taped interviews, which Parker ingeniously edited, filling in the background and circumstances of his encounters with the subjects.

When he came to see me, we discussed various ideas. None of his existing books seemed immediately suitable for television adaptation, but another original idea we discussed seemed very much so. This was the idea of exposing the world of the illicit baby-minder. In a synopsis, Parker described the theme of the proposed play thus:

> This play would highlight this contemporary social situation in which there is totally inadequate provision for unmarried mothers to maintain their children unless they have supportive families or choose to live in the very few mother-and-baby hostels available. Out of initial desire not to give away children for adoption this is what happens.

What happens is that they take the children to private, nonapproved childminders, often with dire results. At the point when I commissioned the play in May 1967, all one knew was the general subject: Parker was going to research it and turn it into dramatic shape, with my help.

Originally I had to commission the script to be done electronically in the studio, as the film effort I had been promised was not yet forthcoming; but when the first version came in, I knew that the only way this play could ever be effective was to put it onto film, for reasons that will be explained.

The shape of *Mrs Lawrence Will Look after It,* as the script came to be called (the first draft was delivered three months after it was commissioned), became, in a sense, the shape of a detective story. Mrs. Lawrence, an elderly woman, collapses in the street and is taken to a hospital where she is heard to moan about her "children." A police officer is sent to her home, and here he finds fourteen tiny children, some of them babies, left on their own. The problem now becomes one for the Children's Department, who have to look after the children while finding out to whom they belong. As each parent is tracked down, a different case history is told. In the end, Mrs. Lawrence (played by Constance Chapman) comes home from the hospital and, despite all warnings that she is liable to prosecution, starts her illicit baby home once more.

It was apparent to me that the story would lose half its impact if the characters were turned into talking heads against studio sets. Only by showing the real circumstances in which the parents lived could one portray their true plight. Moreover, with the fourteen children, one had an insoluble problem as far as the studio was concerned; they would have to be recorded on film. The only way to get good performances out of such young children is to shoot endless takes and edit them; nor, at that time, were such young children allowed in an electronic studio.

So my plea that this project, which I was certain would have a great impact, could not be done without film went into the head of the Plays Department. Eventually, I wrote to Tony Parker telling him that we could do the play on film and that now he would have to take all the interviews with the parents, which he had carefully confined to studio sets, and put them back into their natural environments.

The script went through numerous other major rewrites. A reporter figure whom Tony had invented to string the whole thing together came and went, was turned from a married man who was neglecting his family into a bachelor. The social workers, who came to take over the house and look after the children until their parents were found, also went through several permutations. I felt that, while all the parents' interviews had a ring of total authenticity, being based on real people, the invented characters had less of the breath of real life. It has since been a standing joke between Parker and myself that, every time he gives one of the characters in his plays (usually a social worker) a private life, I take it out again. In this case, it seemed to me to have no relevance to the story at all.

Having got permission to do the entire script on film, I then invited John McKenzie to direct it. I felt that John, who had got his training in "documentary-type" directing while acting as Ken Loach's production assistant, would be good for this subject. We were then lucky enough to get Brian Tufano, a cameraman who was especially skilled at "handheld" work, to shoot the piece.

We started filming on 11 March 1968 (almost a year after the synopsis had been agreed) in various sordid locations around north London. Our main location was a tiny house in Cricklewood from which passersby could hear all day long the collective cries of fourteen small children. Upstairs were crammed fourteen mothers and chaperons, peeping out occasionally to ensure the children's welfare; while downstairs, as in the famous cabin scene in *A Night at the Opera,* the entire crew were squeezed together in one tiny room in which a line of howling babies were laid out on the couch. My favorite moment of filming was the rebellion of one small boy, the eldest of the children. In the scene where the policeman first comes to the house and breaks in, the small boy emerges and the policeman asks his name. After about the third take, the boy stamped his foot and shouted, "I've already told you three times, and I'm not telling you again."

The play was transmitted on 21 August 1969, as the opening play of the new season. The critics greeted it like a long-lost friend. Here was a proper *Wednesday Play.* "This was another *Cathy Come Home,*" said Martin Jackson in the *Daily Express* (23 August 1968). "The *Wednesday Play* is back and bang on target." At least four reviewers mentioned *Cathy,* although, in fact, Parker's entire meticulous approach and reasoned attitude was totally unlike Sandford's impressionism. However, the play received the highest audience figures of the season (9.7 million) and unqualified praise. It dealt with an easily recognizable problem in easily recognizable terms, a problem with which almost everyone could identify. This was obviously the type of journalistic play that could have widespread appeal and demanded no more emotional or imaginative effort from the audience than did a newspaper article.

The next subject Tony and I discussed was perhaps less easy to identify with. The beginnings of *Chariot of Fire* were fairly far removed from the end product. In March 1968, we agreed upon a commission called "The Associates." This was based upon Tony's own firsthand knowledge of voluntary prison "after-care" workers. The play was to be about four of these workers: a young married woman with her own family; an unstable, rather cranky man; an elderly single woman; and a placid, unshakable middle-aged man. These were all actual types whom Tony had personally encountered. The idea was to explore the different motives of people volunteering for this work, the attitude of the prison authorities to them, and their relationships with four prisoners: an elderly con man, a violent criminal, an unemployable inadequate, and a sex offender (all subjects of Tony's different books).

In November 1968, Tony turned up with his research on all these characters but without a script. It struck me then that it would be immensely difficult to develop so many characters and engage an audience's sympathy for all of them in the space of one script. We therefore agreed to select one "associate" and one prisoner and concentrate on them.

For most people, the term *sex offender* conjures up an immediate image of a maniac rapist. Tony, however, had just finished the research for a new book, *The Twisting Lane* (published in 1969), which consisted of interviews with eight sex offenders and revealed most of the subjects to be more pathetic than frightening. One of them (in the play he was to become Stanley Wood) was an innocuous little man in his fifties who, in all other respects, could be considered a model citizen. Wood had spent twenty years of his life in prison for sexual offenses against small boys. These offenses, in fact, were not actual assault (Wood was totally impotent) but mere fondling. Good psychiatric treatment might have helped him, but none was available in the prison system.

We decided that the play should concentrate on the story of Wood and his "associate," a housewife, for his case was, in many respects, the most pathetic illustration of an inadequacy in the existing system. He was also a stock figure of derision and prejudice, and to illuminate his real character seemed worthwhile. The story line showed Wood in prison, the associate's attempts to help his rehabilitation and get him psychiatric help, and her eventual failure to prevent his return to prison.

Originally, I had intended the script to be shot entirely on film. It now appeared, however, that there was not sufficient film allocation or money to do so that year, while for the following year I had two scripts (*Edna, the Inebriate Woman,* and *The Right Prospectus*) that I was anxious to produce and that could not possibly be done other than on film. I decided to save the film effort for these two scripts, and I had once more to ask Tony to rethink the script, this time in terms of turning film into studio. This particular subject, anyway, seemed to be well suited to such a change.

What exactly do I mean by this? In *Mrs Lawrence,* it was absolutely essential to establish, in as realistic a way as possible, the miserable backgrounds of most of the parents involved and the sordid and dangerous conditions of Mrs. Lawrence's "baby-farm." In *Chariot of Fire,* however, it was the interior character of Stanley Wood that counted, as he revealed it to his associate, Shelley Mitchell. This intense study of character through long revelatory conversation pieces was well suited to the electronic camera. This is not to say we did not use film at all. We used it to establish the isolation of Stanley's life at his remote cottage and to show how his involvement with the children came about; we also used it to show fleetingly the lot of the sex offender in prison. Thanks to Tony's influence with the Home Office, we were allowed to film briefly from the roof of Pentonville Prison and showed the prisoners' exercise yard, where Stanley, as a sex offender, was shunned by the others and exercised alone for his own protection; and we showed his release from prison. Apart from these scenes, most of the piece was confined to the studio.

Although I had originally thought of a documentary-type director, now that we had changed to the studio, I asked James Ferman, who I knew was excellent at getting to the heart of artists' performances in studio conditions, to direct the play. We decided to cast Rosemary Leach as the associate and Jimmy Gardner, a very frail actor with the face of a mime and more usually associated with comic parts, to play Stanley. The play went out in May 1970, two years and two months after it was originally commissioned, and was again extremely well received by critics and audiences, many of whom remarked that the play drew attention to a subject that was hardly ever openly discussed and aroused a compassion they had not expected to feel and an awareness of the inadequacies of the prison and social services in dealing with this type of case.

Parker's next play was very much in the same vein. This was *When the Bough Breaks,* which dealt with the subject of baby battering. The play was commissioned in August 1969, delivered in March the following year, recorded a year later, and transmitted almost immediately after that, in May 1971. Like *Mrs Lawrence,* it had a vaguely detective-story structure. A baby is brought to a hospital by its mother and, on being X-rayed, is found to have multiple fractures. The National Society for the Prevention of Cruelty to Children (NSPCC) then sends a social worker to find out which parent is responsible. The father, a giant layabout, seems the obvious choice, but it turns out to be the pretty, fragile mother who is the batterer.

Again, the play was done chiefly in the studio, with a small amount of filming to establish the couple's background on a sleazy caravan site. Again, James Ferman directed it, and we cast a young singer and dancer, Cheryl Kennedy, as the girl, a risk that proved worth taking. In most documentary subjects, the use of unusual or offbeat or unexpected casting goes a long way toward establishing realism.

This play was more obviously didactic than the previous one in that Tony wanted to include a number of discussions at the NSPCC (and, again, wanted to include a personal life for the social workers, which I immediately cut out). The most difficult feat in a documentary drama is to convey statistics, possible remedies, et cetera connected with a social problem without becoming dramatically stilted. Although *When the Bough Breaks* succeeded admirably on a human level, I felt we had never overcome this particular problem and that no amount of humanizing the social workers disguised the fact that they were mouthpieces for the author. There always comes a dilemma in this type of drama-documentary as to whether to go for the drama or the facts. One cannot always succeed on both levels.

The last of Parker's plays on the list, *A Life Is Forever,* was two years in the writing. Our original discussion about depicting the plight of the "lifer" began in May 1970; the script was commissioned in July that year, and Tony went off to research it at the same time as researching a book on the subject. The final script was accepted in May 1972, the play going into rehearsal immediately. It was transmitted the following October.

In the writing of *A Life Is Forever,* which showed the deterioration of Johnson, who was serving a thirty-year sentence for murdering a policeman, and the futility of such long, nonproductive sentences, Parker had, to my mind, shown a great step forward as a playwright in his own right rather than as a documentary journalist. The invented dialogue was far more natural than in any of the previous plays, and the situations seemed to arise more naturally from character, as opposed to being contrived by the author for expository or didactic reasons. I introduced Tony to the director, Alan Clarke, at an early stage, when the first draft was delivered, so that Alan had the chance to gain all the knowledge of prison he could from Parker.

Two policy decisions had to be made early on about this production. For a start, we realized that it would be impossible to get permission to film inside a prison. Our feeling was, therefore, that we should use no film at all; a mixture of film and studio might make the studio part look phony. The designer, Richard Henry, consequently built his prison entirely in the studio, basing it on reference pictures, a viewing of a documentary on prisons, and Tony Parker's advice. Sound also made a great contribution, the soundman, Chick Anthony, attempting to emulate the hollow, clanking sounds of prison. It is a measure of their success that the Home Office phoned up the day after transmission to find out how we had managed to get into a prison to film without their permission. Later they asked to borrow the film as training material for the Prison Service.

The other decision was to cast an unknown actor as the "lifer," as we all felt that a well-known star would lessen the audience's belief in the prisoner's plight. For this part, director Alan Clarke found a saxophonist, Maurice O'Connell, who had only been acting for a year. The rest of the cast were chosen on a similar basis, and amongst them was a young repertory actor called Tony Meyer, who played a snaky little homosexual who had murdered his father. His advances toward the central character, Johnson, who immediately repelled him, were so convincing that I congratulated Tony on writing the first convincing gay scene I had seen on television. His answer was to point out that the only time I had approved his depiction of a sex life for his characters it had to be a homosexual sex life.

The play was generally praised for the realistic picture it gave of the deterioration of a man in prison who knows that he has nothing to live for; for conveying the totally nonproductive nature of the prison system as it exists with no useful work or training program offered for rehabilitation. Like all of Parker's plays, it had a large audience-viewing figure and generally appreciative reviews. Like all of his plays, rather than being blatantly propagandist, it showed all sides of the story and left the audience to think and draw their own conclusions.

Statistically therefore, Parker's plays are proof that audiences like and want plays about realistic and identifiable subjects, treated in realistic terms. In David Rudkin's TV play *House of Character,* a man was locked within his own madness; in Tony Parker's play, the steel bars were more easily recognizable.

Part Three

Criticism: The Quicksands of Politics and History

Stories taken from history and political issues have provided the basic inspiration and jumping-off points for many docudramas. It has been argued that they help us learn about the past and can be a strong influence in shaping public opinion. Yet how authentic and trustworthy are these films? Obviously it is an impossible question to answer in general, but it can be answered in the particular. The authors in part three, therefore, look closely at a number of films that I believe have played a major part in shaping public consciousness on certain topical and historical issues. They look at construction, veracity, effect, and ultimately the films' power to stimulate thought, discussion, and action.

However, one faces a preliminary question. Can history and politics really be taken seriously on television and in feature films? If not, why waste time on the subject? Fraser's and Custen's answers are given in part one, but there has also been intense debate on the subject.

Many historians dismiss television and feature film history (including documentaries) as mere entertainment, lacking in accuracy and having no academic value whatsoever. This fundamental problem is dealt with at length in my book *New Challenges for Documentary,* a good general introduction to the topic. The two most interesting essays in the book are "History on the Public Screen," parts one and two, by Donald Watt and Jerry Kuehl.[1]

Both Watt and Kuehl address the question of *where* and *how* television history (mostly documentary) differs from academic history in its expectations and limitations. Watt, approaching the various topics from an academic point of view, distinguishes between the respective strengths and weaknesses of word-based history and visual history and to my mind lays most of the academic doubts to rest. Kuehl, a historian turned filmmaker, continues the discussion by examining the practical differences between academic and film history, particularly with regard to the nature of the two audiences and the constraints of time on film.

In spite of the work of Watt and Kuehl, it is quite possible that in recent years the hostility to filmed history and politics has in fact increased. This may well be due to the demands by Oliver Stone and others to be taken seriously and the gap between their intentions and their execution.

There has also been a tremendous upsurge in scholarly interest in the means, techniques, and strategies by which history is presented on the screen. In particular, one now sees a great deal of postmodernist questioning regarding the simplistic narrative formulas of most docudramas and Hollywood features.[2]

All of these questions provide the background for part three, in which a number of docudrama films or miniseries are isolated for in-depth criticism and examination. Most of the films discussed were, or still are, influential in shaping our national myths or our attitudes to historic issues and current events. As such, and because of their power, I thought the time had come to bring out the magnifying glass.

Sergei Eisenstein's *Battleship Potemkin* has been cited in the past as one of the world's ten best films.[3] It is certainly one of the best known and is usually discussed in regard to its influence on film development and its use of Eisenstein's theories of montage. However, it is also one of the founders of political cinema, and its images have inspired millions. In fact the film was banned in many European countries in the twenties because of its possible incitement to rebellion.

The propaganda power of *Potemkin,* and its ability to inspire, is largely due to the fact that the film is based on true incidents and events taken from the 1905 revolution. Thus the sailors' act of rebellion, their camaraderie with the townspeople, and the guns of the *Potemkin* roaring defiance have become potent symbols of social revolution over the years.

Myth can obviously inspire as much as truth can, and D. J. Wenden attempts to separate the two by examining the events surrounding the mutiny in detail and comparing them to Eisenstein's film in his wonderful lead chapter, "*Battleship Potemkin:* Film and Reality." The results are fascinating, with invention and reality being almost balanced. Maybe the saddest loss to believers is the discovery that the townsfolk and sailors never really fraternized, that the massacre on the harbor steps took place at night, and that the ship's guns only fired feebly and then missed their target. A possibly more serious historic discovery is that the Odessa locals were much more committed political and social rebels than the sailors.

However, Eisenstein always claimed he was making a feature film not writing history or making a documentary. Nevertheless one suspects he was not averse to having *Potemkin* accepted as truth.

Amidst all the historical analysis, a small piece of research detail suddenly blinds one with its contemporaneity. Following the showing of the film, a sailor wrote to Eisenstein stating he was one of the sailors under the tarpaulin. Moreover, he wanted financial compensation for Eisenstein's use of his story. Clearly, payment for rights has a long history, even in Soviet Russia.

While I was growing up in England, much of my knowledge of British history was gleaned from the adventure films of Alexander Korda and his director brother Zoltan and from MGM's epics. In "Rule Britannia!" George MacDonald Fraser looks at the work of Korda and others with both humor and wit.

In the first section of Fraser's chapter, "Mutiny on the *Bounty,*" he compares the three feature versions of the *Bounty* uprising. None of the films inspired the political passions of *Potemkin,* but then all three were clearly meant for entertainment, dwelling on incidents lost in the mists of time. What gives one pause for thought, however, is Fraser's view that the most truthful film was the weakest as entertainment, and the most historically incorrect film, the most enjoyable.

In Fraser's second section, "The British in Africa," he looks at a series of films, many based on fact, some total fictions, that together provide fruitful material for examining past attitudes and approaches to the colonial landscape. Partially the chapter deals with wasted opportunities and partially with the blind snobbery and prejudice of British imperial practice. Where praise is due it is given, thus Fraser cites the surprising accuracy of *Zulu.* He also raises one criticism about the film with which I strongly agree. At the end of *Zulu,* Lieutenant Bromhead (played by Michael Caine) looks at the carnage and says he feels ashamed. Fraser doubts whether a professional soldier of his time (1880) would have expressed such feelings. I know that Caine's statement in the film expresses the politically correct sentiments of today, but I think modern thinking and historic attitudes should be kept separate.

The imposition onto the past of modern attitudes and idealization are also two of the core problems discussed in Leslie Fishbein's lengthy and painstaking study, "*Roots:* Docudrama and the Interpretation of History." The miniseries itself was based on Alex Haley's book, which the author himself called *faction,* or a study in mythmaking. On the whole, Fishbein found the miniseries to be a well-balanced portrait of slavery but full of a number of historical inaccuracies in regard to eighteenth-century life in Africa and the power of the black family to inspire the flight to freedom.

Roots came out in the late seventies, and besides giving birth to the compacted TV series, it also proved an inspirational base for many Afro-Americans. That seems to me a highly worthy result, which nevertheless has to be treated cautiously. In her book *Not out of Africa* (1996), Mary Lefkowitz warns of the tendency of many Afro-Americans (including many academics) to swallow uncritically a completely false picture of historical life in Africa. In the early episodes of *Roots,* Africa is seen as a demiparadise, or little Eden. This is mythmaking on the grand scale, and as such one has to be aware. It is also interesting to note in Steven Spielberg's film *Amistad* (1997) the involvement of Africans themselves in the capture of slaves.

Much has been written about Warren Beatty's film *Reds,* one of the most interesting discussions being contained in Leger Grindon's *Shadows of the Past.*[4] However, whereas Grindon largely concentrates on Beatty's personal and company problems, Robert A. Rosenstone's chapter, "*Reds* as History," examines historical issues rather than production details. The film fascinates me because of its pivotal quality. It was not the first post-McCarthy radical or protest film, because such films flooded into the cinema in waves following *Easy Rider,* the sixties campus protests, and the Vietnam War.[5] However, *Reds* was the first American film to treat a radical seriously. Nevertheless, as Rosenstone shows, the film ultimately cops out by subtly restructuring history, domesticating Reed, and concentrating on a weak love story.

The two chapters following Rosenstone's are also about politics, but they deal with a desperate and unsolved religious and territorial crisis rather than with the life and machinations of past presidents. The subject is the crisis in Northern Ireland and the problem of continued union or separation from England. Although *In the Name of the Father* is about the imprisonment of Gerry Conlon and his friends, the broader political questions hang heavily over the film.

In the Name of the Father caused a tremendous furor in England when it came out because of its blatant inaccuracies, and both Conor Cruise O'Brien, in "Patriot Games," and Richard Grenier, in "In the Name of the IRA," focus in their different ways on that point. In general, O'Brien attempts to set out the realities of the Belfast situation and the different levels of support for Catholic, IRA, and Protestant points of view. On his side, Grenier presents more of a standard film review, but he dwells heavily on the film's creations and fictions.

Ultimately, what O'Brien and Grenier have to say is fairly simple and goes to one of the root criticisms of docudrama. What both maintain is that *In the Name of the Father* does not just lie in regard to its major points but that those lies will be believed by the ignorant (i.e., most Americans). In turn, those lies will create attitudes and actions that will very much affect an ongoing situation. If the underlying message of *Who Bombed Birmingham?* can be seen as "the truth will set you free," one could say of *In the Name of the Father* that lies will make a complex situation even more difficult to resolve.

Sita Williams has been producing plays for Granada TV since the early eighties, but *The Hostages* is probably her most controversial piece to date. Its subject is the seizure of five men by Hizballah guerrillas and their captivity in Lebanon in the mid eighties. The film has only been shown once in England and was the subject of much praise but also a great deal of criticism.

The source of the newspapers' attack was the fact that the show was made without the authorization of the hostages. The newspapers argued further that, if persons undergo rare and painful experiences, they have a right to keep those experiences private until they decide what use to make of them. These comments followed a public airing of objections to the show by some of the hostages and a generally critical symposium on the subject conducted by the BBC.

Williams, in "The Making of *Hostages,*" counters the argument by citing freedom of expression. She further claims that news reporting would come to a halt and multiple human interest stories could not be presented if one had to wait until all involved agreed to the release.

There is a major point here that affects the very nature of docudrama. Can anybody be said to own the rights to his or her life? And if so, in what cases is that story exclusive? At what point does it enter the public domain? Practically, and as can be seen from the content of Jeff Silverman's chapter in part two, most docudrama producers cover themselves by purchasing story rights. William's battle is to be allowed to go ahead when no consent has been given.

In general, I agree with her argument on that point. My only parting of the ways with Williams is that she appears to accept too easily that scenes can be written for docudrama without authentication, so long as they are "in the spirit" of the situation. This is a long way from Woodhead's demand for chapter and verse to back up every scene.

Rosenstone, by contrast, in "*JFK:* Historical Fact/Historical Film," seems to be saying, Forget chapter and verse, forget facts, don't be bothered that Stone mixes fact and fiction, and above all forget the pursuit of realism. It is soon clear that Rosenstone is not so much writing a critique of *JFK* as he is arguing (as he does in so many of his books) for a new approach to the making of films about history.[6]

What Rosenstone passionately believes is that, to succeed in making us understand the past, a film must engage us with the ideas and arguments of historical discourse. Film is not a window on the past but a construction of the past, and simple realism will no longer do. It is not sufficient for a film to evoke the past. It must, as Rosenstone puts it, "be a *provocation* to thought and intervention into history, a way of revisioning the past" (my emphasis). By all these criteria, *JFK* succeeds admirably.

In practice Rosenstone is arguing toward many of the ideas of postmodernism, a subject treated at length by Sumiko Higashi in "*Walker* and *Mississippi Burning:* Postmodernism Versus Illusionist Narrative." Higashi, in some very strong writing, provides an interesting comparison between *Walker* and *Mississippi Burning.* In the end, *Walker* is praised to the sky and the latter film relegated to the garbage heap. Again, as in Rosenstone's chapter, Higashi's attack goes beyond the fictions of *Mississippi Burning.*

Higashi attacks the simplistic ideal of conventional Hollywood representation. What she argues for is a new kind of film that is skeptical, reflexive, ironic, and absurdist, with the best examples being films like *Hitler: A Film from Germany, Hiroshima Mon Amour,* and, of course, *Walker.* What Higashi wants are films that mix history, fiction, and modernity and in doing so induce you to think about the meaning and construction of the past. This way the viewer is forced to become an *active* rather than passive viewer.

The question of experiment in representation is not as new as postmodernists would have us think. Jean-Luc Godard and Peter Watkins jolted us in the sixties, and Dennis Potter continued the shocks in the seventies and eighties. Even the use of witnesses in *Reds* can be seen as part of the trend. So the game is an old one. I suspect the real question is not whether one form is better than another but whether the chosen form is used with intelligence.

A little of Higashi's argument carries over to the work of Yosefa Loshitsky, where, in "Fantastic Realism: *Schindler's List* as Docudrama," a comparison is made between documentary's and feature docudrama's ways of treating the Holocaust. In this case, the comparison is between Steven Spielberg's *Schindler's List* and Claude Lanzmann's *Shoah.* What Loshitsky suggests is that each film can be seen as a correcting and corrected image of the other. Both set out competing theories of how to resist and overcome the limits of representation.

On the one hand, *Schindler's List* makes a claim for the real by blurring the boundaries of fact and fiction and leaning, at times, toward a deliberate documentary style. So once more we recall Brian Winston's dictum of documentary evoking a higher truth than fiction. *Shoah,* on the other hand, is a dialectic of absent images. It is a film about absent representation whose force depends on the evocation of what Loshitsky calls "involuntary memory."

The comparison is good, the arguments powerful. Both films strongly evoke the past and provoke reactions to the past. However, unlike most, I am not enthralled by Lanzmann's technique or absence of representation, because I believe one factor is always left out of discussions of the film. It seems to me that *Shoah* works only and because we *do* have concrete images of the Holocaust. that, whether from features or newsreels, play in our minds when we see the film. Without those concrete referential images, I suggest, *Shoah* would lose 90 percent of its power.

With Steve Lipkin's study, we find ourselves, in a sense, completing things and back at the beginning. I chose it as the final chapter because, in his "Defining Docudrama: *In the Name of the Father, Schindler's List,* and *JFK,*" he recaps many of the main points running through this book. Among Lipkin's many provocations is the idea that docudrama suggests that lost moral structures can be recovered. Like so many of the essays in this collection, it makes us reflect on the past, question the future, and answer, to a small extent, Why Docudrama?

Notes

1. Donald Watt, "History on the Public Screen 1," in *New Challenges for Documentary,* ed. Alan Rosenthal (Berkeley: University of California Press, 1988), 435–43; and Jerry Kuehl, "History on the Public Screen 2," in Rosenthal (ed.), *New Challenges,* 444–53.

2. See, for example, Paul Smith (ed.), *The Historian and Film* (Cambridge: Cambridge University Press, 1976); Hayden White, *Narrative Discourse and Historical Representation* (Baltimore: Johns Hopkins University Press, 1987); John E. O'Connor (ed.), *Image as Artifact* (Malabar: R. E. Krieger, 1990); Vivian Sobchack, "'Surge and Splendor': A Phenomenology of the Hollywood Historical Epic," *Representations* 29 (winter 1990): 24–49; all the essays in *American Historical Review* 93 (December 1988); and Robert A. Rosenstone (ed.), *Revisioning History* (Princeton: Princeton University Press, 1995).

3. See the annual critics' poll for the world's ten best films in the *Observer* newspaper for any of the years 1950–56.

4. Leger Grindon, *Shadows of the Past* (Philadelphia: Temple University Press, 1995).

5. See, for example, *R.P.M., The Strawberry Statement, Che!, Zabriskie Point,* and *Alice's Restaurant.*

6. See Rosenstone (ed.), *Revisioning History.*

18

Battleship Potemkin: Film and Reality

D. J. Wenden

Battleship Potemkin is one of the best-known and most widely admired films of all time. But it is not only a landmark in the history of the cinema, it is for most people their main source of information about the mutiny of the *Potemkin*. In this chapter, I compare the story of the mutiny and the events in Odessa as portrayed in the film to the real story as reconstructed by a historian, and I discuss possible reasons for the differences.

Making such comparisons is not easy. We can look at the film over and over again, study it shot by shot, and refer to David Mayer's published analysis.[1] We have no such detailed minute-by-minute, or even day-to-day, account of the events it portrays. The motion picture lasts for just over one hour; the mutineers controlled the ship for over eleven days. Unfortunately, no movie cameraman took pictures of the mutiny, of the arrival of the warship in Odessa, or of the battles between strikers and troops in the city. We cannot compare 1905 film with the 1925 reconstruction. Some photographs survived, and several participants in the struggle have recorded their versions in newspapers, books, and official reports.

This chapter is based on a variety of sources yielding information on the risings in Odessa and on the *Potemkin;* but as in all historical investigations, many questions are left unanswered or are given ambiguous answers. Almost as many unsolved mysteries surround the making of the film, how much Sergei Eisenstein knew about the mutiny he portrayed, and why he presented it as he did. A note on the main sources is given at the end of the chapter. Much more, however, remains to be done.

Eisenstein's variation from the truth or failure to tell the whole truth (as he knew it) are not necessarily sinister or reprehensible. He was making a feature film not a work of history. He had been commissioned to produce a work commemorating the 1905 revolution, but it was intended for general distribution and was meant to be an entertainment as well as a revolutionary sermon. To achieve this, and to make a film that would appeal to unsophisticated Russian audiences, Eisenstein had to change and simplify the confused story of the mutiny.

The events he portrayed were only twenty years away, but those two decades had witnessed the 1917 Revolution and the creation of Bolshevik Russia. He had been asked to produce a picture about the 1905 revolution that would justify the political system of 1925. The authorization for the production came from the Official State Committee of the Presidium of the Central Executive Committee of the USSR set up to celebrate the year 1905. As Herbert Marshall explains in his book on *The Battleship Potemkin,* the film was made to "social command" (*sotsial'nyyzakaz*), that is, the command of the Communist Party of the Soviet Union.[2] The propaganda was blunt and direct, unlike Eisenstein's more equivocal treatment of Stalinist agricultural policy in *The General Line* (1928), where occasional hints of disaffection and jibes at the party bureaucracy can be detected. He underlined the contrast between the revolutionary sailors and their reactionary officers, and also by implication the vindictive soldiers on the harbor steps, by falsifying as well as simplifying some of the events he portrayed, even though he assured the All Union Creative Conference of Workers in Soviet Cinematography in 1935 "that we tried to take the historical events just as they were and not to interfere in any shape, manner, or form with the process as it actually took place."[3] Later he wrote of using "the events first taken as unembellished facts themselves so arranged as to form a consecutive whole."[4]

By 1945 he appeared to have had a change of heart. Discussing the controversial role of the tarpaulin in the attempted execution of the mutineers, he quoted Goethe approvingly: "For the sake of truthfulness, one can afford to defy the truth."[5] In the same article, he admitted that his film ended in a false triumph, with the apparent rallying of the whole Black Sea Fleet to the side of the mutinous *Potemkin,* although in reality the revolt ended in ignominy. His excuse for this distortion was,

> But we were justified in ending the film with the historical battleship victorious. Because the 1905 Revolution itself, though drowned in blood, has gone down in history as an objectively victorious episode, the harbinger of the triumph of the October Revolution.[6]

Success in 1917 justified drawing a veil over failure in 1905. However, in putting forward this justification, he contradicted his earlier assertion that he did not "interfere in any shape, manner, or form with the process as it actually took place."

It is possible that Eisenstein by 1945 had become aware of facts about the 1905 struggle he had not appreciated ten years earlier. A more likely explanation of this change of ground is the change in the political climate and in the director's own status. In 1935 the first wave of the Stalinist purge trials had begun. Eisenstein's position was far from secure. He was unable to complete any film project. *Bezhin Meadow* was interrupted by his attack of smallpox and later abandoned owing to political difficulties in 1937. Few men at that time would have risked admitting in Moscow that they had falsified history, even in the cause of great revolutionary propaganda. Confessions of falsification of history were reserved for the Trotskyite criminals who were being destroyed by Andrey Vyshinsky and the NKVD in the most spectacular falsification of history of all time. Ten years later, although Stalin was still in power, the Soviet Union had triumphed in the Great Patriotic War. The regime, politicians, and artists were more self-confident. Eisenstein himself had directed *Alexander Nevsky* and was at work on *Ivan the Terrible.* Minor, harmless distortions of the truth in the revolutionary cause could perhaps be more readily revealed.

In his writings, Eisenstein acknowledged only those few minor distortions. We will probably never know whether he was or was not aware of the more substantial departures from historical accuracy discussed later in this chapter. These have three main sources. Firstly, Eisenstein, like any writer of historical fiction, simplified and distorted the truth in order to make his story more dramatic. Secondly, he had political reasons: the doctored version produced a film more likely to preach the message required by the Communist leaders and by Eisenstein himself. Although his enthusiasm for Stalin may have waned, he never lost his loyalty to the Soviet ideal. Thirdly, he was probably unaware of certain occasions when his version differed from the true course of events in 1905.

Eisenstein had been directed to make a film on the general theme of 1905. Several mysteries surround the process by which this directive was translated into the final production of a comparatively short (and at five reels, 1,850 meters [6,070 feet], *Battleship Potemkin* is short) feature film. The first is the substitution of the story of the revolt on the *Potemkin* and the unrest in Odessa for a general survey of the 1905 revolution. The second is why two films (the lesser-known *Ninth of January,* directed by Viskovsky, was a sister film of *Battleship Potemkin*), intended to mark the twentieth anniversary of a revolution that erupted in January 1905, were not commissioned until the spring of 1925 and not shown until the last month of that year. The third is when and why Eisenstein, who on 2 July 1925 wrote to his mother that he had been given until August 1926 to complete the project, was instructed to deliver a print before the end of the year.[7] The fourth is how much of the grander *The Year 1905* project was begun and what happened to the abandoned material.

There is little information on the last point, but the film library of the British Film Institute has a still photograph that is said to be from the unfinished *The Year 1905.* Whether Eisenstein's deadline was advanced from August 1926 to December 1925 or whether he mistakenly imagined that he had more time is not clear. The project, like the finished film itself, seems to have come to an abrupt, foreshortened close. This, together with the belated commissioning of the work partway through the year, may explain the substitution of *Battleship Potemkin* for the whole of *The Year 1905.* We, the audience, probably have reason to be grateful since, as Bernardo Bertolucci has demonstrated, it is not easy to make a successful film based on a whole year and certainly not easy to make a successful short film on such a theme. In an article in the *Berliner Tageblatt* in June 1926, Eisenstein explains that he had only "three months for production—even in Germany this might be considered a record production schedule. Two and a half weeks were left to me for the montage of the film, for the editing of 15,000 metres of film."[8] It seems likely that lack of time compelled the change of plan from *The Year 1905* to *Battleship Potemkin* and that the brilliant use of the ship's revolt as a symbol for the whole revolutionary effort of the Russian people in 1905 was forced on Eisenstein.

Shooting began in July in Leningrad on a general script prepared by Nina Agadzhanova-Shutko. The end of the Baltic summer and a delay in the completion of the original script drove Eisenstein and his team south to Odessa to film the sequences planned on the naval mutiny. Once there they became the whole film, and the original scenario was replaced by a new outline usually attributed to Eisenstein himself. Here a fifth mystery appears. Did this scenario owe anything to Sergei Tretyakov, the well-known Soviet dramatist? In an article published in 1977, Lars Kleberg advances evidence that suggests strongly an association of ideas between Tretyakov, a former associate of Eisenstein at the Proletkult Theater, and the director of *Battleship Potemkin.*[9] Kleberg's evidence can be summarized as follows.

In December 1925 and January 1926, within four weeks of each other, the two colleagues from the Proletkult unveiled new works, *Battleship Potemkin* at the Bolshoi Theater on 24 December, and a play by Tretyakov, *China Roars,* on 23 January in Meyerhold's Theater. *China Roars* is based on an event in June 1924 in a town on the Yangtze River. An American trader was killed, and the commander of a British gunboat threatened to bombard the town unless the murderers, or two hostages, were handed over for execution. The action of the play alternates between the harbor and the deck of the warship, with confrontations between the British captain and the Chinese coolies. Just as the execution is completed, news comes that riots have started in Shanghai, and the "Roar of China" is taken up by the local townspeople. The theme, and in particular the structure, of the play have many obvious similarities with *Battleship Potemkin.* In November or December 1924, Eisenstein had access to an early version of the play and may even have been asked to work on its production. When Tretyakov returned from China in the summer of 1925, he was added to the advisory board of the studio producing *Battleship Potemkin.* From 1 September for some weeks, he was with the crew in Odessa and in November worked with Eisenstein in Moscow on the cutting and wrote some subtitles. Kleberg suggests that these "coincidences" may explain how Eisenstein was able to concentrate the theme of *1905* so rapidly and effectively into the story of the ship's mutiny and how Eisenstein arrived at the strict, terse dramaturgical structure that characterizes *Battleship Potemkin* but was not developed in either the earlier film *The Strike* or the scenario of *The Year 1905.* In the film credits, the dramatist appears only as a joint author of the subtitles!

The June mutiny on the *Potemkin* is not regarded as a major event by most historians of the 1905 revolution. The crucial disturbances were the strikes and riots in St. Petersburg and Moscow, the disaffection in some military units, and the widespread peasant risings from August 1905 until April 1906. The czar's decisions to grant the concessions made in the October Manifesto and to hasten a revision of the land settlement were prompted by widespread urban and rural revolts not by the *Potemkin* sailors' abortive gesture (eleven days that did not shake the world) nor even by the strikes in Odessa, which were overshadowed in that city by the counterrevolutionary pogroms against the Jews in November.

The *Kniaz'Potemkin Tavrichesky* was a three-funneled battleship of twelve thousand six hundred tons, with four twelve-inch and sixteen six-inch guns.[10] Completed in 1903, it was a Russian version of the United States *Maine* class of warship and was the last large czarist naval vessel based on a British or American prototype. Subsequent ships were built to French designs with French or German equipment and armor. Fred T. Jane, in *The Imperial Russian Navy,* published in 1904, deplored the disappearance of this market for British exports.

> I was told in Russia, not once but a dozen times, that the "Strike Clause" was the stumbling block, Russia insisting on its absence, and British firms (knowing all too well what its absence might mean in these days of agitation) insisting on its maintenance. The agitator helped the British mechanic to kill his goose as far as Russia is concerned.[11]

The *Potemkin* was the most powerful unit in the Black Sea Fleet. Its speed, the weight and velocity of its armament could not be matched by the five other, older battleships based on Sebastopol. This technical superiority explains the czarist admiralty's alarm at its disaffection. It could outmaneuver and outshoot any unit, or almost any combination of units, likely to be sent against it. Moreover, after the Japanese had virtually eliminated the Russian Far Eastern Fleet and the ships of the Baltic Fleet sent to the Pacific, the *Potemkin* was one of the few effective modern czarist battleships left afloat. A British consular report in May 1905 suggests that, together with other units of the Black Sea Fleet, *Potemkin* was being prepared for Asian waters.[12] This appears to have been only a rumor, but it might help to explain the crew's readiness to mutiny. Certainly the attempts to draw drafts of men for service in ships from the Baltic Fleet that were sent to the Far East had occasioned unrest and resistance at Sebastopol, the base of the Black Sea Fleet.[13]

Well before the *Potemkin* uprising in June 1905, there had been agitation among the sailors. Mention is made of unrest in December 1904. A. F. Matyushenko, the ringleader of the *Potemkin* rising, had taken part in this action. Surprisingly Matyushenko, who was known to be an active Social Revolutionary, was not imprisoned but was one of the many political activists designated for service at sea.[14] It was assumed that, dispersed among the ships on maneuvers, they would be less dangerous than if they were concentrated in the Crimean depot. A general rising of the fleet was planned, initially for early June off Tendra Island. This, however, did not take place since the bulk of the fleet was kept in harbor and the *Potemkin* sailed alone for firing practice near Tendra on 12 June. (All dates given are according to the old Russian calendar.) At this stage, the rising seems to have been postponed until early August. The

Potemkin mutiny in June was a premature outburst, roundly condemned by Kirill Orlov, one of the few Bolsheviks involved, as hasty action by "the strong pressure of the Anarchist–Social Revolutionary element."[15] Strangely enough, the ship's crew was deemed to be politically backward, but because of this, and because of the ship's operational preeminence, it had been intended that the general uprising should start on the *Potemkin.*

With the mobilization of the Black Sea Fleet the ship's crew had been brought up to its full complement of 731. Also onboard were fifty or sixty technicians and workmen engaged in repair and refitting.[16] Such men might have been expected to include a high proportion of revolutionary elements. But they seem to have played little or no part in the subsequent troubles and are mentioned only in a comment that no additional rations had been provided for them and that this accentuated dissatisfaction with the food. These shipyard workers were eventually put ashore in Odessa.

On 12 June, the ship sailed to the Tendra Strait to test the linings of the new guns. Captain E. N. Golikov was in command. The officers had little seagoing experience. Service in the Black Sea Fleet brought few opportunities for long cruises. The ratings were mainly peasants, conscripted for seven years' service. One account suggests that many were drawn from the Bessarabian provinces, and this may partly explain their later willingness to seek refuge in Romania.[17] They were poorly paid, harshly disciplined, and forbidden to marry while on active service. Many of the company were raw recruits.

As the ship steamed out of Sebastopol, strikes and disturbances broke out in Odessa. Most Russian cities had experienced spasmodic outbreaks of political and industrial disorder since the massacre of the crowds marching behind Father George Gapon to petition the czar in January. The country was weary of a despotic regime, the incompetence of which had been exposed by defeats at the hands of the Japanese. Odessa, the fourth-largest Russian city, housed a large commercial and industrial proletariat. Over one-third of the population (at the 1897 census 139,984, or 34.65 percent) were Jews. They dominated the grain-export trade and the professions. Their presence had two political consequences. An oppressed minority, they included revolutionary elements who were very active politically: strong branches of the Jewish Bund and Russian Social Democratic Party flourished in Odessa. But the very prominence of the Jews in radical movements enabled the authorities to convert anti-Semitic prejudices among peasants and workers into patriotic counterrevolutionary pogroms. The high proportion of Jews in Odessa made the city more politically conscious, but it also made it possible to split the working-class movement and switch mob energy away from antigovernment riots into attacks on Jewish shops and warehouses. This happened during the outburst while *Potemkin* lay in the harbor and on a larger scale later in November.

The events portrayed in the film arose out of this political ferment in Odessa and on the ships of the Black Sea Fleet. In the opening sequences, Eisenstein establishes the mood with shots of fierce waves breaking on a jetty, followed by examples of the harsh discipline and brooding unrest belowdecks. At midday the men protest at the maggoty meat being prepared for their dinner.

Such an outburst did occur on the ship. While the *Potemkin* waited to begin firing, its torpedo-boat escort sailed off to Odessa to buy food and stores. Owing to the strikes in the city, little fresh food was available. Ironically the carcasses that were to spark off the revolt came from Odessa, and their poor condition was due to earlier revolutionary action in the harbor. Their condition was not improved when on the return journey the torpedo boat ran down a small fishing vessel and could not deliver the stores to the ship's galley until 4:00 A.M. Bad meat did not improve in the Crimean midsummer heat. The next morning, it was crawling with maggots. The ratings protested. Earlier complaints had been made in May. As in the film, the ship's surgeon, Dr. Smirnov, pronounced it fit to eat, saying that it needed only to be washed with vinegar or brine. When the men refused the borscht made from the putrid flesh, Captain Golikov ordered a parade on deck.

Up to this point, the film and the actual events, so far as I can reconstruct them, coincide, except that the film suggests that the mutiny was a spontaneous reaction to bad food and the repression of complaints about the food. The only variation from the truth comes early in the film when Matyushenko and Vakulenchuk are shown talking together, implying that they are fellow revolutionaries. In fact, Vakulenchuk, the martyr of the *Potemkin,* whose lying in state on the Odessa quay and subsequent burial formed an essential, almost the only, link between the ship and the townsfolk, seems, as I show later, to have been an innocent martyr, shot by chance, and not, as the film implies, a leader of the revolt.

We return to the parade on the deck of the ship. In the film, the captain orders those satisfied with the borscht to take two steps forward. A few move but the majority stay still. The captain threatens them with hanging but summons instead a firing squad and proceeds to order the execution of a group of dissidents, who are first covered by a tarpaulin. Vakulenchuk appeals to the guards who refuse to fire and the mutiny erupts.

Eyewitness accounts of the parade contradict each other at several points. Some suggest that the captain, afraid and confused, dismissed the men and walked away, saying that he would report the matter to the commander in chief. As he left, the initiative was seized by the sterner second in command, Gilyarovsky, who re-formed the ranks and proceeded with further threats and action. Others suggest that the captain stayed on deck and in command, ordering those satisfied with the food to move behind him or to pass from port to starboard. All these accounts surprisingly agree that the captain asked those satisfied to move. It would seem better tactics to ask those dissatisfied with the soup to step forward, forcing them to take the initiative and enabling those who were uncertain to remain still and, by implication, content. Again the accounts differ, some suggesting that most of the men moved, others that very few responded.

Eventually a group of sailors, 12, 30, 50 or 60 (the film shows 19), were herded together in the stern. The officers ordered a tarpaulin to be brought. (A tarpaulin, to be placed over or under the men—this point is discussed later—was a warning that a summary execution might take place.) The squad refused to fire, restrained, some say, by Leading Torpedoman Matyushenko, the chief Social Revolutionary Party member onboard and throughout the leading figure. In desperation Gilyarovsky seized a rifle and shot at the petty officer commanding the firing squad whom some say was Leading Seaman Vakulenchuk; others suggest that he aimed at the petty officer but hit instead Vakulenchuk, one of the condemned sailors. In all accounts, Vakulenchuk appeared and was wounded almost by chance. In the film, he and Matyushenko are from the beginning the two leading revolutionaries, shown conspiring in the film's opening shots. Vakulenchuk is the sailor who reads the leaflet in the hammock belowdecks and also the sailor who calls on the guard to ignore the order to fire.

After the outburst, Gilyarovsky was immediately shot dead by Matyushenko. The other officers were hunted down. Dr. Smirnov, the ship's surgeon who had dismissed the complaints about the rotten meat, attempted to commit suicide with his lancet. Several, including Captain Golikov, were killed onboard or in the water as they attempted to swim to the torpedo-boat escort. One account, that of Kuzma Perelygin, a sailor who was, by his testimony, opposed to the mutiny from the outset, claims that even at this stage the crew was divided, and some sailors who opposed the mutiny also jumped overboard and were fired on as they swam away. No other version refers to such an early split in the ship's crew, and it is possible that Perelygin's story was influenced by a desire to stand in well with the Russian authorities. His version was given to Melas, a Russian police agent in the Romanian port of Constansa. It seems clear that the nine hostages were placed under arrest and that three officers unenthusiastically joined the rebels, remaining with them for most of the voyage. Within one hour the mutineers had taken over the ship.

The film conveys a different impression. The captain remains a dominating figure, controlling events until he is seized by the rebels. Gilyarovsky does not shoot Vakulenchuk almost by chance but hunts the unarmed ringleader around the ship until he shoots him down, and the sailor's body falls first into a cradle formed by mast and ropes and finally into the sea. Scores of his comrades leap into the water and bring back the body. In fact Vakulenchuk did not die immediately: he may have fallen into the water, but he certainly lay for several hours in the sick bay.

At several points in the film, a sly, hypocritical priest appears, encouraging the execution and later feigning death to avoid the attention of the rebels. A priest, Father Parmen, was on the ship. He was wounded on the head by Matyushenko during the uprising but remained onboard and was asked by the crew to accompany the body of Vakulenchuk to the military cemetery in Odessa. Even Matyushenko records that, on the evening of the second day, "the drummers summoned the crew to prayers on deck."[18] The religious beliefs of the peasant sailors survived the shock of insurrection. Eisenstein's account of the uprising ends abruptly with the death of Vakulenchuk and moves on immediately to the passage of his body from the ship to its first place of rest on the quay in Odessa, an event that took place twenty-four hours later.

The factual differences between the real mutiny and the film mutiny are comparatively marginal and can be justified by the need to maintain dramatic force and unity. Eisenstein's *Battleship Potemkin* is here more historically accurate than either of the two Hollywood versions of *The Mutiny on the Bounty* (MGM, 1935 and 1962).

Eisenstein does, however, strain the truth in his determination to portray a clear confrontation between the united forces of evil on one side and of virtue on the other. The real Captain Golikov acted much less despotically and decisively than did his film counterpart. He was eventually dragged half dressed from his cabin, where he was contemplating an attempt to swim to safety. He was only killed after a debate among the crew. Eisenstein does not show his end but leaves us in little doubt about what the film mutineers would have done with this overbearing martinet. The officers in the film are united in their infamy. In fact several survived and three joined the insurgents, who appointed Lieutenant Alexeyev as commander of the ship. The ringleaders needed his technical skills and recognized that the bulk of the crew felt happier with an officer as master of the ship.

The crew, whom Eisenstein showed as united and single-minded, were in practice divided and hesitant. As mentioned earlier, one account asserts even that the initial revolt met with strong resistance. Matyushenko and his associates had to prod them into action, and later they had repeatedly to be kept up to scratch by the civilian revolutionaries who came aboard at Odessa. They eventually gave up the revolt, hunger and fear driving them to seek internment in Romania. During their few days in Odessa Harbor, they refused to become directly associated with the town's strikes and riots. The hard-core naval revolutionaries who wanted to link up with the civilian disturbances were afraid to do so and leave the ship in the hands of the apathetic majority. (Eisenstein presented a black-and-white story matching his black-and-white pictures rather than the battleship gray reality.)

A trivial but intriguing confusion surrounds the attempted execution and the role of the tarpaulin. In the film, the sailors selected for execution are herded in the prow, and a tarpaulin is slung over them, placing a barrier between the living and those about to die. But was it to be placed over or under the victims? Either position can be justified. A cover over the men would hide them from their shipmates in the firing squad. Army mutineers on land would almost certainly have faced riflemen from a unit other than their own. A man-of-war at sea is often isolated, and there may be no opportunity to summon anonymous executioners. A naval or marine firing squad may be asked to kill men with whom they have broken bread that morning. A tarpaulin diminishes their anguish.

But Eisenstein, in his essay about the film on *The Twelve Apostles* (1945), claimed that in the czarist navy a tarpaulin would have been placed not over but under the victims, in order to protect the deck from bloodstains in the interests of a cleaner, neater execution.[19] He writes that he deliberately threw the canvas over the men in order to create a spectacular image of "a gigantic bandage covering the eyes of the condemned." A former naval officer acting the role of Matyushenko protested at this falsification. "We shall be ridiculed. . . . This was never done." But Eisenstein "ordered the scene to be shot the way you see it in the film. . . . The scene was left in the film as it was. It became part and parcel of the historical event."

He used this invention to defend himself in a legal case brought by a survivor of the mutiny, claiming payment of a fee for his rights in the story. In a sketchy account of the action against the filmmakers, Eisenstein wrote that the plaintiff claimed to be one of the men "under the tarpaulin during the shooting on the quarter deck," and the lawyers were demanding judgment in his favor "when the whole noisy affair was blown sky high . . . for the simple reason that no one on the *Potemkin* had been covered with a tarpaulin. . . . The scene was the director's invention."

Investigation suggests that the story was a director's fabrication to win a legal battle and not the reversal of naval tradition. Almost all the eyewitness accounts written before the making of the film in 1925 refer to the appearance of a tarpaulin, which was placed *over* and not *under* the ratings. The acting British consul in Galatz, Romania, sent a report of the mutiny by Vasily Barkovsky, a gunner on the ship, to the Foreign Office on 12 July 1905.[20] The gunner explained that the firing squad was ordered to shoot the ringleaders, "first covering them with a tarpaulin." Perelygin reports that the captain ordered the guards to load their rifles, "bring the tarpaulin, and cover these scoundrels."[21] Comparisons between fact and film become even more perplexing when the director claims as a fictional invention an action that seems actually to have taken place. The story becomes even more bizarre when we discover a report in the *New York Times* of 24 October 1926 of a lawsuit in which an unknown Dachenko sued the State Cinematograph Trust, which had paid him the equivalent of $750 for his part-authorship of the scenario of *Battleship Potemkin* but refused to give him a percentage of the picture's earnings. It was suggested that he had written only the scenario and that Eisenstein had introduced ideas and scenes of his own. The "People's Court" decided that Dachenko and Eisenstein were joint authors, and awarded to each 1 percent of the film's earnings. If this is the court case Eisenstein refers to in *Notes of a Film Director,* one's faith in the director is further shaken. He not only distorts the story of the tarpaulin but also claims to have won a case that was lost (unless it was subsequently won on appeal). If it is not the case in question, what is one to make of a total lack of reference to Dachenko and his association with the film in any of the credits or published material on the making of the film?[22]

The third and fourth sections of the film include more substantial deviations from historical truth. Eisenstein presented the citizens of Odessa paying homage to Vakulenchuk's body in a tent on the quayside, while the battleship lay at anchor in the harbor. Sailing boats carry food and gifts to the crew. On the shore, well-dressed crowds in a holiday spirit use the steps leading from the harbor up to the town center as a grandstand from which they can wave to the ship. Suddenly at the top of the stairway a detachment of troops arrives to clear the crowds. They march down the steps, pausing to shoot at the civilians fleeing before their relentless advance. This brilliant film sequence ends with the destruction of the innocents by the sabers of mounted Cossacks at the foot of the staircase. The savagery of the troops is answered by the guns of the *Potemkin,* which bombard the Odessa Theater, the garrison's military headquarters. Their shells are the only contribution from the revolutionaries at sea to help the revolutionaries in Odessa. Eisenstein portrays the townspeople as spectators of events on the ship and, by implication, the sailors as spectators of the massacre on the steps. Once the Cossacks have finished their sweep and the guns have answered, the city plays no further part in the film.

Eisenstein kept to the facts in refusing to exaggerate the connection between the two simultaneous revolts. But in some other respects, he gave a false picture of events between 14 and 16 June in Odessa. The battleship arrived in the harbor at 8:00 P.M., seven hours after the fatal parade on deck. It dropped anchor and remained isolated for the night. The next morning was the second day of the general strike in the town, but the sailors made little response to the appeals for help. Apart from sending Vakulenchuk's body ashore, the crew concentrated on replenishing supplies of food, coal, and water. The two latter items were essential if the ship was to remain mobile. The collapse of the adventure, ten days later in Romania, was hastened by shortage of coal and the damage to the boilers caused by sailing hundreds of miles on seawater. However, on 15 June, they found coal in the harbor and spent most of the afternoon in the laborious and dirty task of transferring the fuel from a collier into their bunkers.

Provisions were bought in the town. The crew paid cash, using some of the twenty-seven thousand rubles (about three thousand pounds) they found in the ship's treasury. The money was used sparingly throughout their brief period of independence. A large sum remained untouched to the end. Before they surrendered to the Romanian authorities, the balance was split up among the crew, Gunner Barkovsky recording that he received eighty rubles. Sightseers as well as supplies came onboard. Eisenstein shows a cheerful passage of food and livestock from small boats into the *Potemkin.* In actual fact, far from welcoming this fraternization, the sailors soon resented the swarm of undisciplined, tiresome visitors. They decided to "clear out the landlubbers." Some women, however, remained onboard for several days, comforting the crew but provoking arguments. The British consul noted three days later the arrival of a party from the ship seeking bandages and medical supplies, since there had been fighting among the crew over the women.[23]

On 15 June, the crew received representatives of the revolutionary parties in the port and sent delegates to land Vakulenchuk's body and to deliver a petition to the French consul but established no close contact with the strikers. They specifically rejected a request to send a large armed party ashore. The local Social Democrats hoped the sailors might persuade the soldiers to defy their officers and repeat the *Potemkin* mutiny in the military garrison. But despite the repeated efforts of representatives of the Odessa political parties (including Feldmann, known as Ivan the Student, and Kirill Petrov), the mutineers made little response and treated the city and its military garrison as a potential threat and the citizens and strikers as almost irrelevant onlookers of their own private concerns.

The film highlights two episodes, the devastating massacre on the steps and the battleship's brief, but seemingly effective, bombardment of the military headquarters onshore. The first is a brilliant invention by Eisenstein to represent the savagery of the forces of reaction; the second flatters the spirit and concern of the crew. Let us examine these two sections in some detail.

Eisenstein was understandably captivated by the cinematic possibilities provided by the Odessa steps. Completed to the design of a Sardinian architect, Boffo, in 1841, the stairway stretched up from the harbor front to the equestrian statue of the Duc de Richelieu and the fashionable shopping streets beyond. The duke was a French Bourbon émigré, appointed governor of Odessa by Alexander I during the Napoleonic Wars. The impression of height and distance was increased by the architect's skill in making the steps nearly twice as wide at the bottom as at the top. From the statue, only the large square landings breaking up the descent were visible. From the bottom, the landings could not be seen, and the eye saw only the steps in a continuous upward sweep.

Eisenstein recalls that

> neither the original script nor the montage drafts provided for the shooting scene on the Odessa steps. The idea flashed in my mind when I saw the steps. . . . Another source might have been the dim recollection of an illustration I had seen in a 1905 magazine, showing a horseman on the smoke enveloped steps.[24]

Marie Seton adds "that in his researches Eisenstein found a series of sketches by a French artist who had witnessed the massacre on the Odessa stairway."[25] Maxim Straukh specifically mentions pictures in the French magazine *L'Illustration* that brought back for Eisenstein memories of the 1905 riots in Riga.[26]

L'Illustration for the summer of 1905 included three articles on the *Potemkin* mutiny but no sketches of a massacre on the steps.[27] Contemporary British accounts record no such massacre, although the *Illustrated London News* published a picture of "where the mob and the Cossacks met, the steps of St Nicholas Church."[28] This church is nearly two kilometers from Richelieu's statue. The Italian magazine *Via Nuovo* has a picture of a crowd on the steps, but it is a peaceful gathering almost exactly matching the opening shot of Eisenstein's sequence.

There was a massacre on the steps, but it occurred on the night of 15–16 June. Four of the five eyewitness accounts left by those onboard the ship mention the outburst, but they express comparatively little concern and no sense of involvement with this drama onshore.

The massacre was not a slaughter of innocents but a desperate, brutal attempt to maintain order in a city in revolt. The strikes in Odessa and other cities in Russia in 1905 were outbursts of primitive anger by industrial workers and peasants. Once the veneer of control exercised by czarist administration was broken, the crowds looted and drank their way through shops and warehouses. By 14 June, that veneer of control had been lost in Odessa.

Matyushenko's own account laid the blame on the town authorities. He accuses them of provoking anti-Jewish riots and leaving cases of vodka about to encourage disorder.

"After the end of the meeting near the body of Vakulenchuk, the crowd at the port consisted merely of curious middle-class elements and hoodlums. There were very few workers and all their attempts to hold back these people or to interfere with them were useless."[29]

The most that the army could hope to do (the mayor had fled to report on the situation to St. Petersburg) was to try to contain the riots in the harbor area and the industrial suburbs and protect the fashionable shopping and residential sections of the town. In 1905 much of the destructive fury of the distressed was unleashed in the vicinity of the poorer homes and commercial centers. The troops adopted a policy of containment, aware perhaps that many of the warehouses belonged to the unpopular Jews, who handled 90 percent of Odessa's grain-export trade. This policy included holding a line on the Odessa steps that separated the center of the town from the quayside. That line was threatened on the night of 15–16 June by the mob that was loose in the harbor area. General Kakhanov, commander of the military district, reported that

> with the coming of dark the malefactors began to hurl explosive bombs at the troops from the port side as well as from the town side, and began to move upon the troops, with inflammatory shouting and with revolver fire. The crowd dispersed at a run on the opening of gunfire, but then throughout the night it tried in various places to move upon the troops; however, each time it was dispersed with shots. By 4 a.m. the crowd had finally dispersed and the exchange of fire had ceased.[30]

This partisan account tallies with evidence from several other sources of a nighttime struggle between troops and civilians, including clashes on the steps, that left hundreds of dead and wounded. The shooting on the steps did take place, but it took place at night and was the frenzied reaction of a military authority trying to prevent a crowd from surging up the steps and not, as portrayed in the film, the cold-blooded daytime murder of a happy crowd innocently waving at the battleship in the harbor.

In his memoirs, Eisenstein himself provides supporting evidence for this interpretation. During his visit to the United States, he was told by the manager of a cinema in Atlantic City, New Jersey, where *Battleship Potemkin* had been shown that the film had reduced one old Russian American to tears. The manager assumed that he must have been one of the sailors or a survivor of the massacre but was told instead that he had been one of the soldiers in Odessa.

> Side by side with the others he had fired volley after volley. They had opened fire at something dark, dim, and indiscernable, huddled far below at the foot of the monumental stairway. And now suddenly after twenty years he had actually seen what he had been shooting at on that day. It was only now that he realised that they had not been firing warning shots, as told, but sending their bullets into living flesh and blood.[31]

Eisenstein's recollection of a cinema operator's story of an old man's remorseful recollections of firing at dark unseen figures does not rank as first-class evidence, but it tallies with several other accounts that speak of rioting and troop action by night but make no mention of a spectacular daytime sweep down the steps.

Eisenstein's invention of the steps sequence is understandable. It is not easy to understand and accept two aspects of his representation of that event, the composition of the crowd and the conduct of the troops. The crowd on the steps in the film include a high proportion of bourgeois figures, and especially well-dressed bourgeois women. One of the prominent victims, who appeals to the troops for mercy, looks like a middle-aged Jewish schoolmistress. The clash was not portrayed as a class struggle between czarist troops and heroic workers, as it is in his first film, *Strike,* or even in the confrontation between officers and men on the battleship itself. Presumably Eisenstein was suggesting that in 1925 and in 1905 urban revolution could still be interpreted as a petit bourgeois preliminary to the full-blooded workers' and peasants' victory in 1917.

In the film, the soldiers display no hesitation or remorse in their march down the steps, shooting unarmed women and children. At the foot of the steps, mounted Cossacks disperse the crowds with enthusiasm. Occasionally Eisenstein gives us a glimpse of an officer giving an order to fire, but he does not stress that the soldiers are being driven to act as unwilling agents of their class enemies. They behave very differently from their comrades on the *Potemkin,* where a firing squad, in the presence of the captain and urged on by Gilyarovsky, refuse to execute their shipmates. This contrast in behavior lies at the heart of the film and gives a confusing political message. It bears out Leon Trotsky's verdict that the 1905 revolution was broken on the bayonets of the peasant army, but that is not an interpretation one would expect to find in a film made in 1925.

This sequence is followed by the sailors' only gesture of solidarity with the townspeople, the bombardment of the military headquarters. There was in fact little cooperation between the two groups. The film excuses the failure of the sailors to join forces with the strikers in subtitles: "The people of Odessa look to you for their liberation. Disembark now, and the army will join forces with you." Answered by, "we cannot disembark. The admiralty squadron has begun to move against us."

On the morning of 16 June, the ship did send a party onshore, to seek permission from the military commandant to bury Vakulenchuk in the military cemetery. They asked permission; they did not seek to dictate terms. The June heat that had putrefied the meat made it essential to bury the martyr quickly. Approval was given, and the ceremony took place at 5:30 P.M. Only twelve sailors and the priest attended from the ship. But the cortege was followed by thousands of townsfolk. Eisenstein surprisingly did not re-create the funeral procession, which, in Matyushenko's words,

> marched through the town. . . . In the streets new masses of people joined us. On the balconies, in the windows and on the roofs of the houses, there were crowds of people. Shouts could be heard. "All honour to the dead hero!" "Down with the tyrants!" "Long live the *Potemkin.*"[32]

Feldmann thought the only incongruous figure was the priest, Father Parmen.

> This minister of God presented a pitiful appearance. During the mutiny somebody had hit him on the nose with a chair, and the bandage would not keep in place on his thick, fleshy nose. It was coming down every minute and he was entirely absorbed in dealing with it.[33]

The funeral was not molested by the troops, but on the return journey the ship's delegation was attacked. Three men failed to return. They were either killed or wounded, or perhaps they took the chance to abandon a losing cause. The attack on the burial party settled the debate on the ship about whether or not to bring the *Potemkin*'s guns into action against a meeting of military officers in the town theater.

Instead of the defiant, accurate bombardment shown in the film as an immediate reaction to the ferocity of the troops, only two live rounds were fired from a six-inch gun after several hours of argument among the crew. The massive twelve-inch guns remained silent. Initially three blank shots were fired. Fifteen minutes later (a delay that presumably enabled all the officers in the theater to disperse), two live rounds were dispatched. One failed to explode, and the other damaged residential property hundreds of yards from the theater and finished up outside the house of the Italian consul general.

Disheartened by their failure to get the range of a target less than two miles away while firing over open sights from an anchored platform, the sailors quickly ended their single act of defiance since the mutiny itself. Eisenstein's picture of an aroused lion flatters this two-shot "barrage."

This section of the story ended not as in the film with a successful counterattack but in anxiety, with the ship's crew awaiting the arrival of heavy land artillery that would force them out to sea and into the arms of the other units of the fleet.

The film ends with the encounter between the *Potemkin* and the ships sent to recapture it. Eisenstein builds up the fear and tension during the approach of the fleet. Action stations are mounted, and the *Potemkin* steams toward the line of ships. Matyushenko emerges at last as the dominant figure and organizes the resistance. But the *Potemkin* is greeted with cheers not shells and passes through in triumph. The film closes on this exultant note, leaving unresolved the fate of the revolt in Odessa and even of the mutineers themselves. *Potemkin* is not shown as victorious, nor has it at that moment been subdued.

This section of the film falsifies nothing, but it conveys less than the truth by ignoring the tragic anticlimax of *Potemkin*'s defiance. The ship's mutiny collapsed as abjectly as the 1905 revolution itself after Czar Nicholas II had made concessions to the liberals in the October Manifesto, splitting the moderate revolutionaries away from the more radical movement. Once the government had recovered from the shock of defeat in the Russo-Japanese War and the internal conflicts of the autumn and winter of 1905–6, many of the constitutional concessions made in the October Manifesto were revoked or watered down. By 1907 the autocracy was back in power, building up fresh resentment for the final collapse in 1917. In that year, whole armies, not single battleships or military detachments, mutinied and could not be defeated in isolation as the crew of the *Potemkin* had been in 1905.

The battleship did sail out of the harbor on 17 June to meet a force of three battleships, a cruiser, and four torpedo boats. Although the numerical odds were against it, the *Potemkin*'s range, weight, and speed of fire made the disparity less marked than it seems on paper. *Potemkin* had two encounters with the squadron. On the first occasion, the czarist forces turned away at a distance of four miles, and the *Potemkin* returned to harbor. Later that day, the force reappeared, strengthened by the addition of two more battleships. *Potemkin,* however, sailed toward them. It was not fired upon, passed through the squadron, and returned back through the lines of ships. Some crews acclaimed it, and one ship, the *Georgy Pobyedonosets,* returned with it to Odessa; the others crept back to their base at Sebastopol. Commander in Chief of the Black Sea Fleet Admiral Chukhnin was so alarmed at the possibility of further disaffection that he sent most of the ratings on leave and immobilized ships' engines so that the vessels could not be made operational. The *Times* suggested that "the Black Sea Fleet has virtually ceased to exist."[34] Up to this point, the encounter was an even greater victory than Eisenstein suggests, but the rest of the story was a humiliating anticlimax.

This brief encounter had solved nothing. The *Potemkin* had not been subdued, but the mutiny had spread to only one other ship. Back in Odessa, the sailors were even less willing to join forces with the rebels on land, who were coming under increasing military pressure. Even the crew of the *Georgy Pobyedonosets* were short-term allies. The ship attempted to slip away to Sebastopol. Discouraged by the menace of *Potemkin*'s guns, the *Georgy* ran aground and the crew abandoned both their ship and the revolutionary cause. The *Potemkin* was desperately short of coal and water. The men were divided about their future course of action. Soon even Matyushenko, the revolutionary leader, agreed that they should sail for a neutral Romanian port.

On 19 June, they reached Constansa. Their welcome was formal and apprehensive. Failing to secure the supplies they needed, but not yet completely cowed, the *Potemkin* sailed away in search of coal. It called at the Russian port of Theodosia, but the townspeople evacuated their homes in terror, and troops opened fire when the crew attempted to take over a coal barge. The ship finally limped back to Constansa. The crew surrendered on 25 June, accepting assurances that they would not be handed over to the Russian authorities.

They did not settle easily in Romania. Some returned home to face trial and varying lengths of sentence. Others found work on the Romanian land harder and even less rewarding than in the Ukraine. In 1908 thirty-two of them arrived in London through the good offices of the German Socialist Party and the "British Friends for Russian Freedom." This organization, the committee members of which included Dr. G. M. Trevelyan, appealed in the *Times* for three hundred pounds to resettle in one of the colonies a party made up of "strong vigorous men of peasant extraction and all under thirty."[35] A letter from Mr. Trautmann, a British resident in Odessa in 1905, reminded potential subscribers that the refugees had murdered their officers and had been guilty of theft, insubordination, murder, and arson in Romania. "Will they be desirable settlers in our colonies?" he concluded.[36] Eventually they departed, not to join the descendants of British convicts in Australia, but to the Argentine.

Matyushenko did not stay long with his shipmates. By the time they surrendered, the crew were bitterly opposed to the man who had driven them so hard for so little purpose. One of the crew, Reshkitin, jumped the ship on its first visit to Constansa, claiming he had fled "because he could not tolerate Matyushenko's earthy and coarse manner towards the crew. Those who dared to oppose either the committee or Matyushenko were threatened with death."[37] The Romanian socialists welcomed Matyushenko and he left Constansa on the first night, according to one report "because he was afraid of being torn to pieces by the sailors of the battleship *Potemkin* for his inhuman conduct towards them.[38] A year later, he was in the United States, working from June 1906 to March 1907 in a Singer factory. On his way through London, he was seen by R. Rocker, a German working with Jewish revolutionary groups in the office of Kropotkin's newspaper in Stepney. Rocker found "it hard to believe that this simple kindly man had been the ringleader of the *Potemkin* mutiny."[39] In the spring of 1907, he returned to Europe and passed through Paris, en route to further underground agitation in Russia. But he was soon picked up by the police on 3 June in Nikolaev near Odessa in the company of a group of Anarchist Syndicalists, living under the name Fedorenko. He was recognized, charged for his part in the mutiny and for a personal responsibility in the murder of the officers, and hanged at dawn on 20 October 1907 in Sebastopol.[40] Feldmann was captured in Theodosia but escaped from prison and resumed his revolutionary career. A police report claimed that he had been seen but not arrested in January 1911. During the preparations for the filming of *Battleship Potemkin,* Feldmann attended an "Evening of Reminiscences of Contemporaries of the Year 1905." Also present were Nina Agadzhanova-Shutko, Grigori Alexandrov, and Sergei Eisenstein, taking notes for the film.[41]

The *Potemkin* itself was punished for its misdemeanors. The ship was collected from Constansa and returned to Sebastopol. Renamed the *St. Panteleimon,* it participated in a second, more extensive mutiny in November 1905. The red flag was run up on the cruiser *Ochakov.* The *St. Panteleimon* and several other ships joined in the revolt led by Lieutenant Schmidt, who sent a telegram to St. Petersburg proclaiming the formation of a Black Sea Republic. The rising was subdued after attacks on the rebels by the guns of the *Rostov* and the *Dvenadtsat'Apostolov* (*The Twelve Apostles*), two of the ships that had failed to overawe the *Potemkin* outside Odessa. This mutiny, although more important historically, is less well known. Lieutenant Schmidt was the hero of a poem by Boris Pasternak, and the *Potemkin* affair provided the subject for an opera by Chishko. In the opera, the sailors to be shot are covered by a tarpaulin. Neither of these works, however, attracted the attention given to Eisenstein's film.

The *St. Panteleimon* continued an undistinguished naval career. In April 1917 it became the *Potemkin* once again but in May was given a third name, *Borets za Svobodu* (*Fighter for Freedom*). It was not in action during the First World War and was finally sunk by order of the Soviet authorities in 1918 to prevent its capture by counterrevolutionary forces. It was later refloated but never brought back into commission.

When Eisenstein made the film in 1925, the *Potemkin* no longer existed. Eisenstein wrote that he used "her sister ship, the once famed and mighty

Dvenadtsat'Apostolov."[42] *The Twelve Apostles* was a contemporary but not a sister ship of the *Potemkin,* a cruiser of 8,560 tons, compared with the 12,600 tons of the *Battleship Potemkin.* In 1925 *The Twelve Apostles* was lying rusting at anchor in a creek near Sebastopol. It was one of the few pre-1905 ships still in existence. Very few Russian naval craft of any vintage were still seaworthy. The Black Sea Fleet consisted of two cruisers and three destroyers. It is not surprising that, for the shots of the main squadron sailing toward the *Potemkin,* Eisenstein had to use pre–World War One stock footage of battleships at sea.

The scenes onboard the *Potemkin* were mostly shot on *The Twelve Apostles,* which was given a face-lift by Eisenstein's technicians. The ship had been neglected and was used as a floating mine store. The decks had to be reconstructed. Belowdecks were thousands of mines. Actors and technicians had to move about carefully for fear of disturbing the dangerous cargo. Later Eisenstein suggested that "the ship on the screen seemed imbued with their explosive power."[43] *The Twelve Apostles* could not move through the water, so some of the material was filmed using another vessel, a 1905 cruiser, the *Pamyat'Merkuriya* (renamed by the Bolsheviks *Komintern*), which was still in service as a seagoing training ship.

These ships were used to create a film the splendid artistry of which transformed an unsuccessful revolt into one of the most famous naval mutinies in history—and in the history of the cinema.

Notes

1. Mayer, *Eisenstein's* Potemkin.
2. Marshall, *Battleship Potemkin,* 5.
3. Eisenstein quoted in Seton, *Eisenstein,* 74.
4. Written in 1939 and included in an introductory essay to Eisenstein, *Battleship Potemkin,* 8.
5. Eisenstein, *Notes of a Film Director,* 23. Ironically Eisenstein makes this assertion when discussing his use of the tarpaulin during the execution of the mutineers and, as I suggest later, claims to be distorting the truth when he was in fact following the true course of events.
6. Ibid., 29.
7. Marshall, *Battleship Potemkin,* 59.
8. Eisenstein quoted in Marshall, *Battleship Potemkin,* 338.
9. Kleberg, "Eisenstein's *Potemkin.*"
10. Jane, *Fighting Ships.*
11. Jane, *Imperial Russian Navy.*
12. Report by G. Woodhouse, British Consul in Riga, 2 May 1905, Public Record Office, London.
13. Kirill Orlov, memoirs published in Nevsky, *Vosstanie Na Bronenostse.*

14. Matyushenko's letter published in Nevsky, *Vosstanie Na Bronenostse,* 337.
15. Orlov, in Nevsky, *Vosstanie Na Bronenostse,* 321.
16. Perelygin, in Nevsky, *Vosstanie Na Bronenostse,* 230.
17. Babin, *L'Illustration,* 22 July 1905, 55.
18. Matyushenko, in Nevsky, *Vosstanie Na Bronenostse,* 302.
19. Published in Eisenstein, *Notes of a Film Director,* 18–31.
20. Report by H. Dundas, Acting Consul General, Galatz, 12 July 1905, Public Record Office, London.
21. Perelygin, in Nevsky, *Vosstanie Na Bronenostse,* 233.
22. Barna, in *Eisenstein,* 98, writes that Eisenstein received a "letter from another surviving mutineer, who also maintained that he had been under the tarpaulin; Eisenstein did not disillusion him, but was amused that the power of empathy could outweigh that of memory." Barna notes that "it is difficult to determine the truth, but there seems no reason for doubting Eisenstein's word." Further study of the stories of the tarpaulin and the court case suggests that there is some reason for so doubting.
23. Report by C. S. Smith, British Consul, Odessa, 1 July 1905 (Western calendar), Public Record Office, London.
24. Eisenstein, *Notes of a Film Director,* 27.
25. Seton, *Eisenstein,* 75.
26. M. Straukh quoted in Swallow, *Eisenstein.*
27. *L'Illustration* (Paris, 8, 15, and 22 July 1905) contains material on the events in Odessa and in Romania.
28. *Illustrated London News,* 8 July 1905.
29. This comment is in the version of Matyushenko's memoirs published in London (1931) as Matyushenko, *Eleven Days on the* Potemkin, but does not appear in the account by Matyushenko in Russian in the work of Nevsky, *Vosstanie Na Bronenostse.*
30. Telegram from the Commander of the Armed Forces of the Odessa Military District, Cavalry General Kakhanov, to the War Ministry, 16 June 1905, published in Nevsky, *Vosstanie Na Bronenostse,* 367.
31. Published in *Soviet Weekly* (London), 7 September 1961.
32. Matyushenko, *Eleven Days on the* Potemkin, 15.
33. Feldmann, *Revolt of the* Potemkin, 75.
34. *Times* (London), 4 July 1905.
35. *Times* (London), 16 September 1908.
36. *Times* (London), 29 September 1908.
37. As reported by Melas, Russian police informant in Constansa, in Nevsky, *Vosstanie Na Bronenostse,* 270.
38. Ibid., 276–77.
39. Rocker, *London Years,* 173.
40. Report by the Temporary Deputy Commander in Chief of the Black Sea Fleet, Rear Admiral Viren, 20 October 1907, in Nevsky, *Vosstanie Na Bronenostse,* 329–30.
41. Marshall, *Battleship Potemkin,* 58.
42. Eisenstein, *Notes of a Film Director,* 20.
43. Ibid., 22.

References

General Works

Baynac, J., L. Engelstein, R. Girault, E. Keenan, and A. Yassoun. *Sur* 1905 (Paris, 1974).
Bennett, G. "The *Potemkin* Mutiny," *Journal of the Royal United Service Institute* (London, November 1959).
Harcave, S. *First Blood. The Russian Revolution of 1905* (London, 1965).
Hough, R. *The* Potemkin *Mutiny* (London, 1975).
Jane, F. T. *Fighting Ships 1905–6* (London, 1906).
———, *The Imperial Russian Navy* (London, 1904).
Mayer, D. *Sergei M. Eisenstein's* Potemkin (New York, 1972).
Rocker, R. *The London Years* (London, 1956).
Taylor, R. *Film Propaganda, Soviet Russia and Nazi Germany* (London, 1979).
———, *The Politics of the Soviet Cinema 1917–29* (Cambridge, 1979).

The Making of the Film

Barna, Y. *Eisenstein* (London, 1973).
Eisenstein, S. *The Battleship Potemkin* (London, 1968).
———, *Film Form* (London, 1951).
———, *The Film Sense* (London, 1968).
———, *Notes of a Film Director* (London, 1959).
Kleberg, L. "Eisenstein's *Potemkin,* and Tretyakov's *Ryci Kiaj,*" *Scando-Slavica,* 23 (Copenhagen, 1977).
Kleiman, N. I., and K. B. Levina. *Bronenosets Potemkin* (Moscow, 1969).
Leyda, J. Kino. *A History of Russian Film* (London, 1960).
Marshall, H. (ed.). *The Battleship Potemkin* (New York, 1978).
Nizhny, V. B. *Lessons with Eisenstein* (London, 1962).
Seton, M. *Sergei M. Eisenstein—A Biography* (London, 1978).
Shklovskii, V. *Eisenstein* (Moscow, 1973).
Swallow, N. *Eisenstein, a Documentary Portrait* (London, 1976).

Accounts of the Mutiny and of Events in Odessa

Reports by the Belgian Consul in Odessa. Archives du Ministère des Affaires Étrangères, Brussels.
Reports by the British Acting Consul General in Galatz, Romania. Public Record Office, London.
Reports by the British Consul in Odessa. Public Record Office, London.
Reports by the British Vice Consul in Sebastopol. Public Record Office, London.
Reports by the French Consul in Odessa. Archives du Ministère des Affaires Étrangères, Quai D'Orsay, Paris.
Reports by the Italian Consul in Odessa and from the Italian Legation in Bucharest. Archives del Ministero degli Affari Esteri, Rome.

Reports by the United States Ambassador in St. Petersburg. Foreign Relations, United States of America. State Department, Washington, D.C., 1906.

Accounts by

Lt. Colonel Budakov
The Gendarme Administration of the City of Odessa
A. F. Matyushenko
Melas (police informant in Constansa)
K. Orlov
K. Perelygin
B. Prokhorov
Colonel Shul'ts
Colonel Zagoskin

(All published in Russian)

Babin, G. *L'Illustration* (Paris, 8, 15, 22 July 1905).
Feldmann, C. *The Revolt of the* Potemkin (London, 1908).
Matyushenko, A. F. *Eleven Days on the* Potemkin: *The Revolt on the Armoured Cruiser* Potemkin (London, 1931).
Nevsky, V. I. *Vosstanie Na Bronenostse, "Knyaz" Potemkin Tavrichesky," Vospominaniya, Materialy Dokumenty,* Moscow-Leningrad, 1924.
St. Petersburg *Official Messenger* (5 July 1905).

19

Rule Britannia!

George MacDonald Fraser

Mutiny on the *Bounty*

The sailing ship, real or not, has been an expensive and unpredictable staple of historical pictures from time immemorial, and out of all the film dramas of fighting sail, piracy, exploration, ghost ships, mad captains, bucko mates, smugglers, and the rest, the story of one small armed transport of the Royal Navy takes pride of place, as it deserves to do. The *Bounty,* subject of three major productions, has been part of film folklore for fifty years; it is also a classic example of the best and worst in Hollywood's treatment of history.

The true story (or rather stories) of the *Bounty* is an epic of the sea to be classed with the *Odyssey* and the voyages of the *Argo,* Christopher Columbus, and Ferdinand Magellan. Hollywood has touched only part of it, and that perforce in condensed form; the full tale of the ship and its company is so complex and sensational—and still mysterious—that it would take several films to tell it properly. It is one of the factual dramas that outstrips fiction.

For the record, the *Bounty* was dispatched in 1787 to Tahiti to collect and transport breadfruit plants to the West Indies. Its young commander, Sir William Bligh, was a fine seaman and navigator of genius, who in later years was to distinguish himself in action, win the praise of Horatio Nelson, and end his days as an admiral. His friend and protégé, Fletcher Christian, sailed in the *Bounty* and was advanced by Bligh to second in command, though he was only twenty-two. The characters of the two men have been dissected and disputed for two centuries, without total success. Bligh was tough, brave, efficient, and (contrary to the false portrait of the first two films) a humane and considerate commander; he was also cursed with an explosive temper and a withering tongue. Christian is more of an enigma. He was inexperienced and possibly incompetent and seems to have been unstable and highly sensitive to criticism.

All went well until Tahiti, where the crew had an idyllic time of it with the native belles. Bligh seems to have let discipline slip (he was not a born manager of men), but once at sea again he bore down, and Christian, who had left a pregnant sweetheart on Tahiti, was eventually driven by Bligh's upbraidings to contemplate jumping ship; in the event, he changed his mind, apparently on the spur of the moment, and with the help of the more discontented elements aboard, mutinied, took the ship, and turned Bligh and the loyal men loose in an open boat.

It was an act of appalling cruelty and tantamount to a slow death sentence: the nearest inhabited settlement was over three thousand miles away, and Bligh had no charts and little food. But in the most remarkable open-boat voyage in maritime history, he made it to Timor and eventually to England. A naval ship, the *Pandora,* was sent after the mutineers and captured some of them but was wrecked. Christian and his fellow mutineers took refuge on Pitcairn Island, far off the sea routes, the *Bounty* was burned, and not for nineteen years was their hiding place discovered, by which time only one of them was left. Christian probably died on Pitcairn, although there is some remarkable evidence to suggest that he got back to England—it includes identification by a former shipmate and a curious letter by the poet William Wordsworth, who had been at school with Christian. It has even been suggested that the "Rime of the Ancient Mariner," by Wordsworth's friend Samuel Coleridge, was inspired by the *Bounty* drama; it is not impossible.

Those are the barest facts. We all know what Hollywood made of them, and history, truth, and fair play took a frightful beating.

The first *Mutiny on the Bounty* (1935) had Bligh (Charles Laughton) as a sadistic tyrant who flogged and abused his crew mercilessly and Christian (Clark Gable) as the stalwart hero driven to desperation. Their relationship was misrepresented; Bligh was made out to be dishonest as well as brutal; ludicrous nonsense about keelhauling was introduced; a key figure, Midshipman Heywood (called Byam in the film and played by Franchot Tone), was distorted beyond recognition; the reason for the mutiny was exaggerated nonsense. The one concession to fairness was in the tribute paid to Bligh's heroic voyage, but he was still left discredited. The film's verdict was spoken by the court-martial president, ignoring Bligh's hand: "I admire your seamanship and courage, but . . ." It was all a libel on a flawed hero, a travesty of truth—and a splendid film.

This could not be said of the 1962 remake. Bligh (Trevor Howard) was, if anything, even more of a villain than Laughton, and to the mutual antipathy between him and Christian a new and farcical element was added. Christian was portrayed as an aristocratic exquisite, with Marlon Brando playing him like an adenoidal Scarlet Pimpernel; Bligh was the despised commoner. (In fact both men were from good but not upper-class families, Bligh's from the West Country, Christian's from the Isle of Man.) The *Bounty* flogged and keel-hauled its way to Tahiti as before; the mutiny took place in a welter of silly epithets; Bligh was seen only briefly in his open boat; his court-martial was an offensive fiction (poor Henry Daniell deserved better at the end of his career); and Christian's final change of heart and gory death were, to put it mildly, in keeping with the rest of a film that seemed to go out of its way to distort history. The first film, if false to the main facts, had been credible in plot and characterization; the second was not.

Why, we may ask, did Hollywood do it not once but twice? The answer is, probably, convention and cliché. The truth of the mutiny is a superb drama—but it is psychological drama, of two conflicting natures, one of which snapped under the strain. Why Christian went out of control we cannot know, because we do not know him, or Bligh, well enough, and we can only imagine what it was like in that unreal floating exile, years and thousands of miles from home: a crew sulking over paradise lost, a captain impatient to reassert authority, an unstable lieutenant possibly heartbroken for his girl in Tahiti and driven beyond endurance by verbal bullying. It is made for sensitive dramatization—and that was not what films were about in 1935. Clear, recognizable "motivation" was needed, right versus wrong; and given the unsavory reputation that Bligh had borne unjustly for 150 years, the temptation to reshape history (with the help of a popular novel) into a spirited, easily understood tale of cruelty and rebellion was not to be resisted. It may well be that no one on the film knew the true story, anyway. But they knew what the customers liked and gave it to them, and the screen officers and crew of the *Bounty* responded with a will.

Laughton was immense, brooding, and scowling, rasping his "Mistah Christian!" into the language; presumably only Victor McLaglen's performance in *The Informer* denied him the Oscar. Gable, who was also nominated, was first-rate, the script was a beauty, the action fast and clear, and there are images that live in the memory—Laughton, beetle browed, sweeping his hand across his mouth, Franchot Tone draped over the crosstrees in a howling storm, Donald Crisp assaulting Ian MacWolfe with a fish, Hiti-hiti in his cocked hat, the solid tramp of the press-gang (the men being pressed were in fact volunteers), the small boats pulling *Bounty* in a flat calm, Bligh roaring defiance from the launch, while Christian, already in doubt, watches in silence. It was all very good and deserved its Academy Award; the pity is that it established a historical falsehood.

The industry made some amends in 1984 with *The Bounty,* which told the essential truths and fell curiously flat. It would be tempting for a Hollywood apologist to say that here is proof of the need to reshape history for good film drama, but that won't do; the fact is that *The Bounty* was not a very good picture. This in spite of a brilliant performance by Anthony Hopkins as Bligh, and a highly creditable effort by Mel Gibson to get inside the skin of the tormented Christian. Perhaps the device of telling the story in flashback from Bligh's court-martial (well conducted by Laurence Olivier and Edward Fox) was a mistake; in the end, what came off the screen lacked conviction. I could believe that ship and its crew in 1935; they seemed realistic in a way that the 1984 *Bounty* did not. A pity, because it was sound history, give or take a few minor details (Bligh's obsession with rounding Cape Horn was emphasized, without, so far as I know, any historical warranty). But once, at least, it came to life, in the moment of mutiny—brawling, struggling confusion, everyone yelling at once, Christian nearly hysterical, and some of the authentic recorded dialogue being used at last. (None of the films really exploited Bligh's splendid gift of invective, examples of which are to be found in the journals of the survivors.[1]) With all his sterling qualities, he must have been a good man to stay away from. Later in life, as governor of New South Wales, he was the object of another insurrection, and his career was well summed up by a friend as "a turbulent journey."

The British in Africa

There are interesting differences between British and American imperial epics. The British films were undoubtedly better historical reconstructions or (since some of the films were contemporary) representations of the imperial scene. There were no zip fasteners on Zoltan Korda's kilts, the technical advisers often worked from firsthand experience, and none of his troops responded to the command "Left face!" The Americans were less meticulous in detail, more prone to take liberties with historic truth, altogether more relaxed in approach. They put across the imperial message just as strongly but more casually; in British prewar films, there is just a hint of self-conscious tendency to show the flag for its own sake, to slip in the quick sermon, to stiffen the upper lip until it touches caricature. Mind you, the British in real life have a tendency to caricature themselves and nowhere more than in the Indian Army; if any young viewer of today thinks that the behavior of some of the screen sahibs is a little over the top and that no one was ever really as clipped-and-Carruthers in real life, rest assured that many of them were. Even send-up does not always exaggerate reality, as can be shown by a comparison of *Carry on up the Khyber* (1968) with the unvarnished truth of one imperial incident.

In the *Carry on* film, there is a lovely take-off of the stiff upper lip. At a residency dinner party, the Governor and his lady (Sid James and Joan Sims) and their guests continue unruffled with their meal while the residency is under attack, ignoring the shells bursting in the dining room, windows crashing in, and the chandelier descending in showers of plaster; polite behavior and protocol are strictly observed—which of course could not happen in such life-and-death circumstances, could it? Compare the case of Brigadier Shelton, held prisoner on top of an Afghan tower during the retreat from Kabul in 1842, in which a British army of fourteen thousand was wiped out. An earth tremor struck, the tower was about to collapse in ruins, and Shelton's only companion, a junior officer, rushed down the stairs followed by his chief. They escaped, and that night, after a day of fearful peril, Shelton rebuked his subordinate: "By the way, Mackenzie, you came downstairs in front of me this morning." Even Talbot Rothwell couldn't top that.

In all imperial films, especially the British productions, there is much that will give offense to modern liberals—the imperial attitude itself, of course, and the apparent patronizing of natives. They are entitled to object, provided disapproval does not interfere with truth. Sentiments are expressed in *Sanders of the River,* for example, that would send a race-relations officer into a decline—which is not to say that it was wrong to have them in the film, or to show the film, which is a true picture of its time, whatever may be thought of it today. There is sometimes a disturbing ambivalence about attitudes to this subject: on the one hand, an eagerness to seize on "racism" as a weapon of anti-imperial polemic and, at the same time, a strange reluctance to face truth because the objector finds it uncomfortable. I offer an example.

In the film *Northwest Frontier,* set in India circa 1905, that fine Indian actor I. S. Johar played an engine driver, and played him extremely well: it was a true rendering of a type imitated successfully by Peter Sellers and others, the quaintly spoken "Oh-jollee-good-sahib" funny Indian—a genuine character familiar to everyone who knows the subcontinent. One critic took violent exception to Johar's performance: it was a disgraceful caricature, and Johar should be ashamed of himself. I'd like to believe the critic thought that was true, but I doubt it. I suspect the critic knew Johar's portrayal was absolutely faithful but preferred to pretend it wasn't because the critic found it embarrassing and didn't like to think that Indians ever really behaved like that—or if they did, it shouldn't be shown onscreen. In other words, damn the truth if it doesn't fit with what one would like to believe is true—an attitude that, honesty aside, seems to me offensively patronizing. I would be less contemptuous of such critics if I thought they would be equally outraged at, say, a British general being portrayed as a pompous, arrogant, blustering clown—which has happened, and some of them were, God knows, so portray them that way by all means. With these thoughts in mind, *Sanders of the River* is a good starting point, since this was imperialism at its most paternal. The book, first of an enormously popular series by Edgar Wallace (and continued by Francis Gerard), appeared in 1910, at the zenith of Empire. Like most of its successors, it is a series of short stories about Mr. Commissioner Sanders, who supervises and keeps the peace among the savage tribes in a British African territory. To call it illiberal and racist by today's standards is like describing *Hamlet* as a family row; Sanders is an absolute ruler who treats his subjects as dangerous children from whom he demands total obedience; he likes and admires them in their primitive state and has no use for Westernized Africans—in short, he has the views of his time. Wallace wrote from African experience, drew an accurate background, and glamorized it heavily. Probably no colonial writer except Sir H. Rider Haggard so shaped Western imagination of Africa and its people, for better or worse. The film of 1935 had Leslie Banks in the title role (bad casting to Sanders fans, who knew that their hero looked more like Roland Young, being small, spare, and quiet), but the star was Paul Robeson as Bosambo, a friendly chief whom Wallace depicted as a likable rogue. Robeson played him straight and also sang magnificently, which was the film's main box-office attraction. It is a middling picture, with some good African location shots and a rather vague plot in which Sanders, assisted by Bosambo, is pitted against a powerful tribal king who turns his enemies into drumskins. There is fine spear work, much dancing, love interest for Bosambo with Nina Mae McKinney, last-minute rescue, and some bad back-projection, notably in the famous "Canoe Song," in which Robeson thunders out "Ai-ee-o-go" while his warriors paddle away (a scene greeted in Oxford cinemas with rapturous cries of "Well rowed, Balliol!"). There was also a fairly toe-curling homily from Banks about the benefits of British rule, which must have gone down well with Jomo Kenyatta, later president of Kenya, who was one of the extras.

Robeson was disappointed with the film, reasonably enough, since he had hoped it would give the black man some dignity. One who took the same view was my father, an old Africa hand who, while a staunch imperialist, had his own quiet, decided view on Africa and its people, formed by soldiering there at a time when Nairobi had not long ceased to be a water hole, and by having his life saved by a Kikuyu warrior (whom I never met but whose name I record simply because I want to. It was Wakibi). All of which was not without influence on my young mind, although it does not affect my judgment of *Sanders of the River* as a film and as a valuable picture of Africa. But I admit it is not one of my favorites; it prompts too many questions, which I cannot answer. It is patronizing. It is also about an unidentified part of Africa whose locality one can only try to deduce from Wallace's stories, which suggest that the territory where Sanders successfully kept the peace may have been that region now called Biafra.

My father and Robeson could have found nothing to complain of in *Zulu,* which in its way is the best African historical film and one of the best in the imperial canon. Purely as a battle picture it compares, on its smaller scale, with *Waterloo* as a piece of meticulous re-creation. I suspect that Stanley Baker, who coproduced and played the lead, was inspired by Welsh patriotism, and it shows. The film depicts the defense of Rorke's Drift in 1879, where 130 British soldiers stood off four thousand Zulus for a day and a night following Isandhlwana, the most catastrophic defeat in imperial history, in which sixteen hundred of Lord Chelmsford's invading army had been wiped out by Cetewayo's impis. Rorke's Drift became a Victorian legend, as it deserved to; eleven Victoria Crosses were awarded, mostly to South Wales Borderers, as well as to Lieutenants Chard and Bromhead, who commanded the little garrison. Half of the film is a splendid buildup: the stricken field of Isandhlwana, with the terrifying plumed and gartered black warriors striding through the burning wreckage, and then a long tranquil sequence at the unsuspecting post on Buffalo River, the troops loafing in the sun or grumbling in the hospital before the message of disaster arrives, and the stillness is broken by the distant, ominous rumble of the advancing impis. There are memorable shots of the massed Zulu ranks, chanting and beating on their shields before launching themselves into attack, and of the post with its red-coated riflemen thinly spread behind their makeshift barricades; the course of the fighting is charted faithfully—the repeated charges driven off with fearful loss, the desperate hand-to-hand fighting in the burning hospital, and the last stand at the mealie-bag redoubts where the Zulu onslaught was finally stopped by the steady volley firing of the Welsh. This, by all accounts, is exactly how it was.

Naturally, the characters are dramatized, and elements of temperament are introduced to charge the atmosphere; so far as I know, there is no evidence of differences between Chard (played by Baker) and Bromhead (Michael Caine, making a striking star debut) in fact, either on the score of Chard's supposed "amateurism" as a Royal Engineer (!) or on the question of command; Chard was undisputed senior. And was the Reverend Witt present at all, and was he a drinker? There was a clergyman, the Reverend George Smith, among the defenders; he distinguished himself but is not in the film. The singing of "Men of Harlech" I assume is borrowed from the incident of the Shanghai Patrol, who are supposed to have sung "God Save the Queen" in similar desperate circumstances, but it made a splendid scene in *Zulu;* and if it is fiction, it is one of the liberties a scriptwriter is entitled to take.

All these are trivial points and in no way affect the film's authenticity, but I do have reservations about opinions being attributed to Chard and Bromhead that seem to reflect modern attitudes to war rather than the views of Victorian soldiers. After Rorke's Drift, the film has Bromhead viewing the carnage and saying he feels ashamed. I doubt if Bromhead really felt or said any such thing; he had no cause to. I question, too, whether Chard expressed such repugnance. They were professional soldiers, doing their duty; and when it was done, I would guess they just felt very tired, very relieved, and not a little bit elated. That may be hard for modern audiences to take, but it is how British soldiers were. I'm sure Chard and Bromhead felt great admiration for the Zulus, but shame or disenchantment with the profession of arms? No. They continued to serve in the army until their deaths, by which time they were both colonels. Baker and Caine were not bad look-alikes, save for Chard's mustache and Bromhead's superb whiskers.

The acting was excellent, with Nigel Green outstanding as the color sergeant; he *was* the old British army, so much so that one viewer wanted to know why he was not among the eleven recipients of the Victoria Cross in the film. The real color sergeant was in fact decorated, although not with the Victoria Cross. There was another interesting piece of casting: King Cetewayo was played by Chief Buthelezi.

Zulu is thoroughly good history, and so, up to a point, is *Stanley and Livingstone,* but it falls far short of the expectations raised by its title and does justice to neither of these remarkable men. David Livingstone, the giant of African exploration, is a supporting player; the film is about how Henry M. Stanley found him and was inspired to carry on the great man's missionary role—which is not what he did. That apart, the film missed a glorious opportunity, for Stanley's career was an extraordinary one. He was born John Rowlands (or Rollant) in Wales in 1841, orphaned, beat up his schoolmaster, worked his passage to America as a cabin boy, was adopted by a New Orleans cotton broker named Henry Morton Stanley, enlisted in the Confederate army during the American Civil War, was captured, changed sides, deserted from the Union navy, became a journalist, covered various campaigns, and was sent to find Livingstone. This success made him famous, and he continued to explore (though not in the missionary sense), founded the state that later became the Belgian Congo, rescued Emin Pasha (who, like Livingstone, stood in no great need of rescuing) from the Mahdists, became M.P. for North Lambeth, and was knighted in 1899, five years before his death.

Something might have been made of this, for the Livingstone search, once the famous greeting has been spoken, is not really enough to sustain a film; some embroidery was necessary, before and after, and it was not very gripping. There was some fine African photography, Spencer Tracy was an acceptable Stanley, but for once Cedric Hardwicke (Livingstone) seemed miscast; and for a film about two successful adventurers, it was strangely unexciting.

So, alas, was another film, which had even less excuse. *King Solomon's Mines* is one of the adventure classics, written for a bet by Rider Haggard to prove that he could match the success of *Treasure Island* and filmed more than once. The 1937 version was the best; it too had Hardwicke, much more at home in the role of Alan Quatermain, with John Loder and Roland Young as his companions, Curtis and Good, and Anna Lee was taken along for love interest—why this was thought necessary is a mystery. The story of the trek into unexplored territory in search of the fabulous diamond mines, the discovery that the explorers' black comrade is the rightful king of the lost land, the subsequent adventures with Gagool the witch, the entrapment in the mines—this needs no romantic embellishment, or if it did, they could have lifted one of Haggard's mysterious African queens from another book for Curtis to fall in love with. Again, the photography is splendid (as it was in the remake, which featured the giant Watutsi as the lost tribe), but the film is really a vehicle for the splendid singing of Paul Robeson, as the claimant king, with pleasing glimpses of wildlife along the way.

Indeed, with the honorable exception of *Zulu,* most African films tend to have a travelogue look about them (*Tarzan* included), and if some student of the future had to rely solely on Hollywood's efforts, he would learn a great deal more about the continent's fauna than about its history. South of the equator, that is; the Sudan has been the scene of two imperial epics, historically linked, and the first deals with the last of one of the great Victorian heroes, Charles Gordon.

He was a weird one, "half-cracked," "mad," "a wild man," according to contemporaries, almost removed from military college for throwing a man downstairs and stabbing another with a fork, asking complete strangers if they believed in Jesus, leading his Chinese storming parties while smoking a cigar and carrying a cane, an eccentric military near genius who administered territories, fought irregular campaigns, combated slavers, and whom a nervous British government was reluctant to put in charge of anything until they sent him, in desperation and without written orders, to evacuate the Sudan, which was being overrun by the Mahdi's army of fanatics. Gordon was cut off in Khartoum and held it for ten months before it fell and he was killed—two days before help arrived.

Khartoum is a spectacular devoted to this last mission, and as an action picture it has its share of good blood-and-thunder sequences, is extremely well acted, and contains beautiful photography of the Nile—turn a movie camera loose anywhere in Africa and the wonder of the place has a beguiling effect on producers, if not on audiences. History has had to be simplified considerably—for example, the decision to send Gordon is taken in cabinet. William Gladstone sees him secretly; Gordon says yes; and that is that. In fact, the discussions took almost two months, and Gordon and Gladstone did not meet. Again, Gordon's screen relations with Stewart, his staff officer, are shown as initially antagonistic; the truth is that Gordon had *asked for* Stewart; they took to each other at once, and apart from one quarrel, got on very well. During the siege of Khartoum, Gordon twice goes to see the Mahdi; in fact, there were no such meetings.

These things, even the last named, do not involve as much tampering with history as might appear. Gordon and the Mahdi were in correspondence during the siege, so there is no question of inventing a relationship that did not exist; the film simply makes them talk to each other instead of writing. Obviously this has dramatic value, and no producer could be expected to forego the opportunity of having Charlton Heston (Gordon) and Laurence Olivier (the Mahdi) confront each other. It may not be historic fact, but it does not involve the distortion of historic sense implicit in bringing Elizabeth I and Mary Stuart face to face. All told, *Khartoum* does well by history in the broad sense, and great pains have been taken with small detail, giving the film an authentic period quality.

Heston looks like Gordon and sounds suitably British (which is a matter of style and manner as much as accent). How close he comes to the eccentric hero of Khartoum, who knows? Gordon's writing during the siege and what we know of his behavior suggest a very complex character indeed, but one thing is certain: however erratic, unpredictable, perhaps even devious he was, his sense of honor was unshakable, and it was that which kept him in Khartoum. This the film brings out fully. As to his death, there are different versions, and the film accepts the popular one showing him being killed, unresisting, on the palace stairs. This is the legendary image beloved by the Victorians, of the stern Christian soldier-martyr, but it rests on unreliable evidence. Khalil, Gordon's attendant, and a Mahdist soldier (both eyewitnesses) told a different story—

that Gordon fought on the stairs, was wounded in the shoulder, fired until his revolver was empty, and was laying about him with his sword when he was shot down. It sounds much more like Chinese Gordon.

Olivier's Mahdi I have heard dismissed as a mere repeat of his Othello. (What did they expect, Hamlet?) I thought he was excellent, possibly because I was looking for the Mahdi not for Olivier. Ralph Richardson did not look much like Gladstone; and while the GOM was no doubt as unprincipled as the next politician, I wonder if he ever appeared quite as cynical as this? Nigel Green was "all Sir Garnet" as Wolseley but did not appear to have a blind eye, and Richard Johnson was a forceful Stewart.

Note

1. For example,

I'll see who will dare refuse the pumpkin, or anything else I may order to be served out! You damned scoundrels, I'll make you eat grass, or anything you can catch, before I've done with you! . . . You damned hound! . . . God damn you, you scoundrels, you are all thieves alike, and combine with the men to rob me, but I'll sweat you for it, you rascals! I'll make half of you jump overboard, before you get through Endeavour Straits.

20

Roots: Docudrama and the Interpretation of History

Leslie Fishbein

Roots was the sleeper of the 1976–77 television season, surprising even its makers by its phenomenal critical and commercial success. An unusual risk, ABC's production of Alex Haley's 885-page opus represented the first time that a network actually made a movie based on a major unpublished book.[1] While blacks had gained visibility on television during the 1970s, their presence had been confined largely to situation comedies and variety shows rather than drama—with the notable exception of CBS's much-touted success with *The Autobiography of Miss Jane Pittman* (1974)—and *Roots'* makers had serious reservations about whether the public would accept a historical drama about slavery as seen from the vantage point of the slave. Advance sales of commercial spots in the miniseries were sold on the prediction of a relatively modest 30 share. Shortly before its airing date, program executive Fred Silverman rescheduled the show: instead of running on twelve successive weeks, it would run for eight consecutive nights, so that if it failed the agony would not be pro-

---

The author would like to thank the Rutgers University Research Council for its fellowship support.

longed.[2] Silverman's decision contributed to *Roots*' phenomenal success, but that decision itself derived from an odd blend of courage and caution. Producer Stan Margulies initially suggested the concept of a *Roots* week, but an ABC executive was fearful of the consequences of a low audience share the first night, so the idea was dropped for a year. "A year later," Margulies noted, "when we had completed production, and the big decision of how to show *Roots* came up again, this was raised, and to his credit Freddie Silverman, who was then head of the network, said, 'We've done something in making this that no one has ever done before. Let's show it in a way that no one has ever shown television before!'" To avoid losing the week in case of *Roots*' failure, Silverman kept strong programs like *Happy Days* and *Laverne and Shirley* and parceled *Roots* out in one- and two-hour segments; his innovative use of consecutive programming made television history.[3] Brandon Stoddard, then the executive in charge of ABC's novels for television, views Silverman's decision as simultaneously bold and circumspect: "It's certain that Fred's idea of scheduling it in one week was at the time very daring and innovative and theatrical and, I think, added a tremendous amount to the success of *Roots*—there's no question about it." Stoddard noted, however, the caution implicit in scheduling the series in January rather than in the more significant sweeps week in February, a rating period in which network audience share is assessed as a means of calculating the attractiveness of each network to advertisers seeking a mass audience.[4]

Roots marked a dramatic shift in the nature of television programming, even though its ultimate format may have been a product of caution as much as daring. Although *Roots* already was in production when Silverman arrived at ABC from CBS, he was primarily responsible for radically altering the format of network programming by introducing limited miniseries in lieu of open-ended weekly series, by abandoning the rigid television season in a shift to real-time programming, and by de-emphasizing the situation comedy and police/adventure series in favor of the drama of the television novel.[5] ABC's previous ratings success with Leon Uris's *QB VII* in 1975 and Irwin Shaw's *Rich Man, Poor Man* in 1976 had paved the way for *Roots* by demonstrating that the miniseries form pioneered by British television had genuine appeal for American audiences.[6] The miniseries format allowed television to achieve the thematic power and narrative sweep ordinarily reserved for film; in reviewing *Roots* as a successful competitor to the movies, film critic Pauline Kael remarked: "These longer narrative forms on TV enable actors to get into their characters and take hold of a viewer's imagination."[7]

The dramatic power of *Roots* sustained audiences' attention for eight consecutive nights, 23–30 January 1977. According to *Newsweek,*

> A. C. Nielsen reported that a record 130 million Americans—representing 85 percent of all the TV-equipped homes—watched at least part of the twelve-hour miniseries. The final episode attracted a staggering 80 million viewers, surpassing NBC's screenings of *Gone with the Wind* and the eleven Super Bowls as the highest-rated TV show of all time.[8]

All eight episodes ranked among the top thirteen programs of all time in terms of estimated average audience.[9] Despite the fact that *Roots*' cast was predominantly black and its villains largely white, none of the ABC affiliates North or South rejected *Roots.* In fact, more than twenty southern cities, all formerly citadels of segregation, declared the eight-day period of the telecast "*Roots* week." More than 250 colleges and universities decided to offer courses based on the television program and the book.[10]

While even during production some critics of the miniseries had feared that *Roots* would exacerbate racial tensions, if anything it served to promote racial harmony and understanding.[11] A handful of violent incidents did follow the broadcast. After a rape episode on *Roots,* black youths clashed with white youths in the parking lot of a Hot Springs, Arkansas, high school, leaving three students injured and eighteen arrested.[12] According to Kenneth Kyoon Hur and John P. Robinson, "*Roots* was also blamed for racial disturbances at schools in Pennsylvania, Michigan, and Mississippi, and for a siege in Cincinnati in which a man took hostages and demanded the return of his son he had abandoned 19 years previously."[13] But apart from these isolated instances of hostility, *Roots* seemed to have had a genuinely humanitarian influence on its audience. An informal survey of National Association for the Advancement of Colored People branch leaders in selected cities nationwide revealed highly positive local response; *Roots* was credited with reviving and strengthening the black-history offerings in schools and colleges, with enlightening whites about the black heritage, and with improving the quality of television programming.[14]

Various local surveys of black and white viewers indicated either that *Roots* had relatively little impact upon viewers' attitudes, since those most sympathetic to the plight of slavery were most likely to watch the programs in the first place, or that its effects were largely humanitarian. A Cleveland, Ohio, survey found that racially liberal whites viewed the programs in disproportionate numbers and were predisposed to be sympathetic to the shows' content; the data suggested that such liberals were most influenced by *Roots*' depiction of the hardships of slavery.[15] An investigation of the response of teenagers in metropolitan Cleveland similarly revealed that the racial attitudes of the teenagers rather than the degree of viewing was the most accurate predictor of perceptions of the hardships of slavery; *Roots* had the most impact on already liberal youths of both races.[16] A study of the racially heterogeneous southern community of Austin, Texas, a city with substantial representation of both nonwhites and Mexican Americans, revealed a generally favorable impact of *Roots* upon its viewing audience. The white community in particular was overwhelmingly positive in its response: "They felt that the program was an accurate depiction of slavery, that the cruel and generally senseless whites depicted in the program were accurately portrayed, and they may have learned a great deal about the black culture and heritage that was previously 'missing.'"[17] A national telephone survey of 971 respondents revealed that, although it was widely hypothesized that whites would react to *Roots* with increased tolerance and blacks with increased hatred or prejudice, in fact both black and white respondents overwhelmingly indicated sadness to have been their predominant reaction to the programs. *Roots* appears to have been a learning experience for both races, to have increased understanding of blacks, and to have fostered interracial communication.[18] A summary of research findings from five studies of the *Roots* phenomenon, including the three mentioned above, indicates that *Roots* either reinforced audience preconceptions or "performed a prosocial, humanistic, and informational role for viewers."[19] At any rate, the miniseries did nothing significant to exacerbate racial tensions and may well have eased them by fostering understanding and communication.

Roots' popular success was matched by the critical attention it received. The dramatization garnered an extraordinary thirty-seven Emmy nominations, far surpassing the record of twenty-three nominations for *Rich Man, Poor Man* the year before. The show actually received nine Emmys in fourteen categories, including that for outstanding limited series.[20]

It also was named program of the year at the Television Critics' Circle Awards.[21] *Roots*' author, Alex Haley, was himself deluged with honors, including a National Book Award and a special Pulitzer Prize.[22]

Roots' extraordinary popularity was the product of a combination of factors, some largely fortuitous and others the result of shrewd programming and marketing techniques. Published 1 October 1976, Alex Haley's book, *Roots: The Saga of an American Family,* on which the series was based, became the nation's top best-seller within a month.[23] Prior to the book's appearance, its author estimated that, as a result of his indefatigable lecturing during the previous six years, more than a million people had learned of his family history and of the book in which it had been reconstructed.[24] Actual publication transformed Haley into an instant public hero: "It was perhaps the first time in history a writer was so quickly elevated to this kind of 'celebrity.'"[25] But the ABC dramatization further fueled the demand for the hardcover edition, and sales hit a one-day peak of sixty-seven thousand on the third day of the TV series.[26] Haley's publisher, Doubleday, expected a favorable public response to the book, but initially the firm projected a first print run of fifty thousand copies. When Doubleday executives met with David Wolper, executive producer of the ABC miniseries, and Brandon Stoddard, both men indicated that such a projection was ludicrously low, that Haley's material was far more powerful than the publisher realized. Nor did the Doubleday executives fully appreciate the degree to which the television version would be a twelve-hour commercial for their product.[27] Perhaps buoyed by Wolper's and Stoddard's optimism, Doubleday proved sufficiently confident of the book's success to risk a record first printing of a hardcover edition of two hundred thousand, which paid off royally once the miniseries was televised; *Roots* remained on the best-seller list for months and sold more than a million copies at $12.50 during 1977.[28] Hence part of *Roots*' popularity as a television miniseries was predicated upon the startling success of the book on which it was based.

Roots' success also may derive from the craftsmanship of its structure. The narrative structure of the miniseries is highly satisfying, combining the lure of end-of-episode teasers with thematic coherence within individual shows. Each show treats a single theme, an approach unique to *Roots* and to its sequel, *Roots: The Next Generation,* and provides thematic resolution for the viewer by the end of the episode. While this thematic approach was employed far more blatantly in *Roots: The Next Generation* two years later, it is already present in *Roots.* For example, the first show deals with the pain and hardship slaveholding caused the whites engaged in the slave trade, a theme treated only marginally in later episodes.[29] We see the gradual corruption of a man of Puritan temperament, Captain Thomas Davies, a man of honor and steel determination, who succumbs to temptation and proves to be corruptible because he is willing to set aside his scruples to carry a cargo of slaves. Captain Davies initially merits our sympathy and respect. The script describes him as "a man who commanded by intelligence and preparation. . . . Any ship of which he's master is going to arrive on time and intact." Davies is a naïf regarding the means of torture employed to subdue the captured slaves; he takes refuge from the troubling world by reading the Bible, and he prefers to sail on the Sabbath to bless even this mercenary voyage—"Seems the Christian thing to do"—a decision that contrasts ironically with his distasteful inspection of the thumbscrews used to achieve compliance from the captured female slaves.

Davies regrets his decision to take command and confides his disenchantment in a letter to his wife, telling her how he rues his separation from his family, leaving unstated the moral degradation this venture has entailed, as first mate Slater enters with a terrified black girl brought to be a "belly-warmer" for the captain: "Little flesh to take the chill off them cold sheets. Didn't figure it'd be any problem to a highborn Christian man like you, sir." Although Davies insists that he does not approve of fornication, he longs for human warmth to allow him respite from his moral struggle, and he attempts to dissolve her terror, ironically introducing himself by his Christian name to the uncomprehending female and invoking heaven when he realizes that she does not understand him. Davies is ordinarily a righteous man who is corrupted by his participation in a mercenary, racist enterprise. The gradual progress of his corruption makes it seem inevitable, and we are meant both to pity him and to identify with him as a man buffeted by forces beyond his control. It is satisfying to unmask him as human and fallible even as we condemn his lapses from Christian morality.

Moreover, the narrative structure of *Roots* is surprisingly upbeat for a drama dealing with so grim a subject as slavery. With the exception of the sixth and seventh shows, which end ominously, each evening's viewing ends with a minor triumph or on a note of promise. *Roots* never sinks into despair regarding the fate of the slaves it portrays. After its harrowing scenes of the Middle Passage, the first show concludes with the exhortation of the Wrestler, a tribal leader, for the slaves to unite as one village, to learn each other's languages, so that they may destroy their enemies, ending with Kunta Kinte's voice repeating in incantatory rhythm: "We will live! We will live!"[30]

The second show ends similarly. The overseer Ames has ordered Kunta to be beaten until he submits to his slave name, Toby. Fiddler ministers to the defeated Kunta, offering him solace, reassuring him of his African identity. Fiddler fondly soothes Kunta and consoles him: "There goin' to be another day! you hear me?—There gonna be another day."[31] The verbal promise is reinforced both visually and auditorily. The camera pulls back from the scene as Fiddler rocks Kunta in his arms, sponging his wrists, a Christological image made more emphatic by the cross formed by the fencing; as we see the final image of the plantation, we hear the drumbeats of Africa, a reminder that Kunta's African identity has not been effaced. The ending of the third show reinforces this theme. Kunta has been maimed by brutal slave catchers, who amputated his foot; he has recovered his health due to the kindly ministrations of the main-house cook, Bell, who has taunted him into walking. Her pleasure at his accomplishment dims as Kunta reasserts his African identity: "Bell—I ain't no damn Toby! I Kunta Kinte, son of Omoro and Binta Kinte. . . . A Mandinka fightin' man from the village of Juffure . . . and I'm gonna do better than walk. (beat) *Damnit! I'm gonna learn to run!*"[32] Kunta exults in his newfound strength, and his forward movement is our last image of him.

The triumphs are proof of human will, of the persistence of identity despite the obliterating impact of slavery. At the end of the fourth show, Kunta has opted to remain with Bell and their newborn daughter rather than follow the Drummer north to freedom. To reassure Bell, whose two children had been sold away from her after her first husband tried to escape, Kunta has given their daughter the Mandinka name Kizzy to remind her that she has come from a special people and that she has a special destiny. The scene ends with the camera tightly focused on the baby Kizzy as we hear Kunta's voice: "Your name mean 'stay put'—but it don't mean 'stay a slave'—it won't *never* mean dat!!!"[33] Although this tiny creature cannot possibly comprehend her father's meaning, his words may serve to chart her future course; in her new life is the family's hope of redemption. In the fifth show, the promise of Kizzy's name is betrayed as she is sold away from her parents because she aided her young beau, Noah, in his futile attempt to escape. Purchased by cockfighter Tom Moore, who rapes her the first night she is on his plantation, Kizzy recovers from her wounds by vowing vengeance against her oppressor. She grimly informs Malizy: "When I has my baby . . . he's gonna be a boy. (beat) And when that boy grows up, I promise you one thing . . . Massa Tom Lea is gonna get what he deserve."[34] Kizzy's eyes glow with a hatred that will give her the sustenance her family no longer can provide.

The sixth and seventh shows end more ominously than the others, but they too bear witness to the small triumphs possible even in slavery. The sixth show was revised significantly for telecast, its penultimate and final scenes transposed. In the 11 August 1976 script by James Lee and William Blinn, the show ends as Kizzy takes revenge on the now-ancient Missy Anne, after the latter refuses her recognition, by surreptitiously spitting into her drinking cup before she hands it to her, small revenge for a betrayal of friendship yet a minor victory that makes life worth living.[35] As actually telecast, that scene precedes another in which Mrs. Moore asks her husband how Chicken George will react when he returns from England only to learn that his family has been sold off. Moore replies cynically: "He won't come back white, my dear . . . he'll still come back a nigger. (*then*) And, really, what's a nigger to do?" He takes up his drink and continues to stare emptily out the window.[36] The televised version reduces the significance of Kizzy's minor triumph and builds suspense regarding how Chicken George will seek to reunite his family and bring it to freedom.

The seventh show also juxtaposes triumph and ominous suspense. Tom has been forced to kill Jemmy Brent, a Confederate deserter caught trying to rape Tom's wife, Irene. In killing Brent, Tom has taken up his father's mantle. When Irene turns to Tom for guidance, "he draws himself up commandingly and suddenly we see the stamp of Chicken George on him, as never before—

father and leader," as he tells her they will "bury him deep . . . and forget his name!" The episode actually ends, however, with Jemmy's brother Evan Brent, suspicious about Tom's battered face, menacing Tom: "You ain't seen the last of me," as he jerks on his horse's bit and rides away. The camera focuses tightly on Tom: "His gaze is burning, fierce and unconquered. As he watches Brent go, a small flicker of triumph forms in his expression as we: FADE OUT."[37]

While the note of promise or minor triumph in the earlier shows is tempered by the bitter reality of slavery, by the end of the eighth show black-white power relationships have been altered significantly, and true optimism is possible. The final show concludes with a series of major triumphs: through a ruse of Chicken George, the family escapes from peonage; it moves to its own land in Tennessee and pays tribute to its African forebear, Kunta Kinte. Chicken George intones:

> Hear me Kunta. . . . Hear me, ol' African . . . you who was took from your father's house in chains . . . an' made a slave in a strange land . . . you who endured because you dreamed of bein' free. . . . Hear me, African . . . the flesh of your flesh has come home to freedom. . . . An' you is free at last . . . and so are we.

By invoking Kunta Kinte, this speech provides dramatic closure for the entire series. Its rhetoric echoes the famous "I Have a Dream" speech by Martin Luther King, Jr., in its final peroration. The show then telescopes the remainder of the family history even more drastically than Haley's own book does and ends with the camera revealing the narrator of that history to be Haley himself, who tells of his obsessive search to learn of his family and its history, a search that took twelve years to complete and that resulted in a book called *Roots.*[38] At this point, the show's optimism is complete: not only have Haley's ancestors achieved freedom and even prosperity but Haley has done what blacks had only dreamed to be possible, he has traced his ancestry back to Africa; he has found his roots, and those roots have made him free.

In translating Haley's epic tale of slavery and emancipation to the television screen, *Newsweek* pointed out, "ABC could not resist applying the now standard, novels for television formula: lots of softcore sex, blood, sadism, greed, big-star cameos and end-of-episode teasers."[39] *Roots* represented the first time nude scenes would be shown on prime-time network television. The frontal nudity, however, was allowed only during the first four hours to preserve the authentic look of the Mandinka women in Africa and on the slave ship.[40] And ABC exerted a bizarre form of censorship to preserve decorum as it titillated its audience: "By the fine calibration of ABC's censors, no bared female breast could be larger than a size 32 or shown within 18 feet of the camera," *Newsweek* reported.[41] The episodes with sadistic appeal included the lashing of young Kunta Kinte to force him to accept the slave name Toby and the brutal amputation of his foot by depraved slave catchers. Yet not all of the sex portrayed was sensationalistic. Haley's ancestors exhibited remarkable sexual restraint, with Kunta and Kizzy experiencing prolonged periods of volitional celibacy. As Brandon Stoddard has noted, however, *Roots* contained "some wonderfully erotic and sexually alive scenes with some of the black families."[42] But with the exception of Genelva's attempted seduction of Kunta, Haley's ancestors are sexually expressive only in love relationships with potential or actual mates. Their marriages are uniformly blessed with sexual fulfillment, with satisfaction lasting even into old age, as in the case of Matilda and Chicken George, so *Roots*' portrayal of sexuality also constitutes a paean to familial values.

Roots debunked the myth that white Americans would reject a black dramatic miniseries of obvious social significance.[43] But the makers of *Roots* ensured this success by deliberately catering to the white middle-class sensibility. *Roots* happened to be telecast during a record cold spell at a time when many people stayed home anyway on account of the gasoline crisis, and it profited from the fact that, anticipating little serious competition, the other networks had scheduled no strong counterprogramming.[44] While such extrinsic factors might account for a greater likelihood of tuning *Roots* in, they hardly explain *Roots*' ability not only to capture but to hold white attention over a period of time. The acting in *Roots* was of a higher quality than that found in much of the contemporary cinema, according to critic Pauline Kael, so *Roots* provided gratis what films no longer could assure their paying public.[45]

Because of the decision to cast the hitherto unknown LeVar Burton in the key role of the young Kunta Kinte, ABC hedged that risk by selecting a star supporting cast for the University of Southern California drama student.[46] The choice of an unknown actor, requiring his introduction to the American audience, provided ABC with what Stoddard calls "a whole new layer of publicity and promotion." But, more important, "from a purely casting standpoint it was essential that Kunta Kinte be seen not as an actor being Kunta Kinte but this being Kunta Kinte, which is exactly what happened."[47] Since the public had no prior image of LeVar Burton, it became easier to suspend disbelief and to forget the fact that this young man was merely acting a role. To tempt whites into viewing, the rest of the cast was laden with familiar television actors. David Wolper, executive producer of the miniseries, explicitly admitted the use of television stars to lure white viewers in particular:

> You have got to remember that the audience, the TV audience, is mostly white, middle-class whites. That's why we picked Ed Asner, Sandy Duncan,

> Lloyd Bridges, Chuck Connors, Lorne Greene, Cicely Tyson, Ben Vereen, and Leslie Uggams, all known TV actors. This was planned like this, because again here, we were trying to reach the maximum white audience.[48]

While Haley's book had devoted more than a fifth of its text to a richly detailed account of Kunta Kinte's life in Africa, the television miniseries extracts Kunta Kinte from Africa well before the first two-hour segment is over.[49] Brandon Stoddard, then a vice president for novels for television at ABC, explained retrospectively why his gamble on *Roots* paid off so extravagantly in terms of its appeal to the parochial interests of its audience:

> What seems to interest Americans most are Americans. A miniseries about the French Revolution wouldn't do it. In Roots, we got out of Africa as fast as we could. I kept yelling at everyone, 'Get him to Annapolis [Maryland]. I don't care how. Tell the boats to go faster, put on more sails.' I knew that as soon as we got Kunta Kinte to America we would be okay.50

The African segment of *Roots* is an exotic, Edenic interlude, an excursion into an explicitly primitive world to which we, like Kunta Kinte, can never return; hence it poses no challenge to the social assumptions of white Americans.

Just as Alex Haley had subtitled his book *The Saga of an American Family,* so too did the miniseries aim at catholicity of appeal by advertising itself as "the triumph of an American family."[51] Critic Karl E. Meyer has noted that *Roots,* in fact, is a dramatic allegory comparable to a medieval morality play, being neither fact nor fiction but a didactic popular entertainment.[52] As such it is concerned with Everyman, a figure representing the problems and limits of the human condition.

Kunta Kinte and his heirs have a universal symbolic significance that overshadows their individual histories. Alex Haley argued that the universal appeal of *Roots* derived from the average American's yearning for a sense of heritage, from the equalizing effect of thinking about family, lineage, and ancestry, concerns shared by every person on earth.[53] This longing for rootedness transcended racial divisions. As James Monaco has noted, "Black Americans are not alone in their search for ethnic roots, and it seems likely that millions of white viewers were attracted as much by the saga of immigration and assimilation as by the racial politics."[54]

Although Haley's slave family was certainly atypical—Kunta Kinte came directly from Africa to American shores, a fate reserved for fewer than 6 percent of all slaves; his family had an exceptionally precise oral tradition; and Haley's ancestors were unusually privileged, both in Africa and in America—the television version of *Roots* consistently presented Haley's family as symbolic of all blacks.[55] Interviewed in his ancestral village of Juffure, Gambia, Haley claimed that his authorial purpose had been more universal than personal: "I began to realize then that the biggest challenge I had was to try and write a book which, although [sic] was the story of my family would symbolically be in fact the saga of Black people in this country." For Haley, the family history of any American black would differ only in detail from that of any other; the fundamental outlines of their heritage remain identical.[56] Since historical details seem irrelevant to such archetypal experience, whites too could respond equally well to the search for roots. Haley argued, "What *Roots* gets at, in whatever its form, is that it touches the pulse of how alike we human beings all are when you get down to the bottom, beneath these man-imposed differences we set one between the other."[57] The television miniseries echoed Haley's approach: LeVar Burton was presented as "a young man everybody could identify with" rather than as "a true African of two hundred years ago," and *Roots* was mounted as "a drama about black people for everybody."[58]

The telecast created burgeoning interest in genealogy and in popular searches for ethnic and familial heritage. "Following the TV-special, letters to the National Archives, where Haley did genealogical research in census manuscripts, tripled, and applications to use the research facilities increased by 40 percent," one scholarly journal reported. Genealogy was absorbed into the university curriculum and inspired books on Jewish and black ethnicity.[59] Alex Haley even donated one hundred thousand dollars of his royalty money to the Kinte Foundation to provide guidance but no financial aid for those engaged in genealogical research.[60] The interest in genealogy may well have eclipsed the concern with slavery for many viewers. Significantly, when Haley himself appeared on *The Tonight Show* following the broadcast of *Roots,* he did not want to discuss slavery or its evils but instead appeared obsessed with genealogy and with the notion that blacks could be integrated into American society because they too had families.[61]

French theorist Ernest Renan once argued that an essential factor in the making of a nation was "to get one's history wrong," that new historical research that illuminated the deeds of violence upon which all political formations must be founded may pose a danger to nationality.[62] *Roots* attempted to correct a political amnesia that had buried the horrors of slavery; but instead of threatening national self-image, *Roots* generated a search for personal heritage that transcended racial lines. In illuminating certain aspects of slavery—the victimization of blacks—it obscured others: the degree of their complicity and the degradation of character that might accompany powerlessness. ABC's promotional material for *Roots* emphasized the veracity of Haley's monumental research, explicitly billing the series as a nonfiction "ABC Novel for Television": "The epic narrative, an eloquent testimonial to the indomitability of the human spirit, involved 12 years of research and writing during a half-million miles of travel across three continents."[63] Despite their claims to essential truth, Haley's *Roots* and the television miniseries create a new mythology to replace the older one: if slavery never robbed Kunta Kinte's heirs of their essential dignity, how oppressive could the "peculiar institution" have been? It is a myth, the epic story of the African, that sustains them during all their trials and tribulations. And Haley and the makers of the miniseries use *Roots* to conjure with, to provide a viable mythology to enable a modern audience to find rootedness in a troubled world.

In an era of mass society, in which the concept of the self-made person seems of only antiquarian value, *Roots* created a compelling symbolic alternative. *Roots,* and even more blatantly *Roots: The Next Generation,* may be viewed as success stories recounting the rise of Haley's family as it achieved not only freedom but respect, prosperity, and status within the community. *Roots* differs, however, from most examples of American fictional or filmic treatment of the success theme. There are very few American success stories with happy endings, perhaps reflecting a national ambivalence toward success that allows Americans to dissipate any guilt regarding their envy of success by noting the psychological price to be paid. Novels like Theodore Dreiser's *Financier* and F. Scott Fitzgerald's *Great Gatsby* and films like *Citizen Kane* and *Mildred Pierce* seem to imply that the acquisition of wealth and personal power precludes true happiness and fulfillment. *Roots* breaks with this pattern, since in the culminating episode the family has achieved freedom and dignity on its own land in Tennessee. In an essay on the rise of ethnic consciousness during the 1970s, James A. Hijiya has noted a significant shift in the American myth of success: "The fascination with the family and the ethnic group signals, I believe, a partial retreat from the traditional ideal of the self-made man. To an unaccustomed degree, Americans are conceiving themselves as products of groups."[64]

In *Roots* what makes the family "special" and, therefore, more worthy than its peers is its preservation of its ethnic heritage and its celebration of familial values. Chicken George returns from his triumphs as a cockfighter in England not to pursue personal success, nor to achieve individual freedom, but to win those accomplishments for his entire family. Because the family never forgets its roots nor its obligations to its patriarch, it remains in Alamance County, North Carolina, after the emancipation until Chicken George returns and sets into motion the chain of events that will lead to its genuine freedom from the debt slavery accompanying Reconstruction. That ultimate success may be acceptable to an American audience because it fulfills certain essential criteria: the blacks were tricked out of their freedom by the duplicity of Senator Justin—hence they deserved a better fate; their success came through cooperation with a good white, Ol' George—hence black success is not necessarily linked to white deprivation; they deserved some reward for their uncompensated hard labor on the former Harvey plantation; and, most important, their success was familial rather than individual, so that it avoided the corruption of the sin of pride. If success is not personal, it can be enjoyed without anguish, since it is not tainted with selfishness. Many American success stories, including those listed above, are bittersweet or tragic precisely because success entails the betrayal of familial values; by effacing the dichotomy between family and success, *Roots* offers a far more tantalizing promise than most other versions of the American Gospel of Success.

Roots also mythologized the African past. For example, Haley and the makers of *Roots* recreated Haley's ancestral village of Juffure as a primal Eden.[65] The African jungle in the dramatization appeared "as manicured as a suburban golf course."[66] In fact, Juffure was no isolated, bucolic haven but rather the center of an active slave trade in which the villagers were complicit. Historical research by Philip D. Curtin places eighteenth-century Juffure in the center of one of the region's most thriving Afro-American trading networks. But Haley preferred to ignore Juffure's complicity in the violence and brutality of the slave trade and instead celebrated it as untouched by sordid reality.[67] In the year in which Kunta Kinte was captured, 1767, a commercial war was brewing between Ndanco Sono, the powerful king of Nomi, and the English, who refused to pay tribute for navigating the Gambia River in pursuit of the slave trade. In reviewing Haley's book, historian Willie Lee Rose noted: "It is inconceivable at any time, but particularly under these circumstances, that two white men should have dared to come ashore in the vicinity of Juffure to capture Kunta Kinte, even in the company of two Africans, as Haley describes it." If such whites had appeared, the king would have exacted a terrible revenge by using his fleet of war canoes, each carrying forty or fifty men armed with muskets. According to Rose, Kunta's childhood was based on a myth of tribal innocence. "In fact history seems entirely suspended in the African section. No external events disturb the peaceful roots of Kunta Kinte's childhood."[68] Although Haley's prose portrait of Juffure had been subject to substantial historical criticism, it was re-created intact in the television miniseries. Haley ultimately admitted his intentional fictionalization of Juffure, which actually had far more contacts with whites than the village he described: "Blacks long have needed a hypothetical Eden like whites have."[69]

The portrait of slavery that appears in the televised version of *Roots* is laden with inaccuracies, including many that had been criticized after the publication of Haley's book. For example, Dr. Andrew Billingsley has noted that the manhood rites of the Mandinka took three or four years, not the several days depicted in the film.[70] John Reynolds is portrayed farming cotton in Spotsylvania County in an era in which the crop would have been tobacco.[71] Chicken George's fate makes little sense after he is taken to Britain for five years by a wealthy Englishman to train his fighting cocks:

> Despite Lord Mansfield's 1771 ruling in the Somersett case, announcing that once a slave set foot on British soil he became free, Haley has George remain a slave to the British lord. Sent back to America in 1860, George continues a slave, even though he stops off in New York, where the personal liberty laws would certainly have guaranteed his freedom, and he returns docilely to the South to entreat his master for liberty.72

Subsequent to the telecast, the genealogical foundations upon which *Roots* was based were challenged on several fronts. A British reporter with a reputation for integrity, Mark Ottaway, spent a week in Gambia studying Haley's factual claims.[73] Ottaway's investigation revealed that Juffure in 1767 was hardly a "combination of third-century Athens and Club Mediterrané with peripatetic philosophers afoot!" but rather was a "white trading post surrounded by white civilization." Its inhabitants were not victims of the slave trade but collaborators in it, aiding whites in the capture of other Africans living farther up the river, hence the improbability of one of its residents being captured in 1767. Haley seems to have chosen 1767 as the year of Kunta Kinte's capture not on the basis of information obtained in Gambia but rather because it was the only year that would coincide with Haley's American research data. Kebba Fofana, whom Haley believed to be a griot who had preserved his family's oral tradition, was in fact not a member of that hereditary caste. A reckless playboy youth, Fofana had been a drummer (*jalli*), which in Mandinka can also mean griot, but he had received no formal training in the griot's complex art and learned his stories from listening to the village elders. There is strong evidence to indicate that Fofana knew in advance the nature of Haley's quest and sought to flatter his guest by reciting a narrative pleasing to him. Shortly before his death, Fofana made a deposition of the tale he had told Haley for the Gambian Archives. The names of Kunta's father and brothers do not coincide with the names used in *Roots.* It seems highly improbable that any resident of Juffure could have been captured by slavers in 1767, since the British were allowed peaceful trade by the king of Barra on the condition that none of his subjects should ever be captured as a slave. The African evidence makes it likely that Fofana's Kunta Kinte was captured after 1829. Ottaway argued, "It is undoubtedly on the assumption of accuracy that the book's commercial success is founded"; while Ottaway's investigation cast doubt on that accuracy, he conceded that the symbolic truth of *Roots* remained untarnished.[74]

More recently Professor Gary B. Mills of the University of Alabama and his wife, Elizabeth Shown Mills, a certified genealogist who specializes in the ethnic minorities of the South, have demonstrated the utter unreliability of Haley's pre–Civil War genealogical research. Crucial to Haley's narrative is the linkage of the identity of the captured Kunta Kinte to that of the American slave Toby. The Millses discovered that the "*Waller slave Toby appeared in six separate documents of record over a period of four years preceding the arrival of the [ship] Lord Ligonier.* Toby Waller was not Kunta Kinte." Strong circumstantial evidence indicates that "*Toby died prior to the draft of the 1782 tax roll which was at least eight years prior to the birth of Kizzy, according to ROOTS.*" Nor is it possible to substantiate that Dr. William Waller ever owned a slave named Bell who had been callously sold away from her infants. Moreover, a "Deed of Gift" by William Waller of 1767 and additional county records indicate that the doctor's niece, Ann, was a fully adult married woman at the time Haley portrayed her as Kizzy's childhood playmate. A thorough study of the Waller documents filed in Spotsylvania County prior to 1810 and a continued study of family probate records filed through 1833 failed to uncover a single Waller slave by the name of Kizzy or by any of the other names Haley used to designate the Waller slaves. Nor does an analysis of county, state, and federal records substantiate Haley's portrait of the Lea family (renamed Moore for television). The only Thomas Lea in Caswell County, North Carolina, who was head of a household in 1806–10 was far more affluent than the cockfighter pictured in *Roots*; Mrs. Lea was not barren and, in fact, bore at least two boys and two girls, with at least one son and one daughter surviving long enough to produce progeny of their own. The members of the Lea household do not correspond with Haley's account in *Roots*, nor could Tom Lea's economic disaster in the mid-1850s account for the dispatch of Chicken George to England in satisfaction of his debts, because Thomas Lea died between October 1844 and March 1845. In short, Haley appears to have misinterpreted or misrepresented the historical record in order to create a dramatic, stereotyped version of his family history, one with enormous popular and commercial appeal.[75]

Even the inaccuracies known at the time of the telecast were allowed to stand because the facts were far less significant than the myths *Roots* wished to generate. Haley himself conceded that *Roots* was not so much a work of history as a study in mythmaking. Haley called his methodology *faction:* "All the major incidents are true, the details are as accurate as very heavy research can make them, the names and dates are real, but obviously when it comes to dialogue, and people's emotions and thoughts, I had to make things up. It's heightened history, or fiction based on real people's lives."[76] Haley's book, much like Harriet Beecher Stowe's *Uncle Tom's Cabin* (1851), is, as Meg Greenfield pointed out in *Newsweek,* "a work of historical imagination and re-creation," ultimately a powerful, provocative fiction.[77]

Subsequent events raised fundamental questions regarding Haley's authorial role in this research. In the wake of the success of the television miniseries, Alex Haley was barraged by a series of lawsuits charging him with plagiarism. While the court dismissed the charges of Dr. Margaret Walker Alexander that Haley had pilfered substantial portions of her 1966 epic novel, *Jubilee,* Haley did agree to a half-million-dollar out-of-court settlement with Harold Courlander, who had charged him with plagiarizing several sizable segments of his 1967 novel *The African.* The trial illuminated the degree to which Haley had succeeded in creating an authorial persona that bore little relation to his actual experience as a writer. He denied ever having read either *Jubilee* or *The African,* an incredible omission for a writer who had spent a dozen years researching his family history. A scholarly journal asserted: "For him to have missed these books is almost akin to someone doing a book on the history of the Black church in America and knowing nothing of W. E. B. Du Bois and E. Franklin Frazier."[78] In testimony given at the trial, Haley conceded that three brief passages in *Roots* had been derived from Courlander's novel. The plagiarism was depicted as inadvertent by Haley's lawyer, but his rationalization of it reveals a new side of Haley to his American audience.

> Haley's counsel, George Berger of Phillips Nizer, said passages from "The African" had probably been given to Haley during lecture tours while he was researching "Roots" when many of his listeners would volunteer material. The collected materials were subsequently culled by graduate students who did not identify their sources, Berger said.[79]

This account contradicts Haley's repeated characterization of his twelve-year search as an arduous solitary one during which the author had to support himself with freelance articles and lectures because any monetary return seemed so unlikely.[80] Clearly *Roots* was not simply the product of one man's quest and suffering as Haley had claimed in so many public forums, nor did it draw strictly upon his own family's authentic historical record.

The television dramatization had no more genuine respect for historical authenticity than the book did. For example, one of the most striking episodes in the televised *Roots,* the slave rebellion aboard the *Lord Ligonier,* did not occur in Haley's original version on account of seasickness and flux among the slaves.[81] There are numerous discrepancies between the miniseries and Haley's 1972 account in the *New York Times Magazine.* That account claims that the doctor, William Waller, was the one who named the African Toby after he had been maimed by slave catchers, whereas the miniseries has Kunta Kinte being beaten into submission less than a year after he has been acquired by the doctor's brother. In the *Times* version, Kunta is captured while chopping wood to make himself a drum; whereas in the film, he is making that drum at his grandmother's request for his younger brother, Lamin. In the *Times* narrative, Kunta Kinte is the eldest of four sons; perhaps to increase the pathos of his capture, he is given only one remaining brother in the film.[82] The character of Fiddler in the film has no historical basis; he is a composite of three characters in the book in order to provide continuity. David Wolper explicitly disparaged scholarly efforts to chide the film for its lack of historical accuracy:

> Some critics complained because we showed a mountain peak in Henning, Tennessee, because that section of the country doesn't have mountains. Nobody cares; it is totally irrelevant. A film is not for reference, but for emotional impact to let you know how it was to live at a certain moment in time. *Roots* was supposed to let the viewing audience feel how it was to be a slave. If you're not moved by watching a film, then the film has failed.[83]

While the genealogy of *Roots* may have been flawed or even fictitious and many of the historical details inaccurate, both the book and the television miniseries provide a valuable corrective of traditional images of slavery. Certainly *Roots* effectively debunks many of the stereotypes of slave life propounded by historian Stanley M. Elkins in his seminal work, *Slavery: A Problem in American Institutional and Intellectual Life* (1959). Elkins argues that the slave experience closely approximated the closed institutional framework of the Nazi concentration camp, with the slaves forced to assume a strategy of accommodation via role playing in order to deal with their oppressors. Elkins claims that the role of Sambo, an infantile and utterly dependent creature, "docile but irresponsible, loyal but lazy, humble but chronically given to lying and stealing," was the most pervasive one assumed by American slaves. *Roots* argues that slaves had a remarkable ability to avoid this role, that the institution of slavery was neither coherent enough nor oppressive enough to coerce predominantly Sambolike behavior. Kunta Kinte never becomes servile despite repeated punishments, including mutilation, for his escape attempts; nor do any of his heirs identify with their owners as "good fathers"—Chicken George has to be restrained from killing his actual father when he realizes that he is no more than valuable chattel to the man. Elkins contends that slaves brought to North America were so shocked by the effectiveness with which they were detached from their cultural background in Africa that they had no choice but to become infantile in the interests of physical and psychic survival. *Roots* shows that the African heritage was not obliterated with the first generation, that remnants of tribal culture might be transmitted even into modern times. Elkins argues that the slave child had no other viable father image than that of the master, since the actual male parent was divested of any effective authority over the child. *Roots* presents Kunta Kinte, Chicken George, and Tom as patriarchal figures, able to command respect and to wield authority within the familial context. The miniseries makes it clear that the slave family was a viable counterweight to the oppressive nature of the "peculiar institution."[84]

In fact, *Roots* reflected the complexities of the slave experience revealed by modern historians who objected to Elkins's monolithic view of slavery. It recognized the persistence of African culture in slave society. As Lawrence W. Levine subsequently noted in *Black Culture and Black Consciousness: Afro-American Folk Thought from Slavery to Freedom* (1977):

> From the first African captives, through the years of slavery, and into the present century, black Americans kept alive important strands of African consciousness and verbal art in their humor, songs, dance, speech, tales, games, folk beliefs, and aphorisms. They were able to do this because these areas of culture are often the most persistent, because whites tended not to interfere with many of these culture patterns which quickly became associated in the white mind with Negro inferiority or at least peculiar Negro racial traits, and because in a number of areas there were important cultural parallels and thus wide room for syncretism between Africans and Europeans.[85]

In *Roots* Kunta Kinte and his heirs are able to preserve vestiges of African language, folk beliefs, and customs, including the ritual of naming a newborn child by lifting it upward toward a full moon, a gesture of symbolic renewal of the link to Africa.

The willingness of modern historians to do "history from the bottom up," to take seriously as evidence slave narratives and other documents illuminating, even if indirectly, the vantage point of the slave, has revealed a hitherto undisclosed pattern of quotidian slave resistance to oppression. Gilbert Osofsky takes note of numerous slave narratives that demonstrate the slaves' "perpetual war to prevent debasement": "The powerful, the self-willed, those whose spirits could not be broken and who sometimes repulsed physically all attempts to whip them, presented the ultimate challenge to the mystique of the master caste."[86] Certainly both Kunta Kinte and Tom Moore fit this rebellious image, one that modern research demonstrates to be far more common than the Elkins model of slavery would assume.

While slave narratives were written from the perspective of those who successfully escaped the toils of slavery and thus may be biased toward expressing resistance and rebellion, the Slave Narrative Collection of the Federal Writers' Project of the Works Progress Administration, compiled during the years 1936–38 as a result of more than two thousand interviews with former slaves, similarly debunks the Elkins thesis. The interviews reveal that the "peculiar institution" left "room for maneuver, for tactics and strategies, for blacks as well as for whites." The editor of these narratives, George P. Rawick, argues that it was the slave community, rather than the more tenuous institution of the slave's nuclear family, subject to dissolution at the master's whim, that was "the major adaptive process for the black man in America." The existence of the slave community ensured that slaves did not suffer total domination by the master class; it enabled its members to alleviate the worst of their oppression and at times even to dominate their masters. Built out of materials from both their African past and their American present, "with the values and memories of Africa giving meaning and direction to the new creation," the slave community provided nurture for its members, who sought dignity and identity despite their physical subjugation.[87] In *Roots* the slave community is similarly portrayed as one largely supportive of its members, whether it be Bell inspiring the injured Toby to walk again or Kunta aiding the young Noah in his plan to flee to the North.

In fact, *Roots* reflects the historiographical insights of Herbert G. Gutman's *Black Family in Slavery and Freedom, 1750–1925* (1976). Relying heavily upon census manuscript materials, Gutman discovered that the prevailing stereotype of the tenuous nature of the slave family was erroneous. "Evidence of long marriages is found in all slave social settings in the decade preceding the Civil War." Despite the oppressive nature of slavery, Gutman argues, blacks were able to retain and develop familial and kinship ties that allowed them to "create and sustain viable Afro-American culture." *Roots,* too, emphasizes the degree to which the family, based as it was on strong affectional ties and preserving remnants of the African heritage, allowed slaves to sustain dignity and identity despite generations of oppression by whites. In debunking the assertion of Daniel Patrick Moynihan that "it was by destroying the Negro family that white America broke the will of the Negro people," both Gutman's work and *Roots* have done a major service to black historiography, for they have demonstrated the essential role played by the black family in transmitting Afro-American culture across generations of enslavement.[88]

If historical details are of only peripheral interest, the miniseries's true concern, much like Haley's, is with mythmaking. And the most potent myth that the television version has to offer is that of the family. It is ironic that Haley himself was a poor family man who had left home as a youth and subsequently was twice divorced.[89] Haley spent little time with his two children as they were growing up; he kept his family life so private that some of his oldest friends in Los Angeles did not know until Haley became a celebrity that he had grown children. Richard M. Levine has written of *Roots*' author: "Clearly, in Alex Haley, television has finally found a man whose insatiable nostalgia for the vanishing dream of the American family matches its own."[90]

The myth of the family may be a source of pride and dignity for its members, sustaining their morale despite adversity; but the family also was an institution that subverted slave efforts at escape and rebellion. The myth of the family perpetuates a nostalgic desire for self-reliance; it nourishes the belief that problems can be solved in small, decentralized units instead of preaching a wider scope for human interdependency. Historian Eric Foner has written of the constrictive effects of *Roots*' notion of the family:

> It is not simply that the narrow focus on the family inevitably precludes any attempt to portray the outside world and its institutions. To include these institutions would undermine the central theme of *Roots*—the ability of a family, through unity, self-reliance, and moral fortitude, to face and overcome adversity. Much like the Waltons confronting the depression, the family in *Roots* neither seeks nor requires outside help; individual or family effort is always sufficient.
>
> Here, I believe, lies one reason for the enormous success of *Roots* among whites as well as blacks. The emphasis on the virtues and self-sufficiency of family life responds to a nostalgia for a time before divorce had become widespread, women had challenged their traditional homemaker role, and children had become rebellious, when the American family existed as a stable entity. Despite the black-nationalist veneer, in other words, the values of *Roots* are quintessentially American.[91]

Roots was acceptable to white audiences because of its essential conservatism; it unabashedly celebrated the family. Despite its own evidence to the contrary, *Roots* upheld the notion that the revolutionary spirit of the slaves was nurtured by the family unit. One film commentator has remarked, "Not for Alex Haley the more disturbing implications of William Styron's *Confessions of Nat Turner*—that it was only when blacks were allowed to separate themselves from that family unit that their revolt became possible."[92] While for over a century historians and sociologists have debated the ravages to the black family wrought by slavery, Alex Haley may well have been the first to suggest that slavery may have made a positive contribution to family life.

But family life, in fact, can constrain freedom. The birth of Kizzy keeps Kunta Kinte from making a final attempt to escape to freedom. Although Kizzy had vowed to avenge her rape by Tom Moore by having her firstborn man-child kill him, Kizzy ultimately dissuades Chicken George from that course by revealing that "it'd be killing your own flesh and blood. He's your papa. You're his son." And even after emancipation the family decides to remain in North Carolina, despite the depredations of the night riders, because George's wife, Matilda, refuses to let the family leave until her husband has returned: "We is a family and we is gonna stay a family." *Roots* fails to acknowledge that family and freedom may be mutually incompatible.[93] Nor does it ever question whether the family, as a product of hostility, may not crumble once prejudice and oppression are removed. The network may have championed *Roots* as "the triumph of an American family," but that triumph may have been purchased at the expense of freedom and social consciousness.

Notes

1. Harry F. Waters with Vern E. Smith, "One Man's Family," *Newsweek,* 21 June 1976, p. 71.

2. David L. Wolper with Quincy Troupe, *The Inside Story of T.V.'s "Roots"* (New York: Warner Books, 1978), 50, 138; Richard M. Levine, "Roots and Branches," *New York Times,* 4 September 1978, p. 54; James Monaco, "Roots and Angels: U.S. Television 1976–77," *Sight and Sound* 46 (summer 1977): 159.

3. Stan Margulies (*Roots* producer), interview and discussion with Margulies and John Erman (*Roots* director) in Arthur Knight's cinema class, University of Southern California, 15 February 1979. Film: *Roots: The Next Generation,* 1 reel, 7″, University of Southern California Special Collections. Also see Wolper with Troupe, *Inside Story,* 136–39.

4. Telephone interview with Brandon Stoddard, vice president for ABC Entertainment, Century City, California, 20 June 1981 (hereafter referred to as Stoddard interview).

5. Monaco, "Roots and Angels," 159.

6. Karl E. Meyer, "Rootless Mini-Series," *Saturday Review,* 20 January 1979, p. 52.

7. Pauline Kael, "Where We Are Now," *New Yorker,* 28 February 1977, p. 90.

8. Harry F. Waters, in Bureau Reports, "After Haley's Comet," *Newsweek,* 14 February 1977, p. 97.

9. "Nielsen All-Time Top 25 Programs," *Nielsen Newscast,* no. 1 (1977): 6. Rankings based on reports through 17 April 1977.

10. Wolper with Troupe, *Inside Story,* 164; Les Brown, *The New York Times Encyclopedia of Television* (New York: Times Books, 1977), 369.

11. Stoddard interview.

12. Waters, "After Haley's Comet," 97–98.

13. Kenneth Kyoon Hur and John P. Robinson, "The Social Impact of *Roots,*" *Journalism Quarterly* 55 (spring 1978): 19.

14. Gloster B. Current, "Cross-Country Survey on *Roots*—The Saga of Most Black Families in America," *The Crisis* 84 (May 1977): 167–72.

15. Hur and Robinson, "Social Impact," 20–24, 83.

16. Kenneth Kyoon Hur, "The Impact of *Roots* on Black and White Teenagers," *Journal of Broadcasting* 22 (summer 1978): 289–98.

17. Robert E. Balon, "The Impact of *Roots* on a Racially Heterogeneous Southern Community: An Exploratory Study," *Journal of Broadcasting* 22 (summer 1978): 299–307. Quo-tation appears on p. 306.

18. John Howard, George Rothbart, and Lee Sloan, "The Response to *Roots:* A National Survey," *Journal of Broadcasting* 22 (summer 1978): 279–87.

19. Stuart H. Surlin, "*Roots* Research: A Summary of Findings," *Journal of Broadcasting* 22 (summer 1978): 309–20. Quotation appears on p. 319.

20. R. Kent Rasmussen, "*Roots*—A Growing Thicket of Controversy," *Los Angeles Times,* 24 April 1977, p. 5; Wolper with Troupe, *Inside Story,* 164.

21. Morna Murphy, "TV Critics' Circle Picks *Roots* as Program of Year, ABC Top Net," *Hollywood Reporter,* 13 April 1977.

22. Rasmussen, "*Roots*—Growing Thicket," 1; Hans J. Massaquoi, "Alex Haley in Juffure," *Ebony,* July 1977, p. 42.

23. "Why Alex Haley Is Suing Doubleday: An Outline of the Complaint," *Publisher's Weekly,* 4 April 1977, p. 25.

24. "*PW* Interviews Alex Haley," *Publishers Weekly,* 6 September 1976, p. 9.

25. Wolper with Troupe, *Inside Story,* 136–31.

26. "Why *Roots* Hit Home," *Time,* 14 February 1977, p. 69.

27. Stoddard interview.

28. David A. Gerber, "Haley's *Roots* and Our Own: An Inquiry into the Nature of a Popular Phenomenon," *Journal of Ethnic Studies* 5 (fall 1977): 87.

29. Stoddard interview.

30. *Roots,* show no. 1, as telecast, by William Blinn and Ernest Kinoy, p. 6. Scripts of all the episodes of *Roots* were provided courtesy of David L. Wolper, David L. Wolper Productions, Warner Brothers Television, Burbank Studios, 4000 Warner Boulevard, Burbank, California, pp. 19, 89, 93–94. Quotation appears on p. 94.

31. *Roots,* show no. 2, as telecast, by William Blinn and Ernest Kinoy, p. 98.

32. *Roots,* show no. 3, teleplay by James Lee and William Blinn, 15 June 1976, fifth hour, p. 56.

33. *Roots,* show no. 4, by James Lee and William Blinn, 17 June 1976, sixth hour, p. 58.

34. *Roots,* show no. 5, by James Lee, second draft, 19 April 1976, seventh hour, p. 57. Note that rather than Tom Moore, in the script the name Tom Lea was actually used, as in Haley's book.

35. *Roots,* show no. 6, teleplay by James Lee and William Blinn, 11 August 1976, eighth hour, p. 51.

36. *Roots,* show no. 6, part 2, 28 January 1977, Museum of Broadcasting, New

York City. All the videotapes of *Roots, Roots, One Year Later,* and *Roots: The Next Generation* were viewed courtesy of the Museum of Broadcasting.

37. *Roots,* show no. 7, by M. Charles Cohen, revised second draft, 30 August 1976, tenth hour, pp. 48, 50. For the last quotation, the line in the actual telecast was: "You ain't seen the last of me, nigger" (*Roots,* show no. 7, 29 January 1977, Museum of Broadcasting).

38. *Roots,* show no. 8, by M. Charles Cohen, final draft, revised final draft, 6 September 1976, pp. 100–101.

39. Harry F. Waters, "The Black Experience," *Newsweek,* 24 January 1977, p. 59.

40. Wolper with Troupe, *Inside Story,* 73, 141.

41. Waters, "Black Experience," 59.

42. Stoddard interview.

43. Waters, "After Haley's Comet," 98.

44. "*Roots* Takes Hold in America," *News-week,* 7 February 1977, p. 26; Monaco, "Roots and Angels," 161.

45. Kael, "Where We Are Now," 90.

46. Waters with Smith, "One Man's Family," 73.

47. Stoddard interview.

48. Quoted in Frank Rich, "A Super Sequel to Haley's Comet," *Time,* 19 February 1979, p. 87; Wolper with Troupe, *Inside Story,* 62, 148.

49. Alex Haley, *Roots: The Saga of an American Family* (New York: Doubleday, 1976; reprint, New York: Dell, 1977), 11–166 out of 729 pages (all references to Haley's book to the mass-market paperback edition, since that would be more widely available for classroom use); *Roots,* show no. 1, as telecast, by William Blinn and Ernest Kinoy, 27.

50. Quoted in Wolper with Troupe, *Inside Story,* 44; Jean Vallely, "Brandon Stoddard Made a Monster Called *Roots,*" *Esquire,* 13 February 1979, p. 76.

51. Haley, *Roots,* cover; Gerber, "Haley's *Roots,*" 94.

52. Meyer, "Rootless Mini-Series," 52.

53. "Haley's Rx: Talk, Write, Reunite," *Time,* 14 February 1977, p. 72.

54. Monaco, "Roots and Angels," 161.

55. Gerber, "Haley's *Roots,*" 90; David Herbert Donald, "Family Chronicle," *Commentary* 62 (December 1976):70–72; Harry F. Waters, "Back to *Roots,*" *Newsweek,* 19 February 1979, p. 87.

56. Kalamu ya Salaam, "Alex Haley Root Man: A Black Genealogist," *Black Collegian,* November–December 1976, p. 32. Also see *Roots,* discussion between Alex Haley and Stan Margulies, 1977, Pacifica Tape Library.

57. Ya Salaam, "Alex Haley Root Man," 33.

58. Wolper with Troupe, *Inside Story,* 81, 172.

59. Quoted in Gerber, "Haley's *Roots,*" 87–88.

60. Lois Armstrong, "*Roots* Is Back with Brando and a Bumper Crop of Stars to Be," *People,* 26 February 1979, p. 59.

61. Stuart Byron, "Family Plot," *Film Comment* 13 (March–April 1977):31.

62. Ernest Renan, *What Is a Nation?* (1882), translated by Alfred Zimmen (London: Oxford University Press, 1939 edition), cited in Ali A. Mazrui, "The End of America's Amnesia," *Africa Reports* 22 (May–June 1977):7–8.

63. "*Roots:* Gripping 12-Hour, Multi-Part Story of an American Family, Traced from Its African Origins through 100 Years of Slave Life, Will Air on ABC Starting in 1977," press release, 14 June 1976, ABC Television Network Press Relations, 1330 Avenue of the Americas, New York, New York 10019. Supplied courtesy of ABC Public Relations Department.

64. James A. Hijiya, "*Roots:* Family and Ethnicity in the 1970's," *American Quarterly* 30 (fall 1978): 549.

65. Paul D. Zimmermann, "In Search of a Heritage," *Newsweek,* 27 September 1976, p. 94.

66. John J. O'Connor, "Strong *Roots* Continues Black Odyssey," *New York Times,* 16 February 1979, p. C1.

67. Gerber, "Haley's *Roots,*" 98–99; Rasmussen, "*Roots*—Growing Thicket," 1.

68. Willie Lee Rose, "An American Family," review of Alex Haley's *Roots, New York Review of Books,* 11 November 1976, pp. 3–4.

69. Quoted in Kenneth L. Woodward with Anthony Collins in London, "The Limits of 'Faction,'" *Newsweek,* 25 April 1977, p. 87.

70. Research cited in "*Roots* Grows into a Winner," *Time,* 7 February 1977, p. 96.

71. "Living with the 'Peculiar Institution,'" *Time,* 14 February 1977, p. 76.

72. Donald, "Family Chronicle," 73.

73. Woodward with Collins, "Limits of 'Faction,'" 87; Robert D. McFadden, "Some Points of *Roots* Questioned: Haley Stands by Book as a Symbol," *New York Times,* 10 April 1977, pp. 1, 29.

74. Mark Ottaway, "Tangled Roots," *Sunday Times* (London), 10 April 1977, pp. 17, 21.

75. Gary B. Mills and Elizabeth Shown Mills, "*Roots* and the New 'Faction,'" *Virginia Magazine of History and Biography* 89 (January 1981): 7–13, 16–19, 24–26. Quotations appear on pp. 8 and 10; italics in original.

76. Lewis H. Lapham, "The Black Man's Burden," *Harper's,* June 1977, pp. 15–16, 18; "*PW* Interviews," 9, 10.

77. Meg Greenfield, "Uncle Tom's Roots," *Newsweek,* 14 February 1977, p. 100.

78. Herb Boyd, "Plagiarism and the *Roots* Suits," *First World: An International Journal of Black Thought* 2 (1979): 32.

79. "Haley Settles Plagiarism Suit, Concedes Passages," *Publishers Weekly,* 25 December 1978, p. 22.

80. Haley, *Roots,* 716–29; "*PW* Interviews," 8–9, 12; Waters, "After Haley's Comet," 98.

81. Haley, *Roots,* 184–207.

82. Alex Haley, "My Furthest Back Person—'The African,'" *New York Times Magazine,* 16 July 1972, pp. 13, 16.

83. Wolper with Troupe, *Inside Story,* 150, 178.

84. This discussion of Elkins's thesis derives from Stanley M. Elkins, *Slavery: A Problem in American Institutional and Intellectual Life* (Chicago: University of Chicago Press, 1964); see especially pp. 82, 88, 128–30.

85. Lawrence W. Levine, *Black Culture and Black Consciousness: Afro-American Folk Thought from Slavery to Freedom* (New York: Oxford University Press, 1977).

While this particular formulation of Levine's thesis was published after the appearance of *Roots* as a television mini-series, Levine's basic argument was readily accessible to historians in paper and article form.

86. Gilbert Osofsky (ed.), *Puttin' on Ole Massa: The Slave Narratives of Henry Bibb, William Wells Brown, and Solomon Northrup* (New York: Harper & Row, Harper Torchbooks, 1969), 40.

87. George P. Rawick (ed.), *The American Slave: A Composite Autobiography,* vol. 1 of *From Sundown to Sunup: The Making of the Black Community,* Contributions in Afro-American and African Studies, no. 11 (Westport, Connecticut: Greenwood, 1972), xv–xvii, 9–12.

88. Herbert G. Gutman, *The Black Family in Slavery and Freedom, 1750–1925* (New York: Pantheon, 1976), xvii, 14, 327–60 passim. Quotations appear on pp. xvii, 14, 360.

89. Gerber, "Haley's *Roots,*" 107; "View from the Whirlpool," *Time,* 19 February 1979, p. 88.

90. R. Levine, "Roots and Branches," 57.

91. Eric Foner, article in *Seven Days* (March 1977), reprinted in Wolper with Troupe, *Inside Story,* 263–64.

92. Byron, "Family Plot," 31.

93. R. Levine, "Roots and Branches," 56.

21

Reds as History

Robert A. Rosenstone

Reds provided me fifteen minutes of fame. After the film's release, I had the pleasure of being misquoted in a number of mass-circulation publications. The Program Committee of the American Historical Association asked me to set up a screening during the annual convention, and I can still see the scene before the show, three hundred historians in the lobby of the Academy of Motion Picture Arts and Sciences, munching on stale pastries provided by the Publicity Department of Paramount Pictures, whose members evidently worried that the film itself might be hard to swallow. Of the (too) many pieces I wrote about the film, this is by far the most substantial. As an early piece of mine, it stands as a testament to traditional thinking, a work of mild outrage by an academic who may suspect but has not yet quite learned that a film can never be a book.

I must begin this chapter on a personal note. At the conclusion of *Reds,* my name appears in the credits as historical consultant. Since on this side of the Atlantic it may seem unusual to criticize a work in which one has taken part (in France nobody blinked an eye when the playful Roland Barthes reviewed his own book), I wish to be quite specific about my role in the production of the film. Beginning in 1972 (three years before my book, *Romantic Revolutionary: A Biography of John Reed* [*RR*], was first published), Warren Beatty and I talked a few times a year about the film on John Reed that he was always just about to make. Our conversations dealt with Reed, Louise Bryant, their friends and associates, and the historical era in which they lived. In 1979, when shooting was about to begin, we formalized our association with a contract. The talks continued not only with Beatty but with others involved in the production. I also read various versions of the screenplay and offered criticism and suggestions (some taken, some rejected), both historical and dramatic. During shooting, I was occasionally asked specific questions about such things as the number of delegates to the Socialist Party convention in 1919, or the contents of Bryant's and Reed's letters when they were separated. In the spring of 1980, I spent some time with the film company on location in Spain.

A major disappointment was that Beatty politely but firmly refused my generous offer to play the role of Trotsky in the film. Trotsky has, I have always thought, the best single line of the entire Russian Revolution. From the podium of the ballroom in the Smolny Institute on 7 November 1917, he looks down "with a pale, cruel face" (John Reed's description) and thunders at those opponents of the Bolsheviks who are withdrawing from the meeting in protest, "They are just so much refuse which will be swept into the garbage-heap of history!" One might equally well use this phrase to describe what most historical films do to their unwitting subjects. In what follows, I wish to examine to what extent John Reed and his associates have suffered such a fate.

I

The title is uncompromising, bold, and forthright. Once the prerelease jokes about catering to a drug subculture or to Cincinnati baseball fans are put aside, once the wry comparisons to that other sharp, four-letter title, *Jaws,* are cleared away, there is no hiding the basic fact: this is a film about radicals and revolutionaries, about people who take upon themselves an appellation despised in America, people unafraid to call themselves communists. Yet, as the advertisements have shown and the reviews have underscored, *Reds* is a love story. But it is a particular love story set in a particular historical period among a particular set of people. By choosing the United States, by taking as his main characters John Reed and Louise Bryant and re-creating aspects of the subculture in which they lived, by overtly confronting the origins of the American Communist Party and the first, stormy days of the Comintern, and by framing the film with a series of historical witnesses who lived through that period, Beatty has chosen to make a historical statement. To see *Reds* as only a love story is to accept a kind of one-dimensionality, to ignore the very real influence of motion pictures on our lives.

This denial of responsibility should not go uncontested. *Reds* is important not merely because of that well-noted irony—thirty-three million dollars, perhaps more, to tell the story of a revolutionary and founder of the Communist Labor Party—but because it is one of those rare Hollywood films that deals with the subject of native radicalism. How odd this seems. In certain quarters a myth persists of a "Red Decade" in Hollywood. Congressional committees in the forties and fifties rather enjoyed investigating the "Communist influence" in Hollywood. One result was the jailing of ten unfriendly witnesses for contempt of Congress; another was a blacklist that kept hundreds of people from working at their trade for many years. Yet the objective record shows how unwarranted were right-wing fears of subversion in Hollywood. Judged by the contents of films, there was no Red Decade. Radicals there were in the film industry, but their politics rarely made it to the screen except in the most oblique fashion. The House Un-American Activities Committee had to be content with lines like "Share and share alike, that's democracy" as baleful examples of Communist influence.

Consider this: only once before *Reds* has a Hollywood film chronicled the life of a historical American radical. It took a Swedish director to make a film about Joe Hill, the organizer and songwriter for the Industrial Workers of the World (IWW) who died at the hands of a firing squad in Utah, and an Italian company to tell the story of Nicola Sacco and Bartolomeo Vanzetti, the anarchists whose Massachusetts death sentences were such a cause célèbre in the twenties. Until now, the only comparable production has been *Bound for Glory* (1977), a work based upon the life of the folksinger Woody Guthrie. (For some reason, Hollywood has done better with foreign radicals, especially Mexican. Whatever their artistic merits, *Viva Villa* and *Viva Zapata* do deal with revolutionaries.) Unlike *Reds, Bound for Glory,* waffles about its hero's political connections, ignores his relationship to the Communist Party, and never mentions his weekly column in the *People's World* (the West Coast Communist Party newspaper). Guthrie comes across as a man of the people, the balladeer of dust-bowl migrants who suffer from ecological disasters and exploitation at the hands of large landowners. His forebears are as much cinematic as historical, for in its message the film is a kind of *Grapes of Wrath* revisited. Guthrie's views seem a combination of those of Tom Joad in his final speech ("Wherever there's a cop beatin' up a guy, I'll be there") and of the Preacher Casey, whose mystical vision of radical togetherness is much closer to Ralph Waldo Emerson's concept of the oversoul than to Karl Marx's dialectics.

This has been typical of the Hollywood approach to radicalism. The thirties brought forth a number of films in which common people were downtrodden and oppressed by rich businessmen or bankers—usually played by portly Edward Arnold, who seemed to have dollar signs on his tiepin—but never did a real radical lead a revolt. Instead, any revolutionary thrust dissolved into a sentimental insistence upon the Christian virtues of "little people" banding together, caring for one another, indulging in brotherly love, and hoping for the future. Frank Capra was the master of the genre; his *Meet John Doe* and *Mr. Smith Goes to Washington* were morality plays in which Evil, no matter how powerful, managed to defeat itself by the end of the third reel. Sixties radicalism on film was more sophisticated about the staying power of evil but equally defensive in stance. Rather than focusing on specific institutions, radical anger was diffused into a generalized hatred for an entire "sick society." The apolitical protagonist of *Easy Rider* became a hero, and his arbitrary death at the hands of rednecks—like the brutal manhandling by police of the virtuous undergraduates of *The Strawberry Statement*—was transformed into a symbol of the Left's ultimate impotence.

Compared to all this, *Reds* is an audacious undertaking. It is the first Hollywood film to make a hero of a communist, the first to suggest the existence of a bohemian-radical subculture during the second decade of the twentieth century, the first to hint at the bitter issues that shattered world radical movements at the time of the Russian Revolution, and certainly the first to have an all-American couple bed down to the stirring strains of the "Internationale." For an American public generally ignorant of, and either indifferent or hostile to, the whole notion of radicalism, it is bound to provide an image—perhaps the only image—of what the native Left is all about. This means that the film's historical contents must be taken seriously and makes it worthwhile to explore just what *Reds* is saying about American radicalism, the history of our century, and—not so incidentally—the nature of history itself.

II

To analyze *Reds* as history, one must begin with its most obvious historical device, the Witnesses. The film is framed by the comments of elderly men and women who were Reed's contemporaries, and their recollections provide its historical backbone. From them we learn of bohemian pranks in New York City's Greenwich Village, of free love and affairs, and who was sleeping with whom. They describe the radicalism of the Industrial Workers of the World, the antiwar movement in the United States, the coming of the Russian Revolution, the Allied attempts to strangle bolshevism, and the repression of dissent in the United States. Most important they recall the relationship of Jack Reed and Louise Bryant and reflect philosophically on the meaning of their turbulent lives.

Judged by reviews, the use of the Witnesses is one of the most successful aspects of the film. The only recurrent criticism concerns the failure to identify them with name tags. It has been suggested that this was an aesthetic decision, a desire not to make the film seem too much like a documentary. Perhaps. But the overall thrust of *Reds* suggests a deeper reason. To name the Witnesses would be to make them individually more accountable for what they say. As it is, they have the effect of a latter-day Greek chorus, one that creates the conditions of a world in which the leading characters play out their destiny. Keeping them anonymous is a technique calculated to impress and lull the audience; never can the viewer be certain exactly which remarks on politics, sex, art, or the main characters fit together. We are left with the powerful feeling that the Witnesses were there, they remember these events; they lived through those turbulent times and survived to tell their tales, to reflect upon history. Collectively, they are worthy teachers, voices of the past speaking in tones at once personal and impersonal, subjective and objective.

When Beatty in our very first conversation outlined the idea of putting Reed's contemporaries onto film, I thought it a brilliant stroke. I still do. But something happened in the execution that transformed an apparently historical device into a profoundly ahistorical one. Beyond the fact that most of the Witnesses did not actually know Bryant and Reed (another reason for keeping their identities vague) lies the troubling implication of the way their remarks are used. Sometimes the Witnesses are an impressive bunch—winning, humorous, informative, and often forceful as they present alternate versions of the same events. But often they are vague, forgetful, and self-contradictory.

For people mostly in their eighties this is natural enough, except that in this case, they—or more specifically, their memories—are being used as the historical framework of a film. (Much has been made in reviews of the fifteen years of research supposedly undertaken by Beatty. In fact, there is nothing in *Reds* that cannot easily be found in histories of the period and biographies of Reed and his friends.) For those who care about history, here is the locus of the problem. In *Reds,* memory is equated with history. Memory is seen as faulty, and thus history is as well. This approach allows the filmmaker to have it both ways. He can at once indulge himself by playing historian and yet ignore—whenever convenient—all known techniques of assessing evidence from the past, as well as the findings of previous research and scholarship. To put it more directly: the Witnesses ultimately suggest that nobody can know the truth about Reed and Bryant. Thus the filmmaker can tell us whatever story he wishes (and history be damned!).

III

Let us take this violation of the very basis of history as a given and go on to see just what story *Reds* chooses to tell. My focus is Reed because, however much one insists that the film has two principals, it never would have been made had he not achieved journalistic fame, written *Ten Days That Shook the World,* and died a left-wing martyr. Nor, I may add, did the notion of Bryant and Reed as equals and of their love story as central enter the first seven years of my conversations with Beatty. In fact, this was never voiced until production was under way.

From the first moments of the film, it is obvious that John Reed is a man who holds unconventional opinions and does unconventional things. He describes the war in Europe—this is 1915, two years before American entry—as being fought for "profits." On their first meeting, he delivers a night-long lecture to Bryant on the connection between capitalism and war (a good progressive might have done the same). He casually asks Louise, a married woman, to come and live with him. In New York, he is part of a lively group of people who reside in Greenwich Village. Most of their time is spent eating, drinking, and partying, except for those late-night moments when they listen to Emma Goldman—whose radical edge occasionally disappears into a motherly concern over a good cup of coffee—warn of the imminent dangers of American involvement in the war.

Eventually it becomes clear that this unconventionality must be radicalism. Reed listens to stories of dreadful conditions among factory workers (who for some reason are gathered in a barn), nods approval to "Big Bill" Haywood's militant appeals for the IWW, defends the workers in a fracas with the police, and gets knocked down. He breaks with an apparently liberal editor who trims his articles ("Nobody edits my stuff") and says he will publish in the *Masses.* He leaves a Provincetown, Cape Cod, summer vacation to cover the 1916 Democratic Convention and returns to bore his friends with an all-night lecture on politics. When he learns Louise is having an affair with Eugene O'Neill, he ignores, in the name of personal freedom, what more bourgeois people would consider a betrayal. When the United States enters the conflict in April 1917, he bravely takes the platform at a mass meeting to announce, "This is not my war," and briefly lands in jail. A socialist tells him that great things are happening in Russia and, blocked from his vocation as a journalist by his antiwar opinions, he journeys there, arrives on the eve of the October Revolution, makes a speech of solidarity with the Russian workers, and in the excitement of the great ten days is reborn as a Bolshevik.

Almost all these events are more or less historically accurate. Liberties are often taken with time and place: Reed certainly did not know in 1916 of Louise's affair with O'Neill (he got wind of it when they separated in the spring of 1917); he married her not because of jealousy of O'Neill but because he faced that dangerous kidney operation and wanted her to be his legal heir; he did not use the marvelous line "Class struggle sure plays hell with your poetry" in 1916 but in 1919 while organizing the Communist Labor Party; he did not go to France to meet Louise in 1917 (she returned to the United States); and certainly they could not have ridden a train from France to Russia in September 1917 without waving away many millions of Allied and German troops (they went by boat from New York to Norway).

Such quibbles aside, one can assert to this point—and indeed in the second half as well, following the Bolshevik takeover of Russia—the film does manage to capture the overall pattern of Reed's life. But only the surface. Underneath the events on the screen, something crucial is missing, something called motivation. Nowhere does *Reds* really come to grips with or satisfactorily explain just why this privileged Harvard graduate from a stuffy, upper-class Portland, Oregon, background takes a journey so far along a radical path. Such a question may never trouble moviegoers who are content that a hero only be committed to defending some sort of ideals. But certainly it is crucial for understanding not only history but the actions that take place on the screen.

To explain Reed's trajectory from Portland through Harvard and Greenwich Village to a grave at the base of the Kremlin Wall, to make sense of his beliefs and death, it is necessary to comprehend the era and milieu in which he lived—not through fallible memories but through history, which does not fuzz the issues of social change. Reed was a hero for the subculture of bohemians, artists, and radicals that between 1910 and 1920 had its headquarters in the Village, outposts in other American cities, and ties both emotional and personal to similar centers across the Atlantic. This role, achieved through a combination of talent, real literary accomplishment, and bravado, was given a kind of official status in 1914 when Walter Lippmann published a *New Republic* article entitled "Legendary John Reed." The burden of the piece—alternately admiring, caustic, and witty—was that just five years out of Harvard, Reed was already larger than life, a man who poured himself into one enthusiasm after another—travel, love affairs, labor strikes, modern art, poetry, being jailed. Others took his actions more seriously. Fifty years later, Louis Untermeyer, a coeditor of the *Masses,* recalled him as "an idealist who combined boisterous humor and a quiet passion for truth. . . . Jack remains in my mind as the most vivid figure of the period" (*RR,* 6).

As a hero figure, Reed embodied and expressed the values and ideals of a subculture. In the decade after 1910, he was surrounded in the Village, Provincetown, and Croton (thirty or so miles north of New York City) by people from the first large generation of middle-class Americans to wrestle seriously with doctrines that had developed in Europe over the course of a century. The intellectual demands on his associates were enormous. Raised as children of late-Victorian America, a society whose intellectual boundaries were capitalism, the Constitution, Christianity, and genteel culture, they confronted an immense variety of new social and artistic visions: the works of Karl Marx, Sigmund Freud, Henri-Louis Bergson, and Friedrich Nietzsche; the politics of anarchism, syndicalism, socialism, and industrial unionism; the visual modernism of cubists, futurists, and fauves; the shocking writings of August Strindberg, Fyodor Dostoevsky, and D. H. Lawrence; the attractive and disturbing worldviews implied by feminism and free love.

Unlike some of their European counterparts, these artists and intellectuals exhibited few signs of morbidity or fears of decadence. Bohemia in the United States was too new and playful for such attitudes; besides, they were good enough Americans to believe in progress, to expect a better future, one in which their divergent visions would blend into some marvelous new reality. Too easily they spoke the word *revolution,* without much idea what it might mean beyond a wide-ranging liberation in the realms of art, lifestyle, economics, politics, and sexual -relationships. To jumble together such diverse spheres was also a national habit. It was an era when the custodians of American culture—editors, critics, professors, art collectors—saw themselves as protecting a kind of castle, threatened at once by the vulgarity of the newly rich and the alien standards of recent immigrants. At the time of the Armory Show in 1913, the *New York Times* equated the cubists with bomb-throwing anarchists. No wonder radicals greeted an attack on any rampart as an assault on the entire old bourgeois order.

The shortcomings of *Reds* in depicting this bohemia lie less in what it shows than in what it ignores, less in doctrines voiced than in the important connections it fails to make. A multi-dimensional, vibrant, creative, radical bohemian subculture is at once flattened and polarized. Reed's friends hang about bars and restaurants, cavort on the beach, don silly costumes, dance a lot, and perform amateurish theatricals. When not with them, Jack is busy sounding off against editors, politicians, police, capitalists, profiteers, and the war (later this extends to right-wing socialists, the American Federation of Labor, and Communist Party members). Nowhere does *Reds* connect these extremes or indicate that, while the Village folk were certainly capable of having fun, they were dead serious about art, politics, and social change, that if they played with life, they also struggled painfully toward new artistic and intellectual visions in works and deeds that have left an enduring legacy. Merely to name Reed's friends and associates is to chronicle an important era in American cultural life: Max Eastman, Randolph Boume, Waldo Frank, Floyd Dell, Edna St. Vincent Millay, Alan Seeger, Crystal Eastman, Susan Glaspell, George Cram Cook, John Sloan, George Bellows, George Luks, Jo Davidson, Robert Minor, Marsden Hartley, Robert Edmond Jones, Eugene O'Neill, Margaret Sanger.

More extreme in behavior than his contemporaries, Reed was at one with this subculture, anxious for great change on all fronts, although vague before 1917 about how it might occur. He arrived in the Village in 1911 with two incompatible desires: to become a great poet and to make a million dollars. At first journalism merely paid his bills, then the vivid reports of Pancho Villa's revolution that appeared in *Metropolitan Magazine* in 1914 made him famous. Yet this success did not extend to serious poetry and fiction (he had no trouble selling light, topical verse and slick stories). His best short stories were naturalistic slices that, like the paintings of the Ashcan school, simultaneously celebrated and criticized the seamy underside of urban life, the world of hookers, cops, con men, and ward heel politicians. These were rejected by the editors of family publications as being "immoral." It was the need for an outlet for this fiction, rather than any political motive, that first drew him to the *Masses.* Then he was swept into the whirlwind of Village life.

Later Reed claimed that "Ideas alone did not mean much to me. . . . It didn't come to me from books that the workers produced all the wealth of the world, which went to those who did not earn it" (*RR,* 111). But the social and intellectual context in which he lived did help to create a structure of connections between the plight of others and his own situation. Theory joined the contradictions of a commercial culture that Reed experienced (the incompatible demands of self-expression and the genteel, literary marketplace) with the contradictions of factory labor (the promise of economic freedom and the reality of inescapable wage slavery). The writer, he came to see, was like the common laborer; he could be hired when needed and fired when what he produced was no longer acceptable to editors or publishers. From there it was but a short step to acceptance of the idea that the World War was also caused by a demand for profits and that those benefiting economically from the conflict were the same people who wished to squelch change in social and cultural matters.

The war brought personal and political issues to a head. For Reed and his contemporaries, Europe was the much-admired cradle both of high culture and of radical movements. With the major powers locked in a struggle that appeared to be destroying "civilization" (including the Socialist International), one reaction was to ignore the war and hold aloft the torch of cultural and intellectual life in the United States. Reed's response was more personal and more complicated.

His best writing had been elicited by labor struggles at Paterson, New Jersey, and Ludlow; then in early 1914, the experience with Pancho Villa's troops touched his prose for the first time with a tinge of greatness. In the autumn he journeyed to the western front and found a senseless slaughter that was excused by patriotic slogans voiced with cynicism by politicians and received with contempt by the troops themselves. That his Village background led him to judge the conflict "A Trader's War" is not surprising, but his critique had a deeply personal component. The meaningless enormity of the European conflict made it difficult to write well; in fact, he could hardly write at all. For Reed, the artist, the problems of the world out there had now become his own. The antiwar struggle that he waged in the following four years was intimately connected to his struggle to write well—or as he put it, to have something worth writing about.

After 1914 Reed may be seen as a man in search of a subject to match his radical beliefs and artistic powers. By 1917 he was growing discouraged. The civilization he had seen "change and broaden and sweeten" in the years before 1914 was now gone in the "red blast of war." The proletariat, which some doctrinaire minds expected to stop the conflict through revolution, seemed hopelessly divided, blind to its class interest. In the spring of 1917, he wrote sadly, "I am not sure any more that the working class is capable of revolution" (*RR,* 270). Then came the journey to Petrograd, the drama of the great ten days, the incarnation of revolutionary visions in the flesh of Vladimir Ilyich Lenin, Leon Trotsky, and the great mass of Russian workers and soldiers. The artist and the radical in Reed caught fire. Now he had a subject worthy of engaging his pen and his deepest beliefs. No wonder his first lengthy article on the revolution reeked with hope phrased in quasi-religious terms: "This proletarian government will last . . . in history, a pillar of fire for mankind forever" (*RR,* 301).

This faith sustained him through the final three years of his life. It carried him through sedition trials and police harassment in the United States in 1918–19, fired him to complete *Ten Days That Shook the World* in two months, buoyed him up during the discouraging schisms and endlessly dull meetings (*Reds* mostly depicts the fiery confrontations) that marked the birth of two Communist parties in the United States. It helps to explain the limitations of Louise's resounding (and apparently telling) speech that in 1919 he had become a power seeker and was returning to Russia to represent "thirty men in a basement." The answer to this is given later in the film when Reed suggests to Emma Goldman that, if she gives up on the revolution, her life will have had no meaning. Here he is obviously thinking of himself.

If Reed's faith seems unwarranted in the film, that may be due to a too-narrow focus on politics. Jack, in fact, never gave up on art (in his Finnish prison cell, he was sketching notes for two novels). At home, war propaganda and repression had shattered bohemia. Friends like the onetime pacifist Floyd Dell had joined the army, while the anarchist George Bellows had gone from drawing anticapitalist cartoons to creating prowar posters. But in Russia, the revolution had apparently unleashed a huge burst of artistic creativity. In 1919–20, Reed met Vladimir Mayakovsky and his circle of poets and some of the artists whose startling abstractions were changing the rules of visual art. Such experimentation, encouraged by Commissar Anatoly Lunacharsky and tolerated by Lenin, seemed final proof of the Village idea that political, economic, and artistic change went together. No wonder Reed endured the abuse of Grigory Zinoviev and the repeated defeats over the labor issue at the Second Congress of the Communist International. The workers' state was also a state for artists. It seemed a dream come true.

IV

Reed's crucial internal struggles are only hinted at during *Reds.* Of the commitment to bolshevism, Max Eastman can say, "With him it's a religion," and in an important scene Louise may confront him with the notion "You're an artist, Jack." But the hints in these remarks are never developed. Yet to say that the work does not depict Reed's conflict over belief and art may be to belabor the obvious. *Reds* is not meant to be a psychological drama but an interpersonal one, set against the movement of great historical events. The focus is clearly on Jack and Louise; on their stormy romance, breakups, and reconciliations; on the inherent conflict of two-career households, the meaning of fidelity in an age of liberation; on the problematics of any relationship between men and women, once the confining strictures of the bourgeois nuclear family are left behind.

Some debate has already arisen over the film's portrait of the relationship. There seems to be general agreement that Louise is the more interesting of the two main characters—after all, she grows, struggles, and changes, whereas Jack is virtually the same in the last frame as in the first. But the extent to which *Reds* may be a feminist statement or merely another sophisticated reassertion of male supremacy is open to dispute. Advocates of the former position may see signs of Bryant's strength and independence in the affair with

O'Neill, her job as a correspondent in France, her demand that she and Reed go to Russia as a nonsexual team, her refusal to sanction his 1919 trip back to Moscow, and in Reed's deathbed recognition that they are "comrades." Opponents may stress her early lack of direction in Greenwich Village, the affair with O'Neill, the jealousy over Reed's affairs, her sexual capitulation during the ten days, and the final journey to his side as an indication that this is business as usual between Hollywood men and women.

That the historical Louise was intelligent, talented, and attractive is true; that she and Jack quarreled over careers is likely; over affairs, certain; that she left him to work in France in 1917 and deplored his return to Russia is accurate; that he loved her from the first week they met and was deeply devoted—in his fashion—to her right to the end is attested to in many letters and personal documents. But, as if fearing that only worldly accomplishment can make people love one another, *Reds* consistently inflates the historic importance of Louise and diminishes that of Jack. It accepts her untrue claim that she wrote for the *Portland Oregonian* before they met; it neglects to mention that Reed obtained for her the job with the Wheeler syndicate for the trip to Europe; it fails to show that during the separation each was miserable without the other and that she happily returned to him in New York; it suggests that during the Russian Revolution they were artistic equals, when a most casual reading of their works will show that Louise was no more than a competent reporter in the presence of a great story and Jack a major journalist at the height of his powers; it shows Louise testifying to a Senate subcommittee, but it fails to indicate that Reed spent a good deal of time at the same witness table and outspokenly proclaimed, "I have always advocated a revolution in the United States" (*RR,* 344). Nor does the film give any indication that he stood trial for sedition with the other editors of the *Masses.*

The final section of the film, Reed's imprisonment in Finland and Bryant's dramatic journey toward reconciliation, contains more fancy than fact. To suggest that Reed was escaping the Comintern is to ignore that, when arrested in Finland (in the hold of a ship, not on a hand-propelled railcar), he was carrying more than fifteen thousand dollars in diamonds and currency to help finance the Communist Party at home. During his confinement, communication did pass between the two; and only when Jack, after his release, cabled that he was returning to Moscow did Louise leave the United States to join him. Her motives were more complex than the loving altruism portrayed in *Reds.* During Reed's absence, Louise had been living in Woodstock, New York, with painter Andrew Dasburg. From shipboard—she did not stow away but journeyed openly with Hearst press credentials—she wrote Dasburg that the reason for going was to keep Reed from coming home, where he would no doubt be jailed for sedition. Of his possible return, she said, "It would destroy us—you can see that. It would destroy all three" (*RR*, 380).

No doubt the crossing into Russia contained elements of danger, but neither fears of frostbite nor fears of a broken leg from skiing could have plagued Louise, who entered the country in August. And no, that scene on the station platform did not really take place. Before leaving for Baku on August 25, Reed had received a telegram saying that Louise would be in Moscow on his return. On September 25, he ran into her hotel room and they spent a pleasant ten days together before he grew ill with typhus. During that final loving period, it is unlikely that Jack told her of the young Russian woman who had warmed his bed during their long separation.

V

Like any work of art, *Reds* is more than the sum of its parts. For all its omissions, errors, and shortcomings, the film contains far more serious historical data than almost any other Hollywood effort. In the first American motion picture to show a communist as a decent human being, Beatty's John Reed is a nice guy, generally moral and upright, with a winsome touch of naïveté. His forebears seem literary and fictional. Reed onscreen is related to that old American type, the frontiersman, to Natty Bumppo and his latter-day incarnation, John Wayne. Strong and active in the world of men, he is occasionally boyish, shy, and inarticulate with women (this despite his extensive sexual experience, always hinted at rather than shown). Reed makes radicalism acceptable by being a kind of left-wing Archie Bunker. That is, Bunker is a lovable bigot, Reed a lovable commie. (Before its opening, Beatty took the film to the White House. President Reagan's reported comment on the work was favorable, though he was evidently upset at the unhappy ending.)

Friends on the political Left have hailed *Reds* as a significant departure for Hollywood. Publications like the *Nation* and the *Progressive* have given the film good reviews, and the newspaper *In These Times* has claimed it "makes socialism sexy." No doubt. How nice to have as a hero a genuine, historic radical. But here is a marvelous irony. So desperate is the Left for media heroes that it may wink at violations of its own, usually ignored, history. For years radicals have exposed the ideology of free enterprise, and in intellectual circles a cottage industry has grown up that applies Antonio Gramsci's powerful notion of cultural hegemony to a variety of historical situations. Yet what is *Reds* but a flowering example of hegemony in full bloom?

Let me be specific here. *Reds* is no outright piece of fiction but a subtle restructuring of history. It humanizes a radical hero by domesticating him, putting his love life at center stage. (In Reed's case, this is particularly problematic, for in his single autobiographical effort, written only for himself, he devotes only a couple of sentences in thirty pages to all his lovers, including Louise.) It plays with the issues of radicalism and revolution just enough to make them serious but certainly not enough to inform the public as to what they really are. Nor does it so much as hint that the underlying conflict of the real John Reed—which was not the struggle between love and revolution but between the demands of an ambitious self and those of a market economy—still very much exists today.

In fact, what better example can we have of this dilemma than *Reds* itself? An immensely rich and popular star worries for a decade before making a film about a radical. When he does, the story is told within the confines of filmic conventions that detract from the basic vision of his hero. Politics and art take a backseat to love. Thus we have all that cute situation-comedy shtick: the puppy that runs upstairs every time Jack and Louise are in bed; Reed cooking dinner and spilling everything, or hitting his head repeatedly on the lamp in Petrograd, or telling a joke that amuses no one (a bit left over from *McCabe and Mrs. Miller*). Thus we have the *Zhivago*-like trek and the tear-jerking reunion. To argue, as some may, that this is necessary for a big-budget film and a mass audience is only to prove the point. From its length, subject matter, and approach, it appears that Beatty wished to make a bid for immortality, to create a great, serious work like *Citizen Kane.* His inability to do so speaks volumes about the hegemony of commercial values.

In no way am I accusing Beatty of cowardice. My argument is simply that he too is trapped by the conventions and standards of our culture (which include the box office but are not exclusively monetary). Once in my presence Beatty said something like "Nobody knows what history really is." Naively I took this to be a sophisticated statement about the multiplicity of interpretations inherent in any historical situation. I was wrong. What it represented was a fascination with history and a fear of its power to judge us. No wonder the film exhibits a deep ambivalence toward its main subject. No wonder it is necessary both to domesticate John Reed and occasionally to make him a bit of a buffoon. To take Reed's life and death seriously would be to see one's own commercial ventures for what they are, to recognize without deception that, while a brave undertaking, *Reds* panders to popular prejudices and expectations and thus avoids the risk that serious art must take. John Reed would, I think, understand the problems with *Reds,* but he might not be inclined to forgive them.

This harsh judgment is not directed at the filmmaker alone. Beatty has done a real service. He has given us a radical hero and more radical history than has ever before been shown in an American film. If the film is popular among a wide spectrum of people, perhaps it is in part because we all want to be a bit radical and yet well-off and comfortable, venturesome and yet safe. So did John Reed. But for him there came a time when contradictory desires could no longer be held together. Trapped by his own beliefs, Reed's deepest responses led to a militant antiwar stance, to growing disillusionment with his homeland, and to death as a Soviet hero. He was a man who knew the taste of comfort and fame but who ultimately found it less savory than that of truth.

The controlling metaphor of *Reds* is that of Reed chasing a military wagon that he never quite catches. This is our first and only glimpse of him in Mexico, and it is repeated in Russia just before the final reunion with Louise. In the shooting—as in history—Beatty/Reed made it onto the wagon in Russia; in Mexico, no such incident occurred. To me, the scene is unconsciously self-referential, a statement more about *Reds* than about its subject. In reality, Reed found his wagon, his cause, his revolution. Once he did so, neither love, nor the desire to write, nor fears that bureaucracy was beginning to sour the revolution could make him back down on his commitment.

The filmmaker is more ambivalent about his own accomplishment. John Reed's story is Warren Beatty's wagon; he chased it for over a decade and even with the completion of *Reds* does not seem to have caught it. One way to understand this is by returning to the roots of our culture, to Thomas Jefferson's prophetic insight that ours is a social order dedicated to the pursuit (rather than the attainment?) of happiness. This notion runs athwart the religious truths of our tradition, the notion that external happiness is an epiphenomenon, that real happiness can only grow inside ourselves ("the kingdom of God is within"). Accepting this older truth may affect our worldly pursuits and entail a loss of the fame and fortune that good Americans—movie stars above all—are taught to equate with being loved. The dilemma, then, is not merely that of Warren Beatty or John Reed. In the profoundest sense, the problems with *Reds* as history are very much our own.

22

Patriot Games

Conor Cruise O'Brien

In the Name of the Father, Jim Sheridan's film based on the book *Proved Innocent* by Gerry Conlon, did not win its Oscar, despite its technical brilliance and its bravura performance by Daniel Day-Lewis. But what follows is anyway not a review of the film. I am concerned, rather, with its political impact. For many Americans, this film will represent most of what they think they know about Northern Ireland. What they are taking away from the film is a plausible but distorted picture; and the distortion is consistently helpful to the Irish Republican Army, the IRA.

The makers of the film deny that it casts the IRA in a favorable light. They (and most of the reviewers) agree that the film shows the British legal establishment in an exceedingly unfavorable light, but this, they point out, is inevitable, given the nature of the tale: the framing of innocent people by British police, upheld by the British legal system, over many years. In 1974 British police arrested four people, including Gerry Conlon and his father, Giuseppe, and charged them with planting a bomb in a Guildford, Surrey, pub that had killed five people and wounded sixty-four. They were convicted. The convictions were overturned after appeals, by which time those convicted had been

From *The New Republic,* 9 May 1994. Reproduced by permission of Conor Cruise O'Brien, © Conor Cruise O'Brien.

in jail for fifteen years. Thus the film's point about the British legal establishment is altogether valid, but it does not exhaust the film's political impact.

The makers of the film acknowledge that it is based only partly on Conlon's written account, on the trial records, and on other historical materials. They acknowledge, that is, that fictional elements have been added. I shall come to the fictional bits later. Let us first consider the historical material of the film. This material is both authentic and misleading, which is a dangerous combination. It is authentic in that it tells a mainly true story of the sufferings of a Northern Irish Catholic family at the hands of the British legal system. The portrayal of the suppression by British troops of a riot in a Catholic area is also authentic, and so is the dialogue among Belfast Catholics. And yet all this authentic material cannot stand as an acceptable picture of life in Northern Ireland today, under British rule.

Most of the inhabitants of Northern Ireland are Protestants, but there are no Ulster Protestants in *In the Name of the Father.* Artistically, this is defensible. Catholics and Protestants in Northern Ireland live largely separated lives, and the Conlons and their friends and relatives are Catholics. So who is to say that a film should not be made about Catholics? And yet the confinement of the narrative to the Catholic population misleads the viewer because the Protestant population, determined to remain in the United Kingdom and not to be incorporated as a minority in a mainly Catholic united Ireland, is one of the two main reasons why British troops are there.

The other reason that the British troops are there is that the IRA has been trying, for more than twenty years now, to force Northern Ireland out of the United Kingdom, against the will of a large majority of its inhabitants. This is the general political background of the specific events narrated in *In the Name of the Father.* The film contains, however, no hint of its own background. Those who are not aware of the complicated political realities in Northern Ireland will see only a Northern Ireland occupied against the will of its inhabitants. And from such a simplification, the inference is clear that the withdrawal of the British is the solution to "the problem of Northern Ireland." In fact, British withdrawal from Northern Ireland would be followed by interethnic Bosnia-like hostilities. The British are now sitting most uncomfortably, and not very competently, on the lid. Should they depart, the civil war would boil over.

No viewer of *In the Name of the Father* would get even a whiff of these dire possibilities. And this political distortion is all the more dangerous in America, where the public is already conditioned to accept it. Most American discussions of Northern Ireland concentrate on the Catholics and ignore the Protestants. This is true even in such newspapers as the *New York Times* and the *Washington Post.* Irish-American pro-IRA propaganda presents the struggle as a simple one, morally and politically, between the British and the Irish (meaning the Irish Catholics). The Protestants do not come in at all, or they come in as dupes, accomplices, or even slaves to the British. I remember hearing Paul O'Dwyer, a distinguished political figure in New York, holding forth on the radio about how all the troubles of Northern Ireland are owed to "British imperialism." The interviewer rightly asked O'Dwyer about the Protestants of Northern Ireland. He said that they were "fine people who would make a splendid contribution to a united Ireland." The interviewer asked, "Why don't they make it then?" O'Dwyer replied, "The British won't let them."

By the intensity of its exclusive focus on Catholics, *In the Name of the Father* tends to validate the explanation from British imperialism and with great emotional force. The popularity of the film thus increases the already significant pressure, originating in the United States and in other parts of the English-speaking world, at several different levels and in several different ways, to bring about British disengagement from Northern Ireland. It is a powerful paradox that the sympathies that American audiences naturally feel toward the sufferings of the Conlons and their associates, as they see them in Sheridan's film, should be enlisted on the side of a policy that would result in even more terrible suffering for hundreds of thousands of people, both Catholics and Protestants, in Northern Ireland. And the Catholics of Belfast, moreover, are most likely the main victims of a British withdrawal.

Aesthetic considerations and a limited basis in reality may extenuate somewhat the film's sins of omission. But they cannot extenuate its great sin of commission. Sheridan and his associates have introduced into the story of Conlon a pure fiction, and this fiction makes the film more acceptable and more useful to the IRA than the plain truth.

The fiction takes the form of a character called Joe McAndrew. McAndrew (who is played by Dom Baker) is cast as an IRA man and presented as a fellow prisoner of the Conlons. McAndrew never existed, but he is supposed to be the actual perpetrator of the bombing for which the Conlons and other innocent people were punished. This nonexistent McAndrew, moreover, even confesses to the British that it was he who blew up the pub. It is at this point that *In the Name of the Father* takes an ugly and tendentious turn. This fictional transaction makes the British legal system look deliberately wicked to a much greater extent than the historical record, bad though it is, would suggest. The fiction, unlike the record, gives the British no benefit of any doubt. They know, out of the mouth of McAndrew, that the Conlons and their associates are innocent, but they keep them in prison anyway, apparently just to save face.

The character of McAndrew not only boosts the case against the Brits, it also makes the IRA look better than it is. On the record, the IRA repeatedly told investigators that they knew who the real perpetrators were and that they were not the Conlons and their associates. But the IRA did not divulge the names of the real perpetrators, nor did the real perpetrators give themselves up. For innocent people to be unjustly kept in prison by the British suited the IRA's propaganda purposes nicely. And it continues to serve those purposes through this film, long after the unfairly imprisoned have been acquitted and released.

As a fictional creation, and as an instrument of propaganda, McAndrew is interesting. He is hardly a saint, but he is shown, in many ways, as an admirable character. In prison, where others (including Conlon) are demoralized, he is dignified, confident, self-respecting, self-controlled, impressive in appearance and demeanor. He is in no way broken, or even abashed, by the prison system. Instead he defies it spectacularly, and so he wins the admiration of the other prisoners and the respect of the wardens. Also, by the fear that he inspires, McAndrew wins better treatment for the other Irish prisoners. This point is important, from a propaganda point of view, because it provides fictional corroboration of a favorite IRA argument: that violence is the only way of inducing the British to treat Irish people with respect.

McAndrew's ferocity is not exactly extenuated by the film, but it becomes a dramatic point in his favor. He is seen as fighting a war against an evil system. In this way, the bombing itself, which McAndrew admits having perpetrated, becomes implicitly meritorious. Reflected in McAndrew, the war of the IRA begins to look like a just war. By the time McAndrew deliberately sets fire to a warden (another invention), the film has so effectively whipped up a horror of the British and their legal system that some in the audiences may even applaud.

All the reviews I have seen miss the point of McAndrew, if they mention him at all. The reviewers who do mention him see his appearance as making an anti-IRA point, and so it does to squeamish liberals, a category into which critics for upmarket publications have a tendency to fall. The reviewers are repelled by the ruthlessness of the character, as exemplified by his burning of the warden. But IRA sympathizers will not be put off by this. They will see McAndrew as a heroic figure.

The makers of the film represent Conlon as repelled by McAndrew's brutality; and so the film has it both ways again. It strikes a pro-IRA note to please the faithful and an anti-IRA note to please the liberals. It is no wonder that the film has been hailed for its objectivity. The *New York Times* critic saw the film as "a fervent indictment of the bitterness between English and IRA parties." This is precisely the impact that the film is intended to have on the *New York Times.* Conlon, moreover, is something of an antihero in the film, as he is in his own memoir; and his father is lovable but helpless. The book doesn't have a hero. But a film must have a hero, and so Sheridan has taken care to provide one with the invention of the outsized McAndrew, at once courageous and repugnant. And so the film is more sympathetic to the IRA than is the book.

Why would the filmmakers want to make such a film? Surely there is no artistic reason for McAndrew, who is out of key with the subtlety of character in the rest of the film. The answer, surely, is that McAndrew's presence brings a moral and historical profit.

Since he is not a straightforward hero, he permits a kind of ideological sleight of hand: terrorism can be accepted with just the right shudder of abhorrence. McAndrew is there to exploit not only the ignorance but also the ambivalence of his audience.

And I cannot help but believe that there was also a business reason for McAndrew. Would it be possible, in the United States or any other English-speaking country, to get general distribution for a film whose political thrust was as anti-IRA as that of *In the Name of the Father* is anti-British? I don't think so, even if it had stars. One of the many advantages of running the world's most durable terrorist business—which is what the IRA is—is that you are in a position to make credible threats. McAndrew, a figure inspiring respect as well as fear, seems designed to meet the IRA's specifications, to win the IRA's seal of approval; and that, I believe, is also what McAndrew is there for. His presence ensures the safe distribution of *In the Name of the Father;* the theaters are fireproofed. The worst thing about blackmail is that it works.

23

In the Name of the IRA

Richard Grenier

In the midst of a highly publicized forty-eight-hour American visit, Gerry Adams, head of Sinn Fein, the political wing of the Irish Republican Army (IRA), found time on *Larry King Live*—that podium of presidents—to issue a rousing endorsement of *In the Name of the Father,* a film honored by seven Academy Award nominations. It was a "very good dramatic presentation," said Adams, and would give Americans an idea of "British injustice in Ireland."

By contrast, well before its release, much of the London press gave the film a particularly frigid reception, calling it a "farrago of rubbish" and claiming that its poisonous portrayal of British justice was based largely on malign fictions, which at this critical juncture could only further envenom Anglo-Irish relations. According to many of the British papers, the film would unquestionably create new sympathy among ignorant American audiences for the IRA, still an unrepentant terrorist organization that refuses either to repudiate violence or to endorse the proposed new Irish-British peace negotiations that are supported, with the lone exception of the IRA by everyone in London, Belfast, and Dublin—including both major Irish political parties. Responding to these and related concerns with a refreshing directness, one of the movie's stars, Academy Award–winning actress Emma Thompson (*Howard's End*), said, "I don't give a f——."

So the battle lines are drawn, as it were, between those attempting to determine whether *In the Name of the Father* will further the cause of justice in Britain and peace in Ireland and those who "don't give a f——" whether the film is truth or lies and care only that it accomplish its didactic goal, which is apparently to vilify the British judicial system—with a somewhat hazier endorsement for the proposition, "Brits out!" (of Northern Ireland).[1]

In the Name of the Father is nominally "based" on an autobiographical book called *Proved Innocent* by Gerry Conlon, one of four persons convicted of killing five innocent people and injuring sixty-four more in 1974 in a pub bombing in Guildford, England—the four thereafter referred to in Britain as the "Guildford Four." Another member of the Guildford Four is Paul Hill, who, in addition to the role he was convicted of playing in the Guildford bombing, still stands accused of an entirely separate IRA murder in Belfast, and who (a quaint detail) has recently married Courtney Kennedy, daughter of the late Senator Robert Kennedy. This makes Paul Hill the nephew of both Senator Edward Kennedy (who strenuously lobbied President Bill Clinton's administration in February 1994 to reverse its position against letting Gerry Adams enter the country) and of Jean Kennedy Smith, the present U.S. ambassador to Ireland.

The story of the "Guildford Four," "Birmingham Six," "Maguire Seven," and other persons accused of being IRA "active agents" in a series of bombings that left forty innocent people dead and hundreds wounded is hardly a minor legal squabble. On the contrary, the 1974 bombings having horrified all of Britain, the case is one of the longest and most bitter chapters in the annals of British justice, unprecedented in modern times, which after years of investigations and trials has cost British taxpayers some thirty million dollars—something on the financial scale of Lawrence Walsh's Iran-Contra investigations but awakening far stronger emotions in the general populace.

Conlon and other members of the Guildford Four were first convicted and served fifteen years in prison. But during the 1980s, amid heated allegations of police brutality and fabrication of evidence, the sentiment grew among British liberals that the Guildford Four had been improperly convicted—in British legal terminology, that their convictions were "unsafe," that they had not been proved guilty "beyond a reasonable doubt." In the eyes of their partisans, furthermore, they were totally innocent, and in time they were freed to great joy in the liberal community. Criminal proceedings were then instituted against the three detectives charged with misconduct during police interrogation of the Guildford Four. But in 1993, these detectives too were found not guilty: not a single one of the accusations of brutality and fabrication of evidence had stuck. A whole chorus of new testimony was heard at this second trial, some of which had not been deemed admissible during the earlier appeal hearing. To be brief about it, it seems that a member of the Guildford Four (the only one under consideration in the second trial) had "sung like a canary."

The not-guilty verdict for the police detectives set off a whole new chorus of protests, to the effect that the Guildford Four had been guilty of the bombings all along and should never have been released. Even the Maguire Seven, close relatives of Conlon, turned against him. His uncle, Pat Maguire—who had spent many years in prison thanks in part to his nephew's testimony—declared that Conlon "should be put back in prison for what he's done to my family" and blamed him for creating the whole tragic mess to begin with. So what with the Guildford Four found on appeal to be not guilty, and with the detectives accused of falsifying evidence against them also found to be not guilty, Britain awaits the results of a special government inquiry into alleged miscarriages of justice under retired Lord Justice of Appeal, Sir John May, who will make his report sometime after the appeal of the conviction for murder of Senator Kennedy's nephew. The London *Sunday Times* suggested in May 1993 that the verdict vindicating the police detectives had changed the story of the Guildford Four completely, and it was therefore very difficult to see how the people then in the process of filming *In the Name of the Father* were going to be able to provide their movie with a "suitably heroic ending." But in this the *Sunday Times* demonstrated a vast innocence of the ways of the movie world and of the curiously low level of honesty displayed by those making films "based on a true story," as *In the Name of the Father* is advertised.

If we were to take its argument as fact, *In the Name of the Father,* directed by Jim Sheridan (*My Left Foot*), is the story of an outrageous miscarriage of justice. We first meet Gerry Conlon (Daniel Day-Lewis), a petty thief, as a rebellious youth in the streets of Belfast, caught up in a riot between Catholic locals and British troops (a fiction; Conlon took part in no such riot). Sent to London by his father, Giuseppe (Pete Postlethwaite), whom Conlon despises for his submissiveness (actually, Conlon adored his father), he arrives in London with his friend Paul Hill in the early 1970s and falls in with a gang of squatter hippies ("We don't believe in property or law—only love") in the seedy flats of Kilburn, London's main Irish district. On the night of the Guildford bombing, Conlon and Hill are shown resting in a park, where they meet a homeless old man lying on a bench. Later in the evening, Conlon robs a prostitute's apartment, which provides him with a nice amount of ready cash. But he and Hill are shortly picked up by police, acting under the new Prevention of Terrorism Act, and after seven days of brutal interrogation under the malign leadership of Police Inspector Robert Dixon (Corin Redgrave), they confess to the Guildford bombing, which has created a tremendous stir. Not only are Conlon, Hill, and two others (the Guildford Four) sentenced to many years in prison, but other friends and members of their families, the Maguire Seven, are also sent to prison as part of the conspiracy, principally on testimony by the Four. In prison, however, Conlon meets the real IRA architect of the Guildford bombing, Joseph McAndrew (Dom Baker), who confesses not only to Conlon but to the police that he is responsible for the bombing and that Conlon, Hill, and their friends are consequently totally innocent. The police believe him without question but, led on by the diabolical Inspector Dixon, refuse to exonerate the Guildford Four. Inspector Dixon knows perfectly well the Four are innocent but does not care. There is "public pressure." They are "Irish scum." And that is enough for him. Knowing the court is condemning innocent people, Dixon visibly gloats when they are convicted. I should point out that there is no Inspector Dixon. He is a fiction. There is also no Joseph McAndrew, the IRA bigwig who in the film plans the Guildford bombing. He, too, is a fiction. Moreover, Conlon's "perfect" alibi, that he was busy on the night of the bombing robbing a prostitute's apartment, is something less than perfect in that he robbed the prostitute's apartment ten days later. And so we sail on through this sanctimonious movie, from one fictitious character to another, with "perfect" alibis whipped up out of thin air, all presented with great polemical fervor.

But to return to *In the Name of the Father*'s "true" story: with the "blatant outrage to justice" represented by the conviction, with totally innocent men rotting for fifteen years in prison, a white knight must surely come forth to free them. And this white knight appears in the person of a female solicitor, Gareth Peirce. One wonders if Emma Thompson gives a f—— about the extent to which the role she plays is fictionalized—indeed, almost entirely fabricated. In the movie, Gareth Peirce is a quite wonderful person, as well as a wonderful solicitor. Poring over police records, she discovers, by an implausible accident, another "perfect" alibi: a police interview with the *man on the bench in the park,* which the prosecution has withheld from her—and which she goes on to use as the winning piece of evidence in the appeal.

In fact, the real Gareth Peirce learned of the police interview with the homeless old man on the bench in the park (actually a young greengrocer in a hostel) because the prosecution—exactly as it should have done—had communicated this information to her. But it was considered of such little importance that it was not even mentioned during the appeal as grounds for quashing the conviction. What the real Gareth Peirce actually discovered in the mountain of papers—none of which was concealed from her—was that some of the interrogation notes for the first trial, which were supposed to have been taken "contemporaneously," were written later, which made them "unreliable."

It was these "noncontemporaneous" notes and two other seemingly technical details that on appeal led the magistrates to consider the original convictions "unsafe." Even before the detectives were put on trial in 1993, the London *Financial Times* editorialized that there might after all be a relatively benign explanation of such modest chronological discrepancies and that, in slightly altering the times and notes of the interrogations, the detectives might have felt "they had done nothing wrong and had nothing to hide." And, indeed, in the detectives' trial, it counted heavily in their favor that they had had the critical notes in their custody for years and could have shredded them at any moment. Yet in Jim Sheridan's movie, during the appeal in 1989 that won the Guildford Four their freedom, solicitor Gareth Peirce works herself into a near frenzy at the Old Bailey pleading the iniquity of the police and the Guildford Four's innocence—a speech that, alas, will not go down in the history of British law for the simple reason that it was never delivered. It is another fiction.

An artistic judgment is hard to deliver on a film as feverishly polemical and as fast and loose in the presentation of its arguments as *In the Name of the Father.* It is rather as if an assemblage of terrorists were tried, convicted, and imprisoned for the bombing of the World Trade Center in New York, whereupon a high-minded person decided to make a movie exonerating them. For this movie, that person falsifies every single known fact of the case and then calls on us to judge this film as a dramatic work and—as Sheridan says of his movie—as being true, if not to the detail then to "the spirit" of the events.

Emma Thompson and Daniel Day-Lewis (who says he completely "loses" himself in his characters and has no objective judgment on them) both turn in excellent performances, as does Pete Postlethwaite as the elder Conlon, who dies in prison. Northern Irish people assure me that the Belfast accents (Conlons, Maguires, and Hill) are impeccable—so impeccable I should imagine that at moments of great excitement American audiences will miss a bit of the dialogue. Jim Sheridan's directing I find heavily melodramatic, even when the events he is dramatizing actually occurred, which is rather rare. The mending of the relationship between the two Conlons, with the transmutation of the son's contempt for his father into deep respect as the two share the same prison cell, is well enough done—except of course that there was no contempt to begin with and that the two at no time shared the same prison cell and were rarely even in the same prison. Even if we disengage *In the Name of the Father* from its heavy didactic thrust, the dramaturgy is crude. The good people (Conlons and other assorted Belfast Irish) are too good.

The evil people (British police authorities up and down the scale) are too evil. The fictitious IRA man imprisoned with the Conlons is shown in the end to be also evil—though he is clearly strategic "cover," a fig leaf.

In Britain, as I remarked at the outset, there has understandably been a violent storm of criticism over *In the Name of the Father.* When the film opened in London in early February 1994, Robert Kee, an Irish historical scholar who wrote a whole book on the case called *Trial and Error,* declared that it "tells so many lies that it makes its central proposition about a miscarriage of justice questionable." The *Sunday Times,* for its part, ran two major feature pieces under the headline: "THE CAMERA THAT LIES."

The movie has also been disowned by not one but both solicitors principally responsible for the defense of the Guildford Four. Gareth Peirce, acutely embarrassed by the prominence given her role (she came into the case at almost the last minute), has said that she considers herself an "extremely unimportant participant." Alastair Logan, on the other hand, who devoted twenty years of his life to the defense of the Guildford Four and without whom they would still be in prison today, was truly horrified by the movie. It shows, he said, court scenes "which not only didn't happen, but which suggest we conduct our criminal cases on a charade basis."

Predictably, Britain's film critics were fuzzier than members of the country's legal profession or its scholars. The *Guardian*'s reviewer declared that, however inaccurate *In the Name of the Father* may be, it should be viewed more as a "parable based on truth than [as] a thorough examination of the truth itself." The critic for the *Times* wrote approvingly that the film's "streamlining" allowed Sheridan to "suck audiences right inside its story of wrongs being righted." The *Daily Telegraph*'s reviewer—alone noting all the ink "already spilled over the film's deviations from the facts"—asked, "At what point does dramatic license shade into unwarranted distortion of the truth?" He concluded that the movie "has no more than a nodding acquaintance with history" and stressed the anomaly of encountering this much lying in a film that makes such a point of "denouncing the lies of others. "

On this side of the Atlantic, the story was rather different. In estimating the potential audience for *In the Name of the Father,* it should be remembered that the cohesion of the Irish-American community is not what it used to be, and one even wonders how many votes were won in the Adams affair by either Senator Kennedy or Senator Moynihan, who also lobbied for lifting the Adams visa ban. The figure usually given for Americans of Irish descent is forty million, but even the IRA's worst enemies only accuse it of raising a mere one hundred thousand dollars a year from American sympathizers. These people's Irish ancestors, needless to say, left Ireland with very real grievances and dreadful memories, and only a generation or two ago an Irish name in America still suggested membership in a tightly knit ethnic and religious minority. But it now tells one nearly nothing. Reagan, Regan, Brady, Murphy, Casey, O'Neill, Foley, Kennedy, Moynihan, Leahy, Walsh, Buckley—politically they are all over the map. And most of them know precious little about present-day Ireland, which has become quite a minor country in comparison with the number of people of Irish descent in America. But *In the Name of the Father* is not playing to an ethnic constituency, it is playing to a moral constituency—and playing very well. Thus American film critics simply proceeded en masse to review this movie as if they were dealing with an unchallenged historical text. The *New York Times* called it "brilliant," "riveting." Other major critics called it "gripping," "impassioned," "powerful," "mesmerizing," "emotionally wrenching," "emotionally shattering." Among the seven nominations *In the Name of the Father* received from Hollywood's Academy of Motion Picture Arts and Sciences were six for major awards: best picture, best director (Jim Sheridan), best actor (Daniel Day-Lewis), best supporting actress (Emma Thompson), best supporting actor (Pete Postlethwaite), and best adapted screenplay (Jim Sheridan and Terry George—the latter, it emerged in late February 1994, a convicted felon with links to the Irish National Liberation Army, another terrorist organization).

The dean of one of this country's major schools of journalism once said that journalists were not liberals, they merely wanted to "right society's wrongs." Such a statement complacently assumes that journalists are capable of unerringly detecting, first, precisely what is wrong with society, and, second, precisely what to do about it. But when we arrive at the entertainment world—where information levels are far lower than among journalists or academics and notoriously lower than the entertainers' self-esteem—the urge to "right society's wrongs" becomes truly unhinged. While at this writing both pictures have been in release for two months, *In the Name of the Father* has brought in only half the money at American box offices of another British import, Richard Attenborough's *Shadowlands,* with Anthony Hopkins and Debra Winger. But *Shadowlands,* an excellent film, is about suffering, death, and man's reconciliation to the will of God, whereas *In the Name of the Father* is about injustice—about society's wrongs, which the movie world must put right. That world simply has not absorbed the fact that the Guildford Four might not have been victims of an injustice at all and that consequently there might not have been a wrong to put right to begin with. No, the American entertainment world, seconded by the American critical establishment, will right wrongs even when there are no wrongs. Surely there is no greater dedication to justice than this.

Note

1. In recent elections in Northern Ireland, Gerry Adams's Sinn Fein, which is determined to achieve the absorption of the North by the Irish Republic by any means including terrorism, won only 10 percent of the vote, a mere one-third of even Northern Ireland's Catholics. Meanwhile, in recent elections in the almost entirely Catholic Irish Republic, the Sinn Fein won a rousing 2 percent. Hence, in any democratic plebiscite, to which both London and Dublin are now committed under the terms of the new Downing Street declaration, Sinn Fein and the IRA are given no chance whatever of winning. Meanwhile, IRA terrorist attacks continued even while Gerry Adams was in New York.

24

The Making of *Hostages*

Sita Williams

The making of *The Hostages* raises two sets of important questions, which in a haphazard way were repeated by the massive press interest in our film. First, is it a true story? Second, whose story is it? The first issue is about the nature of fiction and reality. The second question is a problem of political and social morality. In this chapter, I want to say something about both these issues.

Hostages is the story of not just one individual but a group of very different individuals who suffered the same fate but were of different age, background, and character. Inevitably their interpretation of and attitude to their common experience differed. *Hostages* is not only the story of John McCarthy, Brian Keenan, Terry Anderson, Tom Sutherland, and Frank Reed. It is also the story of how their friends and families fought to bring their plight to the attention of the world. And their fight was not principally against the hostage takers, their's was a fight against governments who, like the British government, said, "We do not negotiate with terrorists," and didn't; the American government, who said they would not negotiate and then were found to be trading "arms for hostages"; and in the case of Brian Keenan, the Irish government, the least

From "The *Hostages* Controversy" (also called "Faction-Fiction and Reality . . . The Making of *Hostages*"). This chapter first appeared as a paper delivered at a conference on docudrama in March 1996, organized by the Department of Drama of Birmingham University, U.K. Reproduced by permission of Sita Williams, © Sita Williams, 1992.

powerful and probably because of it the most successful in negotiating his earlier release.

Whose Story Is It?

Many people, including some of the hostages, have claimed both that our *Hostages* cannot be the true story and that their own account has a moral claim to priority in publication in any medium. Which of the hostages could claim to present the definitive story of hostage taking? Their right to tell their own story and to make profit out of it is not in dispute. But should Brian Keenan not have published his account until John McCarthy has written his?

To assert priority and exclusivity in the exercise of that right raises questions and points up absurdities and contradictions. We know for example that Frank Reed does not want to be written about by Brian Keenan until he, Frank Reed, has published his own version. Does this mean that Brian Keenan's book should not have any reference to him? An individual's right to publish his own version of events cannot and should not exclude any other interpretation of the same events. No one has an *exclusive* to a story that is in the public domain. If any individual or group of individuals could legally and morally claim such exclusivity, then the restriction on freedom of expression would be enormous.

The hostages asked to be allowed to tell their own story in their own time. In a letter to the *Guardian,* four of the hostages portrayed wrote, "We are all writing personal accounts of our experiences." [1] Their decision to publish means that they are prepared to put the story of their ordeal into the public domain. Of the many Europeans held hostage only one, the French hostage Jean Paul Kaufmann, published his story without any attempt at commercial gain. He published his account privately and gave the book to anyone who wanted to learn more about his experiences. This does not imply that the other hostages are somehow wrong to benefit commercially from their trauma, but equally, they cannot plausibly claim foul against a commercial film that is an equally justified and possibly an important and more comprehensive interpretation of events.

Sense and Sensibility

Were we morally wrong in making this film when some of the key characters didn't want to see it made? We have seen why this is not just one person's story but a story in the public domain. It would therefore be an unwarranted restriction on freedom of speech if the hostages were permitted to effectively censor and manipulate public access to the events of which they were the dramatic focus but which were much larger than themselves and which raise issues of international concern and public interest.

It would surely be wrong if we were prevented from re-creating and dramatizing contemporary history because this is not welcomed by some of the main characters. The hostages have suffered, it is true; but in the film, they are not libeled or denigrated. They are no more entitled to control what is told about themselves than any other public figure. And they certainly became public figures, because the campaigns to free them used the media, quite justifiably, to draw attention to their plights. When each of those men stepped out into freedom, he became a public hero. There is more than a little irony in their subsequently trying to silence the very media who helped to "free" them.

Self-Censorship

Perhaps the only way to avoid controversy is not to make contemporary drama-documentaries but to play safe and restrict their subject matter to people who are dead. This raises the whole question of what is the appropriate subject matter to be explored in this form. Granada have been pioneers in the field from *The Man Who Wouldn't Keep Quiet* in 1970, based on the smuggled diaries of Soviet dissident General Piotr Grigorenko, to more recently *Who Bombed Birmingham?,* an investigation into the conviction of the men known as the "Birmingham Six," a conviction that was subsequently quashed, and *Thatcher—The Final Days.*

All these are dramadocumentaries that have explored contemporary issues, arising out of a journalistic base and often making available new and important facts. A dramadocumentary is a form best used in the area of contemporary issues where the public's need and right to know is foremost.

The Hostages, while following the same journalistic route as all previous dramadocumentaries, breaks new ground as well. Many of our previous films have been reenactments, where we have been able to develop the story from perhaps a court transcript, a diary, or a tape recording of events and conversations. *Hostages* is much more a dramatization of events that illustrates circumstances and attitudes and shows context.

Pure Fiction

In their letter to the *Guardian* newspaper two days before the film's transmission, John McCarthy, Brian Keenan, Terry Anderson, and Terry Waite wrote,

> We are all writing personal accounts of our experiences and do not understand how Granada and HBO [the coproducers] can think they have the right to produce a story, reporting [sic] to be true, before those at the centre of it have come to terms with it themselves. Without our co-operation Granada have felt it permissible to invent very intimate aspects of our captivity and liberation. We feel that to do this whilst claiming that film to be "true" is both highly insensitive to the hostages and their families and a serious abuse of public trust.

Granada was also accused of claiming that *The Hostages* presented "a full story for the first time."

We made none of these claims; but which of the hostages could claim to write the full story, let alone one that is the absolute truth? After all, they are asking to be allowed to "come to terms with it themselves." Having done so, would their recollections of times past be entirely "pure"?

Hostages is a dramadocumentary in the sense that it is a drama based on documented facts. It is not a work of pure fiction but one based on eighteen months of painstaking research. Every event in the film is derived from the public record, supplemented by interviews with hostages, including some not featured in the film—their relatives and friends, diplomats and politicians. Every scene in the film had to be supported by a piece of factual evidence.

Reenactment Versus Dramatization

The principal difference, in the case of *Hostages,* is that in a number of scenes the dialogue was created by writer Bernard McLaverty, for example, some of the exchanges between the hostages in the cells. However, with the overall scenes themselves based on fact, what McLaverty created was dialogue that captured the idiom and spirit of the characters. The role of the dramatist was to shape the events and characters portrayed and create, not invent, drama out of reality. Can the hostages themselves remember accurately what they said and did every day for so many years? The point is not that *this* dialogue took place on *that* day but that what we see and hear should "ring true."

The physical appearances of the hostages are well-known all over the world. Even today, over a year after his release, John McCarthy is recognized on the streets. In casting actors to play the roles, impersonation was never considered. The reality of the men was not what they looked like but *who* they were. Therefore we cast actors who could capture the spirit of the men and women in the story. Realism is achieved through the creative participation of writer and actors, working within the constraints of the research.

Creating the Characters

The task of the dramatist was to create believable people. He took as his starting point specific characteristics and used them as broad brush strokes: Keenan, a touchy, Irish Nationalist Protestant (an almost unique combination), who fought the guards; McCarthy, a middle-class Englishman, witty, diplomatic. Using these broad outlines, he developed character and dialogue. In the initial stages of the script, there were conversations about accents, Belfast English as opposed to the "Queen's," the working class versus the middle class, which eventually became a debate about colonialism. This was important within the context of the film as it also reflected the views of their captors, who saw the evils of Lebanon as a consequence of the colonialist ambitions of Israel and its backer, America. Therefore conversations that were valid to the characters themselves were also selected because they illuminated the broader political context of hostage taking.

Selected characteristics informed the more expanded portrayal of the characters. Frank Reed was very arrogant about his ability as a sportsman. Tom Sutherland, an animal geneticist, was known to the others as "the Professor." He gave them lectures on genetics to enliven the tedious hours in captivity. This was transformed into just one scene in the film in which he gives the others a lecture on DNA. Terry Anderson was known to be fearless, a journalist who would never give up on an idea, who claimed to make the best Irish coffee in Beirut. All these important and apparently trivial character details were used by Bernard McLaverty to enrich the audience's understanding of these men and how each of them lived and survived in captivity. It could be that none of the men sees himself as well portrayed, but what is important is whether or not the overall picture the audience takes away is a true one.

Drama out of Suffering

On 22 September, the day prior to the transmission of the program, the *Independent* newspaper editorial accused us of making a "Drama out of suffering." It stated that "the hostages' suffering is uniquely their own." While it cannot be disputed that none of us has directly experienced the trauma of being a hostage, the article arrogantly assumes that the writer, producers, actors, and audience cannot empathize and understand their ordeal. This is like saying we can't understand and hence have a view about the victims of any disaster unless we ourselves have experienced it.

The Role of the Dramatist

One of the most important aspects of using the dramadocumentary form for this particular story was that, by dramatizing it, the trauma became vivid and real. The role of the dramatist is crucial. He is a human being too (if you prick him does he not bleed?). He understands suffering, pain, separation. His craft is to empathize with his characters. The writer uses his own fears to create the reality of an experience. A trivial example is a fear of cockroaches. This fear and loathing enabled McLaverty to know what it is like (and I use the word *know* advisedly) to be lying hour after hour in the dark surrounded by cockroaches. We share with the hostages the common denominator of humanity, which enables us to empathize with their plight.

Technique

In *Hostages* we incorporated documentary footage to illustrate the political landmarks that were of historical importance to the story. It opens with a selection of documentary footage, sketching the background of the war in Lebanon. Into this actuality, we integrated the dramatized kidnappings of Anderson and Sutherland. Within the body of the film, archive is used to illustrate the effect of geopolitical events on the fate of the hostages. A particular example is the shooting down of an Iranian passenger airliner by the U.S. Navy ship *Vincennes.*

This blending of actuality and dramatization describes economically and powerfully the impact of the outside world on the men and their captors. The inability of politicians and the press fully to appreciate the impotence of the hostages in controlling their own destiny is reflected in President Ronald Reagan's dismissal of Terry Anderson's video appeal for something to be done to end their ordeal.

The use of actuality to heighten the drama with the use of dramatization to depict reality is one of the most successful new art forms today, as is illustrated by television dramadocumentary and the films of Oliver Stone, such as *JFK.*

Would a Documentary Have Done More Justice to the Story?

An alternative to the film could have been a documentary made after the release of all the hostages—one in which they participated. Claude Lanzmann's

Shoah is a powerful example of how the documenting of facts can be a vivid retelling of a story. However, in *Shoah* some of the most vivid and memorable events in the film were "dramatized": the train pulling into the station at Treblinka, as it had done when it brought thousands of victims to the concentration camp, and Lanzmann's interview with the barber, Abraham Bomba. The interview consists of Lanzmann asking Bomba to talk about his work as a hairdresser, cutting the hair of women just before they went into the gas chamber. The interview is conducted in a barbershop, where Bomba works, while he is cutting hair—unquestionably Lanzmann's use of dramatization gives an emotional and, importantly, visual authenticity to the reminiscences, making them an event in the present and therefore more powerful.[2]

Visual Truth and Emotional Authenticity

Hostages portrayed not only the hitherto unrealized physical environment in which the men were held but also the tensions between the hostages themselves and, importantly, between the hostages and their captors. To read about or have described the manner in which the hostages were transported like Egyptian mummies in the bottom of a truck would of necessity have less impact than witnessing it for the first time.

However, I am not claiming that this dramatization is justified on the basis that portraying the horrors is the only means of telling the story. The narrative, as we have seen, worked on the three levels: the men belowground, the women above the ground, and the women fighting the men in suits to get their loved ones released. What a dramatization achieves is the successful juxtaposition of these three story lines into a coherent and clear narrative. The drama was structured to place "action against inaction," "darkness against light," and thus illuminate the whole.

Above all, this was a deeply moving story; and the purpose of using dramatization was to inform, inspire, and re-create this emotional response in the audience—surely a not unworthy goal for any drama.

The Failures of the Dramatization

One of the criticisms of the film was that it was impossible to capture

> the horror of their situation—the boredom, the squalor, the wholesale despair. To do so of course, would be far too painful to watch—but to reduce

> their situation [the hostages'] to selective hyper-dramatic scenes from their years of subterranean nightmare is to gloss over the atrocity. (*Daily Telegraph*)

Only the viewer can judge the validity of this claim. However, the critic did touch on one aspect of the story that poses a problem for contemporary drama. How dramatic is inactivity and continual silence—how does one present the reality of boredom? It would have been sufficient to have one or at most two scenes in which nothing happened, not even a cockroach moving up the wall. We did in fact shoot such scenes. However, in the process of editing the final cut, these scenes were sacrificed to make room for those regarded as more crucial to the story. A failure that must be admitted.

The Subject Defies Drama

"No edge of the precipice climax; we know they got out," said the *Guardian.* Knowing the outcome of the story does not invalidate or diminish the power of the drama. We still go to see *Julius Caesar, Tartuffe,* and *Six Characters in Search of an Author,* even though we know the ending. What each of these dramas does for all time is illuminate our understanding of the human condition, and for this reason alone a contemporary dramadocumentary, such as *Hostages,* is not only justified but will, I believe, have equal value in the future.

Selectivity and the Telescoping of Time

In order to cover six years in two hours, time had to be compressed. The time scale of the film is fictional. Certain events are chosen as the key points in the drama. In this respect, however, dramadocumentary is no different from any other documentary. The selectivity of events, the compression of time, and the shaping of events into a coherent narrative are exactly the same.

The Conflicts Particular to Dramadocumentary

Having chosen the dramatic form to portray factual events, the question raised is whether important facts are discarded or distorted because they are insufficiently dramatic. If this were so, *Hostages* could not be classed as dramadocumentary but as *faction.* As a dramadocumentary, it had to be a fair representation of the facts. The only "distortions" were that on some occasions the chronology was changed, events amalgamated, and the names of minor characters altered.[3]

Why Drama Not Documentary?

The simple criterion for choosing a dramatization is that you can take the camera to events that cannot otherwise be filmed. As a documentary, the hostage story would have failed because the central event, the incarceration and survival of the hostages in that almost medieval "hell" would have been offstage.

Fiction and Reality

Finally, nothing in *Hostages* was untrue, but it was not the absolute truth. However, the best definition of fiction that I have heard was from a fourteen-year-old schoolgirl who, when asked for her definition of fiction, said, "It is made up truth."

Notes

1. Letter from John McCarthy, Brian Keenan, Terry Waite, and Terry Anderson to the *Guardian,* 21 September 1992.
2. See also Derek Paget, *True Stories: Documentary Drama on Radio, Screen and Stage* (Manchester: Manchester University Press, 1990).
3. However, any narrative that is not the same length as the events it describes must alter chronology. If McCarthy himself produces an account that takes less than five years to read, he will have transgressed in the same way!

25

JFK: Historical Fact / Historical Film

Robert A. Rosenstone

In 1989 the *American Historical Review* asked me to create an annual section devoted to film reviews. Some historians objected to this intrusion of the fictions associated with the visual media into a world of historical scholarship, but in general the section has been popular, especially among younger members of the profession. So popular that in 1991 the big film of the year, *JFK,* was snatched away from me and made the subject of a special forum. While other scholars used the film as the basis of essays about John F. Kennedy, Lee Harvey Oswald, homophobia in America (and the usual suspects), I focused on the issue of genre—how *JFK* worked as a piece of history within the conventions of the mainstream dramatic film.

To those of us interested in historical films, the fuss in the media over *JFK* feels familiar. Complaints that the film bends and twists history; accusations that the director, Oliver Stone, willfully mixes fact and fiction, fails to delineate clearly between evidence and speculation, creates characters who never existed and incidents that never occurred—these are the sorts of charges that are made every time a historical film on a sensitive subject appears. With *JFK,* the controversy is particularly heated because of both the topic and its treatment. The film hits us with a double whammy: one of America's most popular directors not only explores our recent history's most touchy subject but does so in a bravura motion picture that (maybe it's a triple whammy) also takes a highly critical stance toward major branches of the American government.

Complaints over the misuse of history in film seem to be based upon two notions: first, that a historical film is no more than a piece of written history transferred to the screen and thus subject to the same rules of historical practice; and second, that a fact is a fact and that history is little more than an organized compilation of such facts. We who write history should find these assertions questionable. At least we have to be aware that "facts" never stand alone but are always called forth (or constituted) by the work in which they then become embedded. This means that, in order to evaluate the way in which any work of history—including a motion picture—uses facts (or data) to evoke the past, we must investigate the aims, forms, and possibilities of the historical project in which those data appear.

All this is to say something simple but important: a film is not a book. To judge the contribution of a work like *JFK,* we must try to understand just what a historical film can do.

As a dramatic motion picture, *JFK* comes to us in a form that has been virtually unexplored by people interested in the study of past events. Neither historians nor anyone else have given much thought to the most basic questions about the possibilities and standards of history when it is represented in the visual media. Evaluations of historical films in essays and reviews are always made on an individual basis. Certainly the historical profession has no agreed-upon way to answer any of the following questions: What kind of historical knowledge or understanding can a historical film provide? How can we situate it in relation to written history? What are its responsibilities to the historical "fact"? What can it tell us about the past that the written word cannot?

Such questions are too broad to answer here, but they are good to keep in mind as we think about *JFK.* My aim in what follows here is less to deal with the contributions and shortcomings of the film than to approach it as part of a tradition. I want to situate *JFK* as both a certain kind of film and a certain kind of historical film. Placed in this context, the factual "errors" (if one wants to term them that) of the work will appear to be less the fault of the filmmaker than a condition of both the medium and the kind of movie he has chosen to make. The contributions (if one wants to call them that) of the film, on the other hand, are in large measure its own—they derive less from the form of the film than from the way that form has been put to use.

There is no single way to do history on film. The traditional division into the dramatic work and the documentary is increasingly irrelevant as recent films (*JFK* included) often blur the distinction between the two. My own research has suggested that history on film comes in a number of different forms. *JFK,* despite the many documentary-type elements that it contains, belongs to what is certainly the most popular type of film, the Hollywood—or mainstream—drama. This sort of film is marked, as cinema scholars have shown, by a number of characteristics, the chief being its desire to make us believe that what we see in the theater is true. To this end, the mainstream film utilizes a specific sort of film language, a self-effacing, seamless language of shot, editing, and sound designed to make the screen seem no more than a window onto unmediated "reality."

Along with "realism," four other elements are crucial to an understanding of the mainstream historical film:

- Hollywood history is delivered in a story with beginning, middle, and end—a story that has a moral message, and one that is usually embodied in a progressive view of history.
- The story is closed, completed, and ultimately simple. Alternative versions of the past are not shown; the *Rashomon* approach is never used in such works.
- History is a story of individuals—usually heroic individuals who do unusual things for the good of others, if not all humankind (ultimately, the audience).
- Historical issues are personalized, emotionalized, and dramatized—for film appeals to our feelings as a way of adding to our knowledge or affecting our beliefs.

Such elements go a long way toward explaining the shape of *JFK.* The story is not that of President Kennedy but of Jim Garrison, the heroic, embattled, incorruptible investigator who wishes to make sense of JFK's assassination and its apparent cover-up, not just for himself but for his country and its traditions—that is, for the audience, for us. More than almost any other historical film, this one swamps us with information—some of it, in the black-and-white flashbacks that illustrate the stages of the investigation, tentative or contradictory (so much is thrown at us that, on a single viewing, the viewer has difficulty absorbing all the details of events discussed and shown). Yet even if contradictions do exist, the main line of the story is closed and completed, and the moral message is clear: the assassination was the result of conspiracy that involved agencies and officials of the U.S. government; the aim of the assassination was to get rid of a president who wished to curb the military and end the Cold War; and the "fascist" elements responsible for the assassination and the subsequent cover-up are a clear and ongoing threat to what little is left of American democracy.

Let me put it simply: if the conventions of the mainstream historical film make it difficult for such works to create a past that stays within the norms by which we judge written history, certain other factors make it impossible. It is not just that most of the data by which we know the past come from the realm of words and that the filmmaker is always involved in a good deal of translation from one medium to another, attempting to find a visual equivalent for written evidence. It is also that the mainstream historical film is shot through with fiction or invention from the smallest of details to the largest events. (Historians do not, of course, approve of fiction, aside from the underlying fiction that the past itself can be truly told in neat, linear stories.)

Invention occurs for at least two reasons: the requirements of dramatic structure and the need of the camera to fill out the specifics of historical scenes. Drama demands the invention of incidents and characters because historical events rarely occur with the kind of shape, order, and intensity that will keep an audience in its seats. Inventions are used for a variety of reasons: to keep the story moving, to keep emotions high, to simplify complex events into a plausible structure that will fit within filmic time constraints. When the screenplay of *JFK* creates a fascist, homosexual prisoner named Willie O'Keefe to give Garrison evidence that Clay Shaw was involved with Oswald, or when it invents a Deep Throat character (Donald Sutherland) in Washington to help Garrison make sense of all the evidence he has gathered by providing a theory to hold it all together, one has the sense that Oliver Stone is doing no more than finding a plausible, dramatic way of summarizing evidence that comes from too many sources to depict on the screen.

Invention due to the demands of the camera may be a subtler factor, but it is no less significant in shaping the historical film. Consider, for example, something as simple as the furnishings in a room where a historical character sits—say, Jim Garrison's office or conference room, or Clay Shaw's apartment. Or think of the clothing that characters wear or the words they speak. All such elements have to be approximate rather than literal representations. They say: this is more or less the way Garrison's room looked in 1966, or these are the kinds of clothes a character might well have worn, or these are likely examples of the words he or she spoke.

The same is true of individuals. This is not just a matter of the director's making up characters. Even historical people become largely fictional on the screen. The very use of an actor to portray someone is itself a kind of fiction. If the person is an actual historical figure, such as Garrison, and even if the actor looks like the figure (which is not true in *JFK,* for the actor Kevin Costner looks little like the real Garrison, who in turn does not look much like Earl Warren, the character he portrays), the film on a literal level says what cannot truly be said: not just that this is how the person looked but also that this is how he moved, walked, and gestured, and this is how he sounded when he spoke.

Settings and clothing, the look and sound of characters—to analyze a historical film is to see how small fictions like this shade into larger and larger inventions. Yet even the tiniest sorts of fictions are not unimportant factors. At least not if history is about the meaning of past events. In a medium where visual evidence is crucial to understanding, such pervasive fictions are major contributors to the meaning of the film, including its historical meaning. So, too, is that elusive, extrahistorical element, the aura carried by famous actors and actresses. A star like Kevin Costner, fresh from his award-winning *Dances with Wolves,* cannot simply disappear into the character of Garrison. From his previous film, he carries for many in the audience a strong feeling of the decent, simple, honest American, the war-hero man who more than a century ago was critical of a certain kind of expansionist militarism in American life.

Like a history book, a historical film—despite Hollywood's desire for "realism"—is not a window onto the past but a construction of a past; like a history book, a film handles evidence from that past within a certain framework of possibilities and a tradition of practice. For neither the writer of history nor the director of a film is historical literalism a possibility. No matter how literal-minded a director might be, film cannot do more than point to the events of the past; at best, film can approximate historic moments, the things that were once said and done, but it cannot replicate them. Like the book, film will use evidence to create historical works, but this evidence will always be a highly reduced or concentrated sample; given its limited screen time, the film will never provide more than a fraction of the empirical data of an article on the same topic. Even as a lengthy three-hour film that includes an unusually dense barrage of information, *JFK* must often make major points with sparse evidence or invented images. Within the world of the film, the idea that Kennedy was ready to withdraw American troops from Vietnam, for example, rests on the mention of a single memorandum and the testimony of a fictional character. The notion that black Americans loved Kennedy is conveyed by having a single woman say, "He did so much for this country, for colored people." What I am suggesting is this: the Hollywood historical film will always include images that are at once invented and yet may still be considered true; true in that they symbolize, condense, or summarize larger amounts of data; true in that they carry out the overall meaning of the past that can be verified, documented, or reasonably argued. But, one may ask, how do we know what can be verified, documented, or reasonably argued? That is, how do we know whether Kennedy was about to withdraw troops or whether he was loved by African Americans? Both of these highly debatable points must be answered from outside the film, from the ongoing discourse of history—the existing body of historical texts, their data and arguments. This need for outside verification is not unique to film. Any work about the past, be it a piece of written, visual, or oral history, enters a body of preexisting knowledge and debate. To be considered "historical" rather than simply a costume drama that uses the past as an exotic setting for romance and adventure, a film must engage the issues, ideas, data, and arguments of that ongoing discourse. Whatever else it does or does not do, *JFK* certainly meets these requirements as a work of history.

The practice of written history is not a single kind of practice. And if that practice is dependent upon data, its value and contribution has never been wholly a matter of those data and their accuracy. Certainly different works of history use data in different ways and make different sorts of contributions to our understanding. Some works of history may be chiefly important for the data they create and deliver. Some for their evocation of people and events of a vanished time and place. Some for their elegance of argument or skill at representation. Some for raising new questions about the past, or for raising old questions for a new generation.

It is the same with historical films. They come in different forms, and they undertake different historical tasks. Some evoke the past, bringing it to life, making us intensely feel people, places, and moments long gone—this surely is one of the glories of the motion picture. (Who can sit through *JFK* without reliving many of the agonies of the sixties that it depicts?) But film may do more than evoke: the historical film can be a provocation to thought and intervention into history, a way of revisioning the past. We don't go to the Hollywood historical film for data but for drama: for the way it intensifies the issues of the past, for the way it shows us the world as process, makes us participate in the confusion, multiplicities, and complexities of events long gone.

JFK is a film that takes up more than one historical burden. Because it chooses as its central strategy an investigation of the past, the film has a self-reflexive edge, one that suggests much about the difficulty of any historical undertaking and the near impossibility of arriving at definitive historical truths. More important, perhaps, *JFK* makes an apparently old issue come to life—indeed, the reaction it has evoked makes it seem like a very successful piece of historical work. Not a work that tells us the truth about the past but one that questions the official truths about the past so provocatively that we are forced once again to look to history and consider what events mean to us today. Like a good historian, Stone begins *JFK* with a preface that contains a thesis; he uses Dwight Eisenhower's farewell address, with its warning about the possible effect of the military-industrial complex on the future of our country, to set the stage for a film that will illustrate the prescience of Ike's words. By doing this,

Stone forces us to face the kind of larger issue that a more sober historian, mired in tons of data and worried about the judgments of professional colleagues, might find difficult to raise so sharply: Has something gone wrong with America since the sixties?

Oliver Stone has been faulted for thinking that many changes in the United States stem from the killing of a single president, but others who are less sanguine about the judgments and actions of Kennedy may take him as a symbol—certainly the experience of the film, like that of any important work of history, resonates well beyond the ideas of its creator and speaks to and for those who do not share Stone's strong faith in JFK. When assessing *JFK,* one should ask this question: Who else in America has dared to raise such historical issues so powerfully (or at all) in a popular medium? If it is part of the burden of the historical work to make us rethink how we got to where we are and to make us question values that we and our leaders and our nation live by, then whatever its flaws, *JFK* has to be among the most important works of American history ever to appear on the screen.

26

Walker and *Mississippi Burning*: Postmodernism Versus Illusionist Narrative

Sumiko Higashi

Is history dead? In 1989 *Newsweek, Time,* and the *New York Times Magazine* featured articles about Francis Fukuyama, a State Department official who heralded "the end of history" as communist regimes went bankrupt, even before Pepsi-Cola and AT&T commercials co-opted the dismantling of the Berlin Wall. Fukuyama's postmortem about the triumph of Western capitalism has since become the subject of academic discourse.[1] Charting the postmodern, Fredric Jameson informs us that, since "the waning of the great high-modernist thematics of time and temporality, the elegiac mysteries of *durée* and memory[,] . . . we now inhabit the synchronic rather than the diachronic . . . ,

The author wishes to thank Ronald Gottesman, Robert Rosen, Vivian Sobchak, and Charles Wolfe for comments on previous drafts read at the Society for Cinema Studies Conference in Los Angeles in 1991 and at the American Studies annual meeting in Costa Mesa in 1992.

[and] our daily life . . . [is] dominated by categories of space rather than by categories of time."[2]

Albeit from opposite ends of the political spectrum, both Fukuyama and Jameson associate the eclipse of history with the triumph of late capitalism and Western-style consumerism. Jameson is particularly concerned about the way in which the rapid processing of information by the news media results in "a series of perpetual presents" and induces "historical amnesia."[3] But is not history being prematurely interred? Critics like Fredric Jameson and David Harvey, who comment on the waning of historicity in postmodernist society, do so from a modernist perspective that includes linear time and periodization, as opposed to spatial and atemporal concepts, such as Foucauldian genealogy. Jameson, for example, postulates three stages of capitalistic growth—market capitalism, imperialism, and multinationalism—that correspond to cultural forms labeled *realism, modernism,* and *postmodernism,* a schematic evolution of infrastructure in relation to superstructure. Analyzing twentieth-century capitalism as a progression from assembly-line Fordism to flexible accumulation or global financial systems transcending nation-states, Harvey asserts the relevance of Karl Marx, who "restored historical time."[4] As evidenced by the linear perspective of the very critics who are alarmed by the disappearance of the historical referent in late capitalist society, traditional concepts of history still persist. In fact, a close scrutiny of *Walker* (1987) and *Mississippi Burning* (1988), two very different films about historical events, reveals that history is still sacrosanct and that efforts to reconceptualize it provoke fractious debate.

A brief survey of recent historiographical developments, which include discourse on film as history, reveals that the historical profession is indeed very much divided.[5] Although traditional history rooted in nineteenth-century German historiography could be labeled a modernist (and thus outmoded) discipline, controversy among historians demonstrates that the field has been reconceptualized so that political history about nation-states now coexists with the "new history," a catchall category that includes the social history of groups excluded from access to traditional forms of power, the new economic history (or cliometrics), and the new cultural and intellectual history informed by poststructuralism.[6] Primary in the canon constituting the "new history" is the work of Fernand Braudel (1902–85), the most influential historian of the *Annales* school in Paris and a colleague of structuralist Claude Lévi-Strauss. Contrary to claims that the accelerating displacement of time by space in postmodernist consumer society means the end of history, Braudel boldly reconceptualized historical time in three tiers so that it was spatial and visual. Parallel to rapidly developing political events are social and economic patterns evolving at a slower pace and almost immobile geographical factors that can only be observed over the *longue durée.*[7] Significantly, Braudel used the language of film montage to describe how time could be manipulated and cautioned that history would "not lend itself so easily to . . . juggling with the synchronic and diachronic."[8]

Precisely the juxtaposition of synchronic and diachronic aspects of time that is so difficult to achieve in the writing of history is possible in postmodernist as opposed to illusionist representations of history in film. A consideration of *Walker* (1987), a parody about a nineteenth-century American adventurer who became president of Nicaragua, and *Mississippi Burning* (1988), an account of the events of Freedom Summer in 1964, are the focus of this chapter. As a postmodernist narrative, *Walker* is self-reflexive, ironical, and absurdist, in contrast to *Mississippi Burning,* a social-problem and male-bonding film constructed according to genre conventions. Unfortunately, the powerful reality effect of the civil rights drama, which I discuss later, limited public discourse on historicity to questions of the authenticity of its representation. By contrast, *Walker* cleverly exploits the cinematic apparatus that results in time compression to provoke thought about the meaning of the past and how it is constructed. Specifically, the film's representation of events is chronological and linear, but the present is superimposed on the past so that American foreign policy in Central America is informed by events of the Vietnam War and, more recently, Desert Shield and Desert Storm in the Persian Gulf. In effect, the juxtaposition of contemporary military exploits with previous ones illustrates Braudel's concept of the spatialization of time that yields perspective on history viewed from a distance.[9] *Walker,* in other words, engages in a continuous dialogue about the ways in which past and present are constructed in relation to each other. Further, the synchronic and diachronic dimensions of historical experience are made visible so that the emphasis is upon continuity, as well as change. Consequently, the film does not represent an endorsement of modernization as progress in a linear unfolding of time. As scriptwriter Rudy Wurlitzer concluded, "I've learned . . . about . . . the currents and cycles of history, how history is really not linear, and that it comes around with its own laws."[10]

Given Jameson's observation about the disappearance of the historical referent in late capitalist society, why does *Walker* succeed as history? As a representation of past events, the film exploits a series of contradictions, not the least of which is the concept of postmodernist cinema as history. Director Alex Cox and Rudy Wurlitzer consciously engage in a self-reflexive exercise that frustrates audience expectations with respect to genres traditionally associated with dramatizing historical events, namely, documentary, docudrama, and biopic. As a matter of fact, they eschew any attempt at illusionist narrative, play fast and loose with the facts, and collapse past and present tense by telescoping events. Further, they effect a satirical tone through a disjunction between image and sound in which voice-over narration, dialogue, and nondiegetic music are contradicted by the mise-en-scène. As Charles Jencks observes, a distanced and ironical view of the past, in which innocence is no longer possible, is the essence of postmodernist thought about time.[11] What emerges in *Walker* is thus a sense of history that runs counter to a nostalgic and romanticized construction of past events equivalent to forgetfulness. The film functions instead as a hilarious commentary on the psychosexual character of American Puritans who subordinated women and peoples of color, on the role of capital in the pursuit of Manifest Destiny, and on the relentlessness of modernization, including a commodified media culture.

A montage of events past and present that sharpens our perspective about both, *Walker* is a representation of American spread-eagle diplomacy that ascribes capitalist exploitation of Third World peoples to institutionalized racism and sexism. Although their meeting in the film is apocryphal, industrial magnate Cornelius Vanderbilt (Peter Boyle) summons William Walker (Ed Harris), the filibusterer who was once a household name in this country and is ironically remembered today only in Nicaragua.[12] Arriving on horseback at the site of railroad construction where Chinese workers are laying tracks, a symbolic scene with reference to Manifest Destiny, Walker meets Vanderbilt underling Ephraim Squier (Richard Masur). As Squier conducts him through a series of passenger cars—a scene that is privileged as a transitional moment in the film because the two men emerge outdoors where they began—Walker listens to his guide salivate about imperialistic conquest. "Central America," exclaims Squier, is "land . . . for the taking . . . [with] bare-breasted beauties under trees laden with fruit—seven to every man." A cartoonish figure seated in the midst of railroad construction, Commodore Vanderbilt echoes the business executives coded as villains in black-and-white, as opposed to color, photography in California Newsreel's *Controlling Interest* (1978). Pointing to a map of Nicaragua, dismissed as "a fucked-up little country somewhere south of here," the industrialist exclaims, "What I need is for some man to go down there and take over. I want that country stable." When Vanderbilt fails to appeal to the ambition of his guest, who affects the dress of a clergyman, he is cunning enough to exploit his self-righteous and fanatical belief in the country's ideals. "Do you prize democracy, universal suffrage, the principles of our founding fathers? . . . Nicaragua needs democracy." Affectless throughout most of the film's tumultuous events, Walker is devastated by the sudden death of his fiancée, Ellen Martin (Marlee Matlin), decides to accept Vanderbilt's challenge, and sets sail for Nicaragua with his "Immortals." Chief among his followers is a fictional black fighter who accompanied him on an earlier filibuster in Mexico.[13] According to a convention of historical epics, documentaries, and educational films, a map is superimposed over a sailing ship as voice-over narration first announces a "new era for Nicaragua and all Central America" and then, as Walker is shot in the foreground with a cross, switches to first-person commentary inflected with ironical reference to Vietnam: "We paused at the small, unregenerated hamlet of Realejo."

Walker's complexity as a postmodernist historical film includes its representation of the politics of the "other" as oppressed but nevertheless heterogeneous groups of people. In fact, Walker emerges victorious in Nicaragua after a disastrous series of setbacks because the country is divided by civil war between conservative and liberal factions. Although the Nicaraguan masses have no voice in the film, the members of the ruling class define their interests in economic rather than nationalist terms and are thus easily co-opted. Witnessing an American setback at Rivas, a Nicaraguan sympathizer rails against his countrymen's opposition: "Our American brothers came here to bring Peace, Democracy, and Liberty. . . . To improve our civilization. And strengthen our economy." Walker stumbles onto victory by accident rather than design and forms an alliance with Dona Yrena (Blanca Guerra), a Nicaraguan aristocrat who would rather sleep with an American imperialist than embrace democratic reform. Also divided are American blacks in Walker's ragtag army, the Immortals. After staging an election to declare himself president of Nicaragua, Walker decrees slavery in order to end a labor shortage and court an alliance with the antebellum South. When he announces his intention during a zany performance of *Julius Caesar,* his black followers angrily leave the theater, but their political reactions differ. Walker's most trusted black lieutenant contests his argument that Nicaraguan Indians, like Negroes, are suited for slavery by reason of their "fidelity and docility and . . . capacity for labor," but he remains a steadfast supporter. Another African-American fighter, however, contemptuously tosses his medal in the dirt and rides out of town. As his wife, who accompanied him to Nicaragua, had predicted in contemporary lingo, "Next thing you know they'll reinstitute slavery. It's the same racist, macho, sexist shit we turned our backs on." Since these events are part of a historical continuum that includes the ongoing oppression of African Americans in the United States and the recent Nicaraguan struggle between Sandinistas and Contras, the elusiveness of political and socioeconomic change is underscored.

Aside from its sophisticated vision of the politics of the developing world and of ethnic minorities, *Walker* reverberates with echoes of feminist discourse on the filmic representation of women. The heroines who are romantically or sexually linked with Walker are, not coincidentally, unable to communicate in English and thus are represented as constructs of different forms of language. Unfortunately, not much is known about Walker's brief relationship with Ellen Martin, a hearing-impaired Southern woman who succumbed to yellow fever.[14] Condemning Manifest Destiny as "a cover-up for slavery," she quickly emerges as the moral center of the film. Despite her inability to speak and hear, Ellen reduces Walker to despair during a quarrel sparked by his refusal to convey her political sentiments to Squier, a smug expansionist. She signs to Walker, "You never represent me. You're always paraphrasing everything I say. Censoring me. . . . I don't trust you." Walker is photographed against a painting of a fertile landscape and next to a model of a sailing ship when he swears, "I'll never leave again." Since the film's cinematography and editing contradict the soundtrack, Ellen's hearing impairment questions speech or utterance as symbolic of the diachronic in favor of mise-en-scène as visual evidence of the synchronic. When Ellen suddenly dies of yellow fever, Walker accepts Vanderbilt's offer to invade Nicaragua, only to succumb to the influence of yet another strong-willed woman, Dona Yrena.

Unlike Ellen, the Nicaraguan aristocrat is a completely fictional construct but a necessary one in that sexual politics is symbolic of colonialist expansion. Again, sexual difference, complicated in this instance by cultural difference, is conveyed by the woman's lack of access to the language spoken by male imperialists. Dona Yrena disguises her ability to speak English, decreed the official language of Nicaragua, so that her Spanish dialogue is subtitled on the screen. Although Walker is repeatedly photographed in foreground and at low angle, Dona Yrena, who is sexually aggressive, observes his slight physical stature and reassures him that his performance in bed is "not great, but for a gringo good enough." Walker's decision to execute General Ponciano Corral, the legitimist leader, and to torch the centuries-old city of Granada are vindictive reactions to Dona Yrena's defiance. She contemptuously dismisses him as "a dog's asshole." The representation of territorial conquest as sexual imperative is nothing new, but the film's sex-role reversals and irreverent tone provide more than a little amusement.

Perhaps most telling in *Walker*'s juxtaposition of past and present to emphasize the continuity of capitalist exploitation is the use of twentieth-century icons in the narrative of a nineteenth-century adventurer. When Dona Yrena escapes from Granada with two Nicaraguan legitimists, her companions are reading *People* and *Newsweek,* both featuring cover stories about Walker, self-styled "Gray-Eyed Man of [Manifest] Destiny." As they discuss the politics of "those crazy gringos" in a horse-drawn carriage, a Mercedes overtakes them on the dirt road. During an interview with a news reporter, Walker asserts that the ends, which he has admittedly forgotten, justify the means. As the two men walk down a stretch of beach in an extreme long shot, in the foreground are icons of multinational corporate dominance, an American with a Coca-Cola bottle and a pack of Marlboro Cigarettes. Undoubtedly most disturbing in the film's anachronistic mise-en-scène is the presence of a computer terminal signifying the information age and Foucauldian panoptic surveillance in Vanderbilt's quarters. At the conclusion, when Walker and his men retreat during the burning of Granada, World War II air-raid sirens are heard on the soundtrack and a helicopter, the quintessential symbol of the Vietnam War, descends in front of the Palacio Nacional to rescue men who can produce American passports. Finally, as the credits roll, a video monitor on screen right shows President Ronald Reagan reassuring the public, "Let me say to those who invoke the men of Vietnam . . . there is no thought of sending American combat troops to Central America." But the newsreel footage shows American men involved in maneuvers and lifeless bodies of Nicaraguan victims. An instance of yet another juxtaposition between past and present tense to achieve historical consciousness, the transition from film to television as a medium for reporting news events, especially military intervention abroad, is particularly apt in representing an era dominated by the small screen.

Despite "the evaporation of any sense of historical continuity and memory" attributed to the postmodern condition by critics like David Harvey, *Walker* demonstrates that postmodernist cinema can indeed be compelling as history. Clarification of this argument requires a focus on the narrower issue of modernization because critics are by no means in agreement about definitions of postmodernism versus modernism or about the extent to which these are overlapping and continuous cultural practices. Andreas Huyssen, for example, argues that poststructuralism is "primarily a discourse of and about modernism," whereas Brook Thomas aligns such discourse with the postmodern and thus construes it as existing in tension with the new historicism. Complicating critical discourse even further, T. J. Jackson Lears points out that literary critics and historians do not agree on definitions of modernism, a phenomenon that he labels *antimodernism* for the purposes of his argument. In addition, critics have expressed disagreement regarding the issue of postmodernism in relation to history. Marshall Berman, for example, critiques both structuralism and postmodernism, which in some instances he equates with modernism, as essentially ahistorical. Linda Hutcheon argues, on the other hand, that contrary to Jameson's observation about the waning of historicity, postmodernist writing characterized by self-reflexivity and parody is indeed rooted in the historical world. Given these disagreements, I focus on the more limited subject of *Walker* as discourse on the issue of modernization as a significant aspect of modernity. Although Marshall Berman indicts social scientists for splintering discussions of modernity into compartmentalized subjects, such as industrialization, market formation, urbanization, and nation-states, these issues are significant precisely because historians, not all of whom claim to be social scientists, have traditionally studied processes of political, economic, and social change.[15]

As a historical film, *Walker* is an interesting amalgam because it calls for a critique of American economic domination, in both its imperialistic and multinational corporate phases, and of modernization, albeit in an innovative postmodernist form. Are we then to assume that the film as postmodernist narrative reconceptualizes history? *Walker* does constitute a departure in that it exemplifies Linda Hutcheon's discussion of "historiographic metafiction" as writing that foregrounds both history and fiction as constructs and employs this awareness to rework the "forms and contents of the past." Yet despite the privileging of multiple voices in response to American hegemony, *Walker* is ultimately limited in rethinking history because it focuses on such traditional issues as nationhood, diplomacy, and military conquest. *Annales* historians, it should be remembered, shifted the terms of debate about modernization and rejected as peculiarly Western the notion that the experience of a modern industrialized society should serve as a yardstick by which to measure the history of the rest of the world.[16] Given this perspective, *Walker* remains traditionalist in its subject matter despite elements of satire, irony, and absurdist humor. Suppose the history of Walker's exploits had been represented instead as Dona Yrena's autobiography or memoir, a Nicaraguan perspective that contradicts and overlaps with American accounts, including those written by the filibusterer.[17] Such a representational strategy would produce disjunction resulting from differences in terms not only of culture but of gender.

Walker, to be sure, remains an interesting departure, but reconceptualizing history provokes resistance, as an analysis of its reception demonstrates, because traditional concepts based on empiricism, objective truth, and linear progress are still dominant in bourgeois culture. As historical reenactment, *Walker* does not conform to the legacy of public images of history validated by realistic representation in mainstream cinema. A film that begins with voice-over narration associated with documentaries and a title proclaiming "THIS IS A TRUE STORY"—only to show battle scenes recalling Sam Peckinpah Westerns to the tune of festive Latin rhythms—does not qualify as history. Filmgoers stayed away from the box office, and film critics focused on questions of authenticity and unconventional form. *Newsweek*'s David Ansen, for example, listed several factual errors in the film and concluded, "Wurlitzer's script offers a tinny, underground-commix view of history. What a waste. The real story of

Walker . . . would make a great epic." As a matter of fact, *Walker* questions the adequacy of the historical epic as a representation of the past in its parodic staging of *Julius Caesar. Variety's* critic objected that *Walker* was "completely unconvincing in its presentation of events" and faulted "surrealist anachronisms that have been woven into the visual fabric . . . to emphasize the modern parallels." The *Wall Street Journal* described *Walker* as a "convoluted—and generally silly—spoof" like *Saturday Night Live.* Apparently without humor, Michael Wilmington warned in the *Los Angeles Times* that some audiences may conclude the moviemakers "have gotten confused about what century they're in." [18]

Walker did receive more appreciative notices from Richard Schickel in *Time,* David Sterrit in the *Christian Science Monitor,* and Stanley Kauffmann in the *New Republic.* Vincent Canby of the *New York Times* liked its "hip, cool, political satire" and observed that its "neo-Brechtian believe-it-or-not inventory of character and events . . . must strike most Americans as outlandishly unbelievable, while many Central Americans may simply nod their heads in recognition." In fact, the *Los Angeles Times* reported that contrary to its reception in the United States, *Walker* played to packed houses in Managua, Nicaragua, despite the fact that the price of a ticket exceeded the daily earnings of an average worker. Although Nicaraguan reviewers, like their American counterparts, tallied up factual errors in the film and did not always appreciate farcical humor, filmgoers in Managua reportedly broke into laughter over the juxtaposition of past and present events.[19] Apparently, postmodernist film as history does speak to the "other" in multiple voices.

The fact that most reviewers objected to *Walker's* collapsed temporality, presentism, and ironical sense of time, not to mention its absurdist humor, is instructive regarding the public's definition of historical film. A consideration of critical as well as audience reception, in other words, demonstrates that postmodernist reading strategies are, in effect, addressed to insiders willing to consider a historiographic representation in which constructing history as opposed to subject matter becomes the focus. Director Alex Cox evidently misread moviegoers because his intention was "to steer the film away from a drab *Masterpiece Theatre* presentation" and to "reach a broader audience, not just the people who go to the art houses." On the contrary, *Walker* is the sort of release that would be exhibited in art-film theaters rather than in shopping malls. The negative reception of film critics demonstrates that postmodernist historical narrative is unacceptable to a public still invested in realistic representations of the past as opposed to discourse on the nature of those very representations. Consequently, the commercial and critical success of *Mississippi Burning* is quite revealing because its powerful realism focused debate on questions of authenticity, as did the postmodernist approach of *Walker* but not on the issue of history itself as a construct. Coincidentally, director Alan Parker, like his British countryman Cox, also denigrated public television broadcasting because he wanted to reach a mass audience. Unlike Cox, he succeeded.[20]

In contrast to *Walker, Mississippi Burning* is an illusionist narrative constructed according to the conventions of the social-problem film as well as of the detective and male-buddy genres. One reviewer dubbed it "Dirty Harry beats dirty laundry."[21] The precredit and credit sequences establish the film's concern with racial injustice: as black spiritual music wails on the soundtrack, a white man and a black boy drink from separate water fountains, and a building torched by the Ku Klux Klan (KKK) goes up in flames. Civil rights workers modeled on Andrew Goodman, Michael Schwerner, and James Cheney are stopped at night on a lonely country road and murdered by white Southern rednecks. Assigned to head investigation of the crime are two FBI agents, Alan Ward (Willem Dafoe), a punctilious eastern bureaucrat who is ineffectual, and Rupert Anderson (Gene Hackman), a rumpled but savvy southerner who eventually convinces his sidekick to resort to KKK tactics. Aside from ignoring procedure and playing rough, Anderson shrewdly observes the local citizenry and exploits Mrs. Pell (Frances McDormand), the lonely and sensitive young wife of the deputy sheriff. At the beginning of the film, Ward and Anderson sit in their car and observe a small town shortly after their arrival in Mississippi. What appear to be casual street scenes photographed in extreme long shot and in soft focus reveal potential sources of information to the Southern agent. A symbol of white conscience, Mrs. Pell eventually betrays her husband and discloses to Anderson where the civil rights workers are buried. In fact, the location of the burial site was revealed by an informant who collected a thirty-thousand-dollar reward.[22]

Switching into high gear, the two FBI agents lead a team, including an African-American agent, who trick and terrorize the guilty. Accelerating events lead to a montage of men being arrested and subsequently leaving a courthouse with black-and-white still shots that identify each convicted man by name and jail sentence. Unfortunately, this last tactic, as well as the documentary-style interviews of local denizens voicing their opinions about race relations, tends to historicize events and fuel controversy about the film. At the conclusion, a tracking shot of a cemetery stops to focus on the vandalized tombstone of the black civil rights worker. But this image of persistent racism is undercut by the film's characterization of black men as essentially passive and impotent, a representation that attests to white paranoia expressed in the myth of the black stud and a history of lynching. Consistent with the precredit sequence in which both an African-American boy and a white adult man drink water from segregated fountains, the only fearless black male in the film is a child. A significant aspect of the narrative strategy of *Mississippi Burning* as a buddy film is to displace irreconcilable racial division onto categories of males, both black and white civil rights workers and FBI agents, who are characterized as either macho or impotent. Further, the appeal to male camaraderie provides a means of resolving a particularly heinous crime in the civil rights era. To put it another way, the film achieves narrative closure by encoding a pattern of social organization based on male bonding that cuts across class and racial lines. Such camaraderie, however, is in reality restricted to rituals like professional athletics because macho codes are not only elitist but also sexist. Anderson is able to exploit Mrs. Pell, for example, because she is socially isolated; as a consequence of her betrayal, she is savagely beaten by her husband in the presence of Klansmen.

The reception of *Mississippi Burning,* a release that received far more attention than *Walker,* provides evidence of what the public construes as a legitimate historical film. Distributed in December 1988 according to a phased release schedule involving only nine screens nationwide, the film required strong reviews, especially in New York, for a successful run. As the result of a *Time* cover story, several *New York Times* articles, and a *CBS This Morning* report, *Mississippi Burning* became the subject of controversy, which led to brisk box-office business and primed the audience for a wide release in January and a video release in July.[23] Despite a disclaimer that the film was a fictionalized account based on true events, its strong reality effect influenced reviewers to react in terms of conventional views about history. Put simply, such views equate history with objectivity and truth. *Variety*'s critic wrote, "Approach is fictional, but . . . [the] script captures much of the truth in its telling of the impact of a 1964 FBI probe into the murders of three civil rights workers." But several reviewers objected to two gross distortions in the film: the blatant repression of black activism in the civil rights movement and the glorification of FBI agents who had in actuality thwarted rights workers. Pauline Kael, sounding a note of disagreement among New York critics, claimed, "Alan Parker is essentially putting blacks at the back [of the bus] again." Similarly, Abbie Hoffman responded to Stuart Klawans's positive review in the *Nation* by asserting that "the idea that the FBI brought an end to a segregated South is about as ludicrous as saying that noble elements inside the Joint Chiefs of Staff were essentially responsible for ending the war in Vietnam."[24]

Clearly, controversy about the historical authenticity of this film was based on concern that filmgoers, unable to differentiate between fact and fiction, would accept Parker's representation of the civil rights struggle. Claims to historical truth are vigorously debated because competing visions of the past are invoked to influence social attitudes and to shape public policy. At least since the controversial premiere of *The Birth of a Nation* (1915), film as history has been subject to debate because it is based on realistic representation. As Jack E. White asserted in the *Time* cover story, "Many viewers, whose ability to discern a whopper . . . has been obliterated by an age of TV docudramas, . . . leave the theater believing a version of history so distorted that it amounts to a cinematic lynching of the truth." Significantly, reviewers who defended the film resorted to the strategy of downplaying the importance of historical accuracy. Vincent Canby, for example, asserted that social issues were best represented in documentaries but claimed that "nothing . . . seriously damages the film's validity as a melodrama or as an evocation of recent history." Canby later argued in a convoluted defense of his views that *Mississippi Burning* was such a powerful indictment of racism that it could only be undermined by "finding reasons not to believe the film." Attempting to minimize objections to the film on the grounds of its lack of credibility, he questioned the value of objectivity and was not above firing salvos at *We Are Not Afraid,* Seth Cagin and Philip Dray's monograph about the Freedom Summer murders.[25]

Discourse on *Mississippi Burning* was not restricted to newspapers, magazines, and trade journals but also appeared in scholarly publications. Robert Brent Toplin gave a detailed summary of factual errors in the film in *Perspectives,* the newsletter of the American Historical Association. Why did academics not simply dismiss *Mississippi Burning* as just another movie? Sundiata K. Cha-Jua argued in *Radical History Review* that for most moviegoers, especially youth who were not old enough to recall the civil rights movement, the film might be their only source of information and, moreover, obscured the public television series *Eyes on the Prize.* Similarly, Thomas Doherty expressed concern about the impact of the film on teenaged audiences in *Cineaste,* a journal whose editors condemned Parker's "egregious inversion of historical facts." Ultimately, the argument provoked by the film in the popular press, if not in scholarly publications, probably cost it Academy Awards—though not nominations. Despite a formidable campaign launched by distributor Orion to counteract negative publicity, the film won an Oscar in only one of seven categories, editing. Nevertheless, *Mississippi Burning* earned respectable figures at the box office even though it could not compete with star-studded blockbusters like *Rain Man* (1988) and *Twins* (1989), also released during the Christmas season. When the film last appeared on *Variety*'s charts, its cumulative gross receipts during a period of 178 days totaled more than thirty-four million dollars. Additionally, when *Mississippi Burning* was released in video format, it remained on the list of top ten rentals for more than two months and was more popular than *Twins.*[26]

Controversy about *Mississippi Burning* demonstrates that traditional conceptualizations of history are still widely held not only among professional historians but among film reviewers and their readership. Peter Novick defines the concept of historical objectivity as follows: "The assumptions on which it rests include a commitment to the reality of the past, and to truth as correspondence to that reality; a sharp separation between knower and known, between fact and value, and, above all, between history and fiction."[27] Although most filmgoers are obviously not trained as historians, they would most likely agree with this formulation because it dovetails with their educational experience and ideological beliefs. As Fukuyama stresses, history deteriorates into antiquarianism unless it is enlisted in a larger cause.[28] Despite his belief that the triumph of Western capitalism signaled the end of history, discourse on historical representation in film, most recently the contentious reception of *JFK* (1991), demonstrates that the public is still invested in traditional concepts about the past. As for the historical profession, Lawrence Stone has observed that despite serious challenges mounted by the "new history," political history based on empiricist research is still dominant in the discipline.[29] Critics' proclamation of a new postmodernist age notwithstanding, traditional history remains as one of the bulwarks of modernist thought in which the individual is still constituted as an autonomous subject, however beleaguered, as opposed to being reduced to a textual construct. The epistemological divide between critical theorists and historians, in other words, is underscored to a significant extent by debate on the issue of human agency as opposed to the privileging of reified texts.[30] Whether repeated calls for the historicizing of texts, on the one hand, and greater attention to history as a construct, on the other, will lead to more frequent cross-disciplinary dialogue that will affect future historiography remains a matter of speculation.

A final word about the argument provoked by *Mississippi Burning* is in order. Ultimately, public discourse on the film's authenticity reinforced belief in linearity, progress, and the ability of Americans to accomplish social engineering. The very fact that the film had been made was cited as a sign of improved race relations despite statistics to the contrary.[31] Controversy, however, did not move beyond questions of veracity to include a consideration of either history itself or the ideological function of history. *Walker,* on the other hand, provokes thought about the relationship between past and present through its lack of verisimilitude and its spatialization of time so that the result is cyclical rather than teleological. Progress is not equated with linear development in a patriotic celebration of American civic virtues, as is the case in *Mississippi Burning.* Despite its limitations, *Walker* does provoke thought about the nature of historical representation as a construct that often validates nationalism and patriotism. As such, it succeeds, whereas *Mississippi Burning* does not. But it was the latter film that found favor with most critics, made millions of dollars at the box office and video rental shops, and garnered Golden Globe Awards and Oscar nominations. The lesson is that not only is postmodernist historical representation unacceptable for a public still invested in traditional notions about history so too are the sweeping generalizations of critics about the waning of historicity itself.

Notes

1. Otis L. Graham, Jr., "Premature Reports: The 'End of History,'" *OAH Newsletter* 18 (May 1990): 3, 23; James Atlas, "What Is Fukuyama Saying?" *New York Times Magazine,* 22 October 1989, pp. 38–42; Alan Ryan, "Professor Hegel Goes to Washington," *New York Review of Books,* 26 March 1992, pp. 7–13; and Peter Fritzsche, "Francis Fukuyama, *The End of History and the Last Man,*" *American Historical Review* 97 (June 1992): 817–19. See also Francis Fukuyama, *The End of History and the Last Man* (New York: Free Press, 1991).

2. Fredric Jameson, "Postmodernism, or, The Cultural Logic of Late Capitalism," *New Left Review* 146 (July–August 1984): 64; reprinted in *Postmodernism, or, The Cultural Logic of Late Capitalism* (Durham, N.C.: Duke University Press, 1991). See also Jameson, "Reification and Utopia in Mass Culture," *Social Text* 1 (winter 1979): 130–48; Jameson, "Postmodernism and Consumer Society," in *The Anti-Aesthetic: Essays on Postmodern Culture,* ed. Hal Foster (Port Townsend, Wash.: Bay Press, 1983), 111–25; Jameson, "Progress vs. Utopia; or, Can We Imagine the Future?" in *Art after Modernism: Rethinking Representation,* ed. Brian Willis (New York: New Museum of Contemporary Art, 1984), 239–52; and Jameson, "Nostalgia for the Present," *South Atlantic Quarterly* 88, no. 2 (spring 1989): 517–37. See also Michael Walsh, "Postmodernism Has an Intellectual History," *Quarterly Review of Film and Video* 12, nos. 1–2 (1990): 147–61.

3. Jameson, "Postmodernism and Consumer Society," 125.

4. Jameson, "Postmodernism, or, Cultural Logic," 77–78; David Harvey, *The Condition of Postmodernity: An Inquiry into the Origins of Cultural Change* (Cambridge, U.K.: Basil Blackwell, 1989), part 2, 273.

5. See Robert A. Rosenstone, "History in Images/History in Words: Reflections on the Possibility of Really Putting History onto Film," *American Historical Review* 93 (December 1988): 1173–85. For critical theorists on historical film, see Vivian Sobchack, "'Surge and Splendor': A Phenomenology of the Hollywood Historical Epic," *Representations* 29 (winter 1990): 24–49; and Janet Staiger, "Securing the Fictional Narrative as a Tale of the Historical Real," *South Atlantic Quarterly* 88 (spring 1989): 393–412.

6. See "*AHR* Forum: The Old History and the New," *American Historical Review* 94 (June 1989): 654–98. Essays read at the AHA annual meeting in December 1987 include Theodore S. Hammerow, "The Bureaucratization of History"; Gertrude Himmelfarb, "Some Reflections on the New History"; Lawrence W. Levine, "The Unpredictable Past: Reflections on Recent American Historiography"; Joan W. Scott, "History in Crisis? The Others' Side of the Story"; and

John E. Toews, "Perspectives on 'The Old History and the New': A Comment."

7. On the *Annales* school, see Lynn Hunt, "French History in the Last Twenty Years: The Rise and Fall of the *Annales* Paradigm," *Journal of Contemporary History* 21 (April 1986): 209–24; and Hunt, *The New Cultural History* (Berkeley: University of California Press, 1989), 1–22. See also Georg G. Iggers's introduction, "The Transformation of Historical Studies in Historical Perspective," in *International Handbook of Historical Studies: Contemporary Research and Theory,* ed. Georg G. Iggers and Harold T. Parker (Westport, Conn.: Greenwood Press, 1979), pp. 1–14. On Braudel's concept of structure, see Samuel Kinser, "*Annaliste* Paradigm? The Geohistorical Structuralism of Fernand Braudel," *American Historical Review* 86 (February–December 1981): 63–105. On the *Annales* school critique of narrative history, see Hayden White, "Narrative in Contemporary Historical Theory," in *The Content of Form: Narrative Discourse and Historical Representation* (Baltimore, Md.: Johns Hopkins University Press, 1987), 31–32.

8. Fernand Braudel, "Time, History, and the Social Sciences," trans. Siam France, in *The Varieties of History,* ed. Fritz Stern (New York: Vintage Books, 1973), 424–25. Originally published as "Histoire et sciences sociales: La Longue durée," *Annales* 13 (1958): 725–53.

9. Kinser, "*Annaliste* Paradigm?" 99.

10. Rudy Wurlitzer, *Walker* (New York: Harper and Row, 1987), 41.

11. Charles Jencks, *Post-Modernism: The New Classicism in Art and Architecture* (New York: Rizzoli, 1987), 20–21.

12. For a brief account of Walker's filibusters, see Karl Berman, *Under the Big Stick: Nicaragua and the United States Since 1948* (Boston: South End Press, 1986), 51–102. A standard account is William O. Scroggs's aptly titled *Filibusters and Financiers: The Story of William Walker and His Associates* (New York: Russell and Russell, 1916). Walker wrote an account of his adventures in third person, *The War in Nicaragua* (Mobile, Ala.: Goetzel, 1860).

13. A Broadway musical entitled *Nicaragua, or, General Walker's Victories,* which opened in New York in 1856, included a character named Ivory Black, "a superior nigger." See K. Berman, *Under the Big Stick,* 76.

14. She was actually Helen Martin. See Scroggs, *Filibusters and Financiers,* 14.

15. Andreas Huyssen, "Mapping the Postmodern," *New German Critique* 33 (1984): 37–38, reprinted in Huyssen, *After the Great Divide: Modernism, Mass Culture, Postmodernism* (Bloomington: Indiana University Press, 1986), 178–221; Brook Thomas, "The New Historicism and Other Old-fashioned Topics," in *The New Historicism,* ed. H. Aram Veeser (New York: Routledge, 1989), 182–203; T. J. Jackson Lears, *No Place of Grace: Antimodernism and the Transformation of American Culture, 1880–1920* (New York: Pantheon, 1981), xix; Marshall Berman, *All That Is Solid Melts into Air: The Experience of Modernity* (New York: Simon and Schuster, 1982), 33–34; and Linda Hutcheon, *A Poetics of Postmodernism: History, Theory, Fiction* (New York: Routledge, 1988), 5. See also Thomas, *The New Historicism and Other Old-fashioned Topics* (Princeton: Princeton University Press, 1991).

16. Hutcheon, *Poetics of Postmodernism,* 5; quoted in Iggers, "Transformation," 9. On Marxism and the *Annales* school, see Hunt, "French History," and Hunt, *New Cultural History.*

17. See, for example, Natalie Zemon Davis, *The Return of Martin Guerre* (Cambridge: Harvard University Press, 1983), which was made into a film. See also Staiger, "Securing the Fictional Narrative."

18. David Ansen, "A Yankee Devil's Manifest Destiny: History as a Bad Joke," *Newsweek,* 7 December 1987; "Walker," *Variety,* 2 December 1987; untitled review, *Wall Street Journal,* 3 December 1987; Michael Wilmington, "'Walker' Dramatizes Bizarre Historical Exploit Gone Awry," *Los Angeles Times,* 4 December 1987, in *Walker* clipping file, Margaret Herrick Library, Academy of Motion Picture Arts and Sciences, Los Angeles, Calif.

19. Richard Schickel, "Bananas Republic," *Time,* 7 December 1987; David Sterrit, "'Walker': History as Tragedy . . . and Farce," *Christian Science Monitor,* 7 January 1988; Stanley Kauffmann, "Stanley Kauffmann on Film," *New Republic,* 28 December 1987; Vincent Canby, "Film: 'Walker,' Starring Ed Harris," *New York Times,* 4 December 1987; "'Walker' Is an Amusing Hit in Nicaragua," *Los Angeles Times,* 5 March 1988, in *Walker* clipping file, Margaret Herrick Library, Academy of Motion Picture Arts and Sciences, Los Angeles, Calif.

20. Quoted in Patrick Goldstein, "Hollywood Invades Nicaragua," *Los Angeles Times Calendar,* 19 April 1987, p. 17; Wayne King, "Fact vs. Fiction," *New York Times,* Arts and Leisure section, 4 December 1988, p. 20. According to *Variety, Straight to Hell* and *Walker* "convinced Hollywood [that Cox] . . . couldn't be trusted; as a renegade the director has been making films in Mexico." See "Missing Persons," *Variety,* 8 June 1992, p. 83.

21. Richard Corliss, "Fire This Time," *Time,* 9 January 1989, p. 58.

22. Also cited as an example of blatant racism is the fact that James Cheney, the black civil rights worker, was driving, rather than sitting in the backseat as shown in the film. See Seth Cagin and Philip Dray, *We Are Not Afraid: The Story of Goodman, Schwerner, and Cheney and the Civil Rights Campaign for Mississippi* (New York: Macmillan, 1988).

23. "Orion Giving 'Mississippi' Straight Promo Push, Avoids Controversy," *Variety,* 18–24 January 1989, p. 13. According to *Variety*'s "Weekend Box Office Report," a weekly feature of the trade journal, the film remained on the charts from the time that it was released in December until June 1989. Released in video format in July, the film ranked number 12 among the top fifty video rentals in 1989. See "Top Video Rentals 1989," *Variety,* 24 January 1990. The film even spawned a television docudrama called *Murder in Mississippi* that was aired on CBS in February 1990 and received an Emmy nomination for best comedy-drama special.

24. "'Mississippi Burning'," *Variety,* 30 November 1988, p. 12; Pauline Kael, review of *Mississippi Burning, New Yorker,* 26 December 1988, p. 74; letters, *Nation,* 13 February 1989, p. 182.

25. *Time*'s own Richard Schickel had written earlier that the film's "power finally sweeps away one's resistance to the film's major improbabilities"; see Schickel, "The Fire in the South," *Time,* 5 December 1988, p. 90; Vincent Canby, "Alien Visions of America," *New York Times,* Arts and Leisure section, 18 December 1988, p. 14; and Canby, "Taking Risks to Illuminate a Painful Time in America," *New York Times,* 8 January 1989, p. 13.

26. Robert Brent Toplin, "*Mississippi Burning* Scorches Historians," *Perspectives*

(April 1989): 20; Sundiata K. Cha-Jua, "*Mississippi Burning:* The Burning of Black Self-Activity," *Radical History Review* 45 (1989): 132–35. Cha-Jua argues that depiction of Klansmen as rednecks (more than half the men eventually indicted held white-collar positions) fails to show that racism transcends class and that repressing black activism in favor of FBI heroics precludes an exploration of the economic base of racial injustice. Thomas Doherty, "*Mississippi Burning,*" *Cineaste* 17 (1989): 48; editorial, *Cineaste,* 17 (1989), p. 2; "Weekend Box Office Report," *Variety,* 7–13 June 1989, p. 8; "Who Benefits from the Academy Awards Promo Campaigns?" *Variety,* 22–28 March 1989, p. 5; "Top Fifty Video Titles," *Variety,* 20–26 September 1989, p. 43. *Rain Man,* starring Dustin Hoffman and Tom Cruise, and *Twins,* starring Arnold Schwarzenegger and Danny DeVito, had earned $160 and $110 million, respectively, at the time *Mississippi Burning* disappeared from *Variety*'s charts.

27. Peter Novick, *That Noble Dream: The "Objectivity Question" and the American Historical Profession* (Cambridge, U.K.: Cambridge University Press, 1988), 1–2.

28. Fritzsche, "Francis Fukuyama," 817.

29. Lawrence Stone, "Resisting the New," *New York Review of Books,* 17 December 1987, pp. 59–62.

30. See Sumiko Higashi, "Ethnicity, Class, and Gender in Film: DeMille's *The Cheat,*" in *Unspeakable Images: Ethnicity and the American Cinema,* ed. Lester Friedman (Urbana: University of Illinois Press, 1991), 112–39.

31. Ansen, "Yankee Devil's Manifest Destiny," 73.

27

Fantastic Realism: *Schindler's List* as Docudrama

Yosefa Loshitsky

One of the most memorable images from Claude Lanzmann's *Shoah,* which eventually acquired the status of the film's visual "logo," or signature, is the smiling face of Henrik Gakowski driving a locomotive against the backdrop of a railroad sign proclaiming "Treblinka." He looks back to the imaginary wagons behind him and slashes his finger across his throat in a supposedly "warning" gesture. During the war, this warning gesture was used by the Polish man, who worked for the Germans as a locomotive driver, to signal to the "ignorant" Jews crowded in the transport trains leading them to extermination what kind of fate awaited them. For Lanzmann, this image itself became the truth. Alongside it, he said, "historical footage becomes insufferable."[1] Almost a decade later, a similar image was used in Steven Spielberg's *Schindler's List.* The second time, however, this image of warning bore Spielberg's auteuristic vision. The performer of the warning gesture was not an old Polish man but a small child, and the disturbing ambivalence invoked by Gakowski's facial ex-

---

A slightly different version of this chapter appeared under the title "Holocaust Others: Spielberg's *Schindler's List* Versus Lanzmann's *Shoah,*" in *Spielberg's Holocaust: Critical Perspectives on Schindler's List,* ed. Yosefa Loshitsky (Bloomington: Indiana University Press, 1996).

pression was replaced with an unambiguous childish sadistic expression. In addition, in Spielberg's film the trains full of Jews rumble toward Auschwitz, "the most significant memorial site of the Shoah," and not toward Treblinka.[2]

Was Spielberg aware of the resonance created by these macabre images? Was he consciously using Lanzmann's iconic signature as an homage quotation? Or, perhaps, was he just "stealing" this powerful image and appropriating it into his own vision of the Holocaust? According to Gertrud Koch, Spielberg "recycled every little slip of film that was made before" to produce *Schindler's List*'s authoritarian quality so as to posit his film "at the end of film history."[3] If indeed we subscribe to Koch's thesis (which I do, as I explain later), then Spielberg is not "innocent." He was fully conscious of the enunciative source of the quoted image. Yet, it seems to me that it is more interesting to pose questions than categorically answer them. Whether we have here an example of self-reflexive quotational practice (a postmodernist pastiche) or merely an example of plagiarism, or even sheer ignorance on Spielberg's part regarding the source of the "original" image, the question of relationships (be they intentional or not) is still there. If indeed Spielberg "stole" Lanzmann's visual signature, then we might as well talk about a relationship of envy, based on an attempt to appropriate and assimilate one's object of envy. If, on the other hand, Spielberg used "Lanzmann's image" as an homage quotation, then we may talk about a relationship of pure admiration in which the master's influence is acknowledged. In fact, regardless of our preferred reading, the resonance between the two images points toward the complex relationship between the two films, both of which have already been canonized as the best films ever made on the Holocaust: *Shoah* in the domain of "documentary" and *Schindler's List* in the domain of fiction. Both films have a claim to being the last word on the Holocaust, a master narrative of the ultimate catastrophe endured by the Jewish people. Until Spielberg's film came out, however, *Shoah* was widely praised as a masterpiece and often claimed to be *the* Holocaust film. *Shoah* thus was the privileged site of debates about the representation of the Holocaust, and it is no wonder, therefore, that even a "nondocumentary" film like *Schindler's List* had either to humbly acknowledge Lanzmann's authority or to challenge it.

Many public debates about *Schindler's List* have compared it with *Shoah*. In these debates, one of the films has been valorized or devalorized in relationship to its counterpart. The relationships between the films, the public personae of their makers, and the social dynamics involved in their reception are all based on an essential Otherness. Although this Otherness is not reversible (in that the Other here is not a double who turns out to be the Self), it nonetheless suggests a kind of mirror relationship: each film is seen as a potential correcting and corrected mirror of the other. Hence, the two films offer two competing paradigms of Holocaust cinematic representation. This implicitly suggests two rival formulas regarding how to "correctly" make a film about the Holocaust and demonstrates how both *Shoah* and *Schindler's List* provide two competing models/theories, which simultaneously "explain" how both to resist and to overcome the "limits of representation."[4] In this chapter, I explore how *Schindler's List* makes a claim to "the real" through its manipulation of the docudrama strategy of blurring the boundaries between fact and fiction. I anchor this exploration in a comparative study of *Shoah,* perceived by critics and scholars as the epitome of Holocaust documentary, with *Schindler's List,* perceived as the fictional "master narrative" (and masterpiece) on the Holocaust. Through this respective exploration, I hope not only to make problematical the notion of docudrama but also to further investigate its special relationship with history in general and the Holocaust in particular.

Philosophical/Historical Tale Versus Popular Tale

The public "aura" associated with *Shoah* and *Schindler's List* was, among other things, invoked by the cultural context of the films' production and the evocation of highly invested notions of "Frenchness" versus "Americanness." Despite the interesting history of mutual fascination and repulsion that these two cultures hold toward each other, in the popular as well as midbrow critical imagination Frenchness connotes sophistication and intellectualism, while Americanness connotes populism, vulgarity, and lowbrow entertainment. These evocative connotations go beyond the aesthetic dimension because they imply the traditional binarism between art versus market, culture versus commodity, which obviously has far-reaching economic ramifications.

The national binarism generated by the two films reverberated also in the realm of the public personae projected by the two directors. As a former leader in the French Resistance and a well-known journalist who worked with Jean-Paul Sartre as the editor of *Les Temps Modernes,* Lanzmann obviously has a halo of an intellectual. Furthermore, *Shoah* was based on thorough historical research, which lasted eleven years. Lanzmann taped 350 hours of interviews in fourteen countries so as to create what he called "a film of 'corroboration,'" in which the Poles say "the same thing as the Jews, and 'this is confirmed by the SS.'"[5] For Lanzmann who was inspired by historian Raul Hilberg—whose book *The Destruction of the European Jews* he used as a model for *Shoah*—the details are what matter.

Claude Lanzmann's monumental nine-and-one-half-hour film on the Holocaust was praised not only by critics and "free-floating intellectuals" but also by professional historians. Although, and perhaps because, no archive footage is presented in the film—less shocking now because overfamiliar and recycled—but instead Lanzmann presses Jews, Germans, and Poles to describe their Holocaust experiences before the camera, the film has been celebrated as a product of vigorous and systematic historical method that transcends art in its consistent search for historical truth and transcends history through its melancholic beauty, rhythmic pace, and poetic images. Interviewing witnesses, survivors, and former Nazis detail by detail, their recollections unveil the terrible fate of the Jews against a background of moving trains and bureaucratic minutiae. Lanzmann's method of probing seemed cruel to some of the film's critics, but the survivors of the Holocaust all agreed to reconstruct painful events that many of them had tried to forget because they understood that part of the Final Solution was not only to do away with the Jews but also to obliterate all memory of them. Lanzmann's eleven years' investment of intellectual, emotional, and physical energy resulted in a monumental biography of death, an oral history of the Holocaust as narrated by victims, perpetrators, and bystanders.

Whereas Lanzmann is a professional journalist who uses film as a means to render rich and complex testimony on the Holocaust, Spielberg is a professional filmmaker—known as the most commercially successful director in movie history—for whom film is an end in itself. *Schindler's List* was for Spielberg a vehicle through which he received recognition as a great filmmaker, as well as a reborn Jew. For Spielberg, as for other American Jews, the Holocaust has become central to the self-understanding of their Jewish identity. Hence, Spielberg's road back to Judaism involved a cinematic voyage to the Holocaust, the new locus of Jewish identity in American public discourse. *Schindler's List* thus merges Spielberg's much-publicized rediscovery of his Jewish identity with the public's and critics' rediscovery of Spielberg as a reborn director. Consequently, *Schindler's List* functions as a redemptive rite of passage for Spielberg. It is a narrative of personal and collective redemption. Indeed, the subtext of many reviews of *Schindler's List* is that the true wonder of the film is that Spielberg made it, not that it is a powerful depiction of the Holocaust in and of itself. It is as if in and through *Schindler's List* Spielberg is against himself, Spielberg is against the grain of Spielberg, or Spielberg transcends Spielberg.

As a self-made historian with journalistic training, Lanzmann created a film that, according to Pierre Vidal-Naquet, epitomizes a unique and nontraditional modus of historical writing.[6] As a Hollywood popular teller, Spielberg, on the other hand, produced a classical Hollywood narrative. Whereas Lanzmann presents a collective (yet individually distinctive) hero composed of a variety of Jewish victims, Spielberg, following the Hollywood model of the historical epic, chose an individual (and a nonvictim one) to function as a protagonist in history. The moral implications of this choice perpetuate classical Hollywood's narrative psychohistorical approach, that is, the view that personal history is no less important than public history.

The Fiction of Reality Versus the Reality of Fiction

To a large extent, we might argue, the binarism generated by *Shoah* and *Schindler's List* is the result of genre division. "Documentary and fiction, we are told, appear as different genres and cannot, some might say, be compared."[7] Indeed journalistic accounts celebrated Spielberg's film as the finest nondocumentary film ever made on the Holocaust and *Shoah* as the best documentary ever made on the Holocaust. Yet these comfortable genre boxes should not mislead us. Traditionally, documentaries have been viewed as superior to fiction films because of their pretension to monopolize the market of the truth. Yet the cinematic institution's categories of "documentary" and "fiction" have continuously been thrown into crisis, especially since the emergence of cinema verité, which was so influential in France from the late 1950s to the mid-1970s and to which Lanzmann's *Shoah* is indebted. Lanzmann, for example, described his film as a "fiction of reality," whereas Spielberg based his film on "a real story" and simulated many documentary traditions (including cinema verité features) in order to make the events of his film look more real.[8] Lanzmann's definition of *Shoah* as a "fiction of reality" echoes one of the more famous aphorisms coined by Jean-Luc Godard, which appears as a handwritten slogan in his film *British Sounds (See You at Mao)* (1969): "photography is not the reflection of reality but the reality of that reflection." Godard later modified this aphorism, defining cinema on many occasions as "the fiction of reality and the reality of fiction." Unlike the Eric Rohmer–André Bazin phenomenological approach, Lanzmann—like Godard—distrusts verisimilitude as the means to render reality. *Shoah,* to a certain extent, is influenced by the radical tradition of the political upheavals of 1968 in Europe, hence epitomizing Jean-Louis Comolli's ideal, *le direct* (direct cinema), which extends the original conception of cinema verité. It is not a crude transformation of reality into cinematography but rather a presentation of representation. It is a documentation of the process of producing events in front of the camera. This explains why Lanzmann often called his witnesses the "characters" of the film. Moreover, Lanzmann edited their testimonies very carefully and staged certain scenes in search of a particular "re-enacting" from his interviewees. In the cinema verité tradition, the camera is used in these scenes as a valuable catalytic agent, a revealer of inner truth.

The documentary/fiction dichotomy carries special implications regarding the representation of the Holocaust. The Holocaust has traditionally been conceived as defying representation. This tradition evolved from the debates "that have revolved for several decades . . . around the question of an aesthetics after Auschwitz."[9] In these debates, triggered by Theodor W. Adorno's famous aphorism that after Auschwitz poetry could no longer be written, "silence" emerged as the least "obscene" aesthetic response to this historical trauma. Of course, silence was used in these debates more as a trope marking the appropriate boundaries of aesthetic reaction to the Holocaust (although in some cases it was both meant and read literally) rather than as an attempt at suppressing any expressive response to it. Documentary, due to its claim to direct access to reality, and hence to "truth," was therefore a preferred genre for the representation of the Holocaust. The widespread view of film as immanently the most mimetic of art forms and the notion of documentary as a transparent window reflecting reality accorded this genre a liability to deal with the Holocaust in a nondistortive manner. This explains the privilege traditionally accorded to documentary in discourse on the representation of the Holocaust. Lanzmann's mistrust of documentary's claim to be "truer" than fiction guided his "fiction of reality," which challenges the boundaries of correctness imposed by the debate on post-Auschwitz aesthetics.

Although *Schindler's List* is a classical Hollywood film, it integrates into its narrative various devices traditionally coded as belonging to documentary modes. *Schindler's List* is a realistic film, as most Hollywood narratives are. Yet the realistic code of the film is re-created in documentary style. The scene that epitomizes the assimilation of the documentary code into the fictional narrative is the final scene, when present-day Schindler Jews line up to place stones upon the real Oskar Schindler's grave in Jerusalem. This is, in Simon Louvish's perceptive words, a "Lanzmannesque invasion of the actual into the simulation."[10] As the whole film is shot in black and white, this scene, shot in color against the dazzling, bright light of Jerusalem, stands out. It conveys an impression of a "raw" slice of reality, contrasted with the overstylized expressive black and white of the film and its glossy nostalgic look. But even this seemingly original merging of fiction with documentary mode is part of Hollywood tradition, the historical epic. In *Reds,* for example, real historical figures are interviewed against their fictional "impersonifications." This integration seems to authenticate the fiction, suggesting that the depicted events really happened.

In fact, the assimilation of the documentary style into *Schindler's List* is part of the broader postmodernist aesthetics of the film. *Schindler's List* is a pastiche of a variety of cinematic styles. The film bears the look of, to use Fredric Jameson's words, "the technological 'perfection' of the new nostalgia glossy-film product."[11] It is a visually spectacular and eclectic text, quoting from styles as different and diverse as film noir, German expressionism, Italian neorealism,

World War II newsreels, and CNN news coverage. When Spielberg and cinematographer Janusz Kaminski chose to shoot in black and white, they conformed to a theory that this particular historical event could not be adequately rendered in color. Spielberg claimed: "I have no color reference for that period." Yet, his expressive use of black and white is indebted more to cinematic traditions associated with black and white rather than to any claim of truth. In fact today black-and-white cinematography has more of a glamorous, "arty," nostalgic appeal than an absolute claim to authenticity. Contemporary codes of realism require color as the norm, while black and white is seen as a nostalgic, stylized, and artificial reference. This is the reason also why Spielberg used color for the closing scene. Its "authenticity" is indebted to the use of color and its being shot on location. Spielberg's use of black and white varies in accordance with the cinematic style from which he is quoting. Thus, for example, the opening scene takes place in a cabaretlike milieu and is shot in dramatic contrasting black and white, which create a chiaroscuro interplay of light and shadow associated with German expressionism and film noir (in itself a highly stylized genre inspired by the visual iconography of German expressionism). These brilliant allusions to the chiaroscuro lighting are influenced by the Hollywood studio film particularly as realized in the work of Josef von Sternberg, Orson Welles, and Max Ophuls. This stylized, highly evocative black and white is replaced by grainy black-and-white tonality, embedded with shades of gray in the "more realistic scenes," such as the liquidation of the Kraków, Poland, ghetto or the selection of running naked women by Nazi doctors. These scenes embrace what Jameson has termed the "aesthetic of imperfect cinema," which renounces the perfection of Hollywood products by resorting to the low-quality (but highly authentic) images of newsreels and contemporary television news.[12] Other scenes, in particular those representing everyday life in the Kraków ghetto or in Schindler's factory, invoke the style of Italian neorealism, a movement associated with shooting in black and white and depicting life in Italy during and after WWII. Despite the diversity of styles integrated into *Schindler's List,* the final product (unlike the highly eclectic, "impure" films of filmmakers like Pier Paolo Pasolini and Rainer Werner Fassbinder) does not render stylistic or ideological tensions and contradictions. To the contrary, the transition from one quotational practice to another is almost invisible. Following the tradition of the classical Hollywood narrative, the text never calls attention to itself as a complex, constructed text. Rather, one quoted style flows smoothly onto the other, creating the ultimate images of commodified elegance and perfection produced by postmodern late capitalism. It is very possible that the uninitiated spectator, the "naive reader," is not able to recognize, let alone deconstruct, the different stylistic codes embedded in the otherwise harmonious look of the film. It is left to the critic and the film scholar to accomplish the job.

Word Against Image: Images of Absence, Images of Resurrection

Jim Hoberman in the *Village Voice* opened his introduction to excerpts from the roundtable discussion on *Schindler's List* at The Jewish Museum with the following clichélike truism: "In an age when even children understand that the image of an event transcends the event itself, *Schindler's List* is more than just a movie."[13] Lanzmann, however, rejected Holocaust images borrowed from archive footage partly because he claimed that

> it was not possible to determine which archive footage came from which camp, or which date. Film of Treblinka has come to be used as Auschwitz and vice versa. Lanzmann's obsession was to provide a precise and indeed pitiless verification of the events through their survivors' memories. The word was all; the picture, a means to an end. . . . Steven Spielberg, at the opposite end of the scale, goes back to the old dramatic principle of narrative filmmaking: show, don't tell. The Holocaust will be painstakingly reconstructed, in all its horror and misery.14

Schindler's List's challenge to the traditional view of the Holocaust as confined to the realm of the unimaginable, a liminal zone of human comprehension bound by the "limits of representation," was to penetrate (cognitively and visually) this dark continent by simply imagining it. Demystifying the "heart of darkness," trying literally to reconstruct and resurrect it through visual and oral images was something that had never been done before in mainstream cinema. Of course, many fiction films on the Holocaust have tried to depict the concentration camp universe. A film like *Seven Beauties* (1975) by Lina Wertmueller resurrected the camp universe. However, as a black comedy, invested with anarchistic spirit, its portrayal of the camp's universe never claimed the discourse of the real. By contrast, Spielberg was the first mainstream, Hollywood Jewish filmmaker to break the taboo of explicitly imagining the Holocaust and the gas chamber as its ultimate sacred center and horrifying metaphor.[15] In essence, Spielberg violated the ancient Jewish biblical prohibition on creating images as it has been unconsciously resurrected in the moral taboo on representing the Holocaust. Spielberg's transgression of the taboo on imagining the Holocaust explains partially the enthusiastic reception of the film by critics and audiences alike, as well as the hostile responses on behalf of some Jewish intellectuals who perceived this violation as pornographic and desacralizing. It was as if, finally, somebody violated the horrible taboo, killed the totem, and quenched the universal voyeuristic thirst to see what really happened there. The camera's penetration into the gas chamber was perceived by some as a violation of the Holy of Holies (*Kodesh Hakodashim* in Hebrew). Within this economy of scopophilic desire, *Schindler's List* provided an audience hungry for a spectacle of atrocity the illusion of being there.

Unlike *Schindler's List, Shoah* looks to the present to reaffirm the horrors of the Nazi concentration camps. The nine-and-one-half-hour film avoids footage from the camps, focusing instead on the memories of those who were there. The film is a reminder of the Holocaust as it continues to live in the minds and hearts of victims and perpetrators alike. Spielberg attempted to resurrect the Holocaust through construction. This is the reason why he had to rebuild Auschwitz, this time as a movie set. Lanzmann, on the other hand, resurrected the Holocaust through imagination, through the words of the witnesses, and through images of absence, images of tranquility and beauty of what were once the destruction sites.

Whereas Lanzmann, as Gertrud Koch argues, "remains strictly within the limits of what can be imagined," Spielberg goes beyond imagination.[16] Lanzmann's film never challenges "the limits of representation." There are no images of the extermination itself and "its representability is never once suggested by using the existing documentary photographs that haunt every other film on this subject.[17] Lanzmann thus not only abandons the "succession of endlessly recycled déjà-vu images" associated with Nazism but he continues the tradition of conceiving the Holocaust as defying representation.[18] His subjective camera, as Koch points out, "never exceeds the limit; it takes us just far enough to allow us to sense, on the edge of imagination, the reality of the annihilation."[19] This is, of course, the absolute opposite to Spielberg's intrusive and penetrating camera, which goes right there to the showers of the gas chambers, the most horrible, terrifying, and sacred space of Holocaust memory, and a locus of denial to assassins of memory.

Shoah, as Simon de Beauvoir observes, "succeeds in recreating the past with an amazing economy of means—places, voices, faces."[20] The film's evocation of "involuntary memory" through places (the images of young forests and fresh grass in the former destruction sites in Poland) is in line with a great French tradition—whose most well known representative is Marcel Proust's monumental poetic novel *À la recherche du temps perdu*—of invoking memory through material objects. But not only memory is invoked through places. The shift of scenery from one type of landscape to another (such as the lush and peaceful green of the destruction sites in Poland to the blue Mediterranean in Tel Aviv, Israel—where Abraham Bomba is interviewed—and the gray monumental Washington Mall in Washington, D.C.—used as a backdrop in Jan Karski's interview) echoes the "Babel"-like effect created by the different languages used in the film. While *Shoah* abandons the overfamiliarity of recycled images associated with Nazism, relying entirely on talking-head interviews, *Schindler's List* reconstructs the past through the memory of other movies and images associated with the '40s. It is a film that invokes the memory of the Holocaust through the imaginary collective memory of the movies. Unlike *Shoah,* which invokes memory through the oral recollection of personal experience delivered by different witnesses and through the evocation of expressive faces and landscapes, the memory recaptured and "relived" through *Schindler's List* is not an "authentic," "reexperienced" memory but rather a cinema memory produced and recycled by the movie industry. The conscious reliance of *Schindler's List* on the constitution of film as a collective memory thus weakens the link between public memory and personal experience, a link that is so powerful in Lanzmann's *Shoah.* Although *Schindler's List* is based on a real experience, this experience (except in the last scene) is never subsumed into the narrative, which prefers reconstructed real-like images to evocative ones.

Conclusion

In the last decades, the question, as Marc Ferro has phrased it, "whether or not cinema and television modify our vision of History," has assumed a new importance.[21] It has generated extensive debates among historians and media scholars regarding the right of cinema and television to constitute a new form of expression for history, as well as controversies concerning the contribution of this new form of historical "writing" to the transformation of our understanding of history.

Sergei Eisenstein's *Battleship Potemkin* (1925) provides a classic example of this problem. Images from this film have dominated our "memory" of the Russian revolution of 1905 (they even appear in some history books and historical documentaries on the period), although they belong to Eisenstein's space of imagination more than to any real space of historical events. In much the same way, as Anton Kaes observes, millions of Europeans have "experienced" the Vietnam War through the lens of Francis Ford Coppola's 1979 film *Apocalypse Now* or Michael Cimino's *Deer Hunter* (1978).[22] This applies even more radically to a film like *Schindler's List,* whose popular success on a global scale has surpassed all expectations.

As a historical film, close kin to docudrama, *Schindler's List* crosses the "sensitive line" between fact and fiction.[23] Hence, it creates an imaginative space of "faction," which, to use Gary Weissman's suggestive phrase, creates "a fantasy of witnessing."[24] Furthermore, as the most recent and perhaps most successful popular text to deal with the Holocaust—the most extreme case of historical trauma—to date, the film was seen as far too important to be the object of mere formal questions—stylistic and formal concerns being seen as obscuring the essential "facts" of the events.[25]

As the first studio film to deal directly with the enormity of the Holocaust, made by the most commercially successful director in movie history, *Schindler's List* attempts to provide the popular imagination with a master narrative about the Holocaust. Challenging "the limits of representation," Spielberg's 1993 film has become a media event, generating extensive discourse on the Holocaust and its mediation by popular culture in a way not seen in the United States since the NBC 1978 television miniseries *Holocaust.*

Perhaps what is most fascinating about the current "*Schindler* mania" is the film's engagement with public controversies about group hate. Despite some historians' objections, history on film and television is as much about the present as about the past; often it intervenes in ongoing debates. The Holocaust as memorialized by Spielberg's film has been mobilized as an educational tool in the fight against contemporary racism, reinforcing the thesis of French historian Pierre Sorlin that the historical film always interprets the past from the perspective of the present.[26] This is most evident in the way the film has been used as a "weapon" in the multicultural wars dividing the contemporary ethnic landscape of American society. Spielberg's testimony in the summer of 1994 before a congressional committee on the issue of "hate crimes" itself testifies to the fact that the most successful commercial filmmaker in Hollywood's history has suddenly achieved "expert" status on a controversial and complex social phenomenon—purely by virtue of having directed a film whose subject is the rescue of a handful of Jews from the Nazis.

Historian Peter Burke, reflecting on the idea of "thick narrative"—based on anthropologist Clifford Geertz's notion of "thick description"—suggests that "the so-called 'non-fiction novel' might have had something to offer historians, from Truman Capote's *In Cold Blood* (1965) to Thomas Keneally's *Schindler's Ark* (1982), which claims 'to use the texture and devices of a novel to tell a true story.'"[27] However, these literary models, Burke acknowledges, do not grapple with the problem of structures because they condense the problem of an epoch into a story about a family. We may argue that this incapacity to explore macro-structures is all the more problematic in a film like *Schindler's List,* which, following the model of classical Hollywood narrative, represents the individual as the protagonist in history.

Will *Schindler's List* not only preserve the Holocaust in the world's historical memory but also define the shape and dominant imagery of this memory?

Most historians still hold the view that history books are "our designated preservers of memory."[28] However, many of the official custodians of memory, notably Pierre Sorlin, will admit that it is no longer necessary to justify an interest in films as "important pieces of evidence for any study of the twentieth century."[29] Myths and symbols constructed and perpetuated by Hollywood have become permanent features of America and the world's historical consciousness. The trajectory of the "docudrama" through which *Schindler's List* articulates its vision of history suggests that "Spielberg's Holocaust" will become one of these global myths.

Notes

1. Quoted in André Pierre Colombat, *The Holocaust in French Film* (Metuchen, N.J.: Scarecrow Press, 1993), 335. For a further discussion of this scene, see Colombat, *Holocaust,* 335–36.

2. Deborah Dwork and Robert Jan van Pelt, "Reclaiming Auschwitz," in *Holocaust Remembrance: The Shapes of Memory,* ed. Geoffrey H. Hartman (Oxford, U.K.: Blackwell, 1994), 232.

3. Gertrud Koch quoted in Jim Hoberman, "*Schindler's List:* Myth, Movie, and Memory," *Village Voice* 39, no. 13 (29 March 1994): 25. These are excerpts from a roundtable discussion of *Schindler's List,* held at The Jewish Museum in New York City, on 28 March 1994.

4. The notion of "the limits of representation," which has become so prominent in contemporary scholarly discourse on the Holocaust, was coined by Saul Friedlander. See Saul Friedlander (ed.), *Probing the Limits of Representation: Nazism and the "Final Solution"* (Cambridge: Harvard University Press, 1992).

5. Quoted in Annette Insdorf, *Indelible Shadows: Film and the Holocaust* (Cambridge, U.K.: Cambridge University Press, 1989), 253.

6. Pierre Vidal-Naquet, *Assassins of Memory: Essays on the Denial of the Holocaust,* trans. Jeffrey Mehlman (New York: Columbia University Press, 1992), 111.

7. Simon Louvish, "Witness," *Sight and Sound* 4, no. 3 (March 1994): 14.

8. Lanzmann quoted in Colombat, *Holocaust,* 313.

9. Gertrud Koch, "The Aesthetic Transformation of the Image of the Unimaginable: Notes on Claude Lanzmann's *Shoah,*" trans. Jamie Owen Daniel and Miriam Hansen, *October* 48 (spring 1989): 15.

10. Louvish, "Witness," 15.

11. Fredric Jameson, *Signatures of the Visible* (New York: Routledge, 1990), 9.

12. Jameson, *Signatures,* 219.

13. Hoberman, "*Schindler's List,*" 24.

14. Louvish, "Witness," 12.

15. A testimony to the power of the notion of gas in post-Holocaust Jewish consciousness is the reaction of the Israeli public to the threat of chemical warfare and the use of gas masks during the Gulf War. For a further discussion of this issue, see Brenda Danet, Yosefa Loshitsky, and Haya Bechar-Israeli, "Masking the Mask: An Israeli Response to the Threat of Chemical Warfare," *Visual Anthropology* 6,

no. 3 (1993): 229–70. It is not an accident either that Claude Lanzmann, who was in Israel during the war, spoke out against the government's policy of *havlaga* (restraint) precisely because of the memory of the Holocaust.

16. Koch, "Aesthetic Transformation," 21.

17. Ibid., 21.

18. Anton Kaes, "History and Film: Public Memory in the Age of Electronic Dissemination," *History and Memory* 2, no. 1 (fall 1990): 121. For another interesting discussion on the role of recycled images in the production of public memory of the Holocaust, see Scott L. Montgomery, "What Kind of Memory? Reflections on Images of the Holocaust," *Contention* 5, no. 1 (fall 1995): 79–103.

19. Koch, "Aesthetic Transformation," 22.

20. Simone de Beauvoir, "Preface," in Claude Lanzmann, *Shoah,* iii.

21. Marc Ferro, *Cinema and History,* trans. Naomi Green (Detroit, Mich.: Wayne State University Press, 1988), 158.

22. Anton Kaes, *From Hitler to Heimat: The Return of History as Film* (Cambridge: Harvard University Press, 1989), 195.

23. For a fascinating discussion of the use of the "sensitive line" as a metaphor in *Schindler's List,* as well as in the media coverage of the making of the film, see Gary Weissman, "A Fantasy of Witnessing," *Media Culture and Society* 17, no. 2 (April 1995): 293–307. See also Frank Manchel, "A Reel Witness: Steven Spielberg's Representation of the Holocaust in *Schindler's List,*" *Journal of Modern History* 67, no. 1 (March 1995): 83–100.

24. See Weissman, "Fantasy of Witnessing."

25. I am indebted for this point to Keir Roper-Caldbeck from Sussex University.

26. Pierre Sorlin, *The Film in History: Restaging the Past* (New York: Oxford University Press, 1980).

27. Peter Burke, "History of Events," in *New Perspectives on Historical Writing,* ed. Peter Burke (University Park, Penn.: The Pennsylvania State University Press, 1992), 241.

28. Lucy Davidowicz, *What Is the Use of Jewish History?* (New York: Schocken Books, 1992), xiv.

29. Pierre Sorlin, *European Cinemas, European Societies 1939–1990* (London: Routledge, 1991), 5.

28

Defining Docudrama: *In the Name of the Father, Schindler's List,* and *JFK*

Steve Lipkin

The presumptions underlying the production of a docudrama are that its story "should" be told and that re-creation of actual events remains the best, if not the only, means of delivery. Recent features, including *Schindler's List* (Steven Spielberg, 1993), *In the Name of the Father* (Jim Sheridan, 1994), and *JFK* (Oliver Stone, 1991), exemplify the indexical roots, the melodramatic coding, and the consequent moral and ethical problems that in this chapter I identify as major defining features of docudrama.[1]

As its name suggests, *docudrama* is a hybrid form, wedding "documentary" material with "drama," particularly melodrama. The description of docudramatic form offered here centers on how, distinct from conventional documentaries, docudramas replace indexical, "unstaged" images with a quasi-indexical narrative. Image and story claim a motivated, direct relationship to the events the film references. The docudrama narrative, moreover, foregrounds dramatic codes, assuming melodrama's larger function of emphatically clarifying a broad moral system through domestic imagery.

The Indexical Roots of Docudrama

The status of docudrama relative to documentary proper remains problematic for a number of reasons. It is inviting to view a docudrama as a pseudodocument that would strive to lay claim to historical truth but follows the more marketable path of mass fiction. Changes in the technology of film and video documentation since World War II raise epistemological as well as ethical questions about the choice of a re-creative mode, if one's purpose remains the evaluation of the work as a document. *Schindler's List, In the Name of the Father,* and in particular *JFK* illuminate the problems inherent in docudrama generally—with a moral perspective incorporated within its melodramatic narrative structure, docudrama strikes a moral pose free from the ethical concerns usually applicable when a documentary builds its positions from indexical imagery.

A discussion of docudrama begins logically with some description of its form. As a consequence of its place between fiction and documentary, docudrama remains little explored in film scholarship, its form a problem to the side of historiographic issues raised by dramatic re-creations of actual events, while documentary studies understandably bypass docudrama as belonging more properly in the realm of fiction.[2] Bill Nichols's *Representing Reality,* for example, necessarily maintains an absolute, systematic distinction between documentary (building its cases from materials of the historical world) and fiction (constructed from materials that can only resemble the historical world metaphorically). Nichols's efforts to define documentary preclude any consideration of the "truth value" of docudrama, since its re-creations relegate the form without mitigation to the realm of fiction.

If on these terms docudrama cannot assert documentary truth values about the historical world, it still maintains a close connection to documentary. Docudrama argues with the seriousness of documentary to the extent that it draws upon direct, motivated resemblances to its actual materials. As fictions, docudramas offer powerful, attractive arguments about actual subjects, depicting people, places, and events that exist or have existed. To borrow a page from Nichols, it is on the basis of its close resemblances to actuality that docudrama argues for the validity of its metaphors. The stories of docudrama attempt to persuade us with a logic of motivated iconicity.

Even as docudrama departs from documentary proper, the two modes retain a certain semiotic similarity. The evolving technology of mainstream documentary progressively has aligned representation and actuality. The documentary image functions as an index; comparable imagery in docudrama remains primarily iconic; however, docudrama asks if, under its terms, the two signs might not be all that different.[3] The films' often high degree of resemblance to actual people, places, actions, and/or events suggests that docudramatic imagery combines characteristics of iconic and indexical signs, creating what amount to indexical icons, signs with direct, strongly motivated resemblances to their actual referents. We are offered argument by analogy, the analogies (images) often appearing to be of the most literal kind.

The docudrama narrative may also reference other, earlier texts that offer the initial definition of their actual material. The very existence of a prior text or texts arguably motivates production of the film, as well as its eventual narrative structure. The viewer is invited to accept the argument that re-creation warrants, that what we see might have "really" happened in "much this way." The notion of *warranting* is particularly helpful here, since a warrant locates the basis in common knowledge, common sense, and/or rules of logic that allow an argument to make the necessary shift from fact to value.[4]

In the case of film docudrama, warranting occurs both in the choice of subject and in the choice of mode of presentation. The strength of the argument by analogy that the film's indexical icons will make must stem from these warrants. The warrants forward the claims the film will make, essentially the moral position of the film's melodramatic coding.

Docudramas stem from "known" events and figures. The previous texts tend to include news stories, published accounts, and personal testimonies, such as Thomas Keneally's novel about Oskar Schindler, Gerry Conlon's printed exposé of his case, or Jim Garrison's view of the Kennedy assassination.[5] The existence of prior text and/or narrative warrants the choice of material for filmic treatment: these events "really" happened and were important enough for reportage. We are asked to consider that they might have happened "this" way, in the version now offered as feature film docudrama. The choice of the docudramatic mode of presentation itself offers a second warrant. "Actual" documentary materials either do not exist or by themselves are incomplete or insufficient to treat the subject adequately.

Its premises secured, melodramatic form delivers the docudrama's ultimate moral judgments on its material. Film melodrama places domestic settings and familial imagery within the context of larger social systems revealed in the narrative as powerful and corrupt, repressive to the point of hellishness.[6] The often excessive depiction of domestic life caught up in a constraining, destructive world of social power allows the melodramatic narrative to pronounce emphatically through its re-created actual material a clear moral perspective. Like melodrama generally, docudrama suggests that lost moral structures can be recovered and restored. While the actuality the work re-creates may show the exercise of right and wrong thrown into jeopardy, the treatment of actual people, incidents, and events in the docudrama ultimately allows a literal moral "refamiliarization," a restoration of a moral system in the universe.[7]

Docudrama as Melodrama

As different as they are in scope and subject matter, *JFK, Schindler's List,* and *In the Name of the Father* are comparable in arguing that injustice results when social systems go wrong. In the mode of melodrama, *Schindler's List* and *In the Name of the Father* examine how destructive social powers applied against weak, domestically imaged victims produce explicitly hellish results. The exercise of power accordingly appears random and arbitrary, the viciousness of persecution commensurate with the lack of underlying reason. (I discuss further the ethical implications of *JFK*'s re-creation of its material.)

In the Name of the Father renders the British legal process in images of powerless individuals trapped by large, impersonal, impervious, monolithic instruments of social control. Gerry Conlon, Giuseppe Conlon, and Paul Hill are arrested, interrogated, tried, convicted, and incarcerated because they are Irishmen by chance in the wrong places at the wrong times. Social environments funnel claustrophobically from city streets in Ireland to those in London, to a British courtroom, to the jail in which both Conlons are incarcerated. Images of Gerry Conlon's surroundings feature overpowering vertical lines often viewed subjectively (the buildings of Conlon's home turf surrounded by the massed British army; the spectators, advocates, and judges in the courtroom scenes; the barred walls of the multitiered prison). After a riot, the jail that wrongfully imprisons the Conlons becomes even more tightly barred. The film's series of constraining environments progressively shows how the legal system eliminates individual movement and self-determination. The film depicts injustice as the erroneous suppression of individuality by an increasingly purgatorial system.

To the image of life under the Nazis as wrongful incarceration, *Schindler's List* adds the phenomenon of "selection" and develops throughout the film its moral consequences. "Selection" of Jews for deportation, liquidation (of the Kraków ghetto), and final annihilation in the gas chambers of Auschwitz remains a given from the film's opening sequences, so that the issue is never why Jews have been selected for destruction, it is only which ones will be chosen and with what consequences. The horror of pending death and destruction begins with the irrationally random selection process.

The film's opening explicitly links Judaic culture with the iconography of selection, chaos, death, and destruction. The *Shabbat* candle lit in the opening scene burns out as the prayer for candle lighting finishes. The end of candle and prayer raises a question appropriate to the beginning of a film about Jews in Germany during World War II: What will happen to God in the absence of the rituals, the culture, and the believers who sustain His existence? We are at the advent of a truly "desacralized" world, a world from which most forms of the sacred have been banished (Brooks 5). The smoke of the *Shabbat* candle tapers upward as the image dissolves into the smoke of a railroad engine at a station where the soon frequently seen folding tables are set up for processing deportees.

To underline the consequences of selection, smoke appears throughout the film at key junctures, seen, for example, hovering over the "liquidated" Kraków ghetto from burning debris and gunshots. Arbitrary Nazi persecution appears drawn from an inferno. Ash drops on shoulders and car fenders later as the same victims are exhumed and cremated. Nazi soldiers scream and cackle insanely while they build into blazing pyres stacks of decomposing bodies bulldozed up from the mass graves holding the dead of the ghetto. Near the film's end, Auschwitz is shown *Night and Fog*–like from the front gate, smoke belching from its infamous ovens.

In each environment, the matter of "selection," the choice of who will live and who will die is emphatically arbitrary, underlining the horrific chaos at the core of the ostensibly orderly Nazi-run society. Jews are doubly damned, since they must collaborate in the selection process in order to survive at all. Many receive the precious, lifesaving "blue cards" that verify "essential worker status" only because they are known to Stern, the *Judenrat* leader Oskar Schindler enlists to help administer his enterprise.

Stern's "selections" promote survival. Nazi selection procedures by contrast place arbitrary, irrational violence under the facade of orderly lines and bureaucratic trappings. Amon Goeth, the Nazi commandant running the Plaszgow camp that has become the new "home" of the displaced ghetto residents, stands on his balcony with a telescopically sighted rifle and picks off camp internees at random. The ultimate horror intimated throughout the film, then finally shown, remains "selection" for the gas chambers at Auschwitz.

Within their enormously repressive, arbitrarily destructive, hellish social settings, *In the Name of the Father* and *Schindler's List* erect fundamentally melodramatic narrative structures. The lens of melodrama brings a moral clarity to the brutish violence that the films show destructive social powers inflicting upon helpless victims. Both films place characters within familial and/or domestic settings, employing father figures to mediate moral perspectives. Gerry

Conlon moves through a succession of literal or figurative families in the course of the film. He and Paul Hill are assisted in their escape from the British army at the film's opening by the people of their neighborhood. Their route takes them through homes and yards. Conlon leaves his home in Ireland and takes up temporarily with a hippie commune in London; subsequently his trials become prosecutions of both his actual and surrogate families, as his blood relatives captured at his aunt's flat, as well as the members of the commune, are tried as terrorists. When Conlon and his father are jailed, the other inmates form a final surrogate family, complete with another surrogate father (the actual IRA bomber who has confessed to the murders Conlon and Hill have been convicted of). Conlon "returns" to embrace fully the importance of his father's self-sacrifice. Conlon is ultimately redeemed through the late-found desire to save his "real" father, to right the wrong the system has perpetrated against him.

Schindler's List also features contrasting family settings and even more extremely contrasting father figures. Oskar Schindler and Amon Goeth are morally opposite surrogates of the same "family," the Jews of Kraków. Settings in this film also move through a succession of domestic environments: people are displaced from their original residences and forced to cram together by the dozens, first in reassigned ghetto apartments, then the Plaszgow camp barracks. Schindler's factory provides an opportunity to survive the dangers of the ghetto or the camp. Its imagery turns domestic. The factory manufactures pots and pans. Schindler eats at a table in a corner of his upstairs office, surrounded by houseplants. As a melodramatic icon, the factory stairway figures prominently in the film when a woman comes to Schindler twice to beg him to take on her father and mother as workers. He stands at the top of the stairs, a backlit, smoke-enshrouded figure of mystery, his life-granting power verified in a subsequent scene when the daughter stands across the street, watching unseen, Stella Dallas–like as her parents arrive for work.

By contrast the house of Goeth, quite literally a house on the edge of the Plaszgow camp, consistently and perversely marks its domestic spaces with the ongoing processes of repression, terror, and death. In yet another selection scene (eerily evocative of Schindler interviewing secretarial candidates), Goeth chooses his maid out of a lineup of possibilities drawn from his available internees. Helen works "downstairs," a domestic/kitchen area in which she receives successive "visits" from both Schindler and Goeth. Schindler endows her with "not that kind of kiss" and some paternal encouragement. Goeth, he assures her, needs her too much ever to kill her. Subsequently, when Goeth "visits" Helen in her domestic realm, he does not murder her but assaults her, then backs away, leaving the threat of the exercise of his absolute power intact.

The "upstairs" of Goeth's house stages a succession of decadent dinner parties for Goeth's army and civilian acquaintances and, most predominately, allows us into his bedroom with its balcony overlooking his realm. From here he shoots internees, and discusses the rigors of his job with his bedmate. The fusion of bedroom, bed, half-naked mistress, sunlit balcony, and random snipings characterize his patriarchy by his intertwined venting of sexual and murderous physical aggression.

Goeth's status as a patriarchal bully is underlined by his victims, who tend to be women, children, or men made submissively childlike. A female engineer who is not intimidated by him is shot, apparently because of her competence. An equally competent hinge maker's very competence is viewed twistedly as prima facie evidence that he's slacked off, reducing the man to prayer for his life to be spared (and it is when, once again, chance intervenes and none of Goeth's available pistols will work). Goeth appears to follow Schindler's advice to exercise forgiveness as the most absolute form of power when he confronts Lisiek, a boy who works as another of his servants, with stains still not removed from the bathtub. He tells Lisiek, "I forgive you," but shoots him anyway as the boy is crossing the parade ground reentering the camp.

Schindler's workers are similarly childlike in their deference to him (he orders Stern to keep away from him those workers who, like the one-armed old man, want to thank Schindler for his job) or are literally children (such as a quick-witted boy who saves a large group from execution for stealing a chicken, or a girl who brings Schindler a birthday cake and whom he kisses, resulting in his incarceration by the SS).

Schindler's status as "good" father is warranted by his shift from selfishness to self-sacrifice. He is characterized initially in the film by his material superficiality. Before we see him, we meet him through his clothing (his suits, shirts, and ties being laid out), his cuff links and watch, his money clip, and last, his Nazi Party pin. He tells Stern he needs someone with a head for business to run his company, to free him to concentrate on "presentation."

Stern acts as the alchemist's stone, the means of eventual transformation that turns Schindler from petty capitalist to self-sacrificing humanist. Stern's selfless work to save others provides Schindler with an infectious moral reference. Stern knows business and knows the Jewish populace upon which Schindler must depend for the slave labor that will allow his immense profits. Schindler himself must intervene, however, when Stern is swept up and loaded on a train for deportation. He effects a last-minute rescue, and from that point of direct involvement Schindler progressively sheds the material his workers have allowed him to gain in order to keep his workforce intact. Schindler trades his saddle (from which he watched the liquidation of the ghetto), his lighter, watch, jewels, and entire suitcases of currency for human beings. By the time he has liquidated his own possessions in order to save all of his workers, he knows eleven hundred of their names. Early on in his enterprise, a shot worker is "lost time" and governmental "compensation"; by the war's end, he is faced with the fact of the entire group standing before him, and he grieves, "This car! Why did I keep it? I could have saved two people! Two people!"

The conclusion of *Schindler's List* offers a final warranting of its docudramatic articulation by wedding the moral perspective conveyed through its narrative's melodrama with a succession of documentary images and assertions. The group of Schindler Jews we see at the conclusion of the story walks over a hill and their image dissolves to color, present-day footage of the actual survivors of this same group. In a fusion of document and melodrama, as each film actor escorts the real-life person he or she played in the film (or their spouse or child) to Oskar Schindler's grave, subtitles inform us that Schindler died more than twenty years after the war's end a business failure, is buried in Israel, and while today a total of four thousand Jews survive in Poland, there are more than six thousand descendants of Schindler's Jews. Thus the pictorial and statistical evidence of the group's existence today warrants the view that the film we've just seen offers of its subject.[8]

JFK and the Ethics of Docudrama

As Oliver Stone's *JFK* exemplifies the indexical icons and the melodramatic configurations that form the defining characteristics of docudrama, it also sheds light on the ethical considerations this mode of filmmaking raises. Melodrama forwards clear moral positions. *JFK* functions melodramatically in its efforts to wrest order from the chaos created by John F. Kennedy's assassination. Its "creative use" of actual materials in fact creates a melodramatic search for a moral order. In doing so, perhaps no other recent feature film docudrama has been as controversial, particularly regarding issues of the film's credibility, the accuracy of its re-creations, and the resulting validity of its view of its subject.[9] The case of *JFK* illustrates how ethical problems arise when docudrama steps too far from known, actual events into the realm of speculation. Ironically, *JFK* contains more actual "documentary" material than any of the other films considered here, a fact that fuels the charges of irresponsibility brought against film and filmmaker by a wide range of writers and critics.[10]

Melodrama becomes fused with documentary as *JFK* references well-known actual events and texts about those events in its focus on a key individual's struggle against powerful, corrupt forces of social control. Family structures background New Orleans District Attorney Jim Garrison's investigation into the Kennedy assassination. Garrison's work plays (in the film's view, selflessly) against his literal family, his wife, his children, and their home life. We see his investigation as the function of a more figurative family, the group of assistants who share the investigative chores. The seed that grows into the investigation takes root in Garrison's family room, while television news covers the funeral: Mrs. Garrison tries to pull her husband away from the screen and back into family matters in what becomes a recurring tension between work and family. When the film shows Garrison with his team, they are often in "family"-circle configurations, grouped around a table at a restaurant or in a living room–like conference setting, the figurative father Garrison at the head.

The implicit family context of Garrison's work is a secondary melodramatic configuration compared to the work itself. Garrison is launching nothing less than a search for order within a social system that the investigation finds is far more chaotic and destructive than surface appearance suggests. The murder of the president and the underlying conspiracy Garrison uncovers at the highest levels of the federal government reveal the desacralized nature of the world of the film.

JFK presents itself as a film with a mission. The need to bring to public light *JFK*'s view of this conspiracy with its enormous, ongoing issues warrants the film's production. The fact of *JFK*'s widespread theatrical distribution and its resulting controversy argue that we should see this film, think about it, discuss it.

While *In the Name of the Father* is Gerry Conlon's story, and *Schindler's List* tells its audience about Oskar Schindler, *JFK* is not "about" JFK or even his death so much as it is "about" Jim Garrison. Unlike these other films, *JFK* does not bring a particular point of view to generally accepted facts about known events. Instead it attempts to build on the known to argue its theory. The film is a re-creation of several speculative, controversial works.

JFK raises ethical issues when it violates the warrants that allow docudramas to offer arguments by analogy. Is the film about a "deserving" subject? If Garrison's view of the Kennedy assassination has never received widespread acceptance, then why should this material warrant re-presentation as a feature film docudrama? More particular charges against the film's distortions of "known" history—the David Ferrie "confession," for example, before he is found dead, or the fabrication of "X" in order to validate the same kind of conspiracy charges—arguably result from the effort to bolster the warrant (the Garrison view is valuable to the film's audience and society generally) and inevitably jeopardize the film's entire argument.[11]

If the first level of warranting has been thrown into question (that this story deserves to be told), then the second level of warranting must also be questionable (that the story must be told "this" way, through re-creation); however, it is generally agreed that, if nothing else, *JFK* overwhelms its viewer with its interplay between actual and re-created materials.[12] Janet Maslin argues that the systematic, nearly indistinguishable interplay of real and re-created footage ultimately confuses what is real and what is fictional.[13] Technical proficiency won't make for effective argument if the evidence can't be trusted.

What the film attempts to do, more specifically, is to re-create Garrison's speculations as he gathers evidence. A pattern of inferential thinking based on indexical material emerges from scene to scene in the film: Garrison is confronted with information, for example, from television news sources (early on) or through his associates' reviewing gathered evidence (as the investigation gathers steam). While Garrison stands at a scene, such as at the window of the third floor of the Texas State School Book Depository or in David Ferrie's cluttered apartment, the narration of events becomes illustrated by quickly flashed images, some actual (fragments of the Zapruder film as they discuss the progress of the limousine turning from Houston onto Elm) but more often than not re-created (staged, black-and-white images of other assassins standing at the stockade fence, of Oswald in the Dallas jail, of the murder of Ferrie, etc.). Garrison is thus "getting the picture," formulating an increasingly coherent view of complex fragments that will add up to an explanation of who did what, when, and why. If the speculation has persuasive power, it is because of the re-created material's proximity (both in place and resemblance) to the actual.

Objections to this strategy of sometimes shot-by-shot interplay of re-created and actual material have centered on the potential to mistake document for docudrama. Those most critical of the film charge it with blurring the distinction between historical fact and dramatic embellishment. The vast number of actual and actual-looking images in *JFK* fuels what amounts to a critical backfire: since it's such an "analogic"-looking docudrama it offers a potentially powerful, persuasive view of its subject; however, by the same token, its departures from argument through literal analogies (close resemblances) as it develops its conspiracy theory render it susceptible to charges of irresponsibility.

In sum, concerns over *JFK*'s ethics understandably stem from its choice of subject (Does Jim Garrison's conspiracy theory deserve to be told?), as well as its methods of re-creation (When does re-creation stop and imaginative speculation begin?). The interplay between indexical and indexically iconic materials in *JFK* takes to an extreme the mix of cues characteristic of docudrama as a mode: documentary subject matter and materials appear embedded within a fiction narrative, communicated within a fiction feature film context (including theatrical distribution and exhibition); also the fusion of documentary and narrative stylistics has a rhetorical objective easily confused with a literal claim to historical truth.

The docudramas considered here draw power from similar strategies. They reference actual people and events through melodramatic narrative codes. The evil of monolithic social power stems from its random, arbitrarily murderous exercise. The evil abuse of power in Nazi society is rendered in *Schindler's List* by random choices of victims to be murdered. The same kind of monolithic social power is portrayed in *In the Name of the Father* as a corrupt, arbitrary, abusive judicial process. *JFK* shows the U.S. president murdered by his own government. "Good" characters within these worlds begin as flawed heroes "saved" when they can become redeemed by freedom from self-absorption. Schindler becomes a "good" father when he sheds his materiality; Gerry Conlon learns to transfer his concerns and energies from himself to his own father, who has already sacrificed his health and freedom out of his concern for his son. Jim Garrison neglects his family for the sake of seeking the truth.

As docudramas, *Schindler's List, In the Name of the Father,* and *JFK* argue melodramatically for the worth of thought about their subjects. The films offer alternatives to the kind of sober discourse about history that would be the province of documentary. All operate as artistic perceptions of history, offering viewers the opportunity to share the film artists' reflections upon the historical material the works represent. On these terms, the films allow a sense of closeness to that history, an access made possible by rendering chaotic, destructive horrors understandable as essentially domestic conflicts escalated to vastly larger social scales. The films suggest worlds from which morality has been lost then restored. Proximity to the factual in the films attempts to root artistic vision within the sober ground of historical actuality, suggesting at the same time that good has come out of suffering, that justice has prevailed, that—as it must in melodrama—some order has been restored to a chaotic universe.

Notes

1. Attention here is limited to theatrically distributed feature films.

2. Recently Alan Rosenthal, in *Writing Docudrama* (Newton, Massachusetts: Butterworth-Heinemann, 1995), has identified the fundamental issues of balancing dramatic structure and journalistic documentation in the form and the ethical implications of this fusion for the screenwriter. George Custen, in *Bio/Pics* (New Brunswick, New Jersey: Rutgers University Press, 1992), examines in depth the processing of public history by classic Hollywood narrative film style as it produced biographical fact-based fiction. Jack Ellis, in *The Documentary Idea* (Englewood

Cliffs: Prentice-Hall, 1989), discusses several points where fiction and nonfiction film forms overlap or intersect each other, including the turn toward story form in direct cinema; however, he does not consider dramatic re-creation as a subform of documentary in its own right. Bill Nichols, as discussed here, gives the relationship between fiction and documentary extended attention throughout *Representing Reality* and in his more recent *Blurred Boundaries* (Bloomington: Indiana University Press, 1994). Extensive treatments of the more general problems inherent in the representation of history in fiction films have appeared in a number of works. Hayden White, in *The Content of the Form* (Baltimore: Johns Hopkins University Press, 1989), examines the necessity of representing history by means of narration, suggesting the narrative act itself ultimately asserts what is meaningful regarding the history in question. Robert A. Rosenstone, in *Visions of the Past* (Cambridge: Harvard University Press, 1995), clarifies how invention is necessary in both filmed and written history and illustrates how strategies of alteration, condensation, and anachronism characterize historical portrayals in any medium. An exchange between Robert Burgoyne and Angela Dalle-Vacche (Robert Burgoyne, "Temporality as Historical Argument in Bertolucci's *1900*," *Cinema Journal* 28, no. 3, spring 1989; her response appears in *Cinema Journal* 29, no. 3, spring 1990) broaches issues of history portrayed phenomenologically, noting the impact of the cinematic rendering of order, frequency, and duration on the resulting view of history in Bernardo Bertolucci's *1900.* As a group, these works focus on the implications of narrative fiction as a vehicle for portraying history and provide a necessary framework for considering the more specific issues of film docudrama as a form in its own right.

3. C. S. Peirce's language in describing the index is noteworthy in that he pursues the relationship of icon and index accordingly:

> An *Index* is a sign that refers to the Object that it denotes by virtue of being really affected by that Object. . . . In so far as the Index is affected by the Object, it necessarily has some Quality in common with the Object, and it is in respect to these that it refers to the Object. It does, therefore, involve a sort of Icon, although an Icon of a peculiar kind; and it is not the mere resemblance of its Object, even in these respects which makes it a sign, but it is the actual modification of it by the Object. (Peirce 102)

To rephrase, the signifier not only necessarily "refers" to its signified, but the signified also acts upon and/or changes ("affects"; "modifies") its own signifier. Applied to docudrama, the "action" of original events conceivably includes the evolution of their retelling and reformulation.

4. "Warrants indicate how, given the available grounds, it [is] reasonable for the listener or reader to make the inferential leap from them to the claim[;] . . . warrants are found in things already accepted as true as a part of common knowledge, values, customs, and societal norms" (Rybocki and Rybocki 52).

5. Respectively (in recent editions), Thomas Keneally, *Schindler's Ark* (New York: Simon and Schuster, 1982); Gerry Conlon, *In the Name of the Father* (New York: Plume, 1993)—published originally as *Proved Innocent* (London:

H. Hamilton, 1990); and Jim Garrison, *On the Trail of the Assassins* (New York: Warner Books, 1992). *JFK*'s credits also cite Jim Marrs, *Crossfire* (New York: Carroll and Graf, 1992).

6. *Melodrama* and *domestic drama* have been almost interchangeable terms for scholars of film melodrama, such as Charles Affron, in *Cinema and Sentiment* (Chicago: University of Chicago Press, 1982), and Thomas Elsaesser, in "Tales of Sound and Fury" (*Monogram* 4 [1972]: 2–15). See also Robert Lang, *American Film Melodrama: Griffith, Vidor, Minelli* (Princeton, New Jersey: Princeton University Press, 1989). Lang writes: "the melodramatic imagination that structures the film understands experience in Manichean terms of familial struggle and conflict" (Lang 3).

7. Peter Brooks, in *The Melodramatic Imagination,* discusses extensively the function of melodrama in a "desacralized" universe, that is, a universe otherwise lacking in moral reference. Melodrama's emphatic treatment and clarification of moral issues helps fill that lack (Brooks 5).

8. *In the Name of the Father* ends in a similar fashion, relying more conventionally on subtitles rolling as an epilogue to update us about the status of the actual people the film has portrayed.

9. See, for example, Gerald R. Ford and David W. Belin, "The Kennedy Assassination: How about the Truth?" *Washington Post National Weekly,* 23 December 1991; Roger Hilsman, "How Kennedy Viewed the Vietnam Conflict," *New York Times,* 20 January 1992; Leslie H. Gelb, "Kennedy and Vietnam," *New York Times,* 6 January 1992; William Manchester, "No Evidence for a Conspiracy to Kill Kennedy," *New York Times,* 5 February 1992; David W. Belin, "Oswald Was a Lone Gunman," *Wall Street Journal,* 16 January 1992; "Earl Warren's Assassins," *New York Times,* 7 March 1992; Bernard Welnraub, "Valenti Denounces Stone's *JFK* As A 'Smear,'" *New York Times,* 14 April 1992; and see Stone's response to many of the above in "The JFK Assassination—What About the Evidence?" *Washington Post National Weekly,* 5 January 1992, and in "The Shooting of JFK, Stone's Interview with R. S. Ansen," in *Esquire* (November 1991).

10. These include Tom Wicker, "Does *JFK* Conspire Against Reason?" *New York Times,* 15 December 1991; Kenneth Auchincloss, "Twisted History," *Newsweek,* 23 December 1991; Tom Bethell, "Conspiracy to End Conspiracies," *National Review,* 16 December 1991; John Leo, "Oliver Stone's Paranoid Propaganda," *U.S. News and World Report,* 13 January 1992; and Lance Morrow, "When Artists Distort History," *Time,* 23 December 1991.

11. See Ansen's interview with Stone (cited above), and see Edward J. Epstein, "The Second Coming of Jim Garrison," *Atlantic Monthly,* March 1993.

12. David Ansen, "What Does Oliver Stone Owe History?" *Newsweek,* 23 December 1991; Richard Corliss, "Who Killed JFK?" *Time,* 23 December 1991.

13. Janet Maslin, in "Oliver Stone Manipulates His Puppet," *New York Times,* 5 January 1992, writes:

> Images fly by breathlessly and without identification. Composite characters are intermingled with actual ones. Real material and simulated scenes are intercut in a deliberately bewildering fashion. The camera races bewilderingly across supposedly "top secret" documents and the various charts and models

being used to explain forensic evidence. Major matters and petty ones are given equal weight. Accusations are made by visual implication rather than rational deduction, as when the camera fastens on an image of Lyndon Johnson while a speaker uses the phrase "coup d'état."

Works Cited

Brooks, Peter. *The Melodramatic Imagination.* New Haven, Connecticut: Yale University Press, 1974.

Ellis, Jack. *The Documentary Idea.* Englewood Cliffs: Prentice-Hall, 1989.

Nichols, Bill. *Representing Reality.* Bloomington: Indiana University Press, 1991.

Peirce, C. S. Edited by J. Buchler. *Philosophical Writings of Peirce.* New York: Dover, 1955.

Rybocki, Karen, and D. J. Rybocki. *Advocacy and Opposition.* Englewood Cliffs: Prentice Hall, 1991.

Contributors

Alan Rosenthal was born in England, studied law at Oxford, and has made more than fifty films, primarily in the United States and Israel, mostly about Middle Eastern affairs. He has taught at British and Australian film schools and the Hebrew University in Jerusalem and is the author of five other books, including *New Challenges for Documentary* and *Writing, Directing, and Producing Documentary Films and Videos.* His recent film, *Out of the Ashes,* won a Christopher Award and a George Foster Peabody Award in journalism.

John Corner teaches communication studies at the University of Liverpool. He wrote *Television Form and Public Address* (1995) and *The Art of Record* (1996).

George F. Custen, a professor of communications at the City University of New York, is the author of *Bio/Pics* (1992) and *Twentieth Century–Fox: Darryl F. Zanuck and the Culture of Hollywood.*

David Edgar is one of England's leading political playwrights. He adapted *Nicholas Nickleby* for the stage and is the author of *The Second Time as Farce* (1988).

Leslie Fishbein is a professor of American studies at Rutgers University. She is the author of *Rebels in Bohemia: The Radicals of the Masses, 1911–1917* (1982) and has written for *Film and History* and *American Quarterly.*

George MacDonald Fraser is a novelist, screenwriter, and historian. He is the creator of the Flashman books and wrote the screenplays for *Octopussy* and *The Three Musketeers.*

Todd Gitlin is a professor of culture, journalism, and sociology at New York University and author of *The Whole World Is Watching* (1980) and *Inside Prime Time* (1983).

Douglas Gomery teaches at the University of Maryland. He is the coauthor of *Film Theory: History and Practice* (1986), and he writes "The Economics of Television" column for the *American Journalism Review.*

Richard Grenier is film critic for *Commentary* magazine. His other articles on film docudrama include "The Curious Case of Costa-Gavras" (1982) and "The Gandhi Nobody Knows" (1983).

Sumiko Higashi teaches history and women's studies at the State University of New York–Brockport. She is the author of *Cecil B. DeMille and American Culture: The Silent Era* (1994).

Tom W. Hoffer is a former professor of mass communications at Florida State University–Tallahassee and the current publisher of the *Franklin Chronicle* in northern Florida.

Jerry Kuehl is a historian and television producer. His articles include "Truth Claims" (1988) and "History on the Public Screen" (1988). He worked on the TV series *The World at War* and is currently working on a television series about the Cold War.

Steve Lipkin teaches film studies and film / video production at Western Michigan University and is currently writing an extended study of docudrama.

Yosefa Loshitsky teaches communications at the Hebrew University in Jerusalem. She is the author of *The Radical Faces of Godard and Bertolucci* (1994).

Ian McBride is head of factual drama at Granada TV and was executive producer of *Hostages.* His background is in television current affairs and documentary, and as producer of *World in Action,* he exposed the wrongful conviction of the Birmingham Six.

Richard Alan Nelson, is the associate dean for graduate studies and research at the Manship School of Mass Communication at Louisana State University.

Conor Cruise O'Brien is a journalist, diplomat, and best-selling author. He has written widely on Ireland and the Middle East; his most recent book is *The Great Melody* (1994).

Derek Paget is the reader in drama at Worcester College, U.K. He is the author of *True Stories: Documentary Drama on Radio, Screen and Stage* (1990) and *No Other Way to Tell It* (1997).

Robert A. Rosenstone is a professor of history at the California Institute of Technology. He has written a biography of John Reed, *Romantic Revolutionary* (1975), and is the author of *Visions of the Past* (1995).

Betsy Sharkey is a freelance journalist and also editor at large for *Adweek* magazine.

Irene Shubik has worked widely as a drama producer for both the BBC and ITV. She was the original producer of the well-known *Rumpole* series and is the author of *Play for Today* (1971).

Jeff Silverman writes regularly about the arts for the *New York Times* and other publications and was coproducer of the 1989 docudrama *I Love You Perfect.*

D. J. Wenden wrote *The Birth of the Movies* and, until his death, was a fellow and bursar of All Souls College, Oxford University.

Sita Williams joined Granada TV in 1980 and has since produced three major docudramas, Bernard McLaverty's *Hostages,* Geoffrey Case's *Fighting for Gemma,* and most recently Peter Berry's *Goodbye My Love.*

Leslie Woodhead set up the docudrama division of Granada TV in the late seventies and has produced and directed numerous docudramas, including *Invasion* (1982) and *Why Lockerbie?* (1990).